Difference of a Different Kind

Difference of a Different Kind

JEWISH CONSTRUCTIONS OF RACE DURING
THE LONG EIGHTEENTH CENTURY

Iris Idelson-Shein

PENN

UNIVERSITY OF PENNSYLVANIA PRESS *Philadelphia*

THIS BOOK IS MADE POSSIBLE BY A COLLABORATIVE GRANT
FROM THE ANDREW W. MELLON FOUNDATION.

© 2014 University of Pennsylvania Press

Published by
University of Pennsylvania Press
Philadelphia, Pennsylvania 19104-4112
www.upenn.edu/pennpress

Printed in the United States of America
on acid-free paper

10 9 8 7 6 5 4 3 2 1

A Cataloging-in-Publication record is available from
the Library of Congress.

ISBN 978-0-8122-4609-4

To my parents

CONTENTS

All translations are my own unless otherwise mentioned. All biblical excerpts in English, including those incorporated in the translation of maskilic biblical allusions, are based on the Authorized King James edition. All Hebrew and Yiddish terms have been transliterated according to the guidelines set forth in the *Encyclopaedia Judaica* and the standard YIVO transcription system. The Anglicized form is used for terms or names already familiar in English. Parenthetical explanations of Hebrew and Yiddish terms are given upon first mention.

Difference of a Different Kind

Introduction

There is an amusing scene in V. S. Naipaul's *The Mimic Men*, in which Ralph Singh, a Caribbean immigrant in London, describes his impression of his English landlord, Mr. Shylock: "For Mr. Shylock . . . I had nothing but admiration. I was not used to the social modes of London or to the physiognomy and complexions of the North, and I thought Mr. Shylock looked distinguished. . . . He had the habit of stroking the lobe of his ear and inclining his head to listen. I thought the gesture was attractive; I copied it. I knew of recent events in Europe; they tormented me; and . . . I offered Mr. Shylock my fullest, silent compassion."[1]

Naipaul's portrayal of the enthusiastic young immigrant, who has his heart set on becoming a true Englishman, is, of course, ripe with irony. But there is also something unsettling in this description; as we, the readers, cannot help but notice that Singh's object of admiration is not a *true Englishman* at all, one graced with "the physiognomy and complexions of the North." Rather, Singh's landlord is a Jew, and not just any Jew at that, but one named after the archetypical "ugly Jew" of English literature—Shakespeare's Shylock. Indeed, the man Singh is trying to mimic in order to become an authentic Englishman is in himself a "mimic man." The irony inherent in the situation reaches its climax toward the end of the paragraph, with Singh's implied reference to the Shoah. Here, the tables are suddenly turned, and the Jewish landlord's mimicry assumes center stage, announcing itself most clearly.

Naipaul's short episode offers a tantalizing expression of the dilemma inherent in the "Jewish situation" in Europe. Throughout the history of Europe, Jews have occupied a sensitive location at the discursive crossroads of "sameness" and "otherness." To adapt Homi Bhabha's terminology, they have often been considered "almost the same, but not quite." This ambivalence of Jewish ethnicity goes back all the way to the thought of *Ḥazal*, the ancient Jewish sages. In the canonical text of the Mishnah (the first compendium of rabbinic tradition, c. 200 c.e.), it is noted: "An intense brightness in the German is dark, and the darkness of the Kushite is intense, [but] the Children of Israel are . . . neither black nor white, but in between" (Mishnah, Negaim 2:1). Over the years, this "in between-ness" of the Jews, with its religious, cultural, political, and historical implications, has received a great deal of scholarly attention. Historians, anthropologists, theologians, and others have dedicated studies to exploring the Jews' ambivalent status in Europe; their political and social marginalization have been studied rigorously, the Janus-faced and often tormented relationship between Jews and Christians has preoccupied scholars throughout the ages, and the question of Jewish otherness, uniqueness, or difference continues to excite the imagination of many of our own contemporaries.

In contrast, however, to this scholarly enticement with the question of Jewish-Christian relations, very little attention has been given to the *other side* of Jewish "otherness," so to speak. The question of Jewish perceptions and representations of other Others, and their relationships with them, has been virtually neglected by historians. This scholarly tendency to overlook the question of Jewish agency in the history of race conveys a preconception of what race history—indeed, what race—is all about. It is motivated by two dominant historiographical paradigms: the "colonial paradigm" on the one hand and the "antisemitism paradigm" on the other. The colonial paradigm presupposes that there exists an inherent link between the emergence of race and the histories of colonialism and slavery. According to this formulation, the modern concept of race was invented sometime during the early modern period as a means to justify colonial expansion and plantation slavery. It was then imported into Europe, where it was subsequently applied to various groups that were not enslaved, such as the Jews, the Sami, or the Roma.[2] The outcome of this kind of understanding of the history of race is a tendency to downplay or overlook the intense preoccupation with questions of difference in non-colonial countries, or amongst non-hegemonic groups, such as women or Jews. The past few decades, however, have witnessed a growing dissatisfaction with this scholarly approach. A large corpus of studies has shown that the emergence of racist thought was closely linked to the emergence of other types of biological determinism, such as modern conceptions of gender and childhood. Indeed, racist imagery was often used in order to discuss precisely these other identity groups, and not necessarily in order to convey colonialist messages.[3] In light of this new historiographical trend, more and more research has been dedicated to the study of racial imagery in non-colonialist countries.[4] In addition, scholars have also begun to devote attention to the uses and representations of race amongst non-hegemonic groups, and particularly amongst women.[5] However, these new historiographical trends have somehow overlooked the Jews. Only a handful of studies have been dedicated to the exploration of Jewish attitudes toward race in early modern Europe, and, of these, none have devoted significant attention to the long eighteenth century (as the period between 1660 and 1830 is often called), which is widely considered a formative period in the history of race.

But, of course, Jews have never really been excluded from the history of race. Quite the contrary: they are widely considered to be some of the primary victims of racialist or racist thought. Numerous studies have attempted to unravel the history of antisemitism, of racist or proto-racist attitudes and practices toward Jews. These studies focus on different periods and regions, and offer a wide variety of perspectives and methods, and yet they all seem to share the assumption that in regard to the history of race, Jews are always passive objects of racialist thought and hardly ever its subjects. The reasons for this one-dimensional portrayal of Jews by historians of racial discourse are manifold. Amongst other considerations, they have to do with the traditional distinction between "Jewish" and "general" histories, and the tendency exhibited by scholars of European history to view European Jewish history as "somebody else's business," as it were, an issue to be dealt with by scholars of Jewish history. Clearly, there is also a political aspect to the reluctance to study Jews as active agents in the history of race, which has to do with the understanding of Jewish history as a history of persecution in Diaspora and subsequent liberation in the land of Israel. This meta-narrative of Jewish history dictates an image of the Jews as a persecuted minority that is so strong it completely overshadows other possible images.

This, then, is the lacuna the present book aims to fill. My fundamental premise throughout this study has been that, contrary to their traditional portrayal as mere objects of racialist discourse, European Jews' attitudes toward non-European peoples offer a compelling platform for the study of the history of race in general and in the eighteenth century in particular. Indeed, from their unique vantage point at the central nervous system of European identity, eighteenth-century Jews afford an invaluable view into the ways in which, upon the threshold of modernity, new religious, cultural, and racial identities were imagined and formed. In what follows, then, I attempt to unfold the ways in which those "intimate Others," the Jews, who were the objects of anthropological scrutiny, internalized, adapted, and revised the emerging modern discourse of difference to meet their own ends, and the various roles this discourse played in their perception of the "exotic Other," the "hegemonic Other," and the construction of their own identity. Were European Jews, indeed, "chameleons"—as claimed by Dutch philosopher Isaac de Pinto—who merely assumed the philosophy, culture, and values of their surrounding environments?[6] Were they simply passive recipients of the dominant discourse on identity and alterity, or did they articulate their own unique notions of difference, ethnicity, race, and selfhood?

Of the few studies that have addressed the question of Jewish representations of non-Europeans, almost all have focused on the relationships between Jews and Blacks from ancient times and into the modern period.[7] The vast majority of these studies view Jewish attitudes toward race through a colonialist prism, and ignore such fundamental questions as the connection between notions of gender and race; the Jewish uses of non-European peoples as a means for self-reflection; or the widespread Jewish tendency to utilize the image of the non-European as a means to discuss Jewish-Christian relations. The ensuing result is a small corpus of studies focused almost exclusively on colonial Jews, while ignoring European Jews in general and Ashkenazi Jews (Jews of Western, Eastern, or Central European descent) in particular.

An important exception is Jonathan Schorsch's 2004 *Jews and Blacks in the Early Modern World*. In this seminal work, Schorsch exhibits a keen awareness of the introspective aspect of Jewish discourse on the colonial Other. Indeed, one of the book's primary arguments is that throughout the early modern period, "Blacks served Jewish authors . . . as a rhetorical foil against which their own whiteness shone forth."[8] And yet, unavoidably perhaps, Schorsch's ambitious study, which covers a period of 350 years, has a certain ahistorical quality to it. This is most clearly expressed in the author's characterization of Jewish (and, for that matter, general) discourse on Blacks as almost unchanging throughout the period, a discourse marked by "a remarkable stasis."[9] I would suggest, however, that the static nature of early modern racialism identified by Schorsch is an outcome of the choice to focus on the issue of skin color—a tendency shared by the vast majority of researchers in the field of Jewish racial thought.[10] In fact, it is difficult to see why previous scholarship has focused almost exclusively on Jewish attitudes toward Blacks when most early modern Jewish texts do little to discriminate between Blacks and other non-European peoples, who are most often lumped together under the highly ambiguous term "savages." The term was something of a floating signifier in eighteenth-century literature, and like so many other eighteenth-century terms, it is virtually impossible to pin down. Contemporaries often used it to denote Native Americans, Africans, South-Sea Islanders, at times even Chinese or Jews (particularly, East European Jews). Still, notwithstanding its ambiguities, savagery was the most basic category of eighteenth-century anthropology.

The scholarly focus on Jewish-Black relations appears therefore to be an anachronism, a symptom perhaps of what Roxann Wheeler has diagnosed as "our current preoccupation with chromatism," which in much contemporary research "is reproduced rather than challenged by historical difference."[11] And yet, as I demonstrate throughout the present study, at least up until the late eighteenth century, skin color *did not* play a significant role in European Jews' depictions of other peoples. In fact, most eighteenth-century Ashkenazi writings on "exotic peoples" tended to associate the physical appearance and cultural practices of these peoples with the different climates in which they lived, or with their different nutritional practices. Accordingly, in most cases the opposition between Jews and Christians on the one hand, and non-European peoples on the other, was established not by turning to skin color or other biological traits, but rather by addressing cultural and religious differences. Cannibalism, nudity, homosexuality, infanticide, atheism, lack of technology or manners, polygamy, and other cultural characteristics served as prime markers of difference for Jews and Christians alike. It was only later, toward the end of the eighteenth century, that these contingencies were to be gradually replaced by other, more essentialist notions of difference, most

notably skin color.[12] Indeed, the central thesis of the present study
is that *something did change*—and change radically—in the ways in
which Ashkenazi Jews understood difference during the early modern period.

Throughout the book, I ask two fundamental questions concerning this change. First, I attempt to expose the contours of the change
itself, and tackle the ways in which it affected the uses and representations of race in Jewish discourse over the long eighteenth century.
Second, I review how these Jewish uses and representations of race
correspond with racial discourse in non-Jewish thought during the
same period. These questions are answered in four separate chapters
of the book, which are organized both chronologically and thematically. My method is to begin each chapter by focusing a narrow lens
on one key text, an archetypical test case, and then slowly expand-
ing the view to include other texts. I begin by comparing my key text
to a corresponding non-Jewish text or corpus of texts from the same
period. This technique satisfies the synchronic aspect of my work,
and allows me to arrive at an answer to my question regarding the
difference between Jewish and non-Jewish notions of race. I then continue by comparing my key text with later and earlier Jewish and
non-Jewish texts that are preoccupied with similar issues. This analysis satisfies the diachronic aspect of the work and directs me toward
an answer to the question of change in Jewish notions of difference
throughout the period.

Operating at the level of the text enables an examination of the
racial imagery employed by Jewish authors in all its complexities. It
permits us to view these texts in their proper context, to examine
their intertextual aspects, the ways in which they engage other texts,
both Jewish and non-Jewish, in a multi-faceted and often perplex-
ing dialogue. The focus on four different sets of texts should not be
read, however, as providing an exhaustive account of Jewish attitudes
toward the question of race in the long eighteenth century. Largely
excluded from this study are halakhic (Jewish legal) discussions, such
as those surrounding questions of conversion, burial, and other such
issues. Though I do touch upon some rabbinical texts, such as those
written by Jacob Emden or Abraham ben Elijah, the focus of my
study is on secular conceptions, and halakhic discourse surrounding
race cannot be adequately treated within its confines. For the most
part, this work also excludes Sepharadi Jewry, as well as colonial
Jews, such as the Jewish community of Jodensavanne. For these Jews,

difference was an altogether different matter. The routine encounters with other peoples, the importance of economic considerations, their different status in European society and culture, the different kind of political motives which came into play in their treatment of non-Jews—all these elements make the reality of colonial and Sepharadi Jewry quite different from that of Ashkenazi Jews in Europe, and particularly the maskilim (thinkers of the Jewish Enlightenment), for whom race was a deeply introspective category, and the Other, primarily a conceptual or rhetorical tool.

In terms of corpus selection, the four texts or sets of texts selected for this study correspond with four different literary genres—folktales, philosophical literature, scientific writing, and children's books. These four genres represent the most dominant modes of writing about race during the long eighteenth century, and correlate with the changes in racial discourse throughout the period. In the move from the seventeenth to the eighteenth century, the image of the savage was relocated from the realm of myth and folklore into the philosophical literature of the Enlightenment, where it assumed a dominant position until the rise of anthropological positivism toward the beginning of the nineteenth century. The increasing emphasis on skin color, skull shape, brain size, and other physiological or pseudo-biological traits made the non-European Other a much less appealing philosophical tool. The savage was thus gradually removed from the philosophical laboratory of the Enlightenment and introduced into the physical laboratory of nineteenth-century hard science. A corresponding literary trend may be found in the relocation of colonial discourse from philosophy books and novels into children's books. The latter phenomenon receives poignant expression in turn-of-the-century maskilic literature (literature of the Haskalah), which, for reasons discussed further below, devoted a great deal of attention to Jewish translations of German travel books for children.

Another characteristic of the corpus selected for this study has to do with language. Although the study engages texts written in Yiddish, German, German written in Hebrew characters, and other languages, the reader will notice that particular prominence is given to texts written in biblical Hebrew. This choice stems in part from the prominence given to biblical Hebrew by writers of the Haskalah. Of course, the importance of the Haskalah movement in the construction and proliferation of new modes of thinking throughout the eighteenth century and beyond grants maskilic thinkers a privileged position in the present study. Another reason for focusing on Hebrew works, and particularly Hebrew translations of non-Jewish works, is the unique intertextual nature of the biblical Hebrew used by the maskilim. Writing in biblical Hebrew opened up a world of associations to contemporaneous readers, which are not always immediately available to us today. Significantly, the use of biblical Hebrew was also a nod to thinkers of the non-Jewish Enlightenment(s), for whom the Bible supplied one of the few positive images of the Jew. Here was language that Christians viewed favorably, a language spoken by a people purportedly not corrupted by rabbinical Judaism/Hebrew on the one hand, or by life in Europe/Yiddish on the other. And yet, at the same time, the choice to write in Hebrew was also a choice to remain within the Jewish world, both in terms of language as well as in terms of readership. By choosing to write in Hebrew rather than in German or other non-Jewish languages, maskilic authors asserted their roles as harbingers of Jewish acculturation, while at the same time pledging their allegiance to Jewish tradition, community, and faith. In a way, writing in Hebrew constituted a choice to retain Jewish difference, but render it a difference of a different kind. Forgoing the hybrid Hebrew-Aramaic of rabbinical Judaism, and the equally hybridized Jewish-German or Yiddish spoken by the vast majority of European Jews, maskilic authors declared a kind of intellectual independence that took its inspiration from the image of "the native," in this case the native Israelites. Indeed, one could perhaps say that for a brief moment in the eighteenth century the subaltern could speak in a language of its own. This language was Hebrew.

The first chapter focuses on representations of the savage woman, and particularly the savage mother, through a reading of the memoirs of the German Jewish merchant woman Glikl bas Leib. In her memoirs, written in Yiddish between the years 1691 and 1719, Glikl describes an erotic encounter between a pious Jew and an East Indian woman. Glikl's story is, in fact, part of a tradition of colonial fantasies, such as the story of Pocahontas, or the tale of Inkle and Yarico, which envision the intercultural encounter as an erotic exchange. However, this specific version of the story, with its gruesome infanticidal twist and its incorporation of a highly unorthodox motif of male rape, is intriguing particularly in light of the writer's personal background as a woman, a (bereaved) mother, and a Jew. In my analysis of Glikl's story, I argue that her often radical departures from orthodox European paradigms of cross-cultural contact offer fascinating insights into the ways in which race and gender relate to one another during the early modern period. In addition, throughout the first chapter, I attempt to tackle the assimilation anxieties and inversion fantasies underlying Glikl's story, and to locate them against their Jewish backdrop.

Robert Liberles has warned against overreliance on Glikl as an authoritative source on early modern women.[13] And yet, as the only extant autobiographical text by an early modern Ashkenazi woman, and one of the precious few texts by early modern Jewish women in general, the memoirs should not—or rather *cannot*—be neglected. In the context of Jewish images of race, they afford, when combined with other contemporaneous Jewish and non-Jewish sources, an invaluable view into the ways in which notions of race and gender informed, reinforced, and complicated one another in early modern discourse in general, and in the Jewish and Jewish feminine world in particular. In addition, the folktale, which appears prominently in Glikl's memoirs, turns up in almost identical form in another late seventeenth-century text, a widely read manuscript by the Prague-based couple Beila and Baer Perlhefter. The appearance of the tale in this latter work attests to its positive reception amongst Jewish readers— in particular, it would be safe to assume, Jewish women.

The second chapter follows the image of the savage from its early folkloristic representations in such texts as Glikl's memoirs to the philosophical literature of the mid-eighteenth century. The key text in this chapter is the Lithuanian physician Yehudah ben Mordecai Ha-levi Horowitz's *Amudey beyt Yehudah*, published in Amsterdam in 1766. A prototypical early maskil, Horowitz has been largely forgotten over the years. Like many of his early maskilic peers, his image was overshadowed by later developments that took place during the nineteenth century. A return to this enigmatic author offers an opportunity to view the eighteenth-century Jewish Enlightenment against the context of other Enlightenments of its time, and not through the lens of nineteenth-century developments within the Jewish world.[14]

My reading of Horowitz's book focuses on its paradoxical portrayal of non-Europeans as simultaneously noble and ignoble. Throughout the chapter, I follow this paradox into other eighteenth-century texts such as Daniel Defoe's *Robinson Crusoe* or Steele's "Inkle and Yarico," and argue that the two conflicting images of the savage reflect the Janus-faced character of a strand of religious and conservative Enlightenment, which pursued modernization on the one hand,

while rejecting radicalism on the other. In addition, throughout the
second chapter, I explore the ways in which the maskilim's notions
of nature and savagery correspond with their attitudes toward slavery and colonialism, and attempt to tackle some of the questions surrounding the relationship between colonialism, political hegemony,
and race. Did Jews, as a persecuted minority within Europe, identify
with other subaltern groups? Did they use the image of the colonial
Other as a means to deliver a subversive message regarding European
hegemony and Christian intolerance? Or did they, on the contrary,
utilize the non-European Other as a means to demonstrate a cultural,
religious, or perhaps racial proximity between Christians and Jews?

Chapters 3 and 4 follow the image of the savage from the philosophical literature of the early Haskalah into the very first Hebrew
books for children, written around the turn of the nineteenth century. The choice to focus on children's literature in these two chapters is reflective of the changes that occurred in the uses of the exotic
Other in Jewish (as well as in non-Jewish) thought of the late eighteenth and early nineteenth centuries. Chapter 3 focuses on the Han-
nover-born maskil Baruch Lindau's translation of German pedagogue
Georg Christian Raff's *Naturgeschichte für Kinder*, whereas Chapter
4 discusses the early nineteenth-century Hebrew and Yiddish translations of the widely read works of Joachim Heinrich Campe. My
reasons for focusing on the issue of race in translation are threefold.
First, images of non-European peoples played a significant role in the
building of the maskilic corpus of translations. Second, by comparing
maskilic translations to their non-Jewish source texts, it is possible to
extract and expose some Jewish-specific images and uses of the exotic
Other. Finally, turn-of-the-century Jewish translations demonstrate
the desire of maskilic Jews to acculturate themselves by conforming
to the standards of a hegemonic culture, which was perceived by them
as higher. In this sense, Jewish translators may be viewed as agents of
an internal cultural-colonization. In my discussion of the turn-of-the-
century corpus of Jewish translations, I attempt to identify the relationship between this form of internal colonization and the external
colonization depicted in the translated books.

The final two chapters demonstrate the ways in which Jewish
translators dealt with new, more rigid notions of difference put forth
by the writers of the original texts. Written in 1788, Lindau's Hebrew
translation demonstrates a kind of reluctant resistance to racism by
continuing to employ archaic notions of skin color and ethnicity. It

appears that Lindau, like many other Jewish thinkers of his time, was wary of the new intellectual trends of the late eighteenth century, which called for a more deterministic understanding of physical difference between men. I propose that this reluctance to abandon the environmentalist paradigm was inspired by Lindau's understanding of the hazards inherent in the new notions of race for Jews. As the century progressed, however, it became much more difficult to continue upholding archaic notions of skin color and physical difference. Thus, later texts were less preoccupied with destabilizing the new racial discourse, but rather reproduced it in their own, maskilic versions of the colonial fantasy. This cultural shift is discernible in the early nineteenth-century Hebrew children's books, which are the focus of the final chapter of my work.

The eighteenth century was a period of radical changes in Europeans' understandings of identity and difference. Well versed in the intellectual trends of their time, Jewish writers began turning their gaze eastward, toward the Orient (both far and near), and westward, to the New World. Often, it was a longing gaze, a reflection upon viable cultural alternatives to contemporaneous European (Jewish) life. Other times it was a subversive gaze, which aimed to challenge European notions of identity and alterity. Still other gazes were inspired by these same notions, and utilized the Others out there as a means to establish Jews as part of the White or "civilized" world. However, whether longing or loathing, subversive or conservative, the European Jewish gaze eastward and westward was almost always also a gaze inward. In their scrutinizing of the non-European Other, Jewish thinkers attempted to delineate the borders of their own racial, cultural, or political identity in many different, often conflicting ways.

A few final words of caution; any comparison between cultures runs the risk of simplifying one side of the equation while complicating the other. This is especially true when juxtaposing a subaltern culture with a hegemonic one. In the present study I have attempted to tackle this methodological risk by occasionally drawing the reader's attention to the polyphony not only of Jewish discourse on race, but also to that of non-Jewish discourse. Indeed, it is my hope that by focusing on the nuances and complexities of Jewish racial discourse, new light may also be shed on similar trends within the various non-Jewish discourses.

The reader will also note that the study often employs such politically charged and culturally constructed terms as *savage, civilized, race*, and *exotic*. For reasons of convenience I have chosen not to surround these terms with scare quotes. Their cultural constructedness, however, lies at the very heart of this study. Conversely, the terms *Black* and *White* appear in uppercase throughout the text when signifying social groups, and in lowercase when meant to designate formal color.

An East Indian Encounter

Rape and Infanticide in the Memoirs
of Glikl Bas Leib

Maternal Love! thy watchful glances roll
From zone to zone, from pole to distant pole;
Cheer the long patience of the brooding hen,
Soothe the she-fox that trembles in her den,
Mid Greenland ice-caves warm the female bear,
And rouse the tigress from her sultry lair.
—LUCY AIKIN, 1816

And thou shalt eat the fruit of thine own body, the flesh of thy sons and
of thy daughters, which the Lord thy God hath given thee, in the siege,
and in the straitness, wherewith thine enemies shall distress thee.
—DEUTERONOMY 28:53

The past few decades have seen a growing scholarly awareness to the
fact that notions of gender and race are closely intertwined in early
modern discussions of difference. Scholars such as Susanne Zantop,
Margarita Zamora, and Louis Montrose have called our attention to
the ways in which early modern colonial discourse often employed
eroticism and gender talk in order to narrate, justify, and at times
criticize the conquest, colonization, and subjection of colonial peoples
and lands.[1] But women were not merely a useful colonial analogy.
Rather, for the vast majority of early modern Europeans, they were
much more concrete, immediate, and tangible objects than those wild
savages, who inhabited faraway lands. Indeed, in recent years, more
and more scholarly attention has been given to the ways in which
colonial discourse interacted with gender talk and served to construct
and deliver notions of femininity, as well as to discuss other non-
hegemonic groups within Europe.[2] In many cases, the relationship

between race and gender as discursive tools is merely suggestive, but every once in a while there appears a text that is located right at the heart of this complex discursive web. The memoirs of the German Jewish merchant woman Glikl bas Leib constitute one such text.

In her memoirs, Glikl relates a folktale that is an early variant of the ubiquitous European tale depicting an encounter between a European sailor and an Indian maid. Glikl's idiosyncratic version of the tale affords an invaluable opportunity to investigate the ways in early modern notions of racial difference were informed and complicated by notions of femininity, maternity, and childhood. Her understanding of cross-cultural contact is especially intriguing in light of her personal background as a woman, a mother, and a Jew. At the very center of the tale is another woman—a savage woman—who butchers and devours her own son. Thus, Glikl's story offers a turbulent encounter between notions of savagery and civilization, maternity and femininity, nature and family, Judaism and Christianity. Such encounters would continue to appear in Jewish writings on non-European peoples throughout the long eighteenth century, and would serve Jewish authors as a means to adapt, revise, and deconstruct notions of identity and difference. As in many other Jewish discussions of savages, Glikl's story reveals Jewish-specific fantasies and anxieties, as well as a unique Jewish feminine perspective. However, the story also reflects more general concerns, found also amongst Glikl's non-Jewish contemporaries. As such, it offers an excellent starting point for our present discussion.

GLIKL AND HER MEMOIRS

The growing interest in questions of gender and family within the historical discipline in general, and the field of Jewish studies in particular, has been kind with Glikl. As author of the earliest surviving autobiographical text by a Jewish woman, over the past few years, Glikl has risen to stardom. Her late seventeenth-century memoirs, which remained in manuscript form for almost two centuries, have now appeared in German, Hebrew, and English translations, and have been the subject of several major studies.[3] The most important of the latter are Chava Turniansky's definitive Hebrew translation and critical edition of the memoirs, which appeared in 2006, and Natalie Zemon Davis's discussion of the memoirs in her 1995 *Women on the Margins*.[4] Here, I offer only a concise overview of Glikl's life, and a brief discussion of some of the most important characteristics of the memoirs.

Glikl was born in Hamburg in 1645 to a family of Jewish merchants. At the age of twelve, she was engaged to Chaim of Hamel, and within two years the couple was wed. The marriage was generally a happy one, but it ended tragically in 1689 when Chaim fell on a sharp stone and died. Chaim's demise left Glikl alone with the couple's business debts and twelve children (another two children had died at an early age). But Glikl prevailed; she continued to run the family business on her own and enjoyed a fair degree of financial success. She was not unique in this respect. Even though there had been, since the sixteenth century, a gradual process of excluding women from the world of work in Christian society, this process had not been completed by Glikl's time, and European women, especially single women or widows, continued to support themselves as laundresses, maids, or even merchants throughout the seventeenth and eighteenth centuries. This was especially true in the Jewish community, where women often took an active part in the financial support of their families, and it was not uncommon that a widow should continue managing her late husband's business.[5]

A decade after her husband's demise, however, Glikl tired of her life as an independent merchantwoman and remarried. This second marriage was far from successful, and Glikl eventually came to regret her decision to remarry. She writes: "God laughed at my thoughts and plans, and had already long decided on my doom to repay me for my sins and for relying on people. For I should not have thought of remarrying, for I could not hope to meet another R' Chaim Hamel, and I should have stayed with my children, and accepted the good, as well as the bad, all according to God's will."[6] Before long, Glikl's husband encountered severe financial difficulties and was forced to declare bankruptcy. He died in 1712 and Glikl was once again left to fend for herself. In her desperation, she resorted to seeking the aid of her children and moved into the home of her daughter Esther, where she remained until her death in 1724.

Glikl began writing her memoirs in 1691 as a means to cope with her grief over Chaim's death. And yet, even though Chaim's spirit haunts the text from beginning to end, still the memoirs are not merely a monument to his memory. They do not open with his birth or end with his demise. Rather, they track the course of Glikl's own life, beginning with the history of her parents, and present Glikl's views on such issues as ethics and religion, commerce and family, and Christians and Jews.[7] Contrary to later autobiographies, both Jewish and non-Jewish, such as the memoirs of Salomon Maimon, Henriette Herz, Mordecai Aaron Günzberg, and of course Rousseau, Glikl devotes very little attention to her childhood in the text.[8] This marginalization of what later writers would consider the formative period in the life of the individual bears witness to the perception of childhood amongst Glikl's contemporaries.[9] As shall become clear over the course of our discussion, such disregard for children and childhood stands in direct contrast to the pedagogical thought of the Jewish maskilim, which would begin to take form during the second half of the eighteenth century, and which, inspired by such thinkers as Rousseau, Joachim Heinrich Campe, and Johann Basedow, would put great emphasis on childhood experiences in the formation of the adult personality. Further evidence of a dismissive attitude toward children and childhood is found in Glikl's literary treatment of the deaths in her family. Throughout the memoirs, the younger the deceased, the less attention is given to his or her demise. Thus, Chaim's death, which was the impetus for writing her memoirs, receives far greater attention and is described in much more detail than the deaths of Glikl's four children: three-year-old Mate, an unnamed two-week-old baby, newly wedded Hendeleh, and Lob, who died at the age of twenty-eight.[10] Similar attitudes are exhibited in other memoirs from the period, such as the early seventeenth-century memoirs of Asher Ha-levi or Jacob Emden's *Megilat sefer*, written sometime around 1776.[11]

Another important characteristic of the memoirs is the ubiquitous use of folktales, fables, anecdotes, and stories that serve to deliver Glikl's religious, social, and moral views. Though these stories are most often derived from other sources, they play a central role in the memoirs. As Marcus Moseley explains: "It is the *Mayse* [tale] that provides [Glikl] with the greatest latitude for autobiographical expression, albeit indirect and disguised.... The stories ... constitute a realm of autobiographical play; she can imply and say things in and through her stories that would be unmentionable in the life-account proper."[12] The exact nature and meanings of this "autobiographical play" crystallize in what is the longest and most complex of the stories appearing in the memoirs, the story of the pious Jew and his savage wife.

THE STORY OF THE PIOUS JEW AND HIS TWO WIVES

The story tells of a pious Jew and devout torah scholar who lacks a talent for business. In light of his financial inadequacy, he is forced to borrrow money and is subsequently incarcerated for a debt he could not repay. Following the man's arrest, his wife becomes the family's sole breadwinner, working as a laundress on the beach.[13] One day, she is spotted by a Christian sailor who, captivated by her beauty, abducts her. After his release from prison, the man and his two sons set out on a journey to save the abducted woman, but the boys also disappear, and the pious Jew himself is stranded on an East Indian island. There, he is taken hostage by a band of wild savages and forced into marriage with the tribe's princess, a hairy and cannibalistic beast of a woman. Two years go by, during which the savage woman bears her husband a child. The man remains, however, miserable, and just as he begins to contemplate suicide he is confronted by a heavenly voice, instructing him to dig for a hidden treasure on the island and then seek salvation on the shore. Following these instructions, he discovers a box of riches hidden in the sand and then, while on the shore, sees a European ship. At first, the ship's crew is reluctant to approach the man who, after living with the savages for so long, has grown hairy and has come to resemble them in every way. However, once they hear him speak, they realize that he is indeed a *"mentsh"* like them and they resolve to rescue him.

Upon learning that he has left her, the man's savage wife calls to him from the shore, begging that he take her with him. He mocks her, shouting, "What have I to do with wild animals?" (G. Tur., 92; G. Abr., 26). In response, the savage woman grabs the couple's child by its feet and tears it in half. She then proceeds to throw half of the child's severed body toward her husband in the ship and devours what remains of her son. The story continues with the ship's crew converting to Judaism and forming a small colony on a neighboring island, governed by the pious Jew. During his reign on the island, the man discovers his long-lost wife and sons, and they live happily ever after (G. Tur., 80–106).

As Glikl herself informs her readers, the story of the pious Jew and his savage wife is not her own original creation. The tale's exact source is the focus of ongoing debate amongst Glikl scholars.[14] In a recent study, Nathanael Riemer uncovered another version of the story in a late seventeenth-century manuscript titled *Beer sheva*, by the couple Beila and Baer Perlhefter of Prague. Barring a few linguistic differences, this version is almost identical to Glikl's. In addition, the manuscript contains two additional stories that are also found, in slight variations, in the memoirs.[15] Still, given the linguistic variations between the tales, it is difficult to ascertain whether Glikl was indeed familiar with the Perlhefter's manuscript or whether she copied her story directly from it, perhaps from a copy no longer extant. The inclusion of the story in a second Jewish manuscript may simply attest to its popularity during the period.

The exact origins of the story notwithstanding, it is clear that in her memoirs Glikl appropriated the story for herself and interweaved it into her personal life narrative. Indeed, it is my contention that we should read the story as Glikl's own, not only because it is the longest and most complex tale appearing in the memoirs; more importantly, as Turniansky, has observed, Glikl tends to borrow existing stories and to assimilate them into the framework of her memoirs in such a way as to make them her own.[16] This understanding of Glikl's autobiographical use of existing stories is reinforced by what appears to be her careful and conscientious selection of stories with which to pepper her text. Her choice of stories creates a recurring motif of filicide in the memoirs, which implies a fascination with the issue, almost an obsession with it. Of the seventeen full stories appearing in the memoirs, including the one discussed here, I have counted six in which Glikl discusses parents who killed or almost killed their children, either intentionally or unintentionally, directly or indirectly (G. Tur., 30–33; 107–180; 236–239; 376–383; 504–519). Thus, Glikl tells of a father bird that drops its young into the ocean, and also offers an adaptation of the story of David and Absalom. The child death motif is evident also in the three stories Glikl supposedly took from *Beer sheva*, all of which raise the possibility of the intentional or accidental killing of a child by its parent. Thus, for instance, in both Glikl's memoirs and in *Beer sheva* we find a story about a prince whose friends conspire to have his father, the king, kill him.[17] Additional references to filicide are also made in the memoirs, for instance, when Glikl twice mentions the biblical story of Abraham's willingness to sacrifice his son Isaac, in a comical reference to the story of King Solmon's trial (where once again we encounter the notion of a bisected baby), or when Glikl compares herself to King David, who grieves the slaying of his son by his own men (G. Tur., 34–35, 132–137, 168–169, 552–553). The appearance of the filicidal motif in such a text, which the author explicitly addresses to her children (e.g., G. Tur., 10–13, 26–29), is (to put it mildly) somewhat confounding. It becomes even more surprising when we consider Glikl's own biography as a bereaved mother and widow. How, then, are we to interpret the dominance of child murder in the memoirs?

Glikl's intense preoccupation with filicide challenges the traditional scholarly portrayal of the memoirs as the work of a prototypical "Yiddishe mame," someone constantly preoccupied with her children's well-being and the quest for an ideal family life. One critic complains that scholarly overreliance on Glikl's memoirs has resulted in an inaccurately positive depiction of early modern Jewish family life. Glikl, it is argued, "provides a picturesque portrait of the ideal family in action, but other memoirs fill out the impression by depicting what everyday Jewish life meant for many others."[18] Such readings of Glikl dominate literary, historical, and psychological analysis of the text, and can even be observed in slight deviations from the source text in modern-day translations. Thus, for example, while musing on the issue of divine absolution, Glikl writes: "God forbid if the Holy One had no more mercy on us than parents [*eltern*] have for children! Because if a person [*mentsh*] has a bad child he helps and takes trouble over him two, three times but at length grows tired and thrusts the child, allowing him to go his own way, even though he knows it means his ruin" (G. Tur. 16). Significantly, in two separate translations of the memoirs (one into English, the other into Hebrew), this paragraph is (mis)translated: "God forbid if the Holy One had no more mercy on us than a human father has for his children."[19] In contrast, Glikl discusses the love parents in general (*eltern*) have for their children, not merely paternal love. This telling deviation from the source text demonstrates the scholarly tendency to overlook or downplay Glikl's ambivalence toward the meanings and nature of maternity. In fact, even though a less idealized image of Glikl has emerged in recent years, her doubts, anxieties, and convictions concerning motherhood have yet to be adequately addressed.[20]

I suggest that in her usage of the image of the cannibalistic mother, Glikl unwittingly partakes in two of the most interesting debates of her time: the debate concerning the nature and limits of maternal devotion and the debate surrounding the nature and limits of civilization. Throughout the eighteenth century, these two discussions were often interwoven, and the image of the murderous mother ran through them, binding them together with strands of exoticism, mystery, and horror. A review of these two debates, both together and apart, will allow a better understanding of Glikl's preoccupation with the image of the infanticidal savage, and the ways in which this image corresponds with the major cultural trends of Glikl's time.

THE EROTIC ENCOUNTER IN EIGHTEENTH-CENTURY COLONIAL LITERATURE

Glikl's story corresponds with what was perhaps the most popular short story of eighteenth-century Europe. One of the earliest and certainly the most famous written versions of the story is Richard Steele's "History of Inkle and Yarico," which appeared in *The Spectator* in 1711. Steele tells of an English sailor by the name of Thomas Inkle who is stranded on a Caribbean island inhabited by savage cannibals. Inkle is saved by an "Indian maid" by the name of Yarico, and the two fall instantly in love. However, within time, Inkle tires of his exotic lover, and after being rescued by a European ship he decides to sell Yarico into slavery. In her desperation, Yarico calls to him and tells him that she is pregnant with his child, but he, in response, merely raises her price.[21]

Steele's story was extremely popular throughout the eighteenth century, and it was adapted into ballads, children's stories, songs, a few comedies, and a famous opera by George Colman. It was used in order to deliver various messages concerning such issues as slavery, colonialism, ethical trade, and women's rights.[22] But though they vary in detail, language, and genre, as well as in their meanings and motivations, almost all versions of the story share at least three components: (a) they are all love stories; (b) they all share a sense of sympathy toward the savage woman; and (c) they are all critical of the behavior of her European lover. Let us shortly review each of these components before returning to Glikl's version of the tale.

Stories of the Inkle and Yarico trope are part of a longstanding tradition of colonial romances, which employ eroticism to describe the conquest of the New World. The sexual potential of the colonial encounter is already alluded to in Amerigo Vespucci's 1504 letter to Pier Soderini. Like Columbus before him, Vespucci makes special note of the natives' nudity and adds: "The greatest sign of friendship which they show you is that they give you their wives and their daughters, and a father or a mother deems himself or herself highly honored when they bring you a daughter, even though she be a young virgin, if you sleep with her, and hereunto they use every expression of friendship."[23] Such erotic formulations of the conquest were continued throughout the early modern period, both in literature and in art.[24] An infamous example is Walter Raleigh's graphic 1595 description of Guiana as a country "that hath yet her maidenhead, never sacked, turned nor wrought."[25] A less familiar but no less suggestive formulation is found in Thomas Morton's 1637 description of New England as "a faire virgin, longing to be sped, / And meete her lover in a Nuptiall bed, / Deck'd in rich ornaments t'advaunce her state," or Roger Wolcott's 1725 description of the English settlers who press forward upon "the virgin stream, who had, as yet, Never been violated with a ship."[26] These eroticized descriptions of the conquest were, of course, a pervasive colonialist tool. The feminization of the land and its inhabitants provided Europeans with a language by means of which it was possible to present European hegemony in the New World as a natural and even benevolent state of affairs, much like the husband's authority over his wife.[27] As Zantop has observed, stories like Steele's "History of Inkle and Yarico," which envisioned the conquest as a mutually desirable affair, offered readers "a model for successful, 'humane' colonization."[28] A recurring motif in such colonial romances, one which features in all versions of the Inkle and Yarico story, is the half-European, half-native child, born to a member of the native royalty or nobility. This hybrid child, who appears as a legitimate heir of the native throne, constitutes a further means of establishing a firm and legitimate colonial rule.[29]

A second characteristic of the Inkle and Yarico tales is that of identification with the savage woman. An interesting aspect of this identification is the somewhat odd dichotomy that the various authors implicitly draw between Yarico, the noble Caribbean savage, who is idealized as a naïve and betrayed woman, and her cannibalistic tribesmen, who are often demonized by the tale. In George Colman's famous operatic version, Yarico is portrayed as a noble, generous maid, "beautiful as an angel," who protects Inkle from her cruel countrymen, the cannibals.[30] This dichotomy between the individual noble savage, who often appears in feminized form, and his or her barbaric tribe, which often consists of hairy, monstrous beings, is discussed in some detail in Chapter 2. For the present discussion, suffice to note that this Janus-faced image of the savage is an extremely widespread characteristic of early modern colonial literature, which receives one of its clearest articulations in the Inkle and Yarico trope.

The characteristic of identification with the savage woman is closely connected to the final component of the Inkle and Yarico story discussed above—that of aversion toward the behavior of the European man. This last element is perhaps most pervasive and is found in all previously discussed versions of the tale. In his early version of the story, which is said to have inspired Steele's tale, Richard Ligon explains that the English sailor "forgot the kindness of the poor maid, that had ventured her life for his safety, and sold her for a slave, who was as free born as he: and so poor Yarico for her love, lost her liberty."[31] In Salomon Gessner's German version, even "Yariko's" tribesmen are portrayed in a more sympathetic light, and their attack on "Inkel" is motivated not by cannibalism, but by the desire to protect themselves from their cruel conquerors, the Europeans.[32] Yet even in versions in which a less idealized image of the native woman emerges, the narrator's sympathies still lie with the betrayed savage. One such version is in Jean Mocquet's *Voyages en Afrique, Asie, Indes Orientales et Occidentales*, in which the savage woman is portrayed as infanticidal. Mocquet's version of the story is closest to Glikl's, and is the only non-Jewish version known to employ the infanticidal motif. And yet, even though Mocquet's savage woman resembles Glikl's in having slain her son, still, the object of the writer's scorn is her husband, the English sailor, who abandons his savage wife and their mutual child, after having been saved by her.[33] Aversion toward the European sailor's behavior is evident also in the earliest Hebrew versions of the tale, which appeared in David Zamość's 1819 *Tokhahot musar* and Baruch Shenfeld's 1811 *Musar haskel*, which are, in fact, adaptations of German pedagogue Joachim Heinrich Campe's retelling of the story in his *Sittenbüchlein für Kinder aus gesitteten Ständen* (1777). In all three versions of the story—Campe, Shenfeld, and Zamość's—the narrator's identification with the savage woman receives dramatic expression through the frame narrative, in which the children listening to the tale begin to cry, expressing their deep pity for the savage woman and their outrage at the European sailor's behavior.[34]

Let us return now to Glikl's version of the tale. Of course, Glikl was not directly familiar with Steele's tale, or with Ligon or Mocquet's earlier versions. And yet, the similarities between the tale of the pious Jew and stories of the Yarico and Inkle trope are unmistakable. As Davis points out, there is a clear connection between the Jewish folktale appearing in Glikl's memoirs (and, I would add, in the

Perlhefter's *Beer sheva*) and Mocquet's story of savage infanticide.[35] However, the differences between Glikl's story and other stories of the Inkle and Yarico trope are also striking; in the "Jewish" version of the tale, the three components of love, identification, and criticism of the European sailor's behavior are entirely absent. Glikl offers her readers a uniquely dismal version of the colonial encounter, which is not a love story but a horrendous tale of rape and infanticide in which the savage woman arouses neither empathy nor pity, but rather abhorrence and disgust. She is no different from her cannibalistic and hairy tribesmen, and the only reason she refrains from slaying and eating the Jewish visitor is that her appetite for human flesh is superseded by more intense fleshly desires. Of course, the European Jewish protagonist is in no way attracted to this cannibalistic monster. On the contrary, he is repulsed by the native woman and, in contrast to his non-Jewish doubles, does not wish to marry, domesticate, impregnate, or enslave her. This unique indifference toward the savage woman and her child, which Glikl expects her readers to share, signifies perhaps an underlying indifference to the kind of colonial dilemmas and aspirations that preoccupied her non-Jewish contemporaries. In stark contrast to these authors, Glikl does not view the intercultural encounter as an opportunity for the cultural colonization of the non-European Other. Unlike other Inkle and Yarico tales, her story does not criticize exploitative colonialism, nor does it endorse "colonial benevolence."

In this sense, Glikl is paradigmatic of the problems inherent in attempting to read early modern Jewish texts on the non-European world through a purely colonial prism. In fact, even though some Jews—mainly Dutch, French, and English Jews of Sepharadi origin—did take part in early modern colonialist enterprises, most early modern Ashkenazi Jews, and certainly women such as Glikl, were uninterested parties when it came to their countries' colonialist policies. Being so remote from the locus of political power, they could hardly be suspected of entertaining some form of latent colonial fantasies. And indeed, in her study on representations of the "new world" in early modern Jewish literature, Limor Mintz-Manor finds the same kind of indifferent attitude toward colonialism in other early modern Ashkenazi works, particularly in Abraham Farissol's *Igeret orḥot olam*.[36] Similarly, Martin Jacobs questions the applicability of the Orientalist or colonialist paradigms to medieval Jewish thought and suggests that a new theoretical framework be applied to the writings of non-colonialist Jews.[37] As we shall see, Ashkenazi interest in colonization—both external and internal—would appear only later, in the second half of the eighteenth century, in the writings of the Jewish Enlightenment, the Haskalah.[38]

Not surprisingly, then, Glikl's story cannot be understood as yet another colonial love story, in the same vein as other Inkle and Yarico tales. In fact, in Glikl's version, the victim of the encounter between the European man and the savage woman is not the colonized woman but the man, who is raped by the lustful cannibalistic princess.[39] Correspondingly, Glikl's sympathies lie not with the deserted woman, but rather with the pious Jew. This man, who leaves his child to die at the hands of a savage mother, without showing even a hint of sorrow or remorse, is the hero of Glikl's tale.[40] In Glikl's memoirs, then, the story is shorn of its humanistic and sentimentalist character and becomes a Eurocentric anecdote that draws a sharp distinction between the civilized European and the savage Other. But the question is—why? Why is the only version in which the author sympathizes not with the colonized woman but rather with the European man written by a Jewish woman? Does this difference stem from Glikl's Jewish background? Does it reflect a uniquely Jewish understanding of the meanings of cross-cultural contact? Or does it perhaps reveal a specifically feminine or Jewish-feminine response to the tale? Put differently, if the mutual attraction between the European man and the native woman symbolizes the colonial fantasies of such Christian authors as Steele, Colman, or Gessner, which fantasies, or rather which anxieties, does the rape of the European man by the native woman in Glikl's tale betray?

THE RAPE OF THE COLONIST

Stories of the rape or sexual assault of European men by native women are extremely rare in early modern travel literature.[41] Even though European writers did tend to view native women as more lustful than both European women and native men, and the seduction scenes depicted in their travel narratives may often appear somewhat aggressive, still, the European man is most often portrayed as taking an amused delight in these blunt advances. Thus, for example, in John Thelwall's comic retelling of Inkle and Yarico, the seduction of the European man is presented as an amusing reversal of traditional gender roles: "Aye, I sees how it is: it's the custom here for the women to make love. Why then, of course the men must be coy. I supposes now she'll think nothing of me if I'm won too easy; for I thinks they say we're in the Auntoy's Podes, and so every thing's reversed here."[42]

Another comic description of the somewhat forward advances of native women appears in Diderot's *Supplément au voyage de Bougainville*, in which a French chaplain is seduced by a Tahitian woman and spends the night with her while occasionally crying: "Mais ma religion! Mais mon état!" [But my religion! My vocation!].[43]

A different description, somewhat closer to Glikl's own, may be found in Tobias Smollett's *Humphry Clinker*. Smollett tells of the Scottish traveler Lismahago, who is taken captive by a band of Miami Indians, along with his companion, Murphy. The Indians decide to feast on Murphy and adopt Lismahago instead of their deceased leader.[44] Lismahago has no choice but to join the tribe and marry the widow princess Squinkinacoosta, who is described in the following terms: "Lismahago's bride, the squaw Squinkinacoosta, . . . shewed a great superiority of genius in the tortures which she contrived and executed with her own hands. She vied with the stoutest warrior in eating the flesh of the sacrifice [Murphy]."[45] Smollett's portrayal of the Indian princess as a wild and voracious cannibal parodies the traditional distinction, made by such colonial love stories as "Inkle and Yarico," between the savage princess and her cannibalistic tribesmen. Smollett makes it clear that the tribe's princess is just as savage and cruel as her male counterparts, and that the European visitor has no choice but to marry her. In this sense, Smollett's anecdote bears some resemblance to Glikl's story. However, Smollett promptly departs from Glikl's notion of coerced cross-cultural intimacy and clarifies (ironically, perhaps) that the marriage is anything but coerced and unhappy: "[Lismahago] had lived very happily with this accomplished squaw for two years, during which she bore him a son, who is now the representative of his mother's tribe."[46] Additionally, while Glikl describes the savage princess as being a hairy and physically disgusting beast of a woman, Smollett's Squinkinacoosta is portrayed as beautiful and attractive.[47] Thus we find that even in this case of coerced marriage, the European man is not raped by the native woman, but rather enjoys the sexual contact between colonizer and colonized.

The closest descriptions I have found in a non-Jewish travel narrative to Glikl's portrayal of the sexual victimization of a European traveler by a native woman appear in Jonathan Swift's *Gulliver's Travels*. In this account, Gulliver expresses his disgust at being used as a virtual sex toy by the giant women of Brobdingnag. His aversion to the women is explained by their size, which accentuates every defect in their bodies. Gulliver is once again the victim of sexual harassment during his stay in the land of the Houyhnhms, where he is sexually assaulted by an eleven-year-old Yahoo but is rescued by his protector, the sorrel nag. Here, too, the savage female is presented as not entirely unattractive, as Gulliver notes, contrary to what may be expected: "Her Countenance did not make an Appearance altogether so hideous."[48]

Though they differ vastly in context, purpose, and meaning, all these accounts of sexually aggressive women share a distinct comic aspect, which is also discernible in other tales of sexually aggressive women situated within Europe itself. In Henry Fielding's *Joseph Andrews*, for instance, poor Joseph is attacked by a whole host of lustful and downright sex-crazed women, resulting in several farcical states.[49] Similarly, John Cleland's *Fanny Hill* describes the temptation (or rather, to our modern sensibilities, rape) of a mentally challenged young man by Fanny and a colleague, as a highly amusing episode: "Struck with the novelty of the scene, he did not know which way to look or move; but tame, passive, simpering, with his mouth half open, in stupid rapture, stood and tacitly suffered me to do what I pleased with him."[50] The comic aspect of feminine sexual assault is also found in at least one eighteenth-century Jewish text. In the memoirs of Salomon Maimon, the author relates to his readers what he himself terms "a comical scene," in which an educated widow attempted to seduce him, and at length grasped him by the hand, refusing to let go. "I began to laugh immoderately," writes Maimon, "tore myself from her grasp, and rushed away."[51] Such comical treatment of the sexual assault of a man by a woman is characteristic of eighteenth-century (as well as contemporary) writing. Literary scholar Patricia Spacks explains that in such stories, the women's "sexual aggression is a joke, specifically because it belongs to women, not imagined to present real threats to men."[52]

And yet, the comic dimension of feminine sexual aggression is entirely absent from Glikl's story of the sexual assault of the pious Jew. The latter perceives the savage woman to be a real and concrete threat—not only of a sexual but also of a religious, and indeed mortal, nature.[53]

SAVAGES AND *SEIRIM*

We find that Glikl's portrayal of the European man as sexual victim is not characteristic of the colonial literature of her time. In her discussion of the memoirs, Davis suggests in passing that the story may have been inspired by the widespread folkloristic theme of a marriage between a Jewish man and a she-demon. The particular story Davis has in mind is the "Maaseh Yerushalmy," a popular early modern tale in which a shipwrecked man is saved by a she-demon, to whom he is reluctantly wed. Eventually, the man begins enjoying his life with the she-demon, and the two have a child together. However, at length, he is overcome with longing for his human wife and sons, and escapes his demon-wife. In response, the demon wife sues her husband for divorce and, in some versions of the story, kills him.[54] There are, of course, many differences between this story and Glikl's tale; most importantly, "Maaseh Yerushalmy" presents its Jewish hero in a highly unfavorable light. However, the similarities between the two narratives are also striking. Other demon wife tales also feature some of the prominent motifs of Glikl's tale, such as travel to a faraway land, coerced bigamy, and, in at least two cases, the killing of a child by its (in this case, demon) mother.[55] Of particular interest is the Galician oikotype of the "Maaseh m'Worms," of which, unfortunately, only a late nineteenth-century written version has survived. The tale features three of the most striking motifs of Glikl's story: rape, infanticide, and the shredding to pieces of a child. It tells of a Jewish man who mistakenly marries a she-demon and is physically forced to consummate the marriage. Eventually, the man discovers a certain root to which his diabolical wife cannot be exposed, and he uses it to banish her. Frustrated at her husband's betrayal, the demon woman kidnaps the children she has borne him, shreds them to pieces, and tosses their remains at his feat.[56] The relationship between the tale of the pious Jew and such folktales as "Maaseh m'Worms" or "Maaseh Yerushalmy" is undeniable. It is possible that the tale found in Glikl's memoirs and in the Perlhefter's *Beer sheva* was a kind of modern formulation of the mythical demon wife tale, in which the modern day colonial Other—the savage—took the place of the earlier diabolical Other—the demon wife. Indeed, it has long been recognized that in medieval and early modern European imagination, wild men and savages were closely linked to the world of demons.[57]

The close connection between Glikl's story and the story of the demon wife is also attested to by Glikl's physical description of the savage woman as hairy. The motif of excessive hairiness as a symbol of the demonic is widespread in European literature, both Jewish and Christian. Use of this motif goes all the way back to the Bible, in

Figure 1. Sabbatian demon, from Jacob Emden, *Sefer shimush*,
1758. Reproduced by permission of the National Library Israel.

which the term *seirim* (hairy) is used to denote a type of demons. Use
of the term, and with it the association of body hair with the demonic,
continued in the medieval and early modern periods.[58] Thus, for
instance, in an anti-Sabbatian pamphlet published in 1758, R' Jacob
Emden depicts the Sabbatian movement as a hairy demon, bearing
three faces (one for each of monotheistic religion), hoofs, a tail, and
wings of fire (fig. 1).

It is important to note, however, that the close connection between
Glikl's savage woman and the image of the coercive demon-wife notwithstanding, Glikl leaves no room for doubt as to the humanity of
her savage heroine. Indeed, even though she refers to the woman as
"woman" [וייב, G. Tur., 90, 92] and "animal" [טיר, G. Tur., 90, 92]
interchangeably, she makes a point of mentioning that the woman
wore a large fig leaf to cover her shame. The motif of the fig leaf is of
course an allusion to the biblical story of the expulsion from Eden,
and is ripe with symbolism of primordial sinfulness. Similar images
of hirsute women wearing fig leaves to cover their shame appeared
also in other, non-Jewish sources, particularly in medicine and natural geography books (figs. 2, 3). The presence of the leaf must also be
understood, however, as an indication of the woman's humanity.

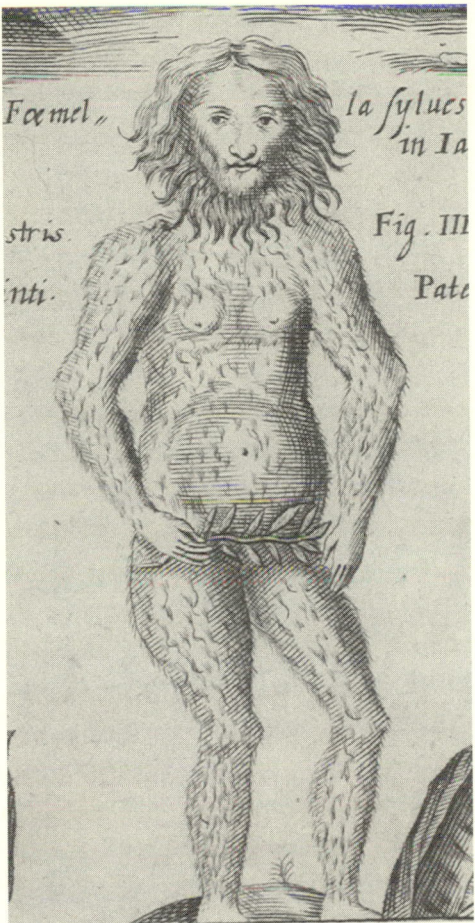

Figure 2. Wild woman of Java (detail), from
Gaspar Schott, *Physica Curiosa* (1662).
Reproduced by permission of the University
of Iowa John Martin Rare Book Room.

After all, only humans, who have tasted from the tree of knowledge, experience the sensation of shame.[59]

The image of the hairy wild man also has its roots in antiquity, and appears as early as the epic of Gilgamesh.[60] Admittedly, the association of savages or wild men with excessive body hair was called into question by early modern "professional ethnographers," but it continued to dominate popular notions of savagery throughout the eighteenth century, and even later.[61] In Carl Linnaeus's acclaimed *Systema Naturae*, for instance, feral children, who had grown up outside

Figure 3. Wild woman (detail), from Gaspar Schott, *Physica Curiosa* (1662). Reproduced by permission of the University of Iowa John Martin Rare Book Room.

of civilization, were characterized as hairy and mute. This kind of characterization was ubiquitous during the eighteenth century and was repeated by later writers as well.[62] In fact, hairy children continued to exist in European imagination well into the twentieth century, as attested by a 1937 newspaper report from Palestine that relates the capture of a "four footed wild-man, in the form of a girl." The image of the child, who is said to have subsided on frogs, snakes, and grass, was probably inspired by the famous case of Marie Angelique Leblanc, who was captured in Songi in 1731 and has since captured the imagination of countless Europeans.[63] The girl was described as "long-haired and long-nailed, her body covered in hair too."[64]

But to return to the early modern period, an interesting feature of the feral children stories is the extreme fluidity that the writers seem to attribute to the characteristic of body hair. In contrast to their demonic corollaries, feral children are imagined to have been born as hairless as any other European. It is their detachment from society, and secluded lives "in nature," which have deemed them hairy. This radical fluidity of the characteristic of hairiness receives startling expression in Glikl's tale, where it is noted in passing that after having spent three years with the savages, the pious Jew came to resemble them in every way, hairiness included. The notion that time spent "in nature" would result in excessive body hair appears to have been widespread in early modern Europe, and it resulted in a host of bizarre hairy beings that inhabited European imagination. Indeed, in the woods of early modern Europe, one could expect to encounter not only hairy demons and wild men, but also hirsute saints, who, due to their reclusive lifestyle, had become almost indistinguishable from beasts.[65] Europeans also turned hairy in the colonies, as may be gleaned from a 1770 illustration depicting the colonial American woman Mary Rowlandson, who had been held captive by Native Americans for three months during the year 1676, as an exceedingly hairy woman.[66] In the mind of the unnamed illustrator, even a three-month "excursion into nature" would suffice to render a smooth European hairy. But perhaps the most striking use of the hairy woman motif in early modern Europe may be found in two Jewish illustrations, which appeared in two separate calendars dating from the seventeenth and early eighteenth centuries (figs. 4, 5). The illustrations portray as hairy no less than the mother of all women everywhere—the biblical Eve.[67]

The use of body hair to signify demons, savages, and "natural people" may have something to do with the unique nature of hair, which, as art historian Angela Rosenthal explains, is a signifier of borders. According to Rosenthal: "Emerging from the flesh and thus both of, and without the body—at once corporeal and a mere lifeless extension—hair occupies an extraordinary position, mediating between the natural and the cultural. It prompts one to scrutinize and question those boundaries defining self and other, subject and object,

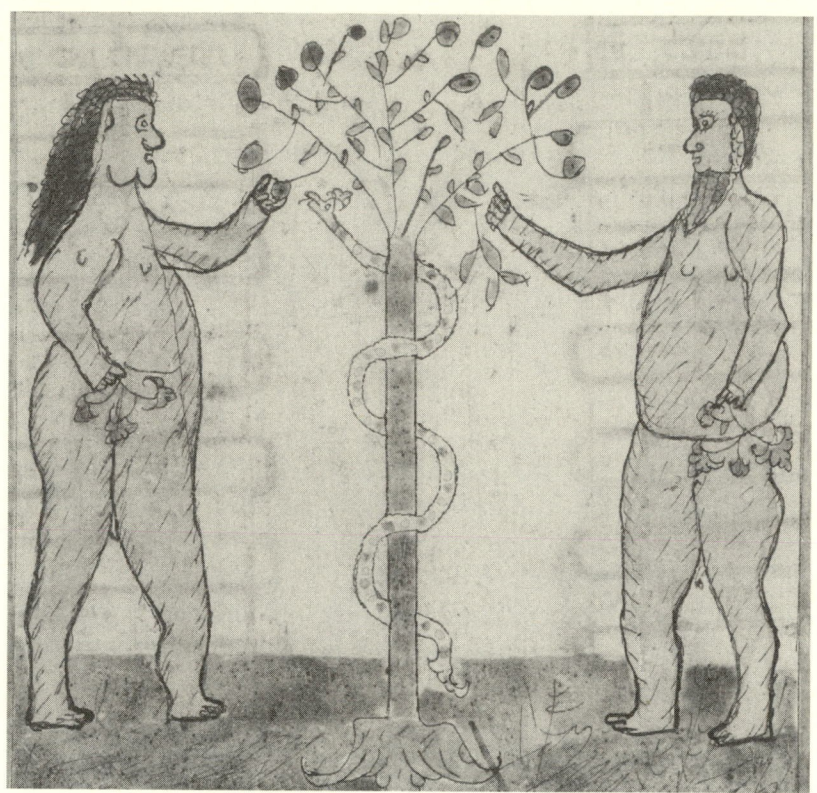

Figure 4. Hairy Eve (detail), from Eleazar ben Joseph of Fulda, "Evronot ve-nosaḥ shetarot," 1627. Image provided by the Library of The Jewish Theological Seminary.

life and death."[68] And indeed, the body hair of Glikl's savage woman positions her in a liminal space, between human and beast, exotic and demonic, life and death. Her hair entangles folktales and medical discourse, travel narratives and mythology, colonial discourse and demonology, images of nature and biblical allusions. It is this final, biblical, element to which we now turn.

RAPE AND EXOGAMY

In her pioneering study on rape imagery in medieval and early modern Europe, art historian Diane Wolfthal explains that even though the vast majority of early modern rapists were male, there was at least one dominant image of a female rapist in European imagination of the

Figure 5. Hairy Eve (detail), from Pinchas Halberstadt, "Sefer evronot," 1716. Reproduced by permission of the National Library Israel.

time: the biblical image of Potiphar's wife. For early moderns, explains Wolfthal, Potiphar's wife was the female rapist par excellence: "Depictions of Potiphar's wife as a sexual aggressor are quite numerous and appeared over a large span of time throughout the medieval and early modern era. Christian, Jewish, and Islamic images . . . attest to the immense popularity of the theme."[69] Significantly, the story of Joseph and Potiphar's wife is just one, albeit the most famous, of a variety of biblical tales that feature Jewish heroes or heroines who are harassed by non-Jews, and especially by non-Jewish kings or persons of authority. Joseph's great-grandmother Sarai also fell victim to the sexual aggression of her non-Jewish superiors, and was forced to become a concubine to the Egyptian Pharaoh and later to King Abimelech (she was also pursued by Og, King of Bashan); the Jewish Dinah was kidnapped and raped by a Canaanite prince; and another Jewish woman, Esther, had no choice but to marry the Persian king Ahasuerus.[70] The Talmud also features several stories of the attempted rape of a Jewish man by a non-Jewish woman. In one case, the man is saved from his female pursuer by running into a burning flame; another man jumps off a roof to escape his temptress.[71] These stories of coveted Jews all share a fear of being coerced or tempted into marriage or concubinage with a non-Jew, an anxiety intensified by a biblical prohibition: "You must not intermarry with them, neither giving your daughters to their sons nor taking their daughters for your sons; if you do, they will draw your sons away from the Lord and make them worship other gods."[72] This biblical prohibition demonstrates the basic fear underlying these stories of coerced intimacy: the fear of assimilation through exogamy.

And indeed, it appears that the assimilation anxiety underlying the biblical stories of Joseph and Sarai is also prevalent in Glikl's tale. In stark contrast to other "Inkle and Yarico" narratives, Glikl's story of the savage princess and her Jewish lover does not express fantasies of a benevolent conquest of the "exotic Other," but quite the contrary: it manifests a fear of being culturally and religiously conquered by the Other. This fear crystallizes in the rape of the pious Jew by the savage woman, but is also foreshadowed in the kidnapping of the pious Jew's Jewish wife by a Christian sailor earlier in the story. As mentioned above, the Jewish woman is coveted by a Christian sea captain and is eventually kidnapped by him and forced into a state of pseudo-concubinage. Glikl, however, stresses that the captain's desire is never realized. When asked by the pious Jew why he did not consummate his passion for the woman, the captain replies that she had threatened to commit suicide if forced to please him, since "it is not appropriate that a commoner should ride the king's horse" (G. Tur., 96; G. Abr., 27). Moseley reads this difference between the two captivity narratives (the pious Jew's captivity and his wife's captivity) as a subversive element in the text, concluding: "The only leading character in this story whose behavior can really be said to be exemplary is the *Talmid khokhem's* first wife, who is indeed Jewish, but more to the point, I think, a woman."[73] That Glikl was in some way critical of the pious Jew's behavior, however, appears unlikely. Though effeminate and unheroic to modern eyes, for Glikl, the pious Jew is a paradigm of sublime morality and proper conduct. He is a man who, much like the righteous Job, manages to uphold his Jewish faith even when faced with the most dire of circumstances.[74] Glikl's approval of her protagonist's conduct is evident throughout the entire story and manifests itself most clearly in its happy ending, in which the pious Jew retrieves his long-lost family, becomes king of his own colony, and converts the Christian sailors to Judaism. Moreover, in stark contrast to other versions, in which the European sailor's abandonment of his savage wife and child inspires harsh criticism, in Glikl's version the pious Jew's story arouses nothing but admiration in its listeners, so much so that the Christian sailors are inspired to convert to Judaism upon hearing it. The sparing of the Jewish wife's virtue in the story could be the outcome of various considerations, not least of which that chastity was an essential indicator of a woman's (but not a man's) moral worth. A virtuous woman was expected to maintain her chastity even under the most extreme circumstances (as exemplified by Richardson's famous *Pamela*), and one who failed to do so could hardly be depicted as a model of pious morality.[75] We must also bear in mind the symbolic elements of the rape of the pious Jew by the savage woman; this form of rape not only emasculates the Jewish man, but also interrupts his Jewish lineage, as any child born out of this unholy union would be a non-Jew (in contrast to the potential outcome of the rape of a Jewish woman by a non-Jewish man). This last element may explain the pious Jew's indifference toward his own son, which stands in stark contrast to his devotion to his Jewish children.[76]

In fact, the female rape motif constitutes part of a recurring motif in the story of the threat of being devoured or consumed, which is a further articulation of Glikl's aforementioned assimilation anxiety. Throughout the story, the pious Jew is delivered from various types of metaphoric or actual consumption. Thus, the story begins with his arrest and imprisonment, and continues with his wife being "swallowed" into the Christian captain's boat and disappearing. Further uses of the motif abound throughout the tale: while in prison, the pious Jew dreams of being eaten alive by wild animals; after his release, his ship sinks and he and his children are in danger of being "devoured" by the sea; finally, during his years as a castaway, he is under constant threat of being literally devoured by his cannibal hosts. This fear of being eaten is accompanied by an even greater fear: that of not receiving a Jewish burial. The non-Jewish, cannibalistic burial signifies for Glikl the complete and eternal loss of Jewish identity through consumption/assimilation. For the pious Jew, who has lived so long among savage people, eating their foods, sleeping in their caves, that he has come to resemble them almost entirely, the final loss of Jewish identity is unbearable. The mere thought of not receiving a proper Jewish burial drives him to attempt suicide by drowning: "One day he stood on a small hill . . . not far from the sea, and reflected on all that had happened to him; the loss of his wise and pious wife and children and—heaviest of all—how he must now spend his years among uncivilized wild animals, who eventually, with time, when they have tired of him, will devour his flesh and crush his bones for marrow, and he will not be laid to rest among other good Jews as befitting a pious Jew. 'Is it not better,' [he mused] 'that I should run from this hill and drown myself. . . ?'" (G. Tur., 90; G. Abr., 25). It is perhaps not surprising, then, that the pious Jew's deliverance is achieved by the act of *digging out* a buried treasure, a counter-reaction to the constant threat of consumption, of being devoured. This act of digging out is the opening scene of the second part of the story, which is a reversed narrative of rediscovery and exposure, including the discovery of the European ship and of the pious Jew's lost wife and sons. Throughout this latter part of the story, the assimilation anxiety is resolved through what Davis has appropriately termed a "fantasy of inversion,"[77] which culminates in the conversion of the Christian sailors to Judaism. In other words, in the second half of the tale, the pious Jew turns from devoured to devourer. But at the very beginning of this reversed narrative of exposure and discovery is one final act of devouring, the devouring of the hybrid child by its savage mother.

EARLY MODERN INFANTICIDE

The scene of infanticide is a troubling one, which rarely appears in contemporary modern culture. Even the most provocative and gruesome horror films will most often avoid this particular horrific motif. But infanticide wasn't always such a taboo literary trope. In fact, the image of the murderous mother, who slays her own child in a horrific moment of vengeance or despair, or, conversely, out of considerations of mere comfort, troubled the minds of a great many thinkers during the seventeenth and eighteenth centuries. Indeed, infanticide and paedophagia (the eating of children) were extremely popular tropes in pre-modern Western imagination. There are numerous examples, of course, dating back to Greek mythology, the Bible, and medieval works. Parents eating children is mentioned in Deuteronomy, Kings, Lamentations, Josephus, and *Sefer Hasidim*, to name just a few examples.[78] In some cases, they are permitted to do so by law. One thirteenth-century Spanish source suggests that paedophaogia was considered acceptable and, what is more, *legal,* during a siege.[79] Other sources reveal that the slaying or abandonment of a somehow disabled child was relatively tolerated by contemporaries.[80] Throughout the medieval and early modern periods, it was also believed that parents may resort to murdering their children as a means of punishment or in order to prevent them from converting to a different religion. In 1694 Prague, for instance, a Jewish man by the name of Laser Abeles was accused of having murdered his son, following the latter's interest in converting to Christianity.[81] Another seventeenth-century Jewish folktale told of a father who killed his daughter after discovering that she had engaged in sexually promiscuous behavior with a bandit.[82] During the eighteenth century, murderous parents were often used for social criticism, for instance in Hogarth's hugely famous "Gin Lane," which shows a drunken mother throwing her son head-first down the stairs, while another gin-crazed mother forces the spirit down her infant's throat (fig. 6). In Jonathan Swift's timeless "A Modest Proposal," it is ironically suggested that the starving Irish begin harvesting their own children for food.[83]

There is an interesting assumption underlying many of these pre-modern depictions of the murderous parent, most often the mother, according to which in cases of severe stress, poverty, or despair a mother or parent may harm, abandon, kill, and at times even eat their own children. Single mothers were considered especially vulnerable to this particular risk, and they were often accused, and found guilty of, infanticide. Indeed, belief in the infanticidal potential of a woman was so pervasive that in seventeenth- and eighteenth-century England, France, and German lands, an unwed woman's concealment of her pregnancy was considered proof enough of infanticidal intentions.[84] In contemporaneous Ashkenazi thought, the notion that a widow may turn infanticidal appears to have been equally widespread, and nursing widows were forbidden to remarry for at least

Figure 6. William Hogarth, *Gin Lane*, 1751. Courtesy of the British Museum, © Trustees of the British Museum.

twenty-four months after giving birth, the underlying premise being that after her remarriage a mother might lose interest in her child and cease nursing it, thus leaving it to starve to death.[85]

The twenty-four-month bar presupposes that a mother's love for her children is, at least to some extent, a function of time. As explained by English satirist Bernard Mandeville in 1732: "Even when Children first are Born the Mother's Love is but weak, and increases with the Sensibility of the Child, and grows up to a pro-digious height, when by signs it begins to express his Sorrows and

Joys."[86] Glikl would probably have agreed, as attested to by her casual mention of the death of her two-week-old son.[87] But there were also those who doubted a remarried mother's devotion toward her *adult* children. The Jewish moralist Ẓvi Hirsch Kaidanover complained in his hugely popular 1705 *Kav ha-yoshar* that remarried mothers tend to leave their sons "ragged and bare-footed. Devoid of their father's wealth, they . . . sit between the oven and the stove, and watch their mother enjoy meat, wine and other delicacies."[88]

A sharp critic of maternal abandonment was the English novelist and pamphleteer Daniel Defoe. In his 1722 *Moll Flanders*, Defoe had his heroine explain that abandonment of children is, in essence, "only a contrived method for murder; that is to say, a-killing [of] children with safety."[89] Moll had a point; studies on the fate of children in eighteenth-century foundling homes show appallingly high mortality rates.[90] Of course, this did not prevent Moll herself from abandoning, after the death of her husband, two of her own children, who were, she explains, "taken happily off my Hands by my Husband's Father and Mother, and that by the way was all they got by Mrs *Betty*."[91] Glikl would probably not have judged Moll's behavior in this particular matter too harshly. In her memoirs, she discusses a granddaughter of hers, daughter of her deceased son Zanvil, who "should be about 13 years old and is apparently a very gifted person." That Glikl does not know the exact age of the girl, and has to rely on second-hand reports of her talents, suggests that that she did not keep in touch with her. Glikl additionally relates that the girl's mother remarried and left her in the custody of her maternal grandfather. Interestingly, Glikl's reportage of her daughter-in-law's behavior is uncritical, and in the very same paragraph in which she relates the situation of her granddaughter she refers to her mother as "this good young person" [דאש גוטי יונגי מענש] (G. Tur., 558–59), regardless of her having abandoned her daughter after remarriage.[92]

This absence of critical undertones may be startling to the modern reader; however, stories of parents, most often mothers, who abandoned, sacrificed, or even murdered their children to better their own situation appeared relatively frequently throughout the eighteenth century, often without any discernible judgmental tone. The Jewish memoirist Dov of Bolichov told of a Mrs. Reisel who refused to pay ransom for her son and allowed him to be slain under her window, all the while screaming, "Mame, Mame, open up and give ransom for my soul!"[93] Salomon Maimon was abandoned by his family when they were pursued by Christian assailants, as was his father before him. Both were miraculously delivered.[94] Another story, this time by a Christian writer, told of a "Negro Woman" who smothered her infant to death during a raid so as not to be discovered. A second woman, a European by the name of Mrs. Clendenin, managed to escape the assailants but left her baby to be ruthlessly slain by them.[95] Interestingly, early versions of the story portrayed Mrs. Clendenin's behavior as brave or heroic, but in a later version, which appeared in Samuel G. Drake's 1839 anthology of captivity narratives, the following passage was inserted into the original text: "This ends the remarkable, though short captivity of a woman, *more to be admired for her courage than some other qualities not less desirable in the female character* [my emphasis]."[96]

Drake's telling addition marks a change in Western attitudes toward maternity, which has been eloquently characterized by Wahrman as "a distinctive shift . . . from maternity as a general ideal, broadly prescriptive but allowing for individual deviations, to maternity as inextricably intertwined with the essence of femininity for each and every woman."[97] Indeed, whereas early reports could often feature praise or appreciation for the murdering or abandoning parent, for instance in the cases of Mrs. Clendenin, in a Yiddish song commending Laser Abeles for the murder of his son, or in the Yiddish folktale of the father who killed his promiscuous daughter, later depictions of infanticide tended to portray the murdering mother as either a pathological figure, a stepmother, or—in some cases—as wishing to protect her infant from a life of slavery or utter poverty.[98] The change in prevailing attitudes toward murdering mothers received expression in diverse realms of European culture, including literature, art, and law.[99] One telling expression of the change may be found in the field of children's stories. Folklore research over the past three decades has shown how some of our favorite fairytales today, which feature vicious and often murderous stepmothers, such as "Snow White" or "Hansel and Gretel," originally featured biological mothers who aim to murder their own children.[100]

Similar changes in perceptions of maternity are found in early nineteenth-century Jewish literature, which features a wide range of loving and devoted mothers. Of particular interest are Baruch Shenfeld's 1826 "Indian Songs," in which a Native American mother is portrayed mourning her deceased son, and Joseph Perl's moving depictions of the maternal devotion found in female birds. Of course,

Shenfeld and Perl's understanding of maternal devotion in "natural peoples" and animals stands in direct contrast to Glikl's earlier stories of infanticidal birds and paedophagic East-Indians.[101]

The changing attitudes toward maternity in general and murdering mothers in particular were supported also by science. In the early nineteenth century, phrenologists Franz Joseph Gall and Johann Spurzheim made a startling discovery: they found a unique area in the female human skull which, they explained, was responsible for women's natural devotion to their children. In writing about this "discovery" in 1815, Spurzheim explained: *"It is objected that love of children is the result of moral sentiments, of self-love, or of the desire of suckling, and not of a peculiar propensity. These causes, so commonly admitted, cannot produce love of offspring; for in many animals which love their progeny, these causes do not exist. No animal, below man, has any idea of duty or religious sentiment; birds do not give suck, yet they love their young. . . . Moreover, in mothers there is no proportion between moral or religious sentiments, and philoprogenitiveness. Consequently, we must admit a particular organ for this propensity."* Spurzheim proceeded to explain that, based on the examination of the skulls of twenty-five murderous mothers, he had discovered that this organ is either exceedingly small or entirely missing in the skulls of infanticidal women.[102] Thus, the murdering mother became a pathology, no longer a social, religious, or legal problem; she was now an anatomical enigma.

SAVAGE MOTHERS

But to return to Glikl's time, it appears that early modern Europeans viewed the act of infanticide not as pathological, but rather as somehow natural (though not necessarily adequate) behavior.[103] It is therefore not surprising that many early modern authors tended, like Glikl herself, to attribute infanticidal tendencies to precisely those persons they considered to be most "natural," non-Europeans, or savages. The rumor that parenting norms outside Europe were somewhat lax appeared in some of the earliest reports describing the New World. Already in his first report on the American natives, Columbus explained that these men and women exhibit very loose family ties. According to his account, whenever the Spanish attempted to approach the natives, they fled so quickly that fathers forsook their children.[104] Reports of somewhat "unconventional" parental relations also appeared in the first detailed Jewish report on the "discovery" of America—Abraham Farissol's *Igeret orḥot olam*. In his book, Farrisol argued that it is the custom of American mothers to have sexual relations with their sons. He added that these people "have no governor or lord, no religion or gods, but they behave according to nature alone."[105] The savage family and its loose ties continued to excite European imagination generations later, in the seventeenth and eighteenth centuries. Stories of child murder were a prominent motif in scientific or travel literature, as well as in the fiction and philosophy of the period. They appeared in such popular and esteemed texts as John Locke's *Essay Concerning Human Understanding*, in which certain Amerindian peoples are said to be fond of eating their children's flesh; or in Adam Smith's *Theory of Moral Sentiments*, in which Europeans are reminded of their own infanticidal past.[106] The British navigator James Cook reported to his numerous readers that child murder rituals were still practiced in Tahiti and constituted the main means of combating the high birthrate on the island.[107] Jews were also accused of infanticide, most famously by Voltaire, who used the Deuteronomic passages cited in the epigraph to this chapter to portray the Israelites as a savage people whose descendants would never be able to integrate into Europe.[108] Savage infanticide was such a popular trope in early modern European thought that even primitivist thinkers were obliged to confront it, lest it taint their own depictions of the "noble savage." In his popular 1777 *Les Incas*, for instance, French playwright Jean-François Marmontel explained that the Incas had recently discontinued the barbaric custom of sacrificing their children.[109]

Some writers attempted to explain the infanticidal customs of savage peoples by turning to climate. Thus, in his magnum opus *Histoire Naturelle*, the leading naturalist Georges-Louis Leclerc de Buffon informed his readers that parental love tends to diminish or even disappear in certain climates. According to Buffon, the damp and relatively chilly American climate produces frigid natives who "lack any enthusiasm for their females, and as a consequence, for their fellow men. As they do not know the most basic attachment, so too their other sentiments are cold and languid. Their love for their parents and infants is feeble; the most intimate social relations, the familial relations, are merely weak links."[110] Buffon added that, by contrast, the Africans who reside in a warmer climate are deeply devoted to their children. And yet, even in the case of the Africans, Buffon appears not to have been entirely convinced of their degree of parental devotion, and he reported that African parents are often willing to sell their own children into slavery in return for gin, a claim that was widely repeated during the eighteenth century.[111] The premise underlying all these reports of savage infanticides was concisely put by Samuel Johnson, who observed: "[Savages] have no affection. . . . Natural affection is nothing; but affection from principle and established duty is sometimes wonderfully strong."[112]

In the minds of Glikl's contemporaries, then, maternal devotion was an attribute of civilization, and infanticide was just one of so many "natural vices," such as cannibalism, homosexuality, atheism, or bestiality that characterized the lives of men and women who had been completely abandoned to the dictates of nature. It should be clarified, however, that if infanticide was indeed considered a natural response under certain conditions, it was certainly not thought of as *adequate* behavior. Much like cannibalism, this was one natural inclination a good parent (and particularly a good mother) was expected to overcome. And indeed, contemporary research suggests that the intense preoccupation with the image of the murderous mother in eighteenth-century Europe was the result of an attempt to construct an opposing image of the civilized European woman as an emblem of domesticity. As we shall see, traces of this kind of thinking are found in Glikl's story.

NOTIONS OF DIFFERENCE IN EARLY MODERN EUROPE

It is time to divert our gaze from the atrocious sight of the savage woman who bisects and devours her child to the fascinating encounter that occurs in Glikl's tale between savages, Christians, and Jews. This triangular encounter affords an unusual view into Glikl and her contemporaries' complex understandings of identity and difference. Upon a first reading of the tale, it appears that Glikl's perception of human variety conforms to a simple binary of savage and civilized, with the cannibal woman's barbarity serving to stress the cultural proximity between Christians and Jews. In her cannibalistic, atheistic, and infanticidal behavior, the savage woman unites Jews and Christians in a mutual bond of civilized people, or "*mentshen*," in Glikl's own phrasing. In this sense, Glikl is part of a longstanding Jewish rhetorical practice, in which the non-European other served as a means to establish a shared Jewish-Christian identity. This rhetorical practice has been previously discussed by such scholars of

Jewish-Black relations as Jonathan Schorsch or Avraham Melamed, who explain that throughout the history of the West, Jewish authors utilized the image of the Black as a means to construct an opposing image of the Jews as White(r).[113] However, it should be noted that skin color does not play a role in Glikl's description of the savage woman or in her identification with Christians. In fact, the savage woman's skin color is never once mentioned in the story, and her other physical traits, such as nudity and hairiness, are depicted as exceedingly mutable. So mutable that, indeed, Glikl mentions that after having lived with the savages for some years, the pious Jew came to physically resemble them in every way, and appeared a complete savage to European eyes (G. Tur., 90). Thus, contrary to Schorsch or Melamed's predictions, skin color does not act as a marker of difference in Glikl's story; rather, she uses the savage woman's cannibalism, infanticidal behavior, and barbarity as a means to contrast between civilized and savage, European and non-European.

The marginality and fluidity of physical designators of difference in Glikl's tale is indicative of the anthropological thinking of her time. Another contemporaneous encounter narrative, from Aphra Behn's popular 1688 *Oroonoko*, exemplifies the fluidity of early modern designators of difference quite vividly. The scene takes place on the banks of the Suriname River and depicts a strange encounter between a group of English settlers, a tribe of Surinamese natives, and an African slave. The encounter is described thus: "Now, none of us [the English] speaking the language of the people . . . , we took a fisherman that lived at the mouth of the river, who had long been an inhabitant there, and obliged him to go with us. But because he was known to the Indians . . . and being, by long living there, become a perfect Indian in colour, we, who resolved to surprise them, by making them see something they never had seen (that is white people), resolved only myself, my brother, and woman should go."[114] Let us look closely at this scene. The narrator explains that she wanted to surprise the natives with "something they never had seen (that is white people)." And indeed, the natives are fascinated by the narrator and her European entourage, and are amazed by the strange visitors' clothes and hairstyles. The Europeans, on the other hand, are impressed mainly by the natives' nudity. A modern-day reader, however, may find all this somewhat confusing, since even though Behn clearly states that the natives had never seen "white people" before, they appear strangely unimpressed with the English visitors' skin color. In fact, throughout

the entire description, skin color plays an extremely marginal role
and is mentioned only once, in Behn's description of the English inter-
preter, who is asked by the narrator to remain hidden in the bushes
so as not to ruin the spectacle of Whiteness. This element of the story
adds to our modern reader's confusion, as it is unclear in what ways
this fisherman, who according to our modern-day understanding of
the term is quite clearly White, could ruin the element of surprise.
There is something awfully strange going on here, for we cannot help
sensing that the natives are not really seeing "something they never
had seen," as claimed by the narrator, since we are told that they have
had many encounters with the English fisherman. However, it is clear
that for Behn, this fisherman is no longer White at all. Indeed, for
Behn, Whiteness is an extremely fluid designator *not of race*, but of
culture, mode of living, degree of suntan, and, perhaps most importantly, choice of clothes. Skin color as Behn perceives it is not an ethnic characteristic at all, but rather a cultural one: being White merely
amounts to being dressed as a European, whereas being non-White
means being nude, or wearing non-European clothes. Thus, Whiteness emerges in Behn's anecdote as an exceedingly fuzzy concept, a
highly mutable designator of difference, which can be assumed or
removed at will.

I will return to the importance of clothes in eighteenth-century
anthropological discourse shortly; however, for the purpose of our
present discussion it is important to note how mutable and unclear
notions of Black and White were for early moderns.[115] Clearly, such
fuzzy concepts could hardly serve as prime markers of difference
between men. And indeed, as scholars such as Roxann Wheeler and
Dror Wahrman have shown, throughout the early modern period skin
color played a much less substantial role in the characterization of
non-European peoples than religion, customs, and climates.[116] Moreover, complexion was most often viewed by early moderns as the mere
outcome of these same customs and climates. Perhaps the most ardent
and influential propagator of this view was Buffon, who attributed
the great variety within the human species ("les variétés dans l'espèce
humaine") to the differences in climate, nutrition, and ways of life.
Buffon went as far as to suggest that the removal of Africans from
their native lands and their incorporation into Europe would result
in the "whitening," within ten to twelve generations, of the African
skin. The exact number of generations required in order to "whiten"
the Africans was a source of controversy during the eighteenth

century, but a great many scientists agreed that it was a material possibility.[117] As Behn's anecdote suggests, it was also widely accepted that a European may turn Black after a time spent under a warmer climate, or after embracing some of the practices of non-European peoples.[118] Some eighteenth-century writers viewed this possibility as a real hindrance to the colonial project. In 1745, for instance, the Dutch Jewish intellectual Isaac De Pinto, director of the Dutch East India Company, expressed his concerns that the Europeans in America were slowly growing to resemble the natives, and this, he prophetically added, may eventually result in a colonial revolution.[119] The notion that humans and other animals change under different climates or upon being subjected to different customs or diets was reiterated by numerous authors throughout the eighteenth century. One persistent rumor, which appeared in a wide range of texts in English, French, German, and also Hebrew, was that dogs imported into America tended to lose the ability to bark.[120]

But how did seventeenth- and eighteenth-century Jews think about physical difference? Did they too attribute the same mutability to physical traits as their non-Jewish contemporaries? In her study on images of Native Americans in sixteenth- and early seventeenth-century Jewish literature, historian Limor Mintz-Manor shows that most early Jewish writers on the Americas tended to associate physical appearance and cultural practices with the effects of climate.[121] This association between climate and appearance continued in Jewish writing well into the eighteenth and even nineteenth centuries. Writing in 1794, the English maskil Elyakim ben Avraham (Hart) explained that natural organisms are highly influenced by climate, which leaves its mark on the nature of animals, countries, and plants.[122] A fellow maskil, the German English Mordecai Gumpel Schnaber Levison, wrote in 1771 that those men and women who live under the equator "are black due to the intense heat, but are rational beings nonetheless."[123] The notion that Europeans tend to darken outside of Europe was also shared by the maskilim. Thus, in an early nineteenth-century Hebrew and Yiddish translation of Campe's description of Willem Bontekoe's voyage to the East Indies, often attributed to the Polish maskil Menachem Mendel Lefin, it is argued that during their journeys the Dutch travelers became "darker than black."[124]

Some Jewish apologists attempted to harness the climatic theory to the debates surrounding Jewish emancipation. Thus, in his 1789 *Apologie des Juifs* the Polish French thinker Zalkind Hourwitz explained that there is no physical difference between Christians and Jews, which may serve to justify the latter's discrimination. "It is recognized by all physicians," explained Hourwitz, "that the physical constitution of the Jews is absolutely identical to that of other peoples who inhabit the same climate."[125] Indeed, as will be discussed in Chapter 3, climatic theory appears to have held particular sway amongst Jewish thinkers, and especially the maskilim, who continued to propagate the theory well after it was, to a large extent, discarded by their non-Jewish contemporaries. Thus, as late as 1828 we read in Shimshon Bloch's *Sheviley olam* that European travelers to Africa "darken, their white skin turns black, and their beauty becomes ugliness."[126]

But for eighteenth-century thinkers, climate was not the sole factor determining the constitution of man. Faced with the reality of colonial expansion and slavery, which had resulted in the large presence of Europeans in the colonies and colonial subjects in Europe, both Jewish and non-Jewish writers sought new ways to account for physical variety. A popular explanation focused on cultural practices. Already in 1707 the Jewish physician Tuviah Ha-cohen explained that a person's physical constitution is modified not only by climate, but also by diet.[127] Later writers attempted to explain skin color by referring to tattoos, hygienic practices, or the application of various potions to the skin. Thus in a manuscript written by an obscure maskil named Shlomo Keysir, we read that "when (the Greenlanders) are born they have white skin like all other humans but because they never wash and their homes are full of smoke and they cover themselves in oil or fat, their skin tends to become green."[128] Another interesting example may be found in a geography book published in 1801 by the rabbinical scholar Abraham ben Elijah of Vilna, son of the famed Vilna Gaon: "It is now time to explain the reason for the difference in appearances and sizes. God created man to live in the divine Garden of Eden, a place protected from heat and cold. . . . But when God dispersed men throughout the entire earth, and each chose his own climate and multiplied there, their sons varied in looks, sizes, and character according to their climates and choice of foods."[129] The attribution of complexion to climate or culture emphasizes its marginality for these thinkers.

In other eighteenth-century texts, both Jewish and non-Jewish skin color and other "racial" characteristics are considered so marginal that they are simply omitted from the description altogether. Thus, in

Diderot's *Supplément au Voyage de Bougainville* or in Françoise de Graffigny's *Lettres d'une Péruvienne*, no note is made of the physical appearance of the Peruvian and Tahitian protagonists, or of their European hosts and visitors.[130] An interesting Hebrew example of the extreme marginality of physical appearance is found in the Lithuanian physician Yehudah Horowitz's discussion of savages in his 1766 *Amudey beyt Yehudah*, which will be discussed in detail in the next chapter. Like Glikl before him, Horowitz neglected to make any note whatsoever of skin color in his description of either the noble or the ignoble savages described in his book. Instead, he used the opposition between civilized monotheist and savage atheist to present a program for the unification of all civilized peoples, meaning Jews, Christians, and Muslims.[131]

It is unlikely, however, that Glikl would have approved of Horowitz's somewhat radical program for monotheistic unification. In fact, reading through her story one can easily detect an ambivalent attitude toward Christians, which complicates her view of the varieties of man. Indeed, Glikl's story does not offer a simple division of humankind into the two traditional groups of civilized/monotheistic and savage/heathen. Rather, it offers a much more nuanced view of identity and difference, which takes into account a multiplicity of axes of identity such as gender, religion, and manners or perhaps class. Indeed, even though Jews are depicted as somehow closer to Christians than they are to savages, their identification with Christians is far from complete. The two captivity stories presented in the tale—the pious Jew and his savage captor on the one hand, and the pious Jewess and her Christian captor on the other—draw an unavoidable analogy between savages and Christians. This analogy, followed by the conversion into Judaism of the Christian sailors and their acceptance of the pious Jew's rule, all point toward Glikl's ambivalent perception of Christians as being at once religiously inferior and politically superior to Jews. This hesitant haughtiness of Glikl's is evident throughout the entire memoirs, in which Christians are often presented in inferior or derogatory roles such as bandits, murderers, or drunks.[132] It would appear, then, that in the great chain of being drawn by Glikl, Christians are located between Jews and savages, and their conversion to Judaism is a prerequisite to their progress.

THE IMAGE OF THE IDEAL WOMAN

A fascinating glimpse into Glikl's understanding of the difference between Jews and Christians—and, more specifically, between Jewish and Christian women—is afforded by the Christian captain's description of his two wives: "The captain . . . said he had two wives—one at home with whom he had had three children. 'Her I keep as a housewife. The other is very delicate and no good at housework, but she is very wise, and so I always take her with me to superintend the affairs of the ship. She collects the money from the passengers and enters it in a book, and manages all my affairs'" (G. Tur., 94; G. Abr., 27). This description warrants a close inspection. Three women appear in Glikl's story, and all three share with her the characteristic of being single mothers. They are all women who have been abandoned by their husbands and left to fend for their children on their own. Their responses seem to signify the three forms of single motherhood as envisioned by Glikl. The most striking form of single motherhood is, of course, the savage woman's, who copes with her abandonment by killing and devouring her child. In this manner, she vents her anger and frustration, while at the same time redeeming herself from the toils of single motherhood. As we have seen, in depicting the savage woman as infanticidal, Glikl shares with many of her contemporaries an intriguing understanding of maternity, not as a biological imperative of women but as an attribute of civilization. As mentioned above, eighteenth-century depictions of savage infanticide often served as a means to construct an opposing image of the civilized European woman as an emblem of domesticity. And indeed, in Glikl's story the image of the Christian housewife stands in stark contrast to that of the monstrous savage mother. Left ashore by an adulterous husband, this woman offers a more civilized response to single motherhood by choosing the path of domesticity. This portrayal of the devoted Christian mother as the exact opposite of the savage murderous mother is consistent with many other contemporaneous treatments of maternity, in which, as Felicity Nussbaum explains, the "civilized notion of motherhood . . . is contrasted with a savage motherhood capable of infanticide and cannibalism yet at the same time described as 'natural.'"[133] Interestingly, however, Glikl shows nothing but disdain for this domestic Christian woman. Both she and the savage wife are depicted as entirely dependent on their husbands, unable to care for their children or to support them financially on their own. The two women are thus contrasted with the pious Jew's Jewish wife: an independent, wise, and resourceful woman, who supports her children financially after the incarceration of their father, and who, even after losing her husband and children, continues to find solace in business and financial success. Interestingly, in a reversal of traditional gender roles, which is characteristic of the entire story, the Jewish woman's economic prowess is also contrasted with the pious Jew's financial ineptness.[134]

Significantly, this kind of resourceful widowhood was embraced by Glikl herself, who, in spite of losing her husband and three of her children, continued to run the family business on her own for many years. In fact, even though Glikl did eventually remarry, ten years after the death of her first husband, she was to view this decision as a woeful mistake. As she stresses in her memoirs, contrary to what could be expected, her dependence on a husband led not to financial relief but to ruin. Furthermore, after the death of her second husband, which left her with almost nothing of her former fortune, Glikl was forced to resort to a second kind of dependent widowhood, which she perceived as most deplorable—a widow in a multigenerational household, dependent on her children.[135] The travails brought about by her second marriage are portrayed by Glikl as a form of divine punishment inflicted on her for her decision to become financially dependent on a husband: "The blessed lord laughed at my thoughts and plans, and had already long decided on my doom to repay me for my sins in relying on people. For I should not have thought of marrying again" (G. Tur., 500; G. Abr., 151).

In her memoirs, then, Glikl constructs an image of the ideal woman, or widow, as one who manages to uphold a respectable household after her husband's demise, without resorting to dependence on others, such as her children or a second husband. In this sense, she presents an understanding of feminine virtue quite different from the sorts of chaste, maternal, or domestic virtue commonly ascribed to women in eighteenth-century novels, conduct books, and other writings.[136] However, it appears that Glikl was not alone in pursuing this ideal. In fact, many of her contemporaries, both Jewish and Christian, appear to have shared this ideal of independence and made every effort "to be independent of material and financial intergender and/or intergenerational transfers."[137] Thus, for instance, in her reading of Eliza Haywood's 1724 *The Rash Resolve*, Toni Bowers demonstrates how the author constructed "a vision of powerful, enabling, and independent motherhood."[138] Haywood confronts her readers with a single mother who succeeds in upholding a respectable household, notwithstanding the absence of her child's father. When, however, toward the end of the tale, the absent father reappears, the heroine dies of shock and heartbreak. In both Haywood's tale and Glikl's memoirs, the appearance of a dominant male figure on the scene, in the form of an estranged father or a second husband, results in ruin.

Traces of early modern women's ideal of independence are also found in other Jewish sources. Thus, for instance, an early seventeenth-century Jewish folktale tells of a Jewish woman who wished to remain single in order to continue her life as a businesswoman.[139] Other writers commended their mothers, grandmothers, or other family women for managing to uphold their own after the deaths of their husbands. The aforementioned Bohemian memoirist, for instance, speaks highly of his grandmother, who "remained a widow with three sons and two little daughters [but] was an *eshet hayil* [a woman of valour], energetic, and clever and supported her family comfortably."[140]

As Glikl's memoirs demonstrate, the ideal of resourceful widowhood also required that widows remain independent of their children. And indeed, a second rare text by an early modern Ashkenazi woman bears further witness to parents' reluctance to turn to the aid of their children. I am referring to the sixteenth-century women's guidebook *Meneket Rivkah*, written by Rivkah bat Meir Tiktiner. Tiktiner relates a story about an old widower of some means who decides to move into his son's household. At first, the relationship between the man and his son and daughter-in-law is friendly, and yet the moment the old man bequeaths his wealth to his son, the young couple begins to abuse him, to the extent that he is resorted to sleeping naked under the stairwell and eating scraps off the kitchen table.[141] The story is repeated in other sixteenth- and seventeenth-century sources, and is just one of a wide variety of stories which express the exceeding suspicion of parents toward the gratefulness and reliability of their children. Similar doubts are frequently voiced in Glikl's memoirs, for instance in the story of the infanticidal bird, which ends with the following moral: "[We see] the difference: how parents toil for their children and with what great devotion they raise them, while they, if they had the trouble with their parents as their parents do with them, would soon tire" (G. Tur., 32; G. Abr. 9).[142]

Glikl's solution to the problem of the unreliability of children and spouses is to offer her readers an image of a woman who is independent and resourceful, and does not rely on the aid of others for her happiness or success. But Glikl does more than justify the authority and adequacy of the independent women/widow as head of the household. In presenting her ideal woman as "no good at housework," and contrasting her sophistication with the image of the simple Christian housewife, Glikl demonstrates an intriguing disdain for domesticity, not only in widowhood but also in marriage. We find hints of this attitude, which values professional success over domestic bliss, throughout Glikl's autobiographical text. As explained by Turniansky: "Though Glikl is constantly busy with pregnancies and labor [during the period described in the memoirs], these are not the only subject of her written memoirs, nor are they their central theme."[143] In fact, the greater part of the memoirs deals with matters relating to Glikl's professional life as a businesswoman: her financial success and the subsequent financial travails brought about by her second husband; her business partners and their deeds and misdeeds and other such matters. Throughout the memoirs, Glikl prides herself on her financial conduct, both during her first husband's lifetime and even more so after his demise. Other women are also commended by Glikl, not only for their piety, modesty, or chastity, but also for their success as businesswomen. Thus, for example, one woman is presented as "a chaste and resourceful woman, very well versed in trade [who] practically kept her family afloat" (G. Tur., 62). Another woman is described as "unprecedented in her integrity and piety, and especially in her being an *eshet ḥayil* who managed her own trade and provided for her husband and children bountifully" (G. Tur., 312). For Glikl, then, a woman's worth is a function of her resourcefulness, wit, and intelligence, and not, as may perhaps be expected, of her domestic virtues.

This understanding of woman as financial agent differs greatly from later representations of true womanhood as being achieved through maternity and domesticity, but it appears to have been shared, at least to some extent, by Glikl's contemporaries. The anonymous Bohemian memoirist commends his mother who "showed her ability in supporting the family by her own efforts, and started to manufacture brandy out of oats. . . . This was hard labor, but she succeeded. In the meantime my father pursued his studies."[144] One eighteenth-century responsum (a rabbinic reply to a question concerning Jewish law) by the great Jewish scholar Yeḥezkel Landau went as far as to accuse married women who refrained from work of being a cause of their husbands' deaths. Landau explained: "A woman who is confined to her home, and is kept by her husband, her luck is such that she causes her husbands' deaths, so that she may live in poverty. And this holds true for regular women. But in a women who is an *eshet ḥayil* we find that even after the deaths of her husbands she succeeds in commerce and manages to support herself adequately, and so it clear that her luck does not cause her poverty, and therefore her husbands' deaths are not caused by her."[145] Rabbi Jacob Emden, for his part, praised his first wife, who worked in loans, and berated his second wife, who, though a descendant of a family of merchants, was financially incompetent.[146] As befitting a rabbi of his stature, Emden's primary concern was that the financial incompetence of his second wife would not allow him to leave matters of business to her and concentrate on his studies. Significantly, Emden's view differs from Glikl's in that, for him, a woman's financial ability is to be commended only to the extent that it enables her husband to devote himself to his religious duties.[147] However, as shown by historian Moshe Rosman, who has studied the lives of early modern Jewish women in Poland and Lithuania, the majority of working women were not the sole breadwinners. Rather, like Glikl herself, they were either partners in their husbands' businesses or working widows. Through an elaborate survey of the financial activities of Jewish women during this period, Rosman concludes that these women's financial roles influenced their social status: "In contrast to the bourgeois ideal of a woman reaching fulfillment through cultivation of the home and family, which was prevalent during the nineteenth century, in the earlier period, women interweaved financial activity and gain into their everyday lives. The family was an economic unit, in which the husband was senior partner, but the woman was also a partner."[148]

ENCOUNTERS IN A THIRD SPACE

Glikl poses a fascinating problem for the historian of race in the long eighteenth century. On the one hand, her story cannot be read by means of a colonialist paradigm; on the other, it cannot be understood as a misogynistic display of male anxieties regarding women.[149] In my reading of the memoirs, I have attempted to show that Glikl's lack of identification with the savage woman expresses a decidedly

Jewish indifference toward the early modern project of cultural and political colonization. In contrast to the traditional image of the European male colonist, who becomes master of the New World through the seduction and romantic conquest of the native, the protagonist of Glikl's story is a highly effeminate man who is raped by the native woman and saved by the more masculine European men. In this sense, Glikl's story gives tantalizing expression to the reality of being Jewish in early modern Europe. Similarly to the androgynous hero of Glikl's tale, so too the early modern European Jew was a hybrid being, simultaneously hegemonic and subaltern, same but different, part of the European "we" but not quite.

Glikl's use of the literary tropes of savage infanticide and the colonial love story differs, then, from other, non-Jewish uses in that it conveys specific Jewish anxieties concerning assimilation and Jewish-Christian relations. In this sense, Glikl can be read as rejecting the dual possibilities of both external and internal colonization: of the acculturation of the non-European Other and of the assimilation of the intimate Other, the Jew.

However, as is most often the case with early modern Jews, Glikl's thought cannot adequately be understood outside the context of the non-Jewish intellectual and cultural trends of its time. Indeed, in her choice of literary motifs, Glikl reflects more general concerns shared by her non-Jewish contemporaries regarding the meaning of civilization, the possibility of cross-cultural encounter, and the differences between men. Throughout the eighteenth century there occurred some radical transformations in the answers European writers provided to these questions. I turn now to review the ways in which these transformations affected Jewish discourse in the decades following Glikl's memoirs.

"And Let Him Speak"

Noble and Ignoble Savages in
Yehudah Horowitz's Amudey beyt Yehudah

It is best to walk the course of nature, and to stray neither left nor right,
for its paths are those of pleasantness, and all its lanes are those of peace.
—SHIMON BAR-ZEKHARYAH, 1788

And Hushai turned to Ittai his master and cried in anguish: have you not heard, oh master, how this man of the
woods has arisen to devour my soul with his questions?
—YEHUDAH HOROWITZ, 1766

In the popular imagination of medieval Europe, Africans, Americans
and other "exotic peoples" were perceived as savage and voracious
beings, creatures that had been cursed by God. Hairy, four-footed,
and mute, they occupied a mysterious limbo between the bestial, the
demonic, and the human. Throughout the sixteenth and seventeenth
centuries, there was some attempt by more "professional" ethnographers to change this imagery and promote a less mythological view of
the non-European world. However, the image of the hairy wild man
endured; wild men and women appeared in folktales such as Glikl's
story of the pious Jew and his savage wife, or the myth of the hairy
anchorite, and were observed by such sixteenth- and seventeenth-century explorers as Antonio Pigafetta or Henry Schooten. Other writers
confronted their readers with ominous beasts, bearing the body of a
man and the head of a dog, or Haitian Satanists, whose skulls could
endure the sharpest blade.[1] Clearly, these were not beings with which
one could engage in rational dialogue. Such dialogue was reserved
to the monotheistic and "civilized" nations—Christians, Muslims,
Jews, at times also Asian peoples—whose cultural and religious proximity crystallized against the context of these ruthless savages.

But this was to change during the eighteenth century. Slowly but surely, non-European peoples were relocated from the realm of folklore and demonology and introduced into the European elite of philosophers and men of science. Already in 1711, an observant Lord Shaftesbury pointed to this burgeoning intellectual trend by complaining that a "Moorish fancy, in its plain and literal sense, prevails strongly at this present time. Monsters and monster lands were never more in request, and we may often see a philosopher or a wit run a tale-gathering in those 'idle deserts' as familiarly as the silliest woman or merest boy."[2] Shaftesbury's complaint notwithstanding, throughout the eighteenth century, non-Europeans began to assume a kind of philosophical prestige, and these formerly mute atheists with whom dialogue was once an impossibility began to open their mouths—and speak. The present chapter is a look at some of their conversations.

AN ENCOUNTER IN THE WOODS

In 1766, a Lithuanian physician by the name of Yehudah ben Mordecai Ha-levi Horowitz published in Amsterdam a book titled *Amudey beyt Yehudah*. The book tells of a society in crisis, split into two rival and equally corrupt camps. The first, the heretical camp, uses Jewish lore and mainly the Kabbalah as a form of magic and entertainment. The second camp, comprising materialists and libertines, uses rational philosophy to undermine religion, morality, and society. Faced with this deepening moral and religious crisis, two Jewish sages, Ittai the Gittite and Hushai the Archite, flee society and find refuge in the woods. The names of the two protagonists are derived from the biblical story of King David and his rebellious son Absalom (2 Samuel 15:19, 15:32). Ittai and Hushai were two advisors who remained loyal to the king during the rebellion. In choosing these names Horowitz refers, of course, to the characters' loyalty to Judaism in a time of moral crisis. The sages' time in the woods is spent in complete solitude, studying the sacred texts of Judaism and reading philosophy, until one day they encounter a savage "unabashed and nude, and collecting wet herbs for his food" (AMBY, 3a).[3] The man's first instinct is to flee back into the woods; eventually, however, he is tempted to taste a loaf of bread offered to him by Ittai, and from that moment on "the savage man followed them as a calf follows a cow" (AMBY, 3a). This encounter marks the savage's entry into society. Initially, Hushai suggests that the man be enslaved; however, Ittai firmly objects and vows not only to acculturate the savage, but also to introduce him into society as a living moral exemplar, which will arouse the remorse and repentance of immoral men. Thus, the savage's domestication begins. He is given the name Ira the Yaarite ("Ira of the Woods," also from the story of David and Absalom), and promptly acquires the Hebrew language, scientific knowledge, morals, religious commandments, and proper laws.[4] Three years go by, until one day a messenger arrives in the woods and announces that the conditions are ripe for the sages' return into society. The men head back to the city, accompanied by their now acculturated savage, and upon their arrival begin a dialogue concerning religion, society, and philosophy. The dialogue, which dominates the greater part of the text, serves Horowitz as a platform from which to rationally justify Jewish faith and traditions and to demonstrate their compliance with the dictates of reason. In so doing, Horowitz wished to deliver a crucial blow to what he viewed as the most dire threats to contemporaneous Jewish tradition: kabbalistic mysticism, Sabbatianism, and Frankism (two influential messianic movements) on the one hand, and radicalism, skepticism, and libertinism on the other.[5] These two forms of heresy are symbolized in the book by the two opposing camps from which the Jewish sages Ittai and Hushai flee to the woods. The sages, in turn, personify the solution to the crisis of eighteenth-century European Ashkenazi Jewry as it is perceived by Horowitz, a careful combination of tradition and reason, religious and secular studies.

YEHUDAH HOROWITZ AND THE CONSERVATIVE ENLIGHTENMENT

Though a relatively well-connected maskil during his lifetime, over the nineteenth and twentieth centuries Horowitz and his works were largely forgotten. It was only toward the end of the twentieth century that some scholarly attention began to turn to Horowitz, and two papers, by Shmuel Werses and Shmuel Feiner, were devoted to this enigmatic maskil.[6] In his compelling reading of *Amudey beyt Yehudah*, Feiner presents Horowitz as a paradigmatic figure of the early Haskalah. A multilingual intellectual, well versed in science and rabbinic lore, he represents the new ideal type of the early maskil who combined secular learning with religious knowledge. Like other maskilim of his time, Horowitz viewed himself as part of the Jewish halakhic world, and saw the new rationalistic discourse as a means to improve and revitalize Jewish faith, not to undermine it. In his approach to non-Jewish science and philosophy, he was an adherent of early maskilic ideology, formulated by such writers as Naphtali Herz Wessely and Moses Mendelssohn, who criticized religious dogmatism and the neglect of secular knowledge on the one hand, and objected to radical skepticism on the other.[7]

Of course, this kind of attempt to reconcile Enlightenment and religion was not exclusive to the Jewish literary world. Similar aspirations were characteristic of a strand of Enlightenment that has been characterized by contemporary scholars as "conservative" or "religious." In a now classic study, Jonathan Israel defines this Enlightenment as one that "aspired to conquer ignorance and superstition, establish toleration, and revolutionize ideas, education, and attitudes by means of philosophy but in such a way as to preserve and safeguard what were judged essential elements of the older structures, effecting a viable synthesis of old and new and of reason and faith."[8] Clearly, the conservative Enlightenment consisted of a cluster of national, religious, and other Enlightenments that often differed quite radically from one another. What united these various Enlightenments, however, was an intense devotion to reform, accompanied by a common concern regarding the possibility of the radicalization of Enlightenment ideals. Conservative thinkers preferred to promote their ideas carefully and gradually, and to bring about the desired reforms in European society through such means as legislation and education.

The framework of a conservative Enlightenment seems particularly conductive as a context for reading Horowitz's work. In his corpus of writings, this early maskil expressed a deep concern regarding the radicalization of reason on the one hand, and faith on the other. Indeed, Horowitz's preoccupation with the split within Judaism between the emerging camps of Hasidim (members of a religious movement which emphasized piety, ecstasy, and divine intervention), mitnagdim (opponents of Hasidism), and maskilim, and his fear of libertinism, Frankism, Sabbatianism, and radicalism, echo the conservative Enlightenment's preoccupation with the problem of political instability and civil unrest. As discussed in some detail below, eighteenth-century thinkers lived in the shadow of the religious and civil wars of the early modern period, and their deep commitment to political stability is a crucial aspect of their thought. Thus too, stability, moderation, toleration, and gradual reform are recurring themes in Horowitz's corpus of works. In the spirit of many other conservative

Enlighteners, he too was acutely aware of the dangers inherent in the new ideas in philosophy and science, and he stressed that they should be consumed responsibly, like delicacies or fine spirits. "Be neither monks nor drunks," he wrote in *Amudey beyt Yehudah*, "for the monk is a sinner, and the drunk—a fool."[9]

Little is known about Horowitz's biography. He was born sometime around 1734, either in the Lithuanian capital of Vilnius or in Padua, and appears to have received a strictly religious upbringing.[10] Later in life he served as a physician in Vilnius and in various small towns throughout Eastern Europe. Some sources identify him as one of the early Jewish students at the Padua school of medicine. Jewish physicians stood at the forefront of the early Jewish Haskalah; they were revered for their knowledge and expertise on the one hand and suspected for their enticement with secular knowledge on the other.[11] A rare glimpse into Horowitz's life is afforded by his 1793 book *Megilat sdarim*, which tells the story of a father, Yedidyah Halevi, who attempts to compromise between his three quarrelling sons: Ovadyah, Ḥashavyah, and Hudeyah.[12] Horowitz utilized the family feud as an allegory for the late eighteenth-century schism between mitnagdic and hasidic Jewry. Through the story of the youngest son, Hudeyah, the author presents the Enlightenment as a golden mean between the two opposing camps. The Haskalah is thus depicted as a project that is beneficial, nay crucial, to the revitalization of Jewish tradition and faith. However, a closer reading of the text reveals a second, less immediately discernible allegory, through which the author delivers his own life story. The biographical details are embroidered into the image of the maskilic son, Hudeyah, whose name is in fact an anagram of the name of the author—Yehudah. Similarly to Horowitz, Hudeyah receives a strictly halakhic upbringing, but goes on to study medicine amongst "the gentiles." As the narrative unfolds, he returns home to his family only to face his brothers' suspicions that his secular learning has compromised his faith. It is soon revealed, however, that not only have Hudeyah's studies not damaged his religion, but they have strengthened it to a great degree.[13] Hudeyah's travails may be understood to represent those of the Jewish maskilim in general, and those of Horowitz himself in particular, who aimed to strengthen Jewish faith and tradition through rational philosophy and science, but was suspected of heresy and radicalism in return. More specifically, the story appears to allude to the negative reception of *Amudey beyt Yehudah* in Vilnius. Indeed, there is evidence to suggest that following the publication of the book, Horowitz was chastised by the local religious elite and forced to leave the city and settle in distant Hrodna (Grodno).[14] The unfortunate episode left Horowitz bitter for many years to come. "Slanderers have maligned me," he wrote several years before his death in 1797, "and bitter enemies have persecuted and injured me."[15]

Looking back from the twenty-first century, it is difficult at first to see how *Amudey beyt Yehudah*, a text so intensely embedded in traditionalist Jewish writing, could have caused such commotion. The text is written in biblical Hebrew in rhymed prose, in the style of the medieval maqama, which was quite popular amongst the early maskilim.[16] Only on rare occasions does Horowitz stray from this structure, as when dealing with an especially important or complex issue (e.g., AMBY, 17a, 28a–b). As befitting a traditionalist text, the first few pages of *Amudey beyt Yehudah* are densely packed with haskamot (rabbinic endorsements of the book). To these are added a few recommendations by the leading members of the early Haskalah, namely, Mendelssohn, Wessely, and the Dutch Jewish publisher Isaac Ha-cohen Belinfante (AMBY, [19], [23]). The inclusion of these recommendations alongside the rabbinical haskamot serves as further indication of Horowitz's mitigative approach and his attempt to present the bourgeoning maskilic movement as part and parcel of Jewish tradition and faith. This attempt to domesticate the Enlightenment is one of the book's most prominent and consistent motifs.

Thus, though he was one of the earliest maskilim and the target of at least one known controversy, Horowitz was no radical. In the preface to *Amudey beyt Yehudah*, he asserted his conservatism by reminding his readers that he was merely following in the footsteps of such great Jewish canons as Maimonides and Yehudah Ha-levi, both of whom had written books that aimed to combine Jewish theology with rationalistic philosophy (AMBY, [24]). In terms of non-Jewish sources of inspiration, Horowitz took special care not to mention any Christian authors by name in his book. The only non-Jewish thinkers cited throughout the text are classical authors such as Socrates, Plato, Galen, and Aristotle, all of whom would have been acceptable reading for an eighteenth-century Jew. And yet, there is a great cultural divide between these early authors and Horowitz's Enlightened endeavor. Indeed, in his attempt to present his book as a continuation of Ha-levi's project, Horowitz was merely complying with the literary norms of his fellow maskilim, who often utilized a spoonful of

Jewish canon to help their modern philosophical or scientific ideas go down. In reality, however, if we are to view Horowitz's text against its proper context, we should divert our gaze neither to Plato's ancient Athens nor to Ha-levi's medieval Spain, but rather to mid-eighteenth-century Europe, where savage philosophers were all the rage.

RATIONALIZING RELIGION

One of the basic assumptions underlying eighteenth-century anthropological thought was that a person's physical constitution is a circumstantial rather than an essential trait. Enlightenment anthropology was dominated by the assumption that there is nothing biologically different between Africans, Americans, and Europeans. In fact, Black Africans or Native Americans are merely Europeans in a different setting.[17] This radical universalism enabled the non-European Other, and especially the savage Other, to assume an exceptional philosophical position. It allowed the philosophers of the Enlightenment to turn the non-European world into a kind of metaphysical laboratory, in which various European norms of behavior could be empirically tested. Eighteenth-century authors utilized the exotic setting as a means to discuss such issues as gender and sexuality, women's rights, family, and class, or as a vehicle to deliver their political sympathies. But the most common norm to be tossed into the philosophical Petri dish offered by the non-European world was religion. Indeed, while it is true that the eighteenth century saw the gradual secularization of science and philosophy, it should be remembered that early Enlightenment discourse was still dominated to a great extent by religious interests and theological agendas. Throughout the greater part of the eighteenth century, religion remained a prime marker of difference between Europe and its Others, and it maintained a prominent place in anthropological descriptions, both in scientific as well as in philosophical works. It is therefore hardly surprising that religious debate was one of the primary functions of the eighteenth-century exotic. Savage idolators, American atheists, African infidels, Chinese philosophers, or Indian Brahmins served as a platform to promote various (often conflicting) religious agendas. Often, these messages were of a deistic or even atheistic nature (such as in the writings of Voltaire or Diderot); other times they were messages directed *against* deism, such as in Defoe's *Robinson Crusoe*.

And indeed, it is religion that stands at the heart of Horowitz's book. The intricate three-way dialogue offered in *Amudey beyt Yehudah* constitutes an ambitious attempt to justify Jewish faith, tradition, and commandments by use of reason. Horowitz's theological use of the image of the noble savage is inspired by a belief in a kind of universal religious intuition, a natural capacity for faith that is instilled even in the wildest savages. God, he wrote in *Amudey beyt Yehudah*, "has granted us the means to elevate any soul from its sordid state. . . . And you will not find anyone who questions His existence amongst peoples of faith from India to Kush, and not one who will deny the wonders He has done in sea and in land and in desert" (AMBY, 27b–28a). This was an extremely widespread approach during the eighteenth century. As an observant David Hume wrote in 1777: "What truth [is] so obvious, so certain, as the being of a God[?]"[18] Hume's question may have been asked in irony, but many eighteenth-century thinkers would have agreed. Mendelssohn, for instance, believed that "all peoples admit the existence of God blessed be He, and even those peoples who worship other gods will admit that the greatest power and abilities are held by the Lord God. . . . The tales of heaven and earth are understood by all, and there is not one thing in them that cannot be understood by any man anywhere."[19] Similar notions were expressed by other maskilim such as Wessely, Isaac Satanov, or David Frisenhausen, who asserted that Christianity and Islam had already banished polytheism almost completely, since "as the pagans heard even a tincture of either of these two faiths, which are based on teachings of the law of Moses, and as they learned how easy it is to follow their commandments, they did not hesitate for a moment but tossed away their idols, which had already become repulsive in their eyes."[20]

But the eighteenth century also saw a growing awareness of other modes of living and other systems of belief, and Enlightenment thinkers were required to grapple with increasing reports of idolatry or even atheism amongst non-European peoples. One popular solution was to claim that such reports were merely false, the outcome of anthropological negligence, or even intentional deception.[21] The English maskil Abraham Tang, for example, explained that the existence of God is a universally accepted fact, and those wild atheists of which one could read in the period's travel literature were merely figments of the travelers' imaginations, or a simple outcome of the language barrier. In reality, claimed Tang, atheism is simply against human nature "which is instilled in every Kushite, or in every man everywhere."[22] Another means of coping with the purported atheism of non-European or ancient peoples was offered by Mendelssohn. The latter shared Tang's skepticism concerning the reports on atheistic nations and tribes, and in his magnum opus *Jerusalem* (Berlin, 1783) he urged travelers to take caution when reporting the norms and behaviors of other peoples.[23] However, contrary to Tang, Mendelssohn did not view the denial of a single God an absolute impossibility. Rather, he claimed, following works of William Warburton, that idolatry is often the result of the misuse of a pictorial script such as hieroglyphs. Pictographs, explained Mendelssohn, tend to confuse men, and it is not long before the symbolic value of the sign is forgotten and the reader confuses the signifier with the signified. Thus, an eagle, a fox, or a lion, which had initially been used to symbolize moral traits, slowly become deities.[24] This theory was shared by many of Mendelssohn's contemporaries, such as the maskilic rabbi Elyakim ben Avraham (Hart), or the German sign-language instructor Samuel Heinicke, who doubted the possibility of delivering abstract ideas to the deaf.[25] But Mendelssohn went a step farther than these thinkers, claiming that even the European alphabetic script is not pure of theological hazards. Roman script, he argued, suffers from a tendency to "displa[y] the symbolic knowledge of things and their relations too openly on the surface [and] creat[e] too wide a division between doctrine and life."[26] It is here that Mendelssohn identifies the advantage of Judaism over all other religions. The ceremonial aspect inherent in Judaism inscribes religious faith into the daily life of the believer, and prompts him to inquire after the spirit and purpose of his beliefs.

The question of ceremonial law is one of the core questions with which Enlightenment and particularly maskilic thought was burdened. Whereas most thinkers would have agreed that the existence of God is a universally recognized fact that can be easily deduced by use of natural reason, the reasonability of the dictates of religion was a much more complex and demanding issue. Some writers shared Mendelssohn's view that there is reason to the commandments. Thus, for instance, Isaac Satanov wrote that while the motivation behind each and every commandment is not always immediately accessible to the mind, still the commandments are never truly contrary to reason. More radical in his commitment to the rationality of religion was Mordecai Gumpel Schnaber Levison, who claimed that the tendency to refrain from a rationalistic discussion of religious commandments leads inadvertently to epicureanism.[27] But other writers were less convinced. German pedagogue Joachim Heinrich Campe, whose works were extremely popular amongst the maskilim, offers a valuable example. In his 1791 rendition of story of the English "discovery" of Palau, Campe stressed that "there exists a theology of the heart [which is] independent of external expressions, and is the only one worthy of its holy name."[28] Campe's book was translated by the Polish maskil Menachem Mendel Lefin in 1818; however, Lefin chose to omit Campe's somewhat subversive observations on Palauan religion, which bordered on deism, and made no mention of Campe's "theology of the heart."[29] And yet, no few maskilim would have agreed with Campe's observations. Amongst these were deists such as Salomon Maimon or Ephraim Kuh, who dismissed the importance of practical religion completely.[30] Others exhibited a more ambivalent approach. Tang, for instance claimed that real religious practice is achieved not through the observance of ceremonial law but through the adherence to universal morals and thought. [31]

A particularly instructive example of the attempt to grapple with the reasonability of the commandments is offered by the Copenhagen-born maskil Isaac Euchel, one of the central figures of the late eighteenth-century Haskalah. In a series of fictional letters published in *Ha-measef* in 1789–1790, Euchel introduced his readers to the image of a Jewish Syrian traveler in Europe by the name of Meshulam ben Uriah ha-Ashtemoy [משולם בן אוריה האשתמועי]. In similar vein to Horowitz before him, Euchel utilized his naïve observer as a means to scrutinize the shortcomings of European society, such as intolerance, greed, and the marginalization of women. And yet, once again like Horowitz's Ira, Euchel's exotic traveler was first and foremost preoccupied with questions concerning religion. In his letters, Meshulam took a stand against religious intolerance, Jewish separatism, and the rabbinical neglect of secular knowledge. Meshulam's observations on these matters were often subversive, at times bordering on the radical. His observations on the Marannos of Madrid offer an interesting case in point. Most of them, writes Meshulam, "do not keep the commandments at all, claiming that their sole purpose is to tie the knot of the people of Israel in Diaspora, but when they are between enemies and at a great risk, a theology of the heart should suffice—indeed, it is the essence of religion. I do not know if these things are true, because to the best of my knowledge the success of every Jewish individual has to do with the keeping of the commandments alone, and if it is possible to be whole and happy without keeping the commandments, why the Greek Socrates and the

Indian Zarathustra would be as happy and as complete as any one of the people of Israel." "Let me know my brother," Meshulam addressed the ever absent recipient of his letters, "let me know your thoughts on this matter, because your faith is pure and whole, and your wisdom great and deep."[32]

Like Horowitz before him, then, Euchel utilized the image of the exotic critic in order to raise some extremely radical questions concerning Jewish faith. But whereas Horowitz presented these questions within the framework of a three-way dialogue, in which each and every one of the savage's inquiries was met by a conclusive answer provided by one of the two Jewish sages, Euchel provided his readers solely with Meshulam's epistles, and the naïve observer's skepticism remained in effect unanswered. In this manner, Euchel's traveler seems to serve precisely the opposite purpose of Horowitz's savage. While Ira's questions conveyed a methodical skepticism, which would subsequently serve as a platform for the fortification of Jewish tradition with the building blocks of science and reason, Meshulam's reflections appear to have manifested Euchel's genuine ambivalence toward some of the essential principles of the Jewish faith of his time. [33]

Skepticism concerning the compliance between reason and religious dictates was shared also by thinkers from the other end of the religious scale, who doubted *not* the necessity of ceremonial law but rather the competence of reason, and viewed its application to religion as useful only insofar as it is complemented by revelation. One such thinker was the famous English novelist and pamphleteer Daniel Defoe. The similarity between Defoe's tremendously popular *Robinson Crusoe* (London, 1719) and Horowitz's *Amudey beyt Yehudah* has previously been noted by Feiner, who writes, "There is no way of knowing whether Hurwitz read Defoe. . . . However, the . . . frame story and the concepts of this tale are unquestionably drawn from the literature of travels in the 'new world.'"[34] In his novel, Defoe introduced readers to a noble savage who, like Horowitz's Ira, acquires Western religion through a rational dialogue. Defoe utilized the story of Friday's religious (mis)education in order to demonstrate the hazards of a religion based solely on reason. Using his natural capacities alone, combined with Crusoe's somewhat inept instruction, Friday is quick to acquire the notion of a single God, of providence, of a redeemer, and of divine punishment.[35] The religious dialogue in *Robinson Crusoe* reaches an impasse, however, with Friday's primitive attempt to grapple with the

problem of theodicy. Friday is simply unable to accept the possibility
of the existence of a devil in a world governed by an omnipotent God.
It is here that the crucial importance of scriptural learning is revealed.
Crusoe's conclusion from the episode is instructive: "It was a testimony to me how the Meer Notions of Nature, though they will guide
reasonable Creatures to the knowledge of God . . . ; yet nothing but
divine Revelation can form the knowledge of Jesus Christ, and of a
Redemption purchased for us. . . . The Word of God [is an] absolutely
necessary instructor of the souls of men, in the saving Knowledge of
God, and the Means of Salvation."[36] As I have argued elsewhere, Friday's illiteracy, his inability to gain direct access to revelation, serves
a powerful rhetorical role in the novel as a means to combat deism
on the one hand and Catholicism on the other. It is this illiteracy that
subsequently legitimizes Friday's enslavement by Crusoe. An illiter-
ate Protestant, he is forever spiritually, and therefore also physically,
enslaved to his European master.[37]

As the century progressed, the differences between the rationalistic approach to religion and the more traditionalist fideistic approach
became more and more discernible, particularly in the Jewish cultural
realm. Traditionalist thinkers were quick to detect the subversive element instilled in the subjugation of faith to reason, and many opted
for an anti-intellectual approach, according to which "the holy spirit,
which is very superior, should not stand trial before acquired wisdom, which is its inferior."[38] The maskilim in turn began to develop a
kind of maskilic self-consciousness, which objected unapologetically
to irrationalism and demanded that all fields of knowledge and faith
be subjected to the scrutiny of science and philosophy. Maskilim such
as Euchel, Satanov, Naphtali Herz Ulman, and others openly rejected
the fideistic approach, and agreed that "there is no judge of truth and
justice in man but reason."[39]

Positioning Horowitz in this debate is difficult. As we have seen,
Horowitz shared with his maskilic peers a belief in the universality of
religious intuition. Indeed, this assumption is what facilitates the very
possibility of a theological dialogue between the sages and their savage. However, at times, he seems to favor revelation over reason. Thus,
for instance, he explains: "If you wish to see signs and emblems—
no sign is greater than the Torah [the Pentateuch] herself, which was
given from heaven. And if in these you do not believe, what good
are to you the sages of Yemen, antiquity, Kalkol and Heman [ancient
sages]" (AMBY, 27b). Elsewhere in the book, Horowitz argues: "If

the ancient fathers had received the light of the Torah as we have they would not have searched other ways in studies and investigations" (AMBY, 30b).[40] But how, then, does Horowitz justify his rationalistic discussion of the commandments in *Amudey beyt Yehudah*? In addressing this issue, Horowitz explains: "Our eyes have been blinded by exile, and the Torah is like the sun in its might, which blinds its viewer's sight. . . . And so there have risen teachers amongst us who have taken pity upon us to guide us in our perplexity[41] . . . and they have prepared for us tools, from the studies of the Greeks . . . , and their writings may serve us as telescopes or glasses, through which to view the great lights which God has put in the skies of our Torah, and in these we observe the complexities of the candle of our commandments" (AMBY, 31a–b). According to Horowitz, then, rationalistic discussion of religion is necessary only in Diaspora, as the conditions of exile do not allow the same access to truth as life in the land of Israel. Further evidence of Horowitz's understanding of the importance of revelation may be gleaned from the process of Ira's education, which begins not with the philosophical dialogue, but by acquiring the tools of Jewish faith, most importantly, perhaps, the Hebrew alphabet. Indeed, we must bear in mind that the dialogue begins only after the savage has already spent three years in the woods with his Jewish benefactors and has become partially acculturated.

Like Defoe before him, then, Horowitz appears to reject reason as a singular tool for religious reflection. He exemplifies the hazards of such use of reason through the roles of the three speakers, Ira, Hushai, and Ittai. The dialogue follows a more or less regular structure in which Ira raises a skeptical question, which is initially addressed by Hushai, who provides an answer based on reason alone. In some cases this answer suffices, but often Ittai is required to complete it using his rabbinical, and sometime scientific, knowledge. [42] Thus, for instance, Ira ponders the benefits of processed and particularly kosher foods, and demands to know why civilized men do not settle for the natural foods consumed by savages (AMBY, 4b). Hushai responds by explaining that civilized men are superior to savages not in their physical build but in their mental make-up: "And if wisdom were tied with courage, why the ox would have been the most wise, and the horned beast—the light of the eyes" (AMBY, 4b). Ira, however, finds this answer unsatisfactory, and demands to know how it is that corporeal foods are able to affect an intangible soul. At this point, Ittai intervenes in order to explain that "indeed, the sages have likened the higher soul, to the tree of life planted in the soil. . . . And man is the tree of the field, and his fruit is his reason. But his drinks and nutrition are what cultivate his wisdom" (AMBY, 4b).[43] This recurring pattern serves Horowitz as a means to demonstrate the limits of reason, which must be complemented by rabbinical but also scientific studies. He thus conveys an approach according to which revelation is superior to reason. But is it, as Defoe would have it, "an absolute must" for the acquirement of faith?

In some places in the dialogue, Horowitz seems to convey a more ambivalent approach, and he admits that it is at least theoretically possible to achieve full religious recognition without revelation.[44] In fact, the dialogic form of *Amudey beyt Yehudah* undermines the fideistic message that is often uttered in the text. Ira's three years of acculturation notwithstanding, it is the rational dialogue between the sages and the savage through which Jewish faith is discovered both by the savage as well as by the readers. Indeed, in contrast to Ha-levi's *Kuzari*, Horowitz's purported source of inspiration, in which the theological discussion is ignited and reinforced by divine revelation; or *Robinson Crusoe*, which displays many similarities to Horowitz's tale, and in which providence plays a decisive role, the hand of God is conspicuously absent from Horowitz's book. Ira's conversion to Judaism is not inspired or even ratified by revelation. Rather, the theological investigations in *Amudey beyt Yehudah* are carried out within the strict confines of the rational dialogue, and do not stray from these borders to other realms of religious experience, such as religious authority or divine revelation. This is significant, as the dynamics of the dialogue present reason and consent as the sole criteria for truth. Indeed, within the dialogue, consent is the only necessary and sufficient term for the progression of the theological investigation.

It is this fundamental rationalism of the dialogue that allows Horowitz to subsequently present Judaism, or at least *his version* of Jewish faith, as a natural religion, agreed upon by all. As Ittai exclaims: "And now, my sons, let us leave these matters of opinion, and delve into our holy Torah, for it will strengthen the souls and unite them in a marvellous union, and it was not given by chance, and it is not contested by anyone" (AMBY, 26a). To be sure, the events of Horowitz's own time had taught him well that religious schisms are prevalent in Judaism no less than in other religions. However, the kind of Jewish faith that Horowitz promotes in his book is not the rabbinical Judaism condemned by Enlightenment thinkers such as

Christian Wilhelm Dohm, the abbé Grégoire, or Voltaire. Rather, it is a form of Judaism based on reason, a natural Judaism, from which all other religions have grown: "And if all religious branches have grown from the stem of our holy faith, then it is clearly better to hold on to the foundations of our religion itself, which are pure of all unclean thoughts, so much so that the [non-Jewish] nations are obliged to agree upon them" (AMBY, 29b). Throughout *Amudey beyt Yehudah*, Horowitz attempts to show that the Jewish faith is, in fact, that natural religion advocated by thinkers of the Enlightenment. He emphasizes the universal and rational features of Judaism, and presents it as a religious doctrine accessible to all through reason. And indeed, the kind of Judaism acquired by Ira, and propagated by Ittai and Hushai, is a "common-sensical," reasonable Judaism. It is a Judaism that, once adequately explained, simply cannot be denied.[45] In this manner, the schismatic aspect of religion is avoided: since all men employ the same reason, and are endowed with the same common sense, a rational faith, a natural religion, may never be the source of schisms. As Horowitz explains in a later work: "Many religions have taught us to hate one another, and commanded that we take up swords against each other. . . . If only men could agree on a religion based on love, then they may rest at ease in this world, and prosper in heaven above."[46] We encounter here a profound yearning for peace that, as discussed in some detail below, is a salient feature of Horowitz's corpus of works.

THE SAVAGE STUDENT: MASKILIC PEDAGOGY IN *AMUDEY BEYT YEHUDAH*

Horowitz's presentation of reason and rational consent as the ultimate tools of religious instruction corresponds with his pedagogical views, as they are expressed in *Amudey beyt Yehudah*. Like other conservative thinkers of his time, Horowitz viewed education as the primary means by which reform may be achieved, and pedagogical thought played a central role in his work. Education, he writes, "should not be related through trickery or chance, the way a beast is tamed in anger and wrath, and when the mule tires from the road they beat it so that it continue to carry its load. But this is not the way of our pleasant Torah, and this is not the city of ḥokhmah [wisdom or science], but you must maintain choice in the truth of the Torah, in piety and love. And let him [the pupil] speak, and let him appeal, and complain as a friend and as a maskil" (AMBY, 3b–4a). This view can be read as an early expression of the pedagogic doctrine that would become characteristic of the later Haskalah and was inspired by the philosophy of Rousseau, as articulated in his 1762 *Émile, ou de l'éducation*. Rousseau explained that education should be based on pleasure or desire, and never on constraint: "Great care must be taken that it does not become a burden to [the student] and get to the point of boredom. Always, therefore, keep on the lookout and, whatever you do, stop everything before he gets bored, for it is never as important he learn as that he do nothing in spite of himself."[47] As discussed further below, there is textual evidence to suggest that Horowitz was an avid reader of Rousseau's works, and it is possible that his pedagogical musings in *Amudey beyt Yehudah* were directly influenced by the Swiss philosopher. However, even if Horowitz did not read *Émile* directly, Rousseau's influence on European pedagogic thought during the second half of the eighteenth century was such that it stands to reason that Horowitz would have encountered his pedagogical ideas one way or another.[48] The Rousseauist demand that the learning child be lured into education rather than coerced into it is a recurring theme in many maskilic discussions. Thus, for instance, the anonymous author of the pedagogic tract *Sefer gidul banim* (London, 1771) recommended that Jewish parents explain to their children the rationale behind the various religious dictates. He also suggested that prayers and blessings be related to the child in his mother tongue, and that teachers employ benevolence and patience rather than the violence and intolerance, which, he complained, characterized the existing educational system of his time.[49] Other maskilim were equally critical of the harsh and uninspired education pursued by eighteenth-century melamdim (religious elementary teachers). Most famous is Salomon Maimon's presentation of the Jewish *ḥeder* (religious elementary school) as a system of tyranny and despotism, and of the melamdim as petty and ignorant sadists who enjoy ripping the ears and beating the eyes of their students.[50]

Horowitz's pedagogic program complies with the sentiments of other early maskilim not only in its general prescriptions, but also in its curriculum. Upon the commencement of his studies, Ira learns the Hebrew tongue and alphabet as well as Jewish religion and prayers, science, and ethics. Horowitz's choice to begin the process of acculturation by teaching "his savage" the Hebrew tongue may be viewed as a further expression of the contemporaneous dissatisfaction with the traditional pedagogical system. One of the most widespread points of criticism against the melamdim, even before the Haskalah, was that both they and their students are incapable of adequately understanding the Hebrew Bible and prayers. As a solution to this problem, it was suggested that more emphasis be put on the acquisition of Hebrew amongst teachers and their pupils or, alternatively, that the sacred texts be taught in a language more accessible to the student, particularly Yiddish.[51] Concern over the inaccessibility of the sacred texts increased during the second half of the eighteenth century and featured prominently in the works of such maskilim as Mendelssohn or Wessely.

This preference for the biblical Hebrew tongue corresponds with a second distinctly maskilic characteristic of Horowitz's curriculum, which is the author's emphasis on the Bible rather than the Talmud. In fact, the Talmud, which was the primary text within the Jewish educational system of the time, is conspicuously absent from the savage's curriculum. This shift of focus from the Talmud to the Bible was characteristic not only of conservative maskilim such as Horowitz, but also served the interests of more radical thinkers such as Lazarus Bendavid, who claimed that Jewish neglect of the Bible, combined with the rise of rabbinical thought, had resulted in a scholastic and superficial way of thinking and contributed to the development of a reckless national pride amongst the Jews. [52]A similar distaste for the Talmud is found in the letters of the American Jewish woman Abigaill Levy Franks, who in a 1733 private letter to her son expressed a yearning for a kind of Jewish Protestant revolution that would overthrow the Talmud once and for all.[53] In the thought of Bendavid, Franks, and other radical Jewish intellectuals, the blame for Jewish "cultural inferiority" rested on the shoulders of the rabbinical elite. Similar notions were expressed by Christian thinkers, particularly apologists for the Jews such as the abbé Grégoire, Christian Wilhelm Dohm, or the Marquis D'Argens, who viewed the Talmud and rabbinical lore as the primary culprits in the narrative of Jewish "degeneration" from antiquity to their present day. [54]

Needless to say, Horowitz did not share Bendavid's or Franks's radical aspirations and was certainly not an adherent of the thought of such reluctant "Philosemites" as Grégoire or D'Argens. However, in *Amudey beyt Yehudah* we find traces of an inadvertently subversive view, which transfers religious authority from the rabbinical elites to the educated individual. Ittai, Hushai, and Ira may be brilliant sages indeed, but they are emphatically not members of the Jewish halakhic authority. In fact, those same rabbinical Jews, who were viewed by D'Argens or Dohm as a hindrance to Jewish regeneration, play no role in the acculturation—indeed, religious conversion—of the noble savage in *Amudey beyt Yehudah*. In effect, Ira is never really converted in the traditional sense; rather, he undergoes what Horowitz presents as a kind of spiritual circumcision, which for this author was more than enough. As explained by Ittai: "And as I circumcise the flesh of the foreskin of his heart, let us rejoice in him" (AMBY, 2b).

It should be emphasized, however, that even if Horowitz may be viewed as inadvertently undermining the traditional conceptions of Jewish faith, in no way did he aspire for the abolition of rabbinical Judaism. Horowitz's incorporation of rabbinical haskamot in the book, as well as his tendency to turn to rabbinical texts where he deemed necessary, points to a deep appreciation for rabbinical Jewry and halakhic authority. In addition, contrary to Ira's somewhat "Protestant" mode of learning, during their time in the woods Ittai and Hushai make a point of studying not only the Bible, but also the Talmud, the Mishnah, and even Kabbalah: "And there they sat and read books of reason and morals, and read the Torah, both written and oral, and often ventured also to explore, the religious truths of Kabbalistic lore. . . . And in the dim hours between night and day . . . , through philosophy books they made their way, so as not to be as foolish as apes" (AMBY, 2a–b). Indeed, it is the sages' and not Ira's mode of learning that Horowitz deemed the most ideal program for the education of the Jewish elite. In his short description of Ittai and Hushai's scholarly activity in the woods, Horowitz casually lays out what would later become the controversial pedagogic program of the conservative Haskalah. One of the earliest and certainly the most famous attempts to formulate this program appeared in Wessely's great pedagogic tract, *Divrey shalom ve-emet*, published more than a decade and a half after *Amudey beyt Yehudah*. To educate the Children of Israel in the adequate manner, Wessely explained, knowledge should be divided into two separate categories: "The first class is the discipline of man [*torat ha-adam*], which includes those things which make us all men, and without which we do not deserve that title. . . . The second class is the discipline of God [*torat ha-shem*], which consists of the laws of the Lord and his Torah."[55] It is doubtful whether Horowitz would have agreed with the order of Wessely's program; to wit, the Jewish sages make a point of learning philosophy

only during the "hours between night and day." However, there is a
great degree of similarity between Horowitz's depiction of the fundamental importance of the study of philosophy (the Jewish sages
study philosophy "so as not to be as foolish as apes") and Wessely's
portrayal of acquiring "the discipline of man" as a prerequisite to
humanity.[56]

The attempt to incorporate secular studies into the Jewish curriculum was one of the main points of contention between maskilim like
Wessely and the late eighteenth-century rabbinical elite. The resource
to non-Jewish sources of knowledge was negatively perceived by
many traditionalists, who viewed secular studies not as a contribu-
tion to faith but as a hindrance to it.[57] Indeed, as attested by Horowitz himself in his aforementioned *Megilat sdarim*, those few Jews who
ventured outside the confines of Jewish knowledge were often suspected by their Jewish peers of straying from tradition. To be sure, the
sweeping objection to secular learning was not shared by all members
of the rabbinical elite. Some, like Emden, Baruch Shick of Shklov,
or the Vilna Gaon exhibited a more tolerant or even favorable attitude to the *hokhmot* [secular studies], and particularly to mathemat-
ics, astronomy, and the natural sciences.[58] But the relative lenience
shown by these figures was hardly representative of the governing
views amongst members of the halakhic elite, and as the eighteenth
century progressed the gaps between the two opposing camps—supporters of secular studies on the one hand and those of halakhic studies on the other—widened into an almost unbridgeable abyss. But
Horowitz's pedagogic program should be read against the context of
mid-century efforts to offer a more balanced curriculum. For Horowitz and his early maskilic contemporaries, secular studies and non-
Jewish philosophy were meant to complement rabbinical knowledge
and strengthen the cultural, religious, and political standing of the
Jews. It is to this end that Horowitz utilized the philosophy of the
Enlightenment and particularly that of Rousseau.

IRA AND THE SPIRIT OF ROUSSEAU

In 1755, just over a decade before the publication of *Amudey beyt
Yehudah*, Rousseau published one of his most influential works,
the *Discours sur l'origine et les fondements de l'inégalité parmi
les hommes*. It is this work, I argue, that set the tone for Horowitz's entire project. The similarities between Rousseau's philosophy

and Horowitz's book seem to have made some impression on previous scholars. Joseph Klausner claimed that "Horowitz read Rousseau's books in their original French." In a similar vein, Werses also mentioned in passing that Horowitz read "some of Rousseau's writings." Both scholars, however, made no attempt to substantiate their claims.[59] In reality, Horowitz did not need to know French in order to read Rousseau's *Discours*; the text was translated into German by Moses Mendelssohn already in 1756. The fact that it was Mendelssohn—an acquaintance, perhaps friend, of Horowitz—who carried out the translation supports the hypothesis that Horowitz was indeed familiar with Rousseau's philosophy and with the *Discours* in particular.

Mendelssohn's own views of Rousseau were critical. He rejected Rousseau's controversial presentation of natural man as a solitary being, and, in a public letter to his close friend Gotthold Ephraim Lessing, which was attached to the translation, explained that man is endowed with a natural propensity for society, an undeniable need for the company of other men.[60] This view was shared by the vast majority of Enlightenment thinkers and was also the prevalent view amongst thinkers of the Haskalah, such as Isaac Satanov, who explained, following Aristotle and Maimonides, that sociability is the very essence of humanity: "Man is by nature a political being," he wrote, "and it is unimaginable that a single man may stand alone on an island." [61]

Horowitz, however, took a different approach. Embracing Rousseau's image of an isolated natural man, he presented Ira as a solitary being, devoid of society or culture. Like Rousseau's natural man, he roams the woods in his nudity, collecting wild herbs for his sustenance, and is hardly distinguishable from other animals. Indeed, his sole claim to humanity lies in his free will and his potential for reason—his perfectibility.[62] Horowitz also accepted Rousseau's view of man as naturally mute. Contrary to many of his contemporaries, who viewed language as one of the prime markers of humanity and subscribed to the notion, eloquently expressed by Pope, that "Man from beast by Words is known,"[63] Rousseau explained that man in his natural state has no need for language, if only because he does not communicate with other men. Language, he stressed, is a product of society, and not an essential marker of humanity.[64] In fact, natural man is depicted by Rousseau as a kind of *bundle of potentials*, a rational, cultural, and social creature by force, but irrational, solitary, and mute in practice. In his natural state, explained Rousseau, man lives,

eats, and thinks like an ape. Indeed, he even communicates like one—
without any real language, but with the use of grunts and shrieks.
Accordingly, in *Amudey beyt Yehudah* language is presented as an
outcome of socialization: Ira acquires language only upon his encounter with the Jewish sages, and his first utterances mark his transition
from natural solitude into the society of men.[65] This may have been
a somewhat unusual view for a maskil, but Horowitz was not singular in his appreciation of Rousseau's work. As noted, Rousseau's
influence on the pedagogic thought of the Haskalah was immense,
and even his *Discours* did not go entirely unappreciated. The radical
German Jewish intellectual Lazarus Bendavid, for instance, accepted
Rousseau's views of natural man as mute, claiming in 1807 that the
natives of Tierra del Fuego ("die Pescheräh") do not possess any language whatsoever.[66]

Though seemingly a mere metaphysical construct, for political
thinkers of the seventeenth and eighteenth centuries the paradigm of
a state of nature had important political implications. The story of
man's emergence from his natural state into civilized society served
as a means to articulate the purpose of the state, and to envision a
legitimate form of government. One of the earliest and perhaps most
familiar examples is found in Thomas Hobbes's 1651 *Leviathan*. In
this trend-setting work, Hobbes painted an exceedingly dismal picture of the state of nature, as a state characterized by an endless,
all-encompassing war. Such a state, he claimed, was simply intoler-
able, and the only rational choice available to men was to abandon
the state of nature in favor of just about any form of (stable) government, and preferably the most stable, absolute monarchy. Other
thinkers, such as Locke or Montesquieu, envisioned a less dismal
state of nature, and accordingly offered less extreme forms of government. But whatever the points of contention between them, almost all
early modern political thinkers agreed that the move from the natural
to the civilized state is inspired by reason, and that it is this reason in
which the legitimacy of sovereignty is grounded. Rousseau, however,
was of an altogether different view. "It is clear," he wrote in the *Discours*, "that the first man who made himself clothing or a dwelling,
in doing so gave himself things that were hardly necessary, since he
had done without them until then and since it is hard to see why he
could not endure, as a grown man, a kind of life he had endured from
his infancy."[67] Correspondingly, the natural state is used in the *Discours*, not to legitimize civilization, society, or the state, but rather to

criticize them. Whereas the natural state is characterized by an endless struggle to fulfill man's basic survival needs, the civil or rather social state is defined by the incessant pursuit of the superfluous, an unquenchable desire to meet false needs.

Returning now to *Amudey beyt Yehudah*, we find that Ira's motivations for leaving the natural state are equally confounding: Ira is initially drawn into society by a mere sandwich, offered to him by Ittai (AMBY, 2b). Thus, like Rousseau before him, Horowitz portrays the emergence from nature into society as an intriguingly random and irrational move, initiated by the allure of the artificial. Horowitz, it should be noted, is more forgiving in his understanding of society; however, he too is aware of the hazards of civilization and uses the savage Ira as a means to contain the threat posed by the pursuit of artificial needs. Thus, the savage's first questions upon having entered society challenge the very basis of civilization and pose an alternative mode of living in harmony with nature. Ira asks, for instance, what are the functions of men's fancy clothes, of built houses, of cooked foods? Is it not better, he asks, "to eat the herbs offered by the earth, . . . than to toil away as a beast, and in the sweat of thine faces to eat bread. And it seems to me that the beast has the better of you, as her foods are prepared without much ado, and we too, the men of the woods, without toil or sorrow find our foods, and we are as healthy and as fit as lions, and our bellies are clear of illness and dirt, while you, the men of the state, are skinny and weak, in spite of your armies of bakers and your cooking techniques" (AMBY, 4b). Following close on the heels of Rousseau, Horowitz presents the satisfaction of natural needs as a healthier and happier mode of living, as opposed to the decadence and degeneration brought about by modern civilization's enticement with the artificial.[68] Civilized man, explained Rousseau, is a domesticated animal, and like other domesticated creatures he too has become a weakling, a degenerate, a slave.[69]

CONFRONTING THE SAVAGE BODY IN *AMUDEY BEYT YEHUDAH*

Thus far, we have discussed the mental or internal traits of Horowitz's savage, but what of his external characteristics? Ira's physical appearance is discussed by Horowitz in two short passages. The first occurs upon the initial encounter between the sages and the savage: "And there fell on a day and they went out into the field to gather herbs, and they saw a man, unabashed and nude, and collecting wet herbs for his food" (AMBY, 2b). Later in the book, Horowitz returns to the issue of Ira's body when describing the savage's emergence from the woods, and his first encounter with the townsfolk: "And they [Ittai and Hushai] came into town with the savage man, and at his dreadful sight there arose a great fright, and upon seeing this naked man of the woods, the masses came, and before him they stood" (AMBY, 3b). In the ensuing discussion, Hushai chastises the towns-folk for passing judgment upon the savage based only on his looks: "You stand aghast at the matter and form you behold, and do not wait for the essence and soul to unfold. I see that you wonder at the soul of this savage man, and do not recognize . . . that he possesses morals and wisdom. And do you really assume that he is immoral and unwise, merely because of his savage disguise? And really, to enter-tain thoughts of this kind, you must be bereft of a rational mind. If morality is merely a matter of shape, then there is no-one more moral than the average ape, dressed up in disguise—call him the most wise! Or cover the mule with bells of pure gold, would he then pos-sess a wisdom untold?" (AMBY, 4a). Horowitz mocks here what he views as his contemporaries' exaggerated emphasis on dress as a sig-nifier of identity. And indeed, clothes played a crucial role in early modern articulations of identity, and they often served as a means to draw the lines between civilized and savage, European and non-European, female and male.[70] A vivid expression of the close connec-tion between identity and dress may be found in the early modern version of the paper doll. Like the modern dress-up doll, these min-iature dolls, which gained popularity during the second half of the seventeenth century, were accompanied by various overlays on which different outfits were illustrated. What is striking about these overlays is that they often feature both male and female outfits, rendering the dolls' gender highly ambiguous. Thus, the National Museum of Wales is home to an oil-on-copper miniature dating to the late seventeenth or early eighteenth century that depicts a smiling woman who can be turned into a man simply by applying one of the seven or eight mas-culine overlays, which consist of masculine clothes and in some cases a beard and a mustache. A similar cross-dressing doll is held at the Los Angeles County Museum (fig. 7). Once again, the female doll is rendered male by aid of a masculine mica (fig. 8).

In European Jewish thought of the period, clothes were equally important. The Italian maskil Shmuel Romanelli, for instance,

Figure 7. Miniature portrait of unknown woman, ca. 1650. Costume
Council Curatorial Discretionary Fund. Los Angeles County Museum of
Art, Los Angeles, California. Digital Image © 2013 Museum Associates /
LACMA. Licensed by Art Resource, NY.

describes in his account of his travels through Morocco (Berlin, 1792)
how both he and his acquaintances assumed a host of fictitious identities merely by changing their clothes, and they roamed the deserts of
Africa dressed at times as Muslim Moroccans, other times as Christians, and on some occasions even as women.[71] This kind of religious
and sexual cross-dressing is an essential element of eighteenth-century

Figure 8. Miniature portrait of unknown woman with mica overlay. Costume Council Curatorial Discretionary Fund. Los Angeles County Museum of Art, Los Angeles, California. Digital Image © 2013 Museum Associates / LACMA. Licensed by Art Resource, NY.

travel narratives, and it appears in a wide variety of Jewish sources from the period, such as Euchel's *Igrot Meshulam*, Lefin's *Masaot ha-yam,* or Mordecai Manuel Noah's *She Would Be a Soldier.*[72]

In *Amudey beyt Yehudah* it is the absence of clothes that attracts the greatest degree of attention. The only other trait besides nudity noted by the sages upon their first encounter with the savage is his nutrition. This focus on the two characteristics of nudity and nutrition is characteristic of early modern representations of savages. Non-European peoples were often described as nude or, as in the case of Glikl's savage woman, wearing nothing but a fig leaf to cover their genitals. Their eating habits also served a major role in their characterization as savages, and they were often described as voracious cannibals, eaters of raw meat or fish, vegetarians, or hunters-gatherers. Indeed, it was often theorized that nutrition was one of the key elements contributing to the physical variety of man, second only to climate.[73] In some accounts, diet played such a central role that it was perceived as a matter of life and death. Thus, for instance, in 1801 Abraham ben Elijah related the case of two feral children who had been captured in England and had almost died of starvation after having refused to eat anything but legumes.[74] Similar tales of savages or feral children who were unable to accustom to "civilized foods" were ubiquitous in the eighteenth century, and appear also in several other Hebrew works, such as in Baruch Lindau's *Reshit limudim* or Shlomo Keysir's *Kohelet Shlomo*.[75]

Of course, diet and dress are highly mutable traits, and eighteenth-century authors were not unaware of their instability as designators of difference. Indeed, the ambiguity of the differences between savages and Europeans is a recurring theme in some of the century's most widely read works. In *Robinson Crusoe*, for instance, Defoe makes a point of deconstructing just about every signifier of European identity available to his readers. Thus slavery, one of the traditional markers of savagery in early modern thought, is portrayed in the novel as a potential characteristic of savages and Europeans alike; throughout the novel Crusoe enslaves men from a whole range of ethnicities (Black African, Morisco, and Caribbean), and is eventually similarly enslaved by a Turkish captain during one of his journeys.[76] Similarly, it is suggested that the civilized European is not immune even to the most sordid depths of savagery, namely cannibalism. This may be gleaned from Crusoe's musings upon the discovery of a shipwreck on the horizon: "I fancy'd they had all gone off to Sea in their Boat [and] were carried into the great Ocean where there was nothing but misery and perishing; and that perhaps by this time they might think of starving and of being in a Condition to eat one another."[77] The fluidity of clothes as markers of difference is also treated by Defoe's novel. Indeed, clothes or their absence play an especially important role in *Robinson Crusoe*, as Roxanne Wheeler explains: "Crusoe reveals an uneasiness about the issue of clothing, indicating that it is impractical in the tropical climate though necessary as a sign of his distinction from naked savages. At different times, Crusoe is nearly naked or burdensomely over clothed."[78]

Another popular early eighteenth-century writer to make literary use of the instability of European notions of difference was Jonathan Swift. In his *Gulliver's Travels* Swift exemplifies the mutability of clothes and eating habits as designators of difference by having his protagonist compared to a Yahoo: "The Beast and I were brought closely together; and our Countenances diligently compared. . . . My Horror and Astonishment are not to be described, when I observed, in this abominable Animal, a perfect human Figure; . . . The great Difficulty that seemed to stick with the Horses, was, to see the rest of my Body so very different from that of a Yahoo, for which I was obliged to my Cloaths, whereof they had no Conception: The Sorrel Nag . . . brought out of the Yahoo's Kennel a Piece of Ass's Flesh, but it smelt so offensively that I turned it down with loathing; he then threw it to the Yahoo, by whom it was greedily devoured."[79] The ambiguity of difference between the European and the savage is similarly pronounced in Horowitz's description of the first encounter between the Jewish sages and savage. Ittai and Hushai meet the savage while all three men are in the process of gathering herbs for their sustenance, and whereas at first sight the sages are struck by the savage man's nudity, their next (somewhat odd) move is to undress themselves.[80] In this narrative move Horowitz creates a fascinating literary moment in which there is absolutely no real physical difference between the Jewish sages and the savage man.

THE PROBLEM OF SLAVERY IN EIGHTEENTH-CENTURY THOUGHT

The highly ambiguous physical construction of the savage in *Amudey beyt Yehudah* enables Horowitz to present his readers with a natural man with whom the reader may identify. But those persons known as "savages" in eighteenth-century discourse were never really pure philosophical constructs whose existence was confined to the eighteenth-century mind. They represented real people, living under the yoke of colonial rule. Colonial interests were thus deeply embedded in eighteenth-century philosophical or literary discussions of "natural people." This close connection between European colonial interests and literary representations of savages is perhaps nowhere more evident than in discussions surrounding the issue of slavery. Horowitz's dialogue treats the issue only in passing, conveying what may perhaps be viewed as a kind of aloof abolitionism. This attitude was, I would argue, characteristic of the Jewish Enlightenment.

As mentioned in the introduction, for several decades Jewish attitudes toward slavery have been the focus of a heated debate amongst scholars. Some studies have argued that Jews tended to refrain from empathizing with African slaves in order to distance themselves from other subaltern groups.[81] Others have painted a more favorable portrait of the Jews in general, and eighteenth-century Jews in particular. In discussing the Galician maskil Samson Bloch, for instance, Joseph Klausner argued that Bloch's objection to the transatlantic slave trade should be viewed against the context of his Jewish heritage. According to Klausner, Bloch's adamant objection to the slave trade (which, he slyly adds, "was tolerated by the European nations of his time") was an attempt to "adapt his work to the spirit of Judaism."[82] Some scholars have expressed the notion that their disadvantaged position in European Christian society led Jews to identify more strongly with Black slaves than their Christian contemporaries.[83] These may be noble expectations; however, as history has sadly taught us time and time again, there is nothing inevitable about the treatment of one subaltern group by the other. Identification is always a deeply subjective matter.

All these conflicting approaches see a close connection between Jewish authors' approaches to the issue of slavery and their Jewish background. If they support slavery, it is because they are Jews who wish to "Whiten" themselves in the eyes of their European peers; if they oppose it, it is because they are Jews who have suffered discrimination at the hands of their European peers. However, in order to adequately assess the "Jewish aspect" in eighteenth-century Jewish attitudes toward slavery, and particularly the attitudes of maskilim such as Horowitz, it is crucial that we review these thinkers' approaches to the issue against the context of the dominant intellectual or cultural trends amongst their non-Jewish contemporaries.

The eighteenth century saw a vast change in attitudes toward the institution of slavery. While early works such as Defoe's *Robinson Crusoe* or Behn's *Oroonoko* could often present slaveholding and the trade in an uncritical manner, later writers were often required to address the issue in more reflective and often apologetic ways. An interesting testimony to the changes that occurred in attitudes surrounding slavery is offered by some later adaptations of Defoe's novel, and particularly the vastly popular German adaptation for children produced by Campe (Hamburg, 1779). In his reworking of Crusoe's story, Campe was obliged to confront the issue of Friday's (or in his version—Freitag's) enslavement. In Defoe's 1719 original, slavery, as Wylie Sypher explains, is "among the countless matters of fact to be estimated by the tradesman's coarse thumb."[84] Friday's enslavement, like the enslavement of others in the book such as the Morisco Xury, is almost a non-issue for Defoe, and to the extent that it requires any justification at all it is justified by religion.[85] Sixty years after the first publication of *Robinson Crusoe*, however, such an uncritical and unsentimental treatment of slavery simply would not do. As the eighteenth century progressed, slavery became more morally burdensome for Europeans, and in adapting Defoe's narrative Campe was now required to readdress the problem of Friday's enslavement. His treatment of the issue is instructive. Robinson, Campe explains, would have preferred to take Friday as a friend rather than a slave, however: "He thought it wise for his own safety that the new visitor, whose character he knew yet nothing of, would remain for a while under the confines of respectful submission. He therefore took it upon himself to play the role of king for a time."[86] Some contemporary scholars have viewed Campe's treatment of this issue as constituting a step away from colonialist thought. Thus, Richard Apgar presents Campe's Krusoe as nothing short of an "accidental colonizer," whose slaveholding position is thrust upon him almost involuntarily.[87] Similarly, in discussing an early nineteenth-century Yiddish translation of Campe's work, which was, as discussed in Chapter 4 below, exceedingly popular with the maskilim, Leah Garrett suggests that it was specifically Campe's distaste for slavery which made him a more appealing source text for Jewish translators than Defoe could ever have been.[88] Indeed, Campe's apologetic treatment of Freitag's enslavement was reiterated in the various Hebrew and Yiddish translations of the book, which began to appear in the decades surrounding the turn of the nineteenth century.[89] Interestingly, though Jewish translators were often exceedingly liberal in their approach to translation, and added, omitted, and changed their source texts quite freely (as witnessed by Lefin's omission of Campe's discussion of the benefits of a "theology of the heart" discussed above), it did not occur to any of Campe's Jewish translators to omit the story of Freitag's enslavement. True, both Campe and his Jewish translators appear to have been troubled by the existence of slavery; however, their presentation of Freitag's enslavement by Krusoe as theoretically justifiable must be viewed as part of the late eighteenth-century attempt to envision a form of legitimate, indeed, of *Enlightened* enslavement. Krusoe's adoption of a kind of benevolent slave-master relationship, combined with his dread at the concept of a liberated savage, are indicative of the widespread anxieties that characterized late eighteenth-century discourse surrounding the question of the emancipation of the slaves.

A similar approach toward slavery is found in a wide range of texts from the period. In his popular play *Die Negersklaven* (Leipzig, 1796), for instance, August von Kotzebue confronted Europeans with the woes of slavery, which corrupts its propagators and abuses its victims. In the course of the play, Kotzebue presents his solution to the problem through the voice of a Black slave who had been "fortunate" enough to be purchased by a benevolent master. After being offered his freedom by his new benefactor, the slave refuses, explaining, "He who is captivated by kindness has no need for chains. You have freed me, and I am your slave forever."[90] A similar storyline is found in English Irish children's writer Maria Edgeworth's 1804 story, "The Grateful Negro." Edgeworth relates the story of Caesar, a Black slave purchased by a benevolent master who, like Kotzebue's slave, prefers his sweet enslavement over emancipation. When informed of a planned slave revolt, which will free him and his fellow slaves, he notifies his master and fights at his side against the revolting slaves.[91] Perhaps not coincidentally, Caesar was also the slave name of Behn's Oroonoko. The differences between the two characters, however, are striking: while Behn's Caesar will give his life and the lives of his loved ones for liberty, Edgeworth's Caesar risks his wife's life as well as his own for their master. This difference serves as further indication of the changes that occurred in European notions of race from the late seventeenth century to the early nineteenth century. As George Boulukos convincingly argues, the emergence of the figure of the satisfied slave, willing to trade his freedom for gratitude, was closely linked to the emergence of modern racism. It entailed the assumption that Black slaves are not endowed with the same innate and unflagging desire for freedom that characterizes their White masters.[92]

Stories such as those by Kotzebue, Edgeworth, or Campe were inspired by anti-slavery sentiments that had been propagating throughout Europe during the eighteenth century, and which had reached an all-time high toward the century's close. But when it came to the solution to the problem, thinkers of the period became somewhat more hesitant. Indeed, even the most ardent opponents of the slave trade viewed the immediate emancipation of colonial Black slaves as an extreme measure, potentially detrimental to European colonists abroad. The concerns underlying this approach were adequately expressed by Thomas Jefferson, who in his infamous "Notes on the State of Virginia" (1781) explained that the immediate emancipation of the slaves would result in "convulsions which will probably never end but in the extermination of the one or the other race."[93] Similar anxieties were shared by many of Jefferson's contemporaries on both sides of the Atlantic, and it was not long before a compromise between the notion of natural rights and the political reality of colonial slavery was reached in the form of ameliorationism. Boulukos characterizes ameliorationism as an ideology that viewed slavery as a problem that can be solved only gradually, by means of reform and not emancipation.[94] Ameliorationist thinkers argued that the gradual improvement of the relationship between the individual slave and his master would improve not only the terms of slavery but also the slaves themselves, thus permitting their subsequent emancipation without those "convulsions" dreaded by Jefferson and his contemporaries.

Not everyone agreed, of course, that Africans would eagerly succumb to their benevolent enslavement. Some, like Lazarus Bendavid, pointed out that "tyranny can never produce esteem."[95] And yet the ideology of ameliorationism became the dominant intellectual trend amongst late eighteenth- and early nineteenth-century intellectuals, viewed as a more responsible and politically sound option than emancipation. Indeed, ameliorationism was a perfect means of soothing the conscience of those Europeans, who lived in an age in which, to paraphrase Sir John Hawkins's 1787 observation, humanity was in fashion.[96]

MASKILIC DISCOURSE ON SLAVERY

It remains to be asked, however, to what extent the maskilim were aware of Enlightenment discourse surrounding slavery, and to what extent they partook in it. According to Jonathan Schorsch, not much: "Eighteenth-century Jewish discourse," he writes, "knew next to nothing about the extensive and growing ethnographic and scientific literature on Blacks, on Africa, on slavery."[97] Doubtless, this observation holds true for many Jews of the period, Glikl being an obvious case in point. In my discussion of her memoirs in Chapter 1, I argued that it is possible to find in the story of the savage woman and her pious husband a kind of unique colonial indifference that envisions colonialism as a threat rather than an opportunity. And yet, this colonial indifference would disappear from the writings of the eighteenth-century Haskalah. A useful way to understand the change is to compare Horowitz's reaction to the encounter with the savage to Glikl's earlier response. Contrary to Glikl, who, it will be recalled, rejected both possibilities of external and internal colonialism, Horowitz envisions the encounter as an opportunity to acculturate both the savage without—Ira—as well as the savage within—the strayed Jews. His description of the encounter is thus constructed through the language of colonialism. This kind of intertwining between colonial and pedagogical discourse would feature prominently in the works of later maskilim, as discussed in detail in Chapter 4.

That said, the centrality of the colonial aspect in Horowitz's work or in the early Haskalah in general should not be overstated. A traditionalist Lithuanian Jew who spent his days pouring over the Mishnah or Maimonides, Horowitz could hardly be expected to empathize with the spirit of colonial calling that informed such writings as Defoe's *Crusoe* or Edgeworth's "Grateful Negro." For Horowitz the savage was first and foremost a literary tool that could be imported from the philosophy of his Christian contemporaries and carefully remolded so as to serve maskilic needs. By utilizing this metaphor of the savage, Horowitz attempted to demonstrate the rationality, indeed, the *naturality* of Jewish faith. In so doing, he hoped to pave the way to a new kind of thinking about Judaism, and perhaps also, as will be presently discussed, about the relationship between Christians and Jews.

The question of slavery arises only once in *Amudey beyt Yehudah*, upon the first encounter between the Jewish sages and the savage. After seducing the savage into joining their company, the sages consider what should be done with this man of the woods. When Hushai suggests that they enslave him, Ittai responds as follows: "The counsel that Hushai hath given is not good at this time, to take a foreign man as a slave for our people, and if this poor man has come to join our estate, we shall not dismiss him, nor take him as our slave" (AMBY, 2b). Horowitz's response to slavery is thus clear-cut; in contrast to other thinkers of his time, who devoted exhaustive tracts to justifying the abolition of slavery on economic, religious, sentimental, or philosophical grounds, this maskil offers his readers no explanation for his objection to slavery but rather presents it as an intuitive reaction to a clearly immoral system.

This casual approach to abolition is characteristic of the thought of other maskilim who often brought up the issue of slavery only to reject it in passing. Romanelli, for instance, had the opportunity to express his thoughts on the issue while strolling early one morning through the city of Tetouan. His attention was caught by a group of "naked Blacks" who were laundering their clothes at the city gates. "I approached one of them," he writes, "[and] asked him about his palms of his hands and the soles of his feet, which were white. He informed me that the Blacks are the descendants of Ham. When Noah, Ham's father cursed him, his skin turned black. He wept and pleaded with him, and his father out of compassion took pity on him so that his palms and the soles of his feet became white again. On account of this, however, they were subjugated and sold into slavery, thus fulfilling their forefather's curse—'Cursed be Canaan, the lowest of the slaves shall he be to his brothers.'"[98] Romanelli utilized this short encounter with the Black slave as a platform to offer a short and critical description of the Moroccan slave trade in Black Africans. He concluded his discussion of slavery with a hint of irony, by reminding his readers that "in olden times even Whites and Jews were also sold as we know from the story of Joseph." By conflating the biblical story of Joseph, who had been sold into slavery in Egypt and had subsequently bought the Egyptian people, with that of the descendants of Ham, who had allegedly been cursed with dark skin and eternal slavery, Romanelli parodies what had at one time been a widely accepted explanation for the dark skin color of the Africans, and a widespread legitimization for Black slavery.[99] And yet, as Romanelli's sly allusion to it suggests, the story of the Curse of Ham had begun to lose sway during the eighteenth century. Addressing the question of slavery, maskilic thinkers now employed the rhetoric of the Enlightenment and expressed their objections to the institute based on moral, philosophical, and sentimental grounds. Support for the institution, and particularly for the slave trade, was now presented by the maskilim as an outdated or archaic approach. To be sure, Isaac Satanov admitted in 1795, "internal speech, which is intelligence, is very lacking in the Kushite. And because of this it was seen fit to allow them to be maltreated and to be sold as animals for they were considered akin to beasts. But the philosophers of our times have signalled that they are human beings like us. Therefore they banned mistreating them."[100]

Schorsch views Satanov's discussion of slavery as a "remarkably non-committal" response, which describes both slavery and abolitionism as "merely developments concerning others, out there somewhere."[101] To some extent, this is quite true; for Satanov, Horowitz, Romanelli, and other maskilim, the institution of slavery was a distant problem, indeed, a problem concerning others, out there somewhere. But it was perhaps this distance from the actual reality of slavery as an economic and political system that facilitated the overwhelming (albeit superficial) rejection of slavery in maskilic thought. The lack of direct involvement in colonial expansion and the slave trade allowed the maskilim to carry out their discussions of slavery relatively unbound by straightforward colonial or economic interests. The ensuing result was the development of a maskilic consensus against slavery and particularly against the transatlantic slave trade. This consensus encompassed authors from almost all shades of the maskilic spectrum: from relatively unknown thinkers such as Joseph Baran, who blamed slavery for the "degenerate condition" of Black Africans, through canonical maskilim like Mendelssohn, who mocked the hypocrisy of Christianity in its treatment of slaves, to radicals such as Salomon Maimon, who stressed the indecency of the trade.[102] As noted, abolitionist or ameliorationist sentiments were also translated into Hebrew and Yiddish, through the translations of Campe and other non-Jewish writers' works. Thus, statements against slavery appeared in the works of such translators as David Zamość, Baruch Shenfeld, Yossef Vitlin, Khaykl Horowitz, Abraham ben Elijah, and Moses Mendelssohn-Frankfurt. Some translators even added their own independent objections to the trade.[103] Abolitionist statements are also found in the German translations of the works of Henri Grégoire and Isaac Weld, produced by Saul Asher and Henriette Herz, respectively.[104]

One maskil who seems to have been particularly troubled by the existence of slavery was Samson Bloch. In his 1828 description of Africa, Bloch treated the issue at some length, expressing his deep dismay at the conditions of the slaves and at the continued existence of the trade. His views against slavery were articulated in the fashion of late eighteenth-century sentimentalism, which emphasized the pains and suffering endured by the slaves. Here, for instance, is Bloch's dramatic description of the slaves' journey across the Atlantic: "They dwell in the bottom of the ship, a narrow dwelling, where they lie naked and pressed against one another. . . . . The floors are covered in blood and mucus like a battlefield after a massacre, or a slaughterhouse floor. Stink and scum contaminate the air. . . . The screams of those tormented by their shackles combine with the cries of the miserable. The dying bray feebly, yearning for your comfort, oh death! Rise up my soul from this sordid view of the human soul, ah, what good is it, what beauty can it hold if these are its actions?"[105] Clearly Bloch was deeply devoted to the issue, more so than any of his fellow maskilim. It remains to be asked, however, to what extent did Bloch or other maskilim identify or empathize with the slaves? Does their almost unanimous objection to slavery imply a sense of solidarity between subalterns, as suggested by previous studies? The literary evidence seems to suggest otherwise. Maskilic authors rarely drew a direct analogy between European Jews and Black slaves, and their aloof abolitionism seems to convey not a Jewish identification with the oppressed but an identification with European patronage over the oppressed.[106] In their attitudes toward the institution of slavery, the maskilim thus corroborate Norbert Elias's observation: "A person's attitude towards the 'simple people'—above all, towards the 'simple people' in their most extreme form, the 'savage'—was everywhere in the second half of the eighteenth century a symbol of his or her position in the internal social debate."[107] Indeed, for the maskilim, opposition to Black slavery constituted a kind of "cultural code," to use Shulamit Volkov's terminology, a means to signify their proximity to European culture.[108] Abolitionist discourse served in maskilic writing not to combat slavery per se, but rather to demonstrate the authors' awareness of the intellectual trends of the Enlightenment, and to construct an image of the maskil as a sensible, sentimental, refined, and up-to-date citizen of the world.

THE TWO FACES OF NATURE

If Horowitz's rejection of slavery is indicative of his awareness of the intellectual trends of his time, his attitude toward "nature" and "natural men" offers further evidence of his absorption of Enlightenment discourse. A useful starting point for our discussion is, once again, Rousseau's Second Discourse. In this article, Rousseau presented the state of nature as the most suitable for human existence. In abandoning this state, man not only turns his back on his most ideal mode of existence, but also awakens nature's wrath: "If you take into account the mental anguish that consumes us," he wrote, "you will sense how dearly Nature makes us pay for the scorn we have shown for its lessons."[109] Rousseau's yearning for a simpler, more "natural" life was characteristic of the primitivist strand of Enlightenment thought. Similar philosophical nostalgia is expressed in the writings of such thinkers as Diderot, Michel Adanson, and Lord Monboddo, who described the "newly discovered" South Sea Islands as a place "where the inhabitants live, without toil or labor, upon the bounty of nature in those fine climates."[110] For primitivistic thinkers, the non-European world represented nature in all its glory. It was a world removed from the hazards of civilization, a world of health and plenty, harmony, liberty, and peace.

An ardent adherent of this kind of primitivism was Horowitz, whose literary protagonists, Ittai and Hushai, turn their backs on a corrupt and decaying civilization, and find refuge and solace in nature. Throughout *Amudey beyt Yehudah*, nature is repeatedly presented as an alternative to a perverse society, as explained by Ittai: "Here shall I live amongst the lions and tigers, and not amongst my ruthless brothers, for the beasts of the woods are by nature confined, and may cause us less malice than damned humankind" (AMBY, 2a). This view of nature as sanctuary is repeated in a wide range of maskilic writing, such as in Shalom Ha-cohen's *Amal u-Tirzah*, Aaron Wolfssohn-Halle's *Avtalyon*, or David Zamośc's *Toar ha-zman*.[111] Its roots are planted in antiquity; already in the Hebrew Bible, nature serves as a sanctuary for righteous men, for instance in the story of the prophet Elijah, who finds refuge from Queen Jezebel in the desert. Similarly, in the Talmud we read that the second-century Rabbi Shimon bar Yoḥai (Rashby) and his son escaped from the Romans to a secluded cave.[112] Indeed, throughout the history of the West, nature, in the form of forests, deserts, caves, and—particularly in the early modern period—the "untamed" world outside Europe, was envisioned as the realm of the righteous, a place for study and observation, pure of the strains and perversions of society.

This view of nature fashioned not only early modern perceptions of the non-European world and its inhabitants, but also the image of those few European men who dared to venture outside of civilized society and into the "natural world." Travelers, navigators, and discoverers such as James Cook, Louis Antoine de Bougainville, or François Péron were some of the greatest cultural heroes of the eighteenth century. They were living legends who were revered and admired throughout Europe. Their travel accounts were read by philosophers, men of science, and lay audiences alike, and constituted one of the most widely read literary genres of the period.[113]

And yet, at the same time, there existed also a very different class of men who made their way to the "newly discovered" lands outside of Europe in the seventeenth and eighteenth centuries. These men were no cultural heroes; quite the contrary, they cluttered the lowest strata of society and their voyages were performed not to enhance European knowledge of the non-European world, or to acculturate, tame, or convert its "savage" inhabitants, but rather to rid Europe of its own problematic elements. Indeed, the non-European world served Europeans not only as a metaphysical laboratory but also as a penal colony, to which convicts and indentured laborers were regularly sent. The perception that accompanied this usage of the colonies was expressed somewhat bluntly by English traveler Henry Whistler who, in a 1655 account of Barbados, described the island as "the dunghill whereon England doth cast forth its rubbish. . . . A rogue in England will hardly make a cheater here. A bawd brought over puts on a demure comportment, a whore if handsome makes a wife for some rich planter."[114] Whistler's views were not uncharacteristic of contemporaneous European thought. For generations, there had existed in the Western imagination two opposing images of nature and the natural world, as both utopia and dystopia, heaven and hell, the realm of the pious as well as the perverse. Interestingly, these two seemingly exclusive images could often appear in the very same text. An early example is offered by the talmudic tale of Rashby and his cave, in which the cave serves initially as Rashby's sanctuary and later in the story, after his initial emergence and unsuccessful reintroduction into society, as his punishment.[115]

In the early modern period, this ambivalence toward nature was transcribed into the image of the colonial world, constructing a dialectical understanding of the world outside of Europe, and, as we shall presently see, a complex view of its inhabitants. An exemplary use of the two faces of nature is found in *Robinson Crusoe*. Upon a first reading, Defoe appears to participate in the primitivist perception of nature as a place of refuge and regeneration. Crusoe, a man corrupted by society, who spends his days in an endless quest for new adventures, finds peace and God in nature.[116] But upon a closer reading we find that contrary to Rousseau and other primitivists, who viewed nature as the ideal mode of human existence, for Defoe the ideal state for man is the life of the English middle class.[117] Interestingly, this "middle state" is presented by Defoe in the same manner in which the natural state is presented by Rousseau; it is a state of contentedness and peace, devoid of the vicissitudes that characterize the lives of the highest and lowest classes of society. Accordingly, while Rousseau mused on the dire consequences of mankind's abandonment of nature, in *Robinson Crusoe*, Crusoe's repeated refusal to settle for this ideal middle state constitutes the prime cause of his misfortunes. Thus, nature for Crusoe is thus not a sanctuary so much as it is a penitentiary. Indeed, throughout his stay on the island, Crusoe repeatedly treats the place as a kind of penal colony; he refers to it as "my captivity" and asks: "Why has God done this to me? What have I done to be thus us'd?"[118] In fact, in stark contrast to Ittai and Hushai, who turn their backs on a corrupt society to find refuge and remedy in nature, Crusoe is a corrupt man who turns his back on an ideal social status and finds his punishment in nature. Defoe's understanding of nature as punishment is reflected in the type of nature Crusoe encounters on the island; this is not the benevolent nature described by Monboddo or Diderot, but a lethal, hazardous nature that actively seeks to devour man through sea storms, earthquakes, and cannibals. It is, as Crusoe exclaims on one occasion, a "Nature entirely abandon'd of Heaven, and acted by some hellish Degeneracy."[119] And indeed, Crusoe is constantly preoccupied with protecting himself from the destructive effects of this godless nature; he builds a wall around his habitation, gathers weapons; in a word, he fortifies himself thoroughly.

And yet throughout Crusoe's twenty-eight-year stay on the island, his attitude to the place changes dramatically, and his status on the island is gradually transformed from prisoner to governor. As John Richetti explains, Crusoe's religious conversion from casual Christian to devout believer subsequently enables him "to leave his paranoid seclusion and to convert his island from a prison into a garden. From this point on Crusoe turns to the island itself, exploring it, domesticating it, and indeed enjoying it in various ways. [Eventually] he is able to speak jauntily of 'my reign or my captivity, which you please.'"[120] Significantly, this double conversion—of Crusoe and his island—is made possible thanks to the many European tools that Crusoe succeeds in salvaging from his ship, tools to which an excruciating degree of attention is given in the book. These tools include a knife, a musket, and a Bible, all of which prevent Crusoe from being consumed, both physically and mentally, by the destructive forces of nature. Instead of being devoured by nature, then, Crusoe subjugates it, and converts it from a "nature abandoned of Heaven" to a heavenly nature, wherein providence is most vividly manifested.[121] Thus, for Defoe man's relationship to nature is either that of a captive or of a conqueror, a man or a beast. This view, according to which in order to enjoy the benefits of nature one must subdue, domesticate, or tame it, was widespread during the eighteenth century. Buffon, for instance, derided the Native Americans who, he claimed, had never attempted to become masters of the land, the animals, or the seas, and had thus rendered themselves "an inconsequential species of impotent automatons."[122] In direct opposition to these impotent savages stood the masculine European colonists, who, as we have seen in the previous chapter, were often described as redeeming nature from her virginity. One such man was Benjamin Franklin, who became a cultural hero in Europe after having invented the lightning rod. In the minds of his contemporaries, Franklin had become a true master of nature, taming one of its wildest and most destructive elements.[123]

The same dialectical view of nature is found also in Jewish literature of the eighteenth and early nineteenth centuries. Thus, for instance, in Baruch Shenfeld's 1825 discussion of the Pacific islands we are told: "To this day there are many island dwellers who live without morals and reason, without righteousness and honesty, without morals or wisdom. They are like beasts to themselves, and they have nothing in common with civilized man. Ignorant and shameless, they know no modesty, until they receive help from afar, and wise men came and their eyes were opened and they shall know that they are naked in body and soul, and they shall be ashamed."[124] Upon a first reading, Shenfeld's representation of the non-European world appears unequivocally negative. Indeed, after presenting the woes of an unrestrained "natural" life, Shenfeld arrives at the almost inevitable colonial conclusion, according to which, far from being an infringement on their native rights, colonization is beneficial to indigenous peoples around the world. And yet there is an almost unnoticeable subversive strain that runs through Shenfeld's description. The subversive element is expressed in Shenfeld's intertextual description of Pacific Island life. In using the biblical allusion "and they shall know that they are naked . . . and they shall be ashamed," Shenfeld refers his readers to the story of the expulsion from the Garden of Eden. He

thus likens the savages to Adam and Eve—a traditional literary analogy in the colonial literature of his time. But more importantly, in
using the ubiquitous Edenic analogy, Shenfeld inadvertently likens the
European colonists to the biblical serpent, thus equating European
civilization with a curse, and the colonization of the non-European
world with the expulsion from Eden. Of course, this is not to say that
Shenfeld was aiming for a subversive reading of his text, only that
the conflicting views of nature as heaven and hell, prize and punishment, dictated an extremely complex and contradictory view of the
non-European world and its colonization. Thus, even the most Eurocentric and self-assured accounts could often be plagued by an under-
current of primitivism. An interesting example is offered by Glikl,
who, it will be recalled, portrays her savage woman as cannibalistic
and infanticidal but also as an Eve-like naked woman, bearing a fig
leaf to cover her shame. The Edenic analogy in Glikl's story complicates the image of the murderous mother, transforming her from an
"unnatural mother" to the universal mother of all human kind, a
kind of infanticidal Eve, as it were. A second story that appears in the
memoirs further complicates Glikl's view of nature and natural men.
The story tells of an ancient people, who, writes Glikl, "were not concerned about the world and ate only that which nature grew. They
had no drink but water and among them there was no envy or hatred,
and they wore no clothes" (G. Tur., 38; G. Abr., 10). Glikl goes on to
sing the praise of this people, at one point even expressing a desire to
share their natural lifestyle. Clearly, this description stands in stark
contrast to the description of the East Indians in the story of the pious
Jew. Such dualistic representations of nature would culminate in the
eighteenth century and give adequate expression to one of the great
dilemmas of the period, between the ideal of acculturation on the one
hand and the worship of nature on the other. Indeed, Enlightenment
thought was dominated at once by a desire for domestication, a will
to conquer and acculturate the savage, to "enlighten" the ignorant,
and domesticate the wild; and an appreciation for nature and the natural, an idealization of the primordial, the ancient or the savage.

FANTASIES OF ACCULTURATION AND ANNIHILATION
IN *AMUDEY BEYT YEHUDAH*

By the end of the Middle Ages, writes Hayden White, "the Wild Man
has become endowed with one of two distinct personalities, each

consonant with one of the possible attitudes men might assume with respect to society and nature." One personality is that of the ignoble savage, representing all the horrors and depravities of human nature. We have met a host of such savages in the previous chapter, which discussed the image of the infanticidal or cannibalistic savage as it appeared in the works of Glikl, Locke, Smith, and others. However, European imagination has also long been preoccupied with a different kind of savage, one which represents a harmonious, benevolent nature; a noble savage who stands for all that is naturally good in man, and questions all that is perverse in European culture.[125] White presents these two personalities of the savage as thematically and chronologically distinct. Each personality, he argues, represents an altogether different view of nature and of mankind and bears its own unique uses. And yet, in Horowitz's woods, we encounter both types of savages, the ignoble and the noble, the wild man and the savage philosopher. The latter is represented, of course, by Ira, who is depicted by Horowitz as an emblem for humanity, a rational, just, and naïve creature, against whose scrutiny Jewish tradition and faith must be justified. And yet, at the same time, other savages are described by Horowitz (through the voice of Ittai) as wild and voracious beings, monstrous beasts, whose only claim to humanity lies in their human form. So degenerate, so horrendously evil—Ittai finds them unfit for life, and, in stark contrast to his treatment of Ira, offers them no acculturation or redemption, but only extermination. When prodded by Ira as to the reason for his harsh treatment of the savages as a whole, Ittai responds: "Why not ask me to take pity on the animals of the woods? Know really that these men differ from the entire human species, and their soul is by nature as filthy as the souls of beasts. But beasts have an advantage over these men . . . for it is set by nature that a beast will not covet another species, if its own species is set before it and these damned men will come upon every beast, animal and bird, they shall lie with mankind, as has been revealed by the new travel literature, so much so that they have set themselves apart even from the cruellest of animals" (AMBY, 28a). Though Horowitz claims that his description is based on the accounts of contemporaneous travelers, the attribution of homosexuality and bestiality to savages is much older. In fact, Horowitz appears to be alluding to the biblical portrayal of the seven nations that inhabited the land of Canaan during the Israelite conquest. The sins of these nations are described in Leviticus 18:22–24: "Thou shalt not lie with mankind, as with womankind. . . . Neither shalt thou lie with any beast to defile thyself therewith: neither shall any woman stand before a beast to lie down thereto: . . . Defile not ye yourselves in any of these things: for in all these the nations are defiled which I cast out before you."[126] The analogy between contemporaneous colonial peoples and the seven nations of Canaan is reinforced by Ittai's usage of the biblical story of the conquest of Canaan in order to justify the Spanish conquest of the New World: "And really, when the Europeans conquered them, they massacred them without pity, for they did not see any difference between them and beasts, as is known from the histories of Edom and Spain. And were God to put them in our own hands, as he did the known seven nations [of Canaan], he would surely have commanded that we slay them one and all, for they are all of one verdict" (AMBY, 28a). In conjuring the story of the conquest of the seven nations by the Israelites in the context of European colonialism, Horowitz once again demonstrates the maskilic tendency to identify not with the victims of colonization but rather with its perpetrators. The Canaanite analogy itself was quite widespread during the early modern period. However, Enlightenment thinkers, amongst them the maskilim, often opted for more "humane" justifications for colonialism. To the extent that the Canaanite analogy endured, it was most often used in order to criticize the conquest, presenting it as barbarous, cruel, and unjust.[127] But if Horowitz's description of savages was somewhat outdated, it was certainly not unique in its harshness. Reports of savage cannibalism, anarchy, infanticide, and blood lust appear frequently in the writings of such authors as Defoe, Steele, Buffon, Cornelius De Pauw, and others. These descriptions can be characterized as displaying a "Hobbesian" view, according to which nature is a state of constant war, in which "the life of man [is] solitary, poore, nasty, brutish and short."[128] Indeed, Hobbes himself identified the Native Americans as men subjected to a real-life state of nature: "It may peradventure be thought, there was never such a time, nor condition of warre as this . . . but there are many places, where they live so now. For the savage peoples in many places of America . . . have no government at all; and live at this day in that brutish manner."[129]

But how does Horowitz's "Hobbesian" view of savage nations comply with the "Rousseauist" depiction of nature and natural man, also expressed in the book? In a previous discussion of this issue, Feiner locates the source of Horowitz's ambivalent treatment of savagery in his Jewish background. According to Feiner, though

Horowitz's use of the image of the noble savage attests to a familiarity with Enlightenment literature, his harsh treatment of the savages as a whole reflects the limits of his reception of Enlightenment culture.[130] To be sure, the question of the fate of non-Jewish non-believers has a distinct "Jewish dimension." It is an issue that has preoccupied Jewish theologians from the Talmud, through Maimonides to the present day. Most famous is Maimonides' position, according to which only the "righteous amongst the Gentiles," meaning only those non-Jews who have received the word of God and observe the Noahide laws (seven commandments that, according to rabbinic thought, apply to all humanity) are entitled to a share in the World to Come. But what of those righteous men who have not accepted revelation but still observe the Noahide code? These men, explains Maimonides, may expect no share in the World to Come.[131] The question seems to have received some urgency during Horowitz's time, given European expansionism, voyages of "discovery," and the growing interest within the Jewish community in the non-European world. A correspondence between Mendelssohn and Emden is dedicated to this question, with Mendelssohn representing Ira's view that savages are not to be blamed for their ignorance, and Emden representing the rabbinical view that only revelation secures a place in the World to Come.[132]

And yet, the dialectic treatment of savagery in *Amudey beyt Yehudah* is not a uniquely Jewish phenomenon, but is found also in the works of non-Jewish writers. A brief encounter with the Janus-faced savage is offered, for instance, by the widespread adaptations of the Inkle and Yarico tale discussed in Chapter 1. As will be recalled, in almost all versions of the tale (barring Glikl's) Yarico is presented as a noble savage par excellence—a pleasant and gentle soul who offers the European sailor all her tender love and care. Yarico's savage nobility stands in stark contrast to her tribesmen's utter barbarism, and her care for Inkle clashes with the tribe's cannibalistic customs. This somewhat odd dichotomy between Yarico and her tribe was a salient feature of the Inkle and Yarico genre, and was repeated uncritically in most versions of the tale. Its ubiquity is indicative of the fact that eighteenth-century authors did not necessarily view the two images of the noble and ignoble savage as mutually exclusive, and the two "personalities" described as distinct by White were, in fact, closely intertwined.[133]

A poignant example of the dualistic treatment of savagery in eighteenth-century literature is offered by Defoe's *Robinson*

Crusoe. During his stay on the island, Crusoe realizes that his new home is the meeting ground for the cannibal feasts of the neighboring savage tribe. From this moment on, he develops a compulsive preoccupation with these savages. "Night and Day," he remarks, "I could think of nothing but how I might destroy some of these Monsters in their cruel bloody Entertainment and, if possible, save the Victim they should bring hither to destroy."[134] Here, too, it is the artifacts of civilization, this time in the form of a musket, which protect Crusoe from nature's all-consuming power. With the aid of his musket Crusoe succeeds in his plan to save the cannibals' victim, and the latter becomes his companion, known to us as the trusty Man Friday. But Friday is not merely a *victim* of cannibalism; indeed, he is also its perpetrator. This noble savage, described by Defoe as being endowed with a conquering "European smile" and a kind and gentle nature, is in fact no less a cannibal than his ruthless attackers. To wit, after his release from the cannibals, Friday offers his new master that he himself indulge in a victorious feast on the defeated men's flesh. And yet, whereas Crusoe sentences the Caribbean cannibals as a group to death, he grants Friday his protection, education, and affection. And while Crusoe spends the remainder of his time on the island acculturating Friday, converting him to Christianity and preparing him for civilization, he makes no attempt to convert or "domesticate" his tribesmen, the savage's pleas notwithstanding.

Such inconsistencies are, I suggest, a salient feature of the anthropological discourse of the Enlightenment. Similar ambivalences are revealed even in the works of some of the century's most unequivocal primitivists, such as Rousseau, who made a point of differentiating between his purely hypothetical and, more importantly perhaps, solitary natural man, and the actual savage societies known to his contemporaries. According to Rousseau:

> As soon as men had begun to appreciate one another, and the idea of consideration was formed in their minds, each one claimed a right to it, and it was no longer possible to be disrespectful toward anyone with impunity. . . . Thus, everyone punishing the contempt shown him by another in a manner proportionate to the importance he accorded himself, vengeances became terrible, and men became bloodthirsty and cruel. This is precisely the point reached by most of the Savage Peoples known to us, and it is for want of having sufficiently distinguished between ideas and noticing how far these Peoples already were from the first state of Nature that many have

> hastened to conclude that man is naturally cruel, and that he needs
> Civilization in order to make him gentler.[135]

For Rousseau, the original sin of socialization is what separates savage societies from men in their natural state. Once united, men may
no longer live in a state of nature, and they require civilization and
responsible sovereignty in order to maximize their survivability. There
is thus an essential, qualitative gap between the life of an *individual
man* in nature and the reality of a *group of men* in nature; the former is an idealized state of existence, whereas the latter is potentially
a dismal state of affairs. This distinction between the individual and
the collective in nature is of paramount importance for our discussion; indeed, I would argue that it is this difference that dictates the
dualistic treatment shown by Horowitz, Defoe, and their contemporaries to the individual noble savage on the one hand and the ignoble
savage tribes on the other. In all these works, the individual savage is
depicted as challenging, tempting, and noble, whereas the savages as
a group are viewed as threatening, dangerous, and barbaric.

This dualistic treatment of the individual savage on the one hand
and fear of savages as a collective on the other extends beyond the
realm of literature. Its effects may be found, for instance, in eighteenth-century attitudes, practices, and legislation surrounding the
institution of slavery. As we have seen, anti-slavery sentiments had
been propagating throughout Europe during the eighteenth century,
and reached an all-time high toward its close. But when it came to the
question of emancipation, thinkers of the late eighteenth and early
nineteenth centuries became somewhat more hesitant. They feared
that the immediate emancipation of the slaves would pose a political
and even mortal threat to European colonists, and offered an alternative solution in the form of amelioration. The ameliorationist program was based on the assumption that the gradual improvement of
the conditions of slavery would result in an even better relationship
between each individual slave and his or her master, to the point that
the relationship would subsequently, almost unnoticeably, become
that of an employer and employee.[136]

The notion that the improvement of the individual is a means to the
gradual and peaceful improvement of society in general is a recurring
theme in these discussions. It is here that the conservative Enlightenment's ambivalence surrounding the Enlightenment project itself is
most clearly pronounced. In their emphasis on the individual, conservative thinkers promoted ideals of liberty, equality, and social reform,

while at the same time containing the revolutionary threat posed by the potential radicalization of these very ideals, which might result in social revolution, moral chaos, and political anarchy. This tension is a recurring theme in the literature and thought of the conservative Enlightenment. It is expressed in Enlightenment thinkers' preoccupation with such binary pairs as nature and culture, liberty and anarchy, noble savages and ignoble barbarians, the individual and the mass, revolution and reform. Thus, in his 1784 *Was ist Aufklärung*, Immanuel Kant stressed that "a public can achieve enlightenment only slowly. Though a revolution may well put an end to personal despotism . . . , it will never produce a true reform in ways of thinking; rather, new prejudices will serve as well as old ones to control the great, unthinking mass."[137] Fear of this same "great unthinking mass" is also evident in Voltaire's famous definition of equality: "Every man has the right to believe himself, at the bottom of his heart, entirely equal to all other men," but in practice, men must accept the role designated to them by society or else "every human society is perverted."[138] In the abbé Henri Grégoire's treatment of the Jews, we find yet again a preference for the individual over the mass. Grégoire explains that in order to improve the state of the Jews, it is best to work on the individual level rather than addressing the Jews as a whole. Indeed, he explains: "Nature does not occupy itself with species but only after having formed the individual."[139] Similar thoughts were expressed by Mendelssohn, who stressed that "progress is for the individual man, who is destined by Providence to spend part of his eternity here on earth."[140] This focus on the individual is, I would argue, a means of containing the threat posed by radicalism. It serves to relieve the basic tension between reform and revolutions, which underlay the project of the conservative Enlightenment.

Returning to *Amudey beyt Yehudah*, we find the same kind of ochlophobia expressed frequently throughout the text. In some cases the mass is presented as truly horrific, no less so than savage nations. Thus, for instance, Horowitz explains: "And the sages are like flocks without a pasture and the mass is like a wolf, who yearns to devour the righteous and good as though they were wasps and flies" (AMBY, 16a); later in the book he adds: "And really, the sages amongst the masses of the earth are like a soul residing in a damned body which pursues its desires" (AMBY, 20b). Significantly, the mirror image of this mindless mass appears in the form of the maskil, or the wise men of all nations. While the mass is characterized by endless wars and hatred, there exists between the sages of all nations, Horowitz explains, a natural affinity, even love: "There is no hate so great as the religious hate between the fools, and no love so deep as the love between the wise. The former will hate for their ignorance and latter will love for their harmony."[141]

The careful reader will notice that in describing the mass Horowitz utilizes the same rhetoric used in his depiction of savages. Both groups are presented as intimidating, violent, hedonistic, and mindless collectives who are at constant war with one another and should be abandoned to their sordid fates. In fact, Horowitz displays the same kind of ruthlessness toward both groups, the strayed masses and the savages. When informed by a messenger from the city that the "men of pride and heresy" have all been lost to madness, hunger, or atheism, he responds: "Thus shall be the fate of all who have strayed from the path of truth" (AMBY, 3b). The message is reinforced in a second work by Horowitz, in which it is suggested that the wise should abandon the fools to their blissful ignorance.[142] Furthermore, Horowitz's attitude toward the mass or the ignorant is characterized by the same kind of dualism expressed in his treatment of savages. After all, Horowitz's primary purpose in *Amudey beyt Yehudah* was to remedy what he saw as the main problems afflicting European Jewry. His was an inherently pedagogic project, inspired by the desire to acculturate his fellow Jews, by exposing them to rationalistic philosophy, scientific development, and the discourse of reason and tolerance. And indeed, in some places, Horowitz expresses a more optimistic approach toward the issue of acculturability, and attempts to construct the image of the maskil as a benevolent Enlightener of his fellow men. Thus, for instance, he explains in the introduction to *Amudey beyt Yehudah*: "God has awakened some precious souls . . . to instruct and to teach, to compose books and treatises . . . and the inkwells of the wise, shall bring on the fools' demise, . . . and as the clouds of foolishness shall rise, the light of wisdom shall shine upon our eyes, and the Children of Israel shall everywhere witness the aura, and keep their blessed Torah" (AMBY, [21]).

John G.A. Pocock explains the fear of radicalism and revolutionary violence that characterized the thought of the conservative Enlightenment, as a reaction to the religious wars of the early modern period. Pocock's Enlightenment is a traumatized historical movement that uses skepticism, etiquette, science, and toleration as a means to preserve peace.[143] And indeed, eighteenth-century thinkers were often preoccupied with the question of keeping the peace in Europe, and offered practical programs for reaching this end. The most famous of these were those programs proposed by the French thinker Charles-Irénée Castel, the abbé de Saint Pierre (adapted and republished later in the century by Rousseau), and by Immanuel Kant. But there were also some more obscure or esoteric programs that proliferated throughout the eighteenth-century literary world. Amongst these was Horowitz's ambitious program for the unification of the three monotheistic religions, which was reiterated in several of his writings, and which is stated most clearly in *Amudey beyt Yehudah*: "The nations of our times, if only we could unite with them, for we share one God and grow from one stem. And we should not quarrel and hate one another, for the small differences in this point or the other, for disagreements are plentiful even in our own wings, and I have yet to meet a family which agrees on all things" (AMBY, 26a).[144] This fantasy of unification is located immediately following Horowitz's discussion of the extermination of the savages, and demonstrates once again the ubiquitous tendency amongst Jewish writers to use the non-European Other as a rhetorical means for achieving a proximity between Jews and Christians. We have seen hints of this tendency in Glikl's memoirs, and it becomes ever more pronounced in the literature of the Haskalah. Thus, in his account of his journey to Morocco, Italian maskil Shmuel Romanelli repeatedly emphasized the cultural affinity between Christians and (both European as well as Moroccan) Jews by juxtaposing them with Arabs. Romanelli explained, for instance, that Christian travelers are loath to spend the night in Arab homes, and prefer sleeping at the purportedly cleaner Jewish homes; that they wear only the clothes and shoes produced by Jews and not those produced by Arabs; that they prefer eating with Jews; and so on. Romanelli's Occidentalism culminates in the observation, midway through the book, that in Morocco "we Europeans were all one society."[145]

To return, however, from Romanelli's Morocco to Horowitz's forest, it appears that savages serve Horowitz not only as a means to envision a Jewish-Christian unity, but also to deliver a crucial message on the importance of keeping the peace in Europe, and in the Jewish community in particular. Through the depiction of the dismal reality of savage existence, Horowitz confronts his readers with the monstrous alternative to peace, a Hobbesian state of nature, a constant, savage war. And indeed, Hobbes himself linked the constant war prevalent in his grim natural state with the wars in Europe, explaining that the natural state exists not only amongst the savage peoples of America, but also in European civil wars and in the international relations between the various states of Europe.[146] This notion was also shared by Locke, who stated that "all princes and rulers of independent governments, all through the world, are in a state of nature."[147]

The pacifistic prism offered by Pocock provides a useful way to approach the dialectic of the noble and ignoble savages in the thought of the conservative Enlightenment. The positive depictions of a benevolent nature and of noble "natural man" reflect a yearning for a peaceful, harmonious Europe, whereas the negative depictions of barbaric savages, trapped in a state of constant violence, convey eighteenth-century anxieties concerning war and particularly civil war and violent revolution. For Horowitz, these anxieties took on added urgency. A particularly observant critic of the Jewish community of his time, he was painfully aware of the increasing animosities between the various cultural camps within Jewish society. The schism between these camps serves as a literary background for the narrative of *Amudey beyt Yehudah*, and is the most pressing issue discussed in this as well as other works by Horowitz. As will be recalled, Ittai and Hushai flee a society torn by dispute and intolerance and find refuge in the woods. There they find a solution to society's problems in the form of the individual noble savage. The story of the domestication and acculturation of the savage serves as a platform to discuss the gradual perfection of society, based on the acculturation of each individual. The image of the savages as a tribe or a people, on the other hand, allows Horowitz to deliver a powerful message against the potential radicalization of Enlightenment ideals and the dreaded outcome of the emerging Jewish Kulturkampf. Horowitz's dualistic treatment of savagery thus reflects a paradigmatic form of conservative Enlightenment discourse in which the individual carries a positive valence, as a subject of a radical reform that does not threaten society, but rather contributes to it; whereas the masses are viewed as the greatest threat posed by and to Enlightenment.

The image of the savage was a central rhetorical tool in these debates. And indeed, when revolution finally erupted, first in America and later in France, one of the most widespread images used to depict the revolutionary pandemonium was the image of the cannibalistic, barbaric savage tribes.[148] Thus, for instance, in a 1792

Figure 9. James Gillray, *Petit souper, a la Parisienne; -or- a family of sans-culotts refreshing, after the fatigues of the day*, 1792. Courtesy of the British Museum. © Trustees of the British Museum.

caricature by James Gilray, the French revolutionaries are depicted as half-naked cannibals (fig. 9). A later illustration by Thomas Rowlandson contrasts English and French forms of liberalism by invoking the two opposing images of nature—the peaceful, acculturated, and tameable nature of the ancients (as implied by the lion resting at Justice's feet, or the ship sailing a peaceful ocean), and the wild, uncontrollable, and murderous nature of the savage (fig. 10).

SOLITUDE AND THE AFTERLIFE OF *AMUDEY BEYT YEHUDAH*

For Enlightenment thinkers, then, individuality was a politically forceful concept. One philosopher who devoted special attention to individuality was Rousseau. Indeed, individuality, and more particularly solitude, is a recurring theme in Rousseau's oeuvre, and he returned to it repeatedly in his various writings. In *Émile* he articulated the philosophical benefits of solitude, claiming that "the surest means of raising oneself above prejudices and ordering one's judgments about the true relations of things is to put oneself in the place of an isolated man and to judge everything as this man himself ought to judge of it with respect to his own utility."[149] An ardent disciple of

Figure 10. Thomas Rowlandson, *The Contrast*, 1793. Courtesy of the British Museum, © Trustees of the British Museum.

the Swiss philosopher, it was precisely this quest that Horowitz set out to achieve in his *Amudey beyt Yehudah*. Throughout the book, Horowitz accepted Rousseau's solipsism and embraced his criterion for truth, the criterion of utility. Using this criterion, he attempted to demonstrate that the principles of Jewish faith answer the strict demands of a noble savage, for whom society itself was a mere European convention. This was, of course, a radical endeavour, perhaps more so than Horowitz could ever have imagined, and it cost this timid maskil dearly. As conservative as he may have been in comparison with other, non-Jewish thinkers of the period, for the Jewish community of Vilnius, Horowitz was still too radical, and after the publication of the book he was accused of heresy and forced to leave his home in Vilnius. Surprisingly, perhaps, Rousseau's own fate after the publication of his *Émile* was not vastly different. After having put Christianity to the test of reason and utility, he, unlike Horowitz, arrived at a deistic position. Now, to be sure, Paris may have been more colorful or cosmopolitical than Vilnius, but it was not much more forgiving. Following the publication of *Émile*, Rousseau was forced to leave Paris and wander through Europe in search of political refuge.

But if posterity has been kinder to Rousseau than his own contemporaries were, Horowitz's solitude has merely intensified over the centuries. In the decades following the publication of his controversial book, he was banished not only from Vilnius, but also from the canon of maskilic literature. Indeed, over the course of time, Horowitz's once sensational text was largely forgotten, and became so esoteric a book that it was plagiarized twice during the nineteenth century, on one occasion being attributed to none other than the great eighteenth-century rabbinical scholar Jonathan Eybeschütz.[150] Other than these two imitations, the book was never reprinted. It was rarely, if ever, mentioned by later maskilim, for whom Horowitz was simply too ambivalent, too compromising in his approach. His ambivalence concerning the possibility and desirability of acculturation, his staunch support of Jewish tradition, his occasional fideism combined with his irresolute rationalism, his outdated and exaggerated artistic style—all these made him a persona non grata in both maskilic and traditionalist camps. And yet in his works, this early maskil reveals some of the ideas and values that would become central to later maskilic thought, such as the belief in the power of pedagogy, the quest for natural religion, and the vision of Jewish equality.

Horowitz's historical defeat was multiplied further by the frustration of his two greatest visions: the unification of Jewish society on the one hand, and the unification of the three great monotheistic faiths on the other. In the years following *Amudey beyt Yehudah*, the rift between the various camps within the Jewish community reached unprecedented degrees, and a vast ideological, cultural, and religious abyss was formed amongst European Jews. As for his aspirations for the unification of Christians and Jews, whereas Saint Pierre's dream for a European Union did eventually come into being, a look back from the twenty-first century at Jewish-Christian relations in the centuries following *Amudey beyt Yehudah* lends a tragic resonance to Horowitz's dreams. Indeed, in retrospect, Hushai's harsh admonition of Ittai's unification program becomes an ominous prophecy: "But where are the sages of Spain and their dead and where are the sages of France and their saints . . . and where are the saints of Poland, who were ruthlessly massacred . . . and in other places they slaughtered young girls with young men, and expelled them from their homes never to return again. And you [Ittai] thought Diaspora a balm for the pain and did not see what the hearts of our enemies contain, and as I reflect upon the agonies and distress, which were inflicted on our forefathers—I confess, I think we would have been better off today had God put us in the hands of beasts of prey. And Hushai could no longer contain his feelings, and he broke out in great and bitter weeping" (AMBY, 45b–46a).

CHAPTER 3

Whitewashing Jewish Darkness

Baruch Lindau and the "Species" of Man

The fabrication of an Africanist persona is reflexive; an extraordinary meditation on the self; a powerful exploration of the fears and desires that reside in the writerly conscious. It is an astonishing revelation of longing, of terror, of perplexity, of shame, of magnanimity. It requires hard work *not* to see this.

—TONI MORRISON, 1992

And I beg you, the educated reader, to consider all the efforts and pains which will encounter the writer of this discipline in German, or Italian or French, and how hard it is for me to write these things in the Hebrew language, whose writers have rarely treaded this course before.

—ZVI HIRSCH NEUMANN, 1808

Over the course of the eighteenth century, *difference* underwent a kind of demystification. Wild men became savages and lost their hair, satyrs became apes, and reports of dog-headed nations were replaced by dialogues concerning natural religion amongst the cannibals. Of course, mythological or ambiguous creatures such as Patagonian giants, Amazon tribes, and pygmy nations would continue to appear in the writings of such leading eighteenth-century naturalists as Buffon, Condamine, and Linnaeus. The first three-quarters of the eighteenth century, however, witnessed a growing interest in the colonial Other, not as a monster, warped in body and in mind, but as a natural man, whose mental capacities equaled those of Europeans. A dominant paradigm amongst Enlightenment philosophers and naturalists, popularized primarily by the Scottish Enlightenment, was the stadial theory, which argued that there were four major stages experienced by all societies universally: a hunting and gathering stage; a pastoral stage; an agricultural stage; and finally a modern, commercial stage. Every new society or culture encountered was neatly categorized according to these four stages. There were thus no different cultures, races, or histories, but rather only one grand narrative of historical and cultural development, in which all human beings necessarily partook.[1]

These new conceptions of difference required new explanations for the physical variety of man; explanations which would center less on scriptural accounts, such as the curse of Ham or the ten lost tribes, and more on secular factors, such as climate, geographical environment, customs, or dietary habits. In eighteenth-century scientific thought, these factors were often considered the primary contributors to the differences between men. As we have seen in the previous chapter, this kind of circumstantial understanding of the meaning and causes of difference entailed a radical universalism, which allowed non-European peoples to serve as a kind of litmus paper for various European norms and beliefs.

Clearly, the notion that all men, regardless of social or geographical situation, physical appearance, or religion, are endowed with the same capacities for truth, knowledge, and reason was an extremely appealing concept for the maskilim. It complied with the pedagogical optimism of the Haskalah and could serve as a basis for Jewish integration into Europe. And indeed, throughout the eighteenth century Jewish apologists harnessed the circumstantial understanding of difference to account for what they perceived to be the cultural, physical, or educational inferiority of the Jews. Thus, in an oft-cited correspondence with Voltaire, Isaac De Pinto explained that the Jews "have been scattered through so many nations, that they have, we may say, adopted in each country, after a certain time, the characters of the inhabitants; a Jew in London bears as little resemblance to a Jew in Constantinople, as this last resembles a Chinese Mandarin! . . . The Jew is a chameleon who everywhere assumes the colours of the different climates he inhabits, of the different peoples he frequents, and of the different governments under which he lives."[2] But as the century progressed, such statements would begin to be called into question by a new generation of naturalists. The positivistic trends that began to dominate scientific thought toward the end of the eighteenth century, and the increasing professionalization of the natural sciences, resulted in a growing dissatisfaction with the ambiguous notions of difference that had dominated early modern anthropological thought. The move away from scriptural explanations, which had characterized the earlier works of thinkers like Buffon or Montesquieu, could no longer suffice; difference now required a further demystification, and a new generation of scientists, comprising physical anthropologists, phrenologists, and craniologists, began searching for newer, more "objective" ways to account for the differences between men. It was under these circumstances that the modern-deterministic understanding of race as a biological attribute of men began to assume scientific and cultural significance.

All these transformations had an immense impact on the literary and scientific functions of the non-European toward the end of the century. Whereas savage philosophers had been all the rage during the earlier period, the shift to a more essentialist understanding of ethnic—or, as late eighteenth-century scientists would have it, racial difference—rendered the savage critic a much less attractive literary tool; for how could Europe hope to learn anything about itself by looking at creatures who are biologically and fundamentally different? The savage gradually ceased to be a philosophical construct and became a biological one. Race now took the place of religion, and the eighteenth-century philosophical laboratory was replaced with the physical laboratory of the modern world.[3]

There is, of course, an inherent danger in diachronic accounts, and the cultural shift described here should not be understood to have taken the form of a clear linear progression from pre-modern to modern notions of race. As we shall see presently, the changes in European understandings of difference took place gradually and adopted different meanings in the works of different authors. In addition, it is critical that these changes be viewed as only one aspect of a larger and more complex cultural transformation, whose effects we have briefly encountered in our discussion of gender in Chapter 1.[4] Indeed, the growing dissatisfaction with mutable notions of difference affected a wide range of social, cultural, and generational groups throughout Europe, including (but not limited to) women, children, and Jews.

As the eighteenth century progressed, differences between Jews and non-Jews came to be defined less through religious and cultural terms and more by turning to the realm of the physical, to notions of biology and race. Thus, in a 1786 passage discussing the physiognomy of the Jews, Dutch anatomist Petrus Camper explained: "There is no nation which is as clearly identifiable as the Jews: men, women, children even when they are first born, bear the sign of their origin."[5] Similar remarks concerning the innate nature of "Jewishness" were made by such leading late eighteenth-century naturalists as Johan Friedrich Blumenbach and Charles White, who claimed that, contrary to the assertions of earlier naturalists, "The truth is that the Jews are generally swarthy in every climate."[6] There is, of course, a radical difference between this understanding of physical alterity, as innate and unchangeable, and the notions of difference we have thus far encountered in the writings of Glikl, Horowitz, Buffon, or De Pinto. Something was changing in Europe, and the Jews were required to adjust.

And indeed, the new intellectual trends of the turn of the century did not go unnoticed by members of the Jewish Haskalah. Faced with the increasing biological determinism of their time, many Jewish writers such as Samson Bloch and Joseph Perl attempted to go against the grain, and continued to uphold a climatic and circumstantial anthropological worldview. Others, such as Mordecai Aaron Günzberg, turned their backs on anthropology, claiming that it is simply impossible to account for the differences between men.[7] Then there were those who attempted to harness the new notions of racial difference to a Jewish-maskilic agenda. But whatever their responses to the cultural transformations of their time, it is clear that toward the end of the century Jewish authors became more and more interested in questions of anthropological variety or "racial" difference. This growing interest in anthropology was articulated most clearly in a new genre of Jewish and particularly Hebrew writing, the genre of popular science books, which were almost always translated from non-Jewish sources,[8] and particularly from German children's literature. It is in these innovative works that we find the first and most widespread attempts of maskilic Jews to confront the new notions of identity put forth by their Christian peers, and it is to a reading of these texts to which we now turn.

BARUCH LINDAU'S *RESHIT LIMUDIM*
AND THE MASKILIC TRANSLATION PROJECT

The Hebrew translation project of the late eighteenth century encompassed writers from all corners of the Jewish literary world, from militant maskilim such as Joel Brill and Aaron Wolfssohn-Halle to conservative authors such as Pinchas Horowitz and Baruch Schick of Shklov. There is evidence to suggest that even the Vilna Gaon was an ardent supporter of the project and encouraged his disciples to produce translations of their own.[9] At least one, his son Abraham ben Elijah, adhered.[10] But most Jewish translations of non-Jewish books were produced by members of the Haskalah. Beginning in the last

decades of the eighteenth century, maskilic writers turned their attention to the translation of German popular science books, in the hope
of using these books as a means to acculturate their fellow Jews. The
vast majority of these books were rarely read. They were written in
biblical Hebrew, a language long forlorn by European Jews, were often
tediously didactic in nature and tone, and promptly fell into oblivion.
But there were some exceptional translations that succeeded in reaching a relatively large audience. One of the first and most popular of
these was Baruch Lindau's *Reshit limudim*. Published in two volumes
in 1788 and 1810 as a natural history textbook for young students in
the newly formed maskilic schools, *Reshit limudim* promptly became
a popular scientific lexicon for Jewish readers of all ages, appearing
in several editions throughout the nineteenth century.[11] The book's
appeal crossed geographical and cultural boundaries, and we find evidence of its use amongst both conservative thinkers such as Pinchas
Horowitz and R' Ḥanokh Zundel, as well as more radical maskilim
such as Joel Brill and Isaac Euchel.[12]

Very little is known of Lindau's biography. He was born in Han-
nover around 1758 and moved to Berlin, where he worked as a private tutor and where he subsequently died in 1849.[13] During his time
in Berlin he befriended the maskilim and published several works in
the maskilic journal *Ha-measef*, including some essays on natural history. It was here that Lindau first announced in 1787 his intent to
publish a Hebrew book on natural history. In a kind of promotional
ad for the book, he explained:

> For many days I have set my mind to study and explore the ways of
> nature, and to discover whereupon are her foundations thereof
> fastened, and how she is divided into her various genera [and] species
> [סוגיה ומיניה]. . . . And I have labored and found, digged and drunk
> water from the wells of sages . . . who came before in the generations
> of the rishonim [Hebrew for "first ones," meaning early halakhic
> sages], and those whom they knew not and that came newly up, and
> how great are the works of God, in wisdom hath he made them all,
> by understanding hath he established them, the heavens and all that
> is therein; the world, and all the things that come forth of it, the seas
> and all that is therein, all will act in one true order, directed towards
> the whole. . . . [14]

As any contemporaneous Hebrew reader would immediately recognize, almost every sentence in Lindau's declaration is a biblical allusion to such books as Deuteronomy, Isaiah, Psalms, and Proverbs.
Such use of biblical Hebrew and intertextuality was one of the

defining features of maskilic prose.[15] Yehuda Friedlander and Chaim Shoham explain that the maskilim tended to "incorporate into their text linguistic allusions . . . which created an interesting associative texture, thus allowing for the reception of the text in the desired way."[16] There are ample examples of this literary norm. In David Zamość's Hebrew translation of the story of Inkle and Yarico, for example, the translator changed the name of the English sailor Thomas Inkle into the biblical "Bera," after the evil king of Sodom mentioned in Genesis 14:2. In Jewish imagination, the name conjures images of evil and corruption, both in its literal meaning ("ברע"—"in evil") as well as in its historical context. Thus, in a literary maneuver that allows for the smooth reception of the text amongst its Jewish readers, the immoral English trader is transformed into an infamous biblical villain.[17]

Another characteristic maskilic convention found in Lindau's announcement of his forthcoming book is the resource to the authority of the sages. We have already encountered this maskilic norm in Horowitz's *Amudey beyt Yehudah*, in which the author attempts to legitimize the pursuit of secular knowledge by identifying precedents of such pursuits in the thought and writings of such canonical thinkers as Maimonides and Yehudah Ha-levi. Another means of legitimizing scientific knowledge, also discernible in Lindau's ad, was to stress its theological aspects. Authors of scientific works made every attempt to demonstrate that the new scientific discoveries of the Enlightenment were not detrimental, but were rather instrumental to Jewish faith and tradition. A rather extreme example is found in Pinchas Horowitz's *Sefer ha-brit*. The book, an encyclopedia of sorts, was written under the pretext of supplying readers with a text to accompany Chaim Vital's *Shearey kedushah*.[18] Horowitz seems to have taken this literary convention a step too far; indeed, he was chastised for his presentation of the book in a scathing review in *Hameasef*, but the tendency to present scientific pursuit as a form of theology was extremely widespread in the literature of the Haskalah. In fact, even Horowitz's unimpressed reviewer was unable to end his review without a few words on the relationship between science and theology.[19] The presentation of scientific knowledge as instrumental to faith was not a mere maskilic smokescreen. Inspired by the works of such Jewish philosophers as Maimonides, on the one hand, and non-Jewish thinkers such as Linnaeus, on the other, maskilic authors believed that the study of nature reveals some divine master plan, and that through scientific observation it is possible to admire, work, and behold God. Mendelssohn went as far as to suggest that natural revelation even supersedes written revelation, since nature reveals God "not by sounds or written characters, which are comprehensible here and there, to this or that individual, but through creation itself, and its eternal relations, which are legible and comprehensible to all men."[20] In the fashion of his fellow maskilim, then, Lindau presented his forthcoming natural history book as a devout and traditionalist Jewish text, whose main aim was to reveal the glories of creation. However, in practice, religion occupied only a marginal position in the book, compared with other texts from the period.[21]

The first volume of *Reshit limudim* was dedicated to what we would now call geology, biology, geography, and anthropology, while the second focused mainly on physics, astrology, and chemistry. In the introduction to the first volume, Lindau reiterated the standard maskilic lament of the absence of scientific textbooks for Hebrew readers and presented *Reshit limudim* as an attempt to fill this lacuna. He claimed to have gathered information from some of the most prestigious sources of eighteenth-century scientific thought. Two sources were mentioned in particular: Buffon's immensely popular *Histoire Naturelle*, published in thirty-six volumes between 1749 and 1789; and Anton Friedrich Büsching's geographical magnum opus *Neue Erdbeschreibung*, published in seventeen volumes between 1754 and 1792 (RL, [4]). These were, of course, some of the highest authorities of eighteenth-century scientific thought; however, Lindau's "bluff" was exposed as early as 1797, when Pinchas Horowitz, himself a rather frequent borrower from other writers' works (amongst them, ironically, Lindau), claimed that *Reshit limudim* was in fact no more than a wholesale translation of a natural history book for children, originally written by Göttingen pedagogue Georg Christian Raff.[22] More recently, Horowitz's claims have been corroborated by Tal Kogman who, in an extensive comparison between Lindau's book and its German source, shows how the bulk of scientific detail which appears in *Reshit limudim* was translated from Raff's *Naturgeschichte für Kinder* originally published in 1778.[23]

The tendency to present translations as original work was widespread amongst turn-of-the-century maskilim. Of course, this was not a uniquely Jewish phenomenon. As Percy Adams famously observed, eighteenth-century authors often exhibited an extremely "liberal attitude to the borrowing of other writers' works."[24] Still, there seems to have been something distinctive about the dominance that this particular convention held in the Hebrew literary world of the time. In fact, the late eighteenth century saw the rise of new translational norms within the various non-Jewish literary systems, and particularly amongst German translators, which required that translators provide their reader with adequate translations that would accurately deliver both the content and spirit of their source texts. Late eighteenth-century German translators tended to present themselves as mere mediators between the German reader and the non-German text, and a good translation was viewed as one in which the translator himself was almost transparent. The desire for transparency in these writers' translations is evident already on the title pages of their works, from which the translators' names are often absent.[25] Interestingly, Jewish translators who took part in the German system, such as Henriette Herz, Saul Asher, and Moses Mendelssohn, tended to adhere to these new norms when writing in German, though not necessarily when writing in Hebrew.[26] Thus, Mendelssohn omitted his own name from his 1756 German translation of Rousseau's Second Discourse, whereas in his 1750 Hebrew translation of Edward Young's "Night Thoughts," he chose to omit the name of the original author.[27] The difference between Mendelssohn's behavior as a German translator and as a Hebrew one stems, I would argue, from the difference between the contemporaneous Hebrew and German translational norms. Indeed, the two translational systems were almost diametrically opposed; whereas adequacy and transparency were the primary requirements for German translations, Hebrew translators stressed not the transparency of the translation but rather the marginality of the source text and its original author. Correspondingly, they often chose to omit not their own names, but rather the names of the authors of the original text, and in many cases to present the text as their own original work. This widespread and, to our modern sensitivities, somewhat shady translational norm is indicative of a translational ideology that emphasizes the pivotal role of the cultural mediator, and strives not for adequacy but for acceptability.[28] Indeed, translation was perceived by the maskilim as creative work, perhaps even more so than the writing of the original. In effect, adequacy was never an ideal for Hebrew translators. Rather, the source text was viewed as a starting point from which a new and often radically different work would spring.[29]

Reshit limudim offers a paradigmatic case in point. As Kogman has shown, Lindau had no reservations about altering the style and content of Raff's book completely; he discarded the dialogic form of the original, and diverted from the text freely, at times conveying messages which stood in direct opposition to the ones put forth by Raff.[30] Such deviations from the source text were most often made in order to render the text more suitable for Hebrew readership. Thus, for instance, Hebrew translators such as Lefin, Zamość, or Joseph Vitlin tended to clothe their non-Jewish source texts in Jewish garment by "Judaizing," to a greater or lesser degree, names, places, ideas, and language.[31] Other translators deviated from their source texts due to theological considerations, linguistic difficulties, or the need to abbreviate; still others, as we shall presently see, were motivated by scientific or political concerns.[32] Whatever their reasons for diverting from the source text, however, the maskilim were never merely passive recipients of their source texts but rather very active translators, who adapted and domesticated their texts in order to better suit their own agendas and the needs of their target audience. They mistranslated both deliberately and accidentally, added and omitted, gave new meanings to stories and words, and harnessed the Enlightenment's scientific discourse to meet their own maskilic agenda. Throughout the process of translation, then, a new text was created, one that was uniquely Jewish in character and yet corresponded with the ideology and the scientific and naturalistic discourse of the "general" Enlightenment.

Another important characteristic of the turn-of-the-century Hebrew translations was the translators' tendency to translate works from the German. Even works by English or French authors were most often translated into Hebrew not from their original languages, but by use of mediating texts in German.[33] An interesting example is offered by Abraham ben Elijah's 1800 translation of Buffon's *Histoire Naturelle*. A renowned talmudic scholar, Ben Elijah was the first to offer a Hebrew translation of this pivotal natural history book. And yet, in translating Buffon, he chose to base his translation not on the great naturalist's original French text, but rather on an adaptation of the book for children, published in 1778, by the Italian pedagogue Giovanni Ferry di San Constante.[34] Even though there were rumors according to which Ben Elijah was fluent in French, his direct source text appears not to have been Ferry's French adaptation but a German translation of the book that appeared—once again, as we have come to expect, anonymously—in 1783 under the title *Büffons Geist, oder Kern seiner Naturgeschichte* (Buffon's spirit, or an abridgement of his Natural History).[35]

Such use of German children's books as primary sources for the transfer of scientific knowledge is paradigmatic of the early Haskalah. Kogman suggests that Hebrew translators such as Lindau utilized these sources simply because they derived their own scientific knowledge from these same books for children.[36] However, it seems to me that the maskilim's use of children's books as mediating texts was motivated not by the translators' own scientific incompetence, but rather by their paternalistic approach toward their readers and their colonialist understanding of the meaning and aims of translation.[37] In this context, it should be stressed that it was not only science books that were translated into Hebrew through the mediation of children's adaptations, but also, as will be discussed in further detail in Chapter 4, travel narratives such as Defoe's *Crusoe* or Steele's "Inkle and Yarico." To some extent, it was only natural that children's literature be used as a source text for translation. In its essence, the Haskalah was a pedagogic project, and a great deal of maskilic translations, including *Reshit limudim*, were intended either implicitly or, less often, explicitly for the use of children in maskilic schools. However, most translators were decidedly ambiguous as to their target audience, and their verbose translations, which were most often written in obscure biblical Hebrew, were consumed primarily by adults, and particularly by proponents of the Haskalah.[38] But even those books not intended primarily for children valued the extreme didacticism of German children's prose. The foremost purpose of maskilic translations was to acculturate their Jewish readership, and in the eyes of the maskilim both children and adult Jews required such acculturation. The maskilim themselves, however, appear to have acquired their own knowledge from more "professional" sources. A close reading of Lindau's book reveals an author well versed in the scientific literature, lingo, and concerns of his time. In fact, there is evidence to suggest that Lindau occasionally turned to the use of other, more "sophisticated" sources whenever Raff's discussion appeared to him too simplistic or outdated. It is these instances in which Lindau's own attitudes toward the emerging notions of race and difference are most clearly revealed.

LINDAU'S SOURCES

There is no room for doubt that Lindau's primary source in writing the first volume of his book was Raff's *Naturgeschichte für Kinder*. However, in writing the ninth chapter, on man, and the tenth chapter, on geography, Lindau appears to have also turned to other sources. The resource to alternative sources of information seems to have been the product of Lindau's dissatisfaction with Raff's views on these issues, which were, indeed, somewhat outdated. Raff's discussion of anthropology was succinct and focused primarily on strange tales of exoticism, which, in the spirit of eighteenth-century children's literature, were meant to lure the young reader to the book. Lindau, it seems, required something more serious. In his chapter on man he turned, therefore, to higher authorities, namely, to the works of Buffon and Linnaeus.

Lindau's use of Linnaeus was limited and most probably indirect. In contrast to Buffon, whose usage he boasts in the introduction to his book, Lindau made no mention of the Swedish botanist in his work. And yet, there is no denying that Lindau used Linnaeus's work at least once, in his description of a strange variety of men, termed "White Kushites" [(בלענדענד וייסע מאהרן) כושים לבנים]. Lindau's description of the "White Kushites" is clearly fashioned after Linnaeus's description of "Kakurlacko," a monstrous nation that appeared in his *Systema Naturae* under the species *Troglodytes*, one of the two species of *Homo* (the other being the *Homo Sapiens*). A careful reader may notice that the Kakurlacko's human status in Linnaeus's work is quite ambiguous. Taken at face value, Linnaeus seems to be suggesting that there are two separate humanoid species, thus promoting a polygenistic view, a belief in the multiple species of man. However, Linnaeus himself emphasized that though it is clear that the Troglodytes are not men, he did not wish to espouse polygenism. A conservative and highly religious thinker, Linnaeus's reluctance to define the Troglodytes as a separate, preadamic species may have been motivated by the theological hazards of polygenism, which will be discussed in detail shortly. To return, however, to Lindau, a short comparison between the two somewhat odd descriptions leaves little room for doubt that Lindau indeed utilized Linnaeus as a source:

Lindau

White Kushites (blendend weiße Mohren). . . . Usually live no longer than twenty five years. And they see only during the night, in the darkness, and in the day they stumble like blind men in the mist and see nothing[.] Their pupils are red and octagonal. Their hair is curly and short like lambs' wool[.] [They speak] poorly, and their voice is thin and shrill[.] Of this species [min—מין] there are only few left today who are known to us. (RL, 74b)

Linnaeus

[Kakurlacko. . . .] Habitat in Ethiopia. . . . Body white, walks upright, height less than half our own. Hair white and curly. Eyes round: irises and pupils golden. . . . Vision lateral, nocturnal. Fingers, when stretched out, reach knees. Life span 25 years. During the day sees unclearly, hides. At night sees, exits, marauds. Speaks in a whistle.[39]

In both descriptions, these mysterious albinos are depicted as nocturnal, possessing curly hair and strange eyes, a shrill voice and a lifespan of no more than twenty-five years. It is unlikely that these similarities are coincidental, and it seems safe to assume that Lindau borrowed his description of the "White Kushites" from Linnaeus, most probably through some German mediating text.

The Kakurlacko appears to have been the only group that Lindau took from Linnaeus's *Systema Naturae*. In his description of other peoples he preferred to turn to Linnaeus's great adversary, Buffon. His preference for Buffon is not surprising. This prolific French naturalist enjoyed a somewhat privileged status among Jewish writers of the period. Parts of his *Histoire Naturelle* were translated into Hebrew by Abraham ben Elijah of Vilna; both Lindau and Pinchas Horowitz alluded to him in discussing their sources of information; and he was further mentioned by Mordecai Gumpel Schnaber Levison in his 1792 *Shlosh esreh yesodey ha-torah*.[40] Indeed, Buffon continued to maintain a favorable position amongst Jewish writers well after being discarded, to some extent, by non-Jewish thinkers toward the beginning of the nineteenth century. Thus, for instance, in the preface to his 1862 translation of Harald Othmar Lenz's *Gemeinnützige Naturgeschichte*, Sholem Avramovitsh's praised the naturalist, claiming that of all the methods offered for the study of natural history, his was doubtless the best.[41] Avramovitsh was referring to Buffon's methodological trademark, the explanation of various natural and anthropological phenomena by turning to environmental factors such as climate, or cultural and dietary practices. In contrast to Linnaeus, who attempted to categorize the natural world into rigid scientific taxonomies, Buffon's perception of nature was of a world in constant motion, a world that cannot be organized into synchronic taxonomies but must rather be described diachronically. Accordingly, in his *Histoire Naturelle*, Buffon made a point of describing each natural phenomenon, including human beings, against a specific historical and geographical context. Needless to say, this method resulted in exceedingly long and elaborate descriptions of the various peoples of the world.

The lengthiness of Buffon's descriptions vis-à-vis Lindau's succinct accounts makes it difficult, upon a first reading, to note the similarities between the two texts. However, upon closer scrutiny, the overlaps between the two authors' discussion of man reveal themselves quite clearly. Here, for instance, are Buffon and Lindau's descriptions of Northern peoples:

> Lindau
>
> The short, fat and ugly inhabitants of Greenland which is in the cold area in Europe, close to the northern axis[;] the inhabitants of north America adjacent to the axis, and the people of the island of Kamchatka which belongs to the kingdom of Russia in Asia[;] Samoyeds[,] Ostiacks adjacent to the ice sea of the kingdom of Russia in Asia, and the people of Lapland[:] their hair is black, their lips thick and blunt, they eat nothing but fish and wild animals, and grow no more than seven quarters of an arm[.] They all live in the cold climates, and are all stupid, ignorant, cowardly and meagre. They are superstitious and will believe anything. (RL, 74b)

> Buffon
>
> The Danish, Swedish, and Muscovite Laplanders, the inhabitants of Nova- Zerabla, the Borandians, the Samoeides, the Ostiacks, of the old continent, the Greenlanders, and the savages to the north of the Esquimaux Indians, of the new continent, appear to be of one common race, which has been extended and multiplied along the coasts of the northern seas, in deserts and climates considered uninhabitable by other nations. These people have broad faces and flat noses; . . . hair black and straight, and skin of a tawny colour. They are small in stature, and, though meagre, they yet are of a squat form. In general their size is about four feet, and the tallest exceed not four feet and a half. . . . . Incivility, superstition, and ignorance, are alike conspicuous of them all. . . . Their food consists principally of dried fish, and the flesh of bear and reindeer. . . . Immersed in superstition and idolatry, of a Supreme Being they have no conception; nor is it easy to determine which is most conspicuous, the grossness of their understandings, or the barbarity of their manners, being equally destitute of courage and shame.[42]

It is plain to see that Lindau and Buffon refer to the same peoples in their descriptions; both mention the Sami ("Laplanders"), the Samoyeds, the Khanty ("Ostiacks"), the Greenlanders, and the American Inuit. Lindau omits a few of the peoples described by Buffon, such as the Northern Tartars or the Borandians (who were considered by many in the late eighteenth century to be a mythical nation), and adds the people of Kamchatka.[43] The omissions may be a means of abbreviating Buffon's lengthy discussion; however, evidence that Lindau did take at least the Northern Tartars into account is found in the description of the second human variety described in *Reshit limudim*, which refers to the Southern Tartars only, thus conveying an assumption that the Northern Tartars belong to the first variety presented earlier in the text. In addition, both authors depict Northern peoples as dumb, cowardly, and superstitious, and as small and thick yet at the same time meager. Both also comment on these peoples' odd diet, which consists of only fish and meat. It is probable that Lindau derived the information from a German translation of Buffon; however, he appears not to have used one of the German children's adaptations of the *Histoire Naturelle* that were utilized by his fellow Hebrew translators.[44]

After discussing the Northern peoples, Buffon turns his attention to the Southern Tartars and the Kalmyk people. Accordingly, so does Lindau. Once again, the descriptions bear unmistakable similarities; both authors describe the Tartars and the Kalmyk as short and ugly and as having short noses, small eyes, and wrinkled faces.[45] Lindau continues to adhere to Buffon's order of presentation of the varieties of man throughout the remainder of his anthropological discussion, barring the occasional characteristic omissions. Only once, in his description of the Peruvians and the Brazilians, does he stray from Buffon's sequence; whereas Buffon discussed these peoples after a lengthy discussion of Blacks (Nègres), Lindau included them in his discussion of White nations. This difference is of no small significance and will be discussed in some detail below.

Returning to the question of Lindau's sources, as may be recalled, Lindau boasted of his use of Buffon in the introduction to his book. While previous studies have taken his pretences as entirely bogus, a comparison between Lindau's discussion of man in *Reshit limudim* and Buffon's famous discussion of the varieties of man in his *Histoire Naturelle* leaves little room for doubt that Lindau was indeed familiar with the great naturalist's work. Another source explicitly mentioned by Lindau in his introduction was the German geographer Anton Friedrich Büsching's *Neue Erdbeschreibung* (New description of the earth). Büsching was held in high esteem by eighteenth-century men of letters, and his popularity seems to have infiltrated the Haskalah as well. The Uman-born maskil Khaykl Hurwitz, for instance, refers to him as "the sage Büsching" [החכם בושינג], and at least two other maskilim, Joseph Perl and Shlomo Keysir, translated parts of his description of the Greenlanders into Hebrew. Both descriptions remained in manuscript form and appear never to have been published. They are quite similar to one another and may attest to the popularity of some adaptation of Büsching amongst the maskilim.[46]

Evidence of Büsching's popularity is also found in the works of Raff, author of Lindau's main source text. Geography wasn't discussed at all by Raff in his *Naturgeschichte für Kinder*, but he did devote a separate book to the topic. The book, titled *Geographie für Kinder* and published in 1776, was a loose adaptation of parts of Büsching's *Neue Erdbeschreibung*.[47] Lindau may well have been familiar with Raff's geography, which was well received at the time, and he may have been inspired by Raff to make use of Büsching's *Erdbeschreibung* in his *Reshit limudim*. However, he appears to have preferred in this case to turn directly to the source text and not to use Raff's mediating children's text. His motivation for preferring the more complicated source text may have been that, contrary to *Naturgeschichte für Kinder*, which was designed for young readers in general and could be adapted to meet the needs of adult readers, *Geographie für Kinder* was meant for the use of younger children, and was written in a more childlike tone.[48] Clearly, Lindau, who made a point of omitting each and every childish feature that appeared in Raff's *Naturgeschichte*, could hardly make use of such a text.

Evidence that Lindau utilized Büsching's source and not Raff's book may be found in the inclusion in *Reshit limudim* of various details that appear in the *Erdbeschreibung* but were not made available to the readers of Raff's geography. Thus, for instance, in his discussion of Greenland, Büsching explains that Greenland is in all probability an island whose east coast is inaccessible. He then goes on to discuss periods of light and darkness on the island, reflects on its association with Europe on the one hand and America on the other, and describes its natives as people who are unfamiliar with money and who use the intestines of animals to sew their clothes. All these details are conspicuously absent in Raff's short description of Greenland.[49]

There is perhaps some further evidence that Lindau read Büsching's work without Raff's mediation. Raff used information from the *Erdbeschreibung* not only in his geography but also in his natural history. Thus, in his discussion of man, he claims, following Büsching, that the earth inhabits one billion people.[50] After introducing this estimation, Raff goes on to describe various anthropological exotica, such as feral children and acrobats, whereas Büsching turns to the introduction of a short human taxonomy, in which he divides humanity into three different groups or varieties (*Sorte*): Blacks (*schwarze Sorte*), Whites (*weiße Sorte*), and Mediums (*mittlere Sorte*). Inspired by Buffon and the environmental paradigm, Büsching makes a point of noting that the differences between these various groups are the result of their respective circumstances.[51] Raff chose to ignore this taxonomy altogether, both in his *Naturgeschichte* as well as in his *Geographie*; Lindau, however, chose a different course. Raff and Büsching's estimation of the number of inhabitants of the earth appears also in *Reshit limudim*, but contrary to Raff, Lindau chose to continue Büsching's course, and to divide these one billion men into groups, thus presenting a short but significant taxonomy of his own. The taxonomy, to which we will turn our attention presently, differs from Büsching's, and the information provided within it derives not from the *Erdbeschreibung* but rather, as we have seen, from the works of Buffon and Linnaeus. It is probable that Lindau viewed Büsching's taxonomy as outdated. Indeed, contrary to Lindau, Büsching was unaware of the existence of a fifth continent and, in the spirit of early modern geographies, divided the world into four parts. Lindau's taxonomy, by contrast, introduced Hebrew readers to a fifth part of the world, which Lindau terms "South India."[52] However, it could be that Lindau's choice to add a taxonomy to his discussion of man was inspired by Büsching's *Erdbeschreibung*.

This short survey of Lindau's sources of information sheds new light on this enigmatic yet influential maskil. It appears that Lindau's choice of primary source text was inspired not by his own intellectual shortcomings, as has been previously argued by researchers, but was rather a conscious decision to translate what he viewed as a text ideally suited for his target audience. In fact, Lindau was so well versed in the scientific advances of his age that he occasionally strayed from Raff's text when the information found therein appeared to him too outdated or anecdotal to be of use to the reader. On such occasions he chose to turn directly to Raff's own sources of information, namely to Buffon, Büsching, and Linnaeus, all of whom had been used by Raff in various parts of the book.[53] Our reading of Lindau, then, reveals a highly active and critical translator, who felt a clear intellectual responsibility toward his readers and strayed from his source text not only to domesticate or "Judaize" it, but also in order to make it more scientifically accurate, updated, and complete.

This sense of scientific responsibility is reflected not only in Lindau's additions to the text, but also in his omissions. There is a recurring motif in Lindau's treatment of three of his source texts, Raff, Büsching, and Buffon. Each of these writers offered his readers an explanation of the causes of physical variety between men, focused on environmental factors. Lindau, however, consistently chose to omit these discussions, and, in the spirit of Linnaeus, provided his readers with a synchronous presentation of human variety without attempting to explain its sources. These omissions are not to be taken lightly; as noted above, the diachronic aspect of human variety was a major theme in Buffon's thought, and it was to the discussion of these transformations that the French naturalist dedicated his greatest efforts. Büsching, too, put a great deal of emphasis on the mutability of man. In his description of Greenland, for instance, he explained that the skin of the Greenlanders tends to become brown or red due to their "dirty lifestyle."[54] These claims were reiterated by Büsching's other two Hebrew translators besides Lindau, Joseph Perl and Shlomo Keysir, both of whom explained that the Greenlanders are born White, but gradually assume a darker color due to their lacking hygiene.[55] This rationalization of the Greenlanders' skin color is, however, conspicuously absent from Lindau's account. Indeed, it appears that, like many naturalists of his time, Lindau was unsatisfied with the environmental explanations for human variety, which had dominated earlier texts. This dissatisfaction is most apparent in the original human taxonomy he offered his readers in the chapter on man, a taxonomy so rigid in its presentation of human variety that it raises some pointed questions about Lindau's understanding of the meaning of physical difference between men.

LINDAU'S HUMAN TAXONOMY

To the best of my knowledge, the human taxonomy that appears in *Reshit limudim* constitutes the first Hebrew taxonomy of its kind. Lindau's inclusion of this taxonomy is indicative of this maskil's awareness of the intellectual fashion of his time. Indeed, whereas earlier in the eighteenth century the taxonomical approach was identified primarily with Linnaeus, during the last quarter of the century taxonomies became such a pervasive scientific tool that they appeared even in the writings of such thinkers as Kant or Blumenbach, who identified as followers of Buffon.

In his own taxonomy, Lindau divides the human species into two groups according to skin color: the White and the Black. He defines the two groups as two "sugim" [סוגים], a term that in Modern Hebrew is identifiable with the scientific group of "genera." Each "sug" is further subdivided into "minim" [מינים], or "species" as the term translates from Modern Hebrew. Thus, the White "sug" is classified into: (a) people who are white as snow, or "snow Whites," as it were; and (b) "reddish Whites." These groups are then further divided into a second class of "minim" according to climate and constitution. A corresponding division is found in Lindau's discussion of Blacks, who are divided into three primary "minim": (a) Black as coal; (b) Reddish Brown; and (c) Greenish or Yellowish Brown. These three "minim" are then subdivided once again according to geographical distribution. Figure 11 offers a simplified illustration of Lindau's taxonomy.

Lindau describes each geographical group (meaning each group within the second class of "minim") according to several parameters, including complexion, facial characteristics, physical, mental, and moral attributes, and, finally, beauty. Thus, for instance, Northern peoples are described as "ugly"; East Asians are presented as "more beautiful and more White" than other non-European peoples; and finally, of course, Europeans, Arabs, and Persians are presented as "Beautiful and White, of high stature and high morals, educated and intelligent" (RL, 75a). Clearly, Lindau viewed the aesthetic, moral, and mental value of each human group as a direct function of its Whiteness.

The notion that the lighter the skin, the more beautiful, is ancient in the White West, and it continued to be widespread during Lindau's time in the works of such thinkers as Buffon, Kant, Blumenbach, Georges Cuvier, and others.[56] Indeed, even in cases in which dark-skinned figures were presented in a positive light, as noble savages, for instance, their idealization usually entailed their "Europeanization," often by contrasting them with their fellow savages and likening them to fair-skinned men. Defoe, for instance, did not neglect to inform his readers that Friday's skin color was "not quite black, but very tawny, and yet not of an ugly yellow nauseous tawny, as the Brazilians . . . and other Natives of America are; but of a bright kind of a dun olive Colour, that had in it something very agreeable."[57] Defoe also stressed Friday's "European smile," his thin lips, and his

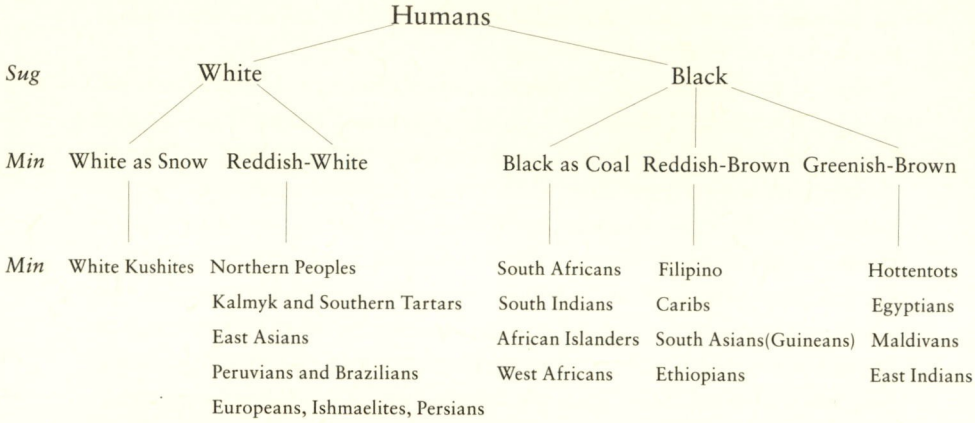

Figure 11.   Sketch of Lindau's taxonomy.

small nose, which, he stressed, was "not flat like the negroes." Some writers claimed that aversion toward Blackness is universal and natural, reflecting perhaps fear of the night and its perils.[58] Though they were often depicted as swarthier than the average European, Jewish thinkers appear, for the most part, to have held similar aesthetic preference.[59] Moses Mendelssohn-Frankfurt, for instance, likened those writers who peppered their idle musings with biblical verse to "a Kushite woman who will paint her face, . . . and all who observe her from afar will consider her the perfection of beauty, but when they approach her—the colours are removed and there she stands as black as the night."[60] A similar preference for the fairer skin is found in a later Hebrew taxonomy that appeared in the 1811 maskilic journal *Bikurey ha-itim*. Inspired by the works of Blumenbach, the author of the taxonomy, Baruch Shenfeld, divided the human species into five distinct races. Of these, he explained, the most handsome was the Caucasian or White race "whose colour is pure and reddish, whose hair is long and soft . . . and whose face is elegant and beautiful."[61] Similar observations on the beauty of Whiteness appeared in the works David Zamość, Abraham ben Elijah, or Samson Bloch.[62]

However, during the eighteenth century some authors began to express doubts concerning the universal nature of White beauty, suggesting that not all people necessarily prefer the fairer skin. Interestingly, traces of such doubts are found in Lindau's description of Blacks. The Black people, writes Lindau, "treasure the black colour and detest the white. For this reason, they paint their idols black, so as to render them most beautiful, and paint their devil white, as it is the worst and most detestable colour in their minds" (RL, 75a). The notion that, in the eyes of Black peoples, black is beautiful, seems to have fascinated Lindau and his contemporaries, and it is repeated in the writings of such thinkers as Herder, Henri Grégoire, Johann Zimmermann, and maskilim such as Bloch and Mendelssohn-Frankfurt.[63] Other writers such as Buffon, Françoise Péron, Moses Mendelssohn, Markus Herz, and even polygenists such as Voltaire and Lord Kames stressed the "odd" aesthetic preferences of Africans and other "exotic peoples," which were not limited to the preference of the color black but extended to the love of filth and dirt, long ears, flat noses, and so on.[64] These descriptions were often written in a tone of amused delight, as exemplified by Shmuel Romanelli's observation concerning the norms and conventions of the Moroccan: "Could any person control himself and not break out laughing at such a sight? But then man is vanity. The children of man are a fallacy on the face of the earth. Just as the practices of the Westerners seem strange to our eyes, so our practices seem strange to theirs. The truth is that all is vanity. We scoff at a child when we know his crying is for some immaterial reason, and the heavenly hosts above laugh at us because we are like infants until the time we become old and gray."[65] This approach is not to be confused, however, with relativism. Pallid demons and filth-covered "Hottentots" were nothing more than an exotic and amusing attraction for most eighteenth-century writers. They were used as a form of comic relief, or for sheer shock value. Sensational, yes, but hardly subversive. If this is relativism, it is, to quote anthropologist Stanley Diamond, relativism at its very worst: "The bad faith of the conqueror, who has become secure enough to become a tourist."[66] And indeed, Lindau's contemporaries viewed the norms of other cultures with the secure and paternalistic eyes of the naturalist and rarely deduced any relativistic conclusions from their white devil anecdotes. Accordingly, aesthetic evaluations continued to play a central role in their anthropological writings.

But let us return to Lindau's taxonomy. At first sight the classification of man into two separate groups according to skin color appears to be a step away from the more fluid notions of ethnic difference which we have thus far encountered in earlier works. And indeed, previous studies have viewed Lindau's anthropology as inspired by modern racism and even late eighteenth-century polygenism.[67] However, as we have seen throughout the preceding chapters, eighteenth-century vocabulary was often highly ambiguous. In order to adequately understand Lindau's taxonomy, we must therefore devote some attention to his usage of terms, and particularly the terms "sug," "min," as well as "Black" and "White."

POLYGENISM AND THE TAXONOMIC CONUNDRUM

Lindau was not the only eighteenth-century Hebrew author to discuss the various "minim" or "sugim" of man. A second example is found in Abraham ben Elijah's translation of Buffon's *Histoire Naturelle*, in which the Sami people are described as "a species [min] of human beings short in stature and odd in appearance and manners."[68] As one of the most vocal advocates of monogenism, the belief in the unity of the human species, Buffon, of course, would have objected vehemently to the classification of the Sami as a species. And indeed, in his source text (as well as in the German adaptation of the text used by Ben Elijah), the Sami are presented not as a species but rather as a "race" ("une race"; "eine Race").[69] An earlier example is afforded by the early maskil Aaron Gumpertz. In 1765 Gumpertz wrote: "I have seen man after his kind [adam le-minehu, אדם למינהו], and have marvelled at his image and pondered creation."[70] In his use of the phrase "man after his kind" Gumpertz alludes to the story of Genesis 1, in which we are told that God created "fruit after his kind"; "the beast of the earth after his kind"; "the cattle after their kind, and everything that creepeth upon the earth after his kind," and so on. Conspicuously absent in the biblical narrative, however, is a description of the creation of man "after his kind." Man in Genesis is created in the singular, a lone male and female pair. It is here, in the scriptural account of creation, that one of the most problematic aspects of polygenism is revealed. In its fundamental premise that mankind is composed not of one but of many species, polygenism is deeply incompatible with the biblical account of the origins of man, according to which God created only a single pair of human beings. But the problem doesn't end here. A second theological issue has to do with the problem of fertile hybrids. As Buffon famously explained in his *Histoire Naturelle*, species are defined by their constancy, whereas varieties are formed by circumstance. The constancy of species, observed Buffon "is the most fixed point that we have in Natural History; all other resemblances, and differences that we can make in the comparison of beings, are neither so constant, real, nor certain. . . . each species, each succession of individuals which reproduce and cannot mix, will be considered apart, and treated separately. . . ."[71] Buffon's criterion for the identification of species, the criterion of fertility amongst the members of the species, was widely accepted by eighteenth-century naturalists, and served as the dominant paradigm in natural history until the appearance of the first works of transformist thinkers such as Jean Batiste Lamarck, Erasmus Darwin, and finally Charles Darwin.[72] It was often used in order to defend monogenism, for instance by Kant, who explained that as humans universally generate fertile children between them, it is clear that they all belong to the same species.[73] Polygenism, however, entailed a rejection of Buffon's criterion of species. Clearly, the ability of Black women and White men, for instance, or less often, White women and Black men, to produce fertile offspring between them had been proven time and time again throughout history.[74] But the problem of fertile hybrids was not only scientific, it was also theological. The existence of fertile hybrids meant that not all beings had been created by God in the act of Genesis. In fact, the notion of fertile hybrids endowed human beings the ability to create an endless succession of new species at will. This was not a possibility that could be tolerated by religious thinkers. And indeed, from its modest beginnings in the preadamic musings of such thinkers as Issac Le Peyrère or Spinoza, the theory of the multiple species of man was a heretical theory and was vehemently rejected by the vast majority of European thinkers. It continued to be considered a radical option well into the eighteenth century, and only began to gain a significant scientific following during the nineteenth century.[75]

This is not to say that all polygenists were atheists or radicals. Though polygenism was often linked with anticlericalism and materialism, there were those few odd polygenists, such as the Scottish philosopher Lord Kames, who attempted to reconcile their belief in the multiple origins of man with their Christian faith. Kames postulated that though there was originally only one human species, after the fall of the Tower of Babel humankind had been divided into various species, each uniquely fitted for a different climate.[76] However, most conservative or religious thinkers were adamant in their opposition to polygenism, and as a rule the theory was considered tantamount to radicalism and heresy. As a perceptive abbé Grégoire observed in 1808, polygenism was most often adopted "by those who by every means seek to materialize man and to rob him of the hopes dearest to his heart; . . . by those who look on the original existence of a diversity of human races as an argument with which to deny the story of Moses; and, . . . by those who have a material interest in colonial agriculture and wish to use the supposed absence of moral faculties in the Negro as another reason for treating him, with impunity, like a beast of burden."[77] Jewish authors were not oblivious to the problems inherent in the possibility of fertile hybrids. In 1791 Isaac Satanov explained that "the species created by God shall not become multiplied nor extinct for all the days of the world."[78] Satanov's English contemporary Elyakim ben Abraham elaborated further on this point, writing that "God . . . has ordained that if two animals of two different kinds shall mix—like a horse and a donkey—their offspring, which is the mule shall not produce offspring, as He desires that no new species shall be created after the creation of the world."[79]

Clearly, Gumpertz and Ben Elijah were not the kind of thinkers to challenge this axiom. Both authors were devout Jews who put together extremely religious texts. And indeed, they both voiced utterly monogenistic claims in their books. Thus, for instance, Gumpertz explained that men are identical in their physical makeup, and the only differences between them—the mental differences—are to be understood not by turning to anatomy, but rather to the Kabbalah.[80] Ben Elijah was even more adamant in his rejection of polygenism, and he stressed several times throughout his work that "the appearance and complexion [of men] are determined by climate, whereas the form and figure are moulded by customs."[81] It is evident, then, that the taxonomic ambiguities in Ben Elijah's translation of Buffon, and in Gumpertz's discussion of divine creation, are not the result of any polygenistic convictions, but rather stem from the unique nature of the Hebrew language of the time, and the absence of an accepted scientific jargon in Hebrew.

In fact, the terms "sug" and "min" had a plethora of meanings in eighteenth-century Hebrew. Some authors used the terms in their medieval sense, as merely a collection of particulars with some common denominator, while others used them in the context of a scientific nomenclature.[82] The latter usage became increasingly popular toward the end of the century, although the terms continued to maintain a certain ambiguity for many decades to come. In some works the term "sug" was used to signify what in modern taxonomies would be defined as "kingdom," whereas in others it indicated what we today might term "race."[83] In many texts, the terms "sug" and "min" were used interchangeably, thus creating an indecipherable taxonomical labyrinth.[84] Another problematic Hebrew term was the term "geza" which in Modern Hebrew signifies race. In eighteenth-century Hebrew however, "geza"—similar to its German, French, and English corollaries, "Stamm" or "race"—was most often used to indicate pedigree.[85]

It is worth noting that ambiguity characterized eighteenth-century biological discourse not only in Hebrew but also in other languages. Buffon himself tended to use the terms "variety" (variété), "species" (éspece), "people" (gens, peuple), and "race" interchangeably.[86] Similarly, in the German literary system of the time, the term "Gattung" was often used to denote both species and genera.[87] However, the problem appears to have been particularly acute in the Jewish world, due to the limited vocabulary at Hebrew writers' disposal, and the archaic nature of biblical Hebrew. In fact, taxonomic ambiguities would continue to afflict Jewish writers well into the nineteenth century, and even as late as the early twentieth century. This is evident, for instance, from Joseph Klausner's 1900 anthropological treatise, in which he expresses a hope that "if all [Hebrew] science books were to add lexicons, the great shortage of words that is felt in our language would slowly be relieved by specialists, each of whom would know the matter at hand and the words by which the thing might be expressed in full."[88] Hebrew translators of scientific texts had no choice, then, but to create their own scientific vocabulary as they went along.[89] The end result was a corpus of scientific literature filled with confusing and vague anthropological, biological, and taxonomic Hebrew terms. It is therefore impossible to deduce a polygenistic worldview merely from Lindau's use of the terms "sug" and "min" in his taxonomy. In his taxonomy, Lindau could indeed be arguing for a multiplicity of species, but he could just as well be attempting to divide humankind into different varieties, races or groups.

Some authors attempted to tackle the problem of jargon by importing scientific terms from European languages. Shenfeld, for instance, made a point of using the new German term "Rasse," which he transliterated in Hebrew characters in his 1811 classification of man. Inspired by the works of Blumenbach, Shenfeld identified five separate "races" of man: the Ethiopian, the Mongolian, the Caucasian, the American, and the Australian.[90] Clearly, Shenfeld was aware of the ambiguities entailed in using taxonomic terms in Hebrew, and, his zeal for the Hebrew language notwithstanding, he preferred to use a more accurate and professional German term.

Shenfeld's taxonomic accuracy allows us, prima facie, to locate him safely within the monogenistic camp. And indeed, he makes a point of noting that "the multitude of climates and airs in which a man is raised is clearly expressed in his figure, size and colour."[91] However, as the essay on man progresses, a more ambivalent view of humanity unfolds. "Still," he writes, "there is, for every family and family, every tribe and tribe, every people and people . . . a certain general sameness which is passed on in that family, tribe or nation from its very establishment to this very day."[92] It may be that Shenfeld, like many authors of his time, was unsure of how to accommodate environmentalism within the new racial discourse. Thus, in discussing innate differences between peoples, he abandoned taxonomic precision and resorted to the ambiguous Hebrew terms of "family" [mishpaḥa], "tribe" [shevet], and "nation" [am]. Shenfeld's essay on man may be seen as emblematic of the late eighteenth-century shift from the radical environmentalism of Buffon to what Mark Harrison has termed a kind of "weak transmutaionism," in which "climate [is] a 'remote' rather than an immediate influence on human development." This view enabled authors such as Kant or Michaelis to continue upholding monogenistic and climatic views, while at the same time accepting the fixity of racial difference.[93]

Lindau would probably have identified with Shenfeld's skepticism regarding the immediate effects of climate. This is evident from his aforementioned tendency to omit from his various source texts all mention of environmental factors for physical variety. Indeed, it appears that, like many of his contemporaries, Lindau felt a kind of dissatisfaction with the environmental paradigm, and sought other explanations for the differences between men. But was polygenism indeed one of them?

THE QUESTION OF SPONTANEOUS GENERATION

As we have seen, polygenism entailed the rejection of the biblical account of creation on the one hand, and of the notion of the constancy of species on the other. One way to solve the problem of Lindau's approach to polygenism would be to analyze his point of view on these two issues. As is evident already from Lindau's announcement of his forthcoming book in Ha-measef, Lindau was a somewhat conservative maskil who recognized the authority of the ancients and saw Enlightenment as a means to revitalize Jewish faith.

Further evidence of his traditionalist worldview is scattered through-out *Reshit limudim,* most conspicuously in the author's occasional resource to scripture as an explanatory tool in scientific discussion. Thus, for instance, Lindau opens his discussion of human anatomy by explaining that the origin of man is in the earth, as stated in the book of Genesis (RL, 75a). Elsewhere, he notes that some sages believe that Europe is inhabited by the descendants of Japheth (RL, 82a). Lindau's acceptance of scripture is also expressed in his tendency to assign bib-lical names to newly discovered animals such as the zebra, which he terms "taḥash" [תחש] or "pere" [פרא]; the panther, which Lindau iden-tifies with the biblical "shaḥal" [שחל]; or the bowhead whale, which Lindau identifies with the "tanninim gedolim" [תנינים גדולים] of Gene-sis 1. Of course, the choice of biblical names was inspired primarily by the maskilic ideology of writing in biblical Hebrew, but it also con-veys a traditionalist worldview which assumes that all recent scientific discoveries were already known to the biblical author, and that all creatures that roam the earth were initially created in the act of Gen-esis.[94] This last point, of course, bears particular significance to our present debate. Indeed, Lindau appears to have been a staunch sup-porter of the notion of the consistency of species, a position he articu-lates with utmost zeal in his treatment of the problem of spontaneous generation.

The theory of spontaneous generation dates back to antiquity. Its main premise may be succinctly put as a belief that certain organisms may, given certain conditions, spontaneously generate from inanimate matter. During the early modern period it was, for instance, widely believed that some insects, such as maggots, lice, or bees, originate from heat, fluids, or decomposed matter. An equally widespread view held that the salamander is born of fire. Even though the theory of spontaneous generation bore similar problems as the theory of fertile hybrids, it managed to infiltrate both Christian and Jewish theology, at first through the Mishnah and Talmud, and later through the writ-ings of Artistotle, which were embraced by scholastic authors. Belief in spontaneous generation is therefore evident in some of the most canonical works of Christianity and Judaism, such as in the works of Augustine, Thomas of Aquinas, Maimonides, or Yehudah Ha-levi. The theory even dictated a Jewish halakhah, according to which, even though the slaughter of animals is prohibited on Shabbat, it is permis-sible to kill a louse because it does not procreate and is therefore not a true animal.[95]

The first real challenges to the theory of spontaneous generation appeared in the late seventeenth century. Especially notable in this respect are the experiments of the Italian Francesco Redi, who in 1668 demonstrated that maggots do not appear in meat that has been disinfected and sealed.[96] During the eighteenth century, thinkers of the conservative Enlightenment promoted such skepticism toward spontaneous generation, as the theory could hardly comply with the Enlightenment's view of an orderly, harmonious, and rational nature, in which God is revealed in all his splendor. Radical, materialist, or atheistic thinkers, on the other hand, were quick to reject Redi's findings, as well as those of his disciples and, ironically, became ardent supporters of the scholastic approach. For these thinkers, spontaneous generation served as a means to banish God from nature and to describe a godless and chaotic world made up of atoms or pure matter. In the works of these writers, spontaneous generation was used as a means to debunk the widespread argument from design, according to which the order found in the universe clearly proves the existence of a divine plan.[97]

The eighteenth-century debates surrounding spontaneous generation also reached the European Jewish community. David Ruderman relates a fascinating debate that took place between the Italian rabbi and physician Isaac Lampronti and his former teacher Judah Briel. Following Redi's experiments, Lampronti challenged the halakhic permission to kill lice on shabbat, claiming that science had clearly debunked the theory of spontaneous generation, thus rendering lice as animals for every intent and purpose. Briel, however, responded that gentile scholarship can hardly serve as a basis for challenging the authority of the ancients.[98] Another early example is found in Israel of Zamość's *Ozar neḥmad*, in which we are told that even though the ancients believed that bees are borne of meat and mosquitoes of wine, "it has already been proven that they were mistaken and believed a lie."[99] These sentiments were reiterated later in the century by Isaac Satanov, who explained that spontaneous generation was nothing more than mere illusion, and the fact is that bees, lice, flies, and other such creatures are born of eggs that are hidden in fowl meet, thus creating an illusion of the emergence of life from matter.[100] A particularly interesting discussion is found in the works of Mordecai Schnaber Levison. In his 1792 work *Shlosh esreh yesodey ha-torah*, Levison, an ardent monogenist and keen reader of scientific literature, addressed the rising polygenistic trend, arguing: "Many gullible persons who have sealed their hearts, have recently claimed that the sun shone on the earth and in her warmth produced all kinds of animals and beasts, and also many species of very strange men, before producing proper man, and really this is a great gullibility, with which we cannot be bothered. . . . And the answer is as clear as the day, for the aharonim [Jewish sages from the early modern and modern periods] have shown in their experiments that no living being may generate from heat or rot and in all species, even of the smallest kind, we find males and females, and also in plants."[101] Levison's tying together of the two theoretical strands of spontaneous generation and polygenism is indicative of the close connection between these two scientific theories. Indeed, already in medieval literature we find evidence that spontaneous generation was utilized to promote preadamic accounts. Thus, for instance, in his thirteenth-century *Sefer shaarey ha-shamayim*, Gerson ben Solomon Catalan wrote that the sages were divided on the question of human spontaneous generation, and that there was at least one school of thought that conceded that it was indeed possible that humans may be generated from inanimate matter.[102] The two theories continued to serve one another well into the nineteenth century, for instance in the works of the famed American polygenist Charles Caldwell, who claimed that throughout history various animals, plants, and indeed people had spontaneously generated all over the world.[103] Even the great Goethe, in a conversation with the naturalist Friedrich von Martius one evening in 1828, toyed with the idea of dozens, if not hundreds, of different human species simply appearing from the void. Von Martius's response demonstrates once again the theological dimension forever in the background of this discussion. "Even if I could," he replied, "as a naturalist, accept your Excellency's position, why as a good Christian I find it difficult to embrace an idea which cannot, it seems, comply with the biblical account."[104]

Lindau's take on the issue appears to have been similarly motivated both by theological considerations as well as by his background as a maskil who subscribed to the harmonistic worldview of the conservative Enlightenment. He had the opportunity to express his views on the problem when, in the course of translating Raff's source text, he stumbled upon a short fragment in which Raff denied the possibility of spontaneous generation: "Insects do not arise from rags, rotten wood or other impure things, as is often the belief of uneducated folk. Rather they spring from eggs, which hatch in the warm air."[105]

Lindau's treatment of this fragment is instructive. Contrary to his tendency, in other parts of the book, to deliver Raff's discussions in highly abbreviated form, Lindau chose to expand on this issue, and add some thoughts of his own on the theological hazards entailed by the theory of spontaneous generation: "And there will be found no insect or any animals which will arise from rags, or from rotting foods, or from other impure things as the masses believe, as this would require a new creation, which is against the laws of nature. Because in the six days of creation God created the heaven and the earth and all that is therein. All species of creatures that have been and ever will be, and the number of species will forever be the same, and it shall not grow or diminish. But the truth of the matter is that all kinds of insects which are unseen to us, are hatched from the eggs, that their mothers lay in the air, and which fall to these things [inanimate objects]. And the heat will bring forth from them all kinds of maggots and worms."[106] Clearly, given his own perception of the grand purpose of his literary project as it is articulated in *Ha-measef* and throughout the book itself, Lindau could not accept the notion of spontaneous generation. A chaotic nature, which produces living things from inanimate matter, is hardly a place in which a divine creator is revealed. But Lindau's response to the challenge of spontaneous generation demonstrates not only his traditionalism, but also brings us back to the question of his purported polygenism. In his denial of the possibility of spontaneous generation, Lindau betrays an unequivocal adherence to the notion of the constancy of species, as well as to the scriptural worldview, two convictions that are, as we have seen, quite incompatible with polygenism. Indeed, his position on the question of spontaneous generation undermines previous readings of his taxonomy as betraying a polygenistic approach, and underscores the need for a more nuanced reading of the taxonomy, which takes into account the historical context of the Jewish and "general" Enlightenments of the late eighteenth century, and the changes that occurred during this period in European conceptions of identity, difference, and race.

ALBINISM AND THE MEANING OF WHITENESS

It seems clear that Lindau was dissatisfied with the climatic agenda that had been promoted by many of his predecessors, and that, as we shall presently see, continued to be propagated with some zeal by

Jewish authors well into the nineteenth century. Contrary to many of his maskilic peers, such as Joseph Perl, Samson Bloch, Shlomo Keysir, and others, he preferred to refrain from the use of climatic or other environmental explanations for the varieties of man. And yet though such skepticism was exceptional amongst the maskilim, it was becoming almost the norm within the non-Jewish scientific realm. Indeed, toward the end of the eighteenth century Buffon's climatic and environmentalist theories of difference, so popular after the first publication of the *Histoire Naturelle* in 1749, began to lose sway amongst naturalists. Turn-of-the-century authors such as Christoph Meiners, Julien-Joseph Virey, and Immanuel Kant began searching for newer, more "objective" ways to account for the differences among men. Some thinkers, such as Kant or Blumenbach, began to promote a more closed view of environmentalism, claiming that, once imprinted by climate or other circumstances, physical traits were irreversible. Other explanations focused on diseases of various sorts to explain the differences between men.[107] Less popular but also available were religious explanations, which focused on the story of Noah's son Ham, considered to be the ancestor of African peoples. According to some accounts, Ham had been cursed not once, but twice by God, and had thus been inflicted with both slavery and dark skin.[108]

Whatever the explanation for "racial differences," however, the emergence of modern notions of race was marked by a growing tendency to describe difference between various groups in binary terms. Cultural, religious, geographical, and physical differences were gradually homogenized, and national or ethnic identities, previously described in complex terms, were now reduced to the rigid categories of "Black" and "White." It was in this new world of Manichean identities that late eighteenth-century Jews were required to locate themselves. These Jews, whose Whiteness had always been a bit of a grey area, were now required to align themselves with the one or the other group. *Reshit limudim* appeared at the very height of these transformations and, upon a first reading, appears to adhere to the positivistic trends of the late eighteenth century. In dividing humanity into two groups according to skin color, Lindau appears to betray a preoccupation with color that far exceeds anything we have seen in Ashkenazi literature before. However, a certain degree of caution is required before determining that Lindau's taxonomy complies with modern understandings of racial difference. Let us not forget that the terms "Black" and "White" are often unstable in their precise meanings; they are never, as it were, simply black and white terms. It is therefore crucial that we ask: what exactly did Whiteness mean to Lindau?

An answer to this question may be gleaned by taking a close look at one of the stranger organs of Lindau's taxonomy, the White Kushites, categorized under the White type. Lindau describes these albinos as men who "for the most part, live no longer than twenty-five years [and] are able to see only in the darkness, whereas during the day they stumble as blind men. Their pupils are red and octagonal, their hair is short and woolly . . . and they speak in a shrill voice." Note the interplay on notions of darkness and light in Lindau's description—the White Kushites are depicted as men whose entire existence is the essence of paradox, they are Black and yet they are White; they are as light as can be, but they see only in darkness. Lindau was not unique in his discussion of this mysterious anthropological group. Hoards of White Africans starred in the writings of such leading naturalists as Linnaeus or Buffon. These thinkers offered a corrective to earlier conceptions of albinism, which viewed albinos as monstrous creatures, products of a misguided maternal imagination, or simply beings cursed by God.[109] Early eighteenth-century naturalists, on the other hand, tended to view albinism not as a monstrosity but as an ethnographical phenomenon, one which often aroused some radical explanations. Thus, as we have seen, Linnaeus categorized the albino nations under a separate human species. In a 1770 discussion of his own, Voltaire agreed, claiming that though the albino nations of Africa and America were indeed human, they were certainly not of the same species as Europeans.[110] Other authors, such as Buffon or the American physician Benjamin Rush, disagreed, claiming that albinism amongst the Africans or the Americans is indisputable evidence of the natural Whiteness of man.[111]

However, during the last quarter of the eighteenth century, something began to change in European writers' understanding of the phenomenon of "Black Whiteness." Already in 1765 the anonymous author of the entry "Negres blancs" in Diderot's famous *Encyclopédie* noted that there are those who believe that the origin of Whiteness in Blacks is in a form of leprosy, but he vehemently rejected this hypothesis, claiming that the Black albinos are normally strong and healthy men.[112] Later encyclopedias, however, seem to imply a consensus surrounding the origin of Black albinism. In an entry on man in the 1809 Nicholson Encyclopaedia, for instance, it is noted that

"[Albinism] was first observed in the African, as the great difference of colour would render the variation more striking; . . . So far however, is this variety from being peculiar to the Negro, . . . that there is no race of men, nor any part of the globe, in which it does not occur."[113] Similar suggestions are to be found in a litany of late eighteenth- and early nineteenth-century sources, ranging from encyclopedias, through travel literature to children's books.[114] Thus, toward the end of the eighteenth century, Black albinos began to be viewed not as an intriguing anthropological phenomenon but rather, as one contemporaneous author put it, as "unhappy individuals, rendered anomalous by disease."[115]

Inspired by these changes, the French naturalist Julien-Joseph Virey used the image of the Black albino to stress that skin color was not a sufficient criterion for the determination of race. There are, explained Virey in 1818, "many other considerations which demonstrate that this species [the Blacks] is quite different from us, regardless of its skin colour. . . . Suppose for instance that due to some particular degeneration [a] black would become white . . . , certainly the conformity between his visage and that of a negro, his elongated lips, his flat nose, his woolly hair, . . . and above all his animalistic character . . . would help identify his species."[116] Virey's discussion of the Black albinos is symptomatic of how, in spite of the growing emphasis on skin color in late eighteenth-century thought, the formal color of one's skin was marginal in respect to other physical attributes, such as physiognomy, brain size, or hair. As the German naturalist Samuel T. Sömmering explained in 1785: "Colour is not a sufficient difference."[117] It was what was under the skin that mattered most, and in the eyes of Virey and his contemporaries, Black albinos may indeed be white skinned, yet they are, for all intents and purposes quite clearly Black.

The changing discourse surrounding Black albinos is indicative of the wealth of physical traits that were assembled during the last decades of the eighteenth century under the term "Black." This assembly of physical traits stands in direct contrast to earlier formulations of Blackness, which stressed not physical but rather cultural characteristics such as religion, clothing, cultural practices, or traits considered to be environmental, such as the formal color of one's skin. In fact, while earlier writers such as Aphra Behn or Bartolomeo Stibbs could categorize what we today would consider White Europeans as Black because of their religion, clothing, or degree of suntan, later writers tended to offer more stable and essentialistic understandings of Black and White.[118] One of the earliest Hebrew examples of such a modern understanding of Whiteness is found in an 1827 children story by Polish maskil David Zamość. In this story, which is discussed in some detail below, Zamość tells of two children, Miriam and Yoḥanan, who grow up on their own desert island in the East Indies. The children are subsequently discovered by a savage tribe from a nearby island, to whom Zamość repeatedly refers as "the Blacks" [השחורים]. Conversely, throughout the course of the tale, Zamość refers to the children as "the Whites," even though we are told that their skin had darkened considerably due to the heat of the climate in which they had been raised.[119] For Zamość, then, the terms "Black" and "White" have nothing to do with the tanning of one's skin. Indeed, they are essences that seep somewhere deep below the skin, to some mysterious undefinable core. Other writers attempted to define this evasive racial essence by turning to various measurable and immutable parameters such as the structure of the skull, the size and weight of the brain, the facial angle, and so forth. These physical characteristics, it was claimed, also determined the mental and intellectual capacities of each and every race. "It is quite plain to see," claimed Virey in 1801, "that the intelligence of the negro is much less active than our own, due to the narrowness of his cerebral organs."[120] Thus, the cultural tables were turned; whereas earlier thinkers tended to describe the physical traits of man as a function and product of his cultural practices and the climate under which he lived, late eighteenth-century thinkers began reducing the cultural and mental characteristics of the non-European to his physical make-up.

But where did Lindau stand on all this? Following close on the works of Linnaeus and other early eighteenth-century naturalists, Lindau viewed albinism not as a medical anomaly but rather as an anthropological type. In this respect, he seems to have favored earlier formulations of albinism over the late eighteenth-century understanding of the phenomenon. But what is even stranger is Lindau's choice to classify the White Kushites under the White group, thus rejecting the contemporaneous tendency to focus on "racial" traits besides skin color in designating the races of man. In effect, the first White group to appear in Lindau's classificatory system is comprised of men who, in the eyes of many of Lindau's contemporaries, were not White at all (their lowercase whiteness notwithstanding). Lindau's use of the term "Kushite" in this respect is interesting; Schorsch explains that "from the Bible to the Middle Ages, the term 'Kush' referred to a geographical and political entity. By the late medieval period, however, 'Kushite' was being wielded as a synonym for 'Black people.'"[121] And indeed, we find evidence of the use of the term "Kushite" to denote Blackness in many eighteenth-century Hebrew texts. An interesting example is found in Ben Elijah's *Gevulot arez*, in which the Black Sea appears as "Yam ha-kushi" [ים הכושי].[122] However, in Lindau's taxonomy Blackness is denoted by the term "shahor," literally meaning "black," and Black people are defined as "anashim shehorim." In his presentation of Kushites, then, Lindau seems to be resorting back to the earlier meanings of the term, which denoted not a racial group but a geographic one. Accordingly, he proposes as an equivalent German term the somewhat outdated "Mohren" and not the more modern "Negern." The difference in terms is telling; while "Negern" denotes "racial" and anatomical characteristics, "Mohren" conjures a whole repertoire of geographic, political, and religious motifs.[123]

As we continue reading Lindau's taxonomy, we find that the category "White" also contains other groups that would not be considered White by many of Lindau's contemporaries, such as the Inuit, the Tartars, the Peruvians, and the Brazilians. The inclusion of these groups in the "White men" category is further indication that Lindau perceived skin color not as a racial designator, which implies certain mental and physical qualities, but rather as a mere formality, a particular shade, which is only skin deep. Thus, even though upon a first reading Lindau's taxonomy seems to employ modern notions of race, a closer scrutiny of the text reveals a view much closer to early modern notions of physical variety than to late eighteenth-century positivistic trends. In spite of its central place in the taxonomy, skin color as Lindau perceives it is an exceedingly fluid designator of difference, an almost meaningless marker of men.

And indeed, Lindau does not settle for a taxonomy based on skin color or other "racial traits"; rather, in his description of the various "minim" of man, he proceeds to divide humanity into different groups according to geography. In this division of man a great deal of emphasis is placed on cultural practices, complexion, religion, climate, and height. Conspicuously absent from the description are the more modern means of describing difference, such as physiognomy or craniology. Lindau's description is dominated by climates, complexions, and culture, and not, like so many other descriptions of his time, by skulls, brains, and facial angles. It appears, then, that in employing the terms "sugim" and "minim," Lindau was aiming for neither modern meanings of species or races, but rather for the more ambiguous early modern or even medieval meanings of the terms.

But what does all this mean? Could it be that Lindau employed such decidedly archaic notions of difference simply because he was unaware of more recent trends in anthropological thought? An absolute answer to this question, it must be admitted, is impossible. But I would venture to suggest that Lindau, an ardent reader of the scientific literature of his day, was well aware of recent scientific and anthropological "advancements." As we have seen, in his *Reshit limudim*, he made use of such canonical Enlightenment thinkers as Linnaeus, Buffon, and Büsching. In addition, throughout the book he exhibits a certain degree of familiarity with recent developments in the fields of craniometry and geography, and often deviates from Raff's source text to make note of these developments. Thus, he makes a point of mentioning the "discovery" of a fifth continent, or, in another place, uses craniometry and the brain-body mass ratio, as a means to separate men from beasts.[124] In fact, Lindau's very choice to deviate from Raff's source text and to include an original Hebrew taxonomy in his discussion of man betrays a keen awareness of the intellectual trends of the late eighteenth century. The emerging picture reveals a maskil well versed in the scientific trends of his age and who makes a point of deviating from his source texts whenever they appear to him too outdated. On the other hand, this same author chose to employ an archaic meaning of Whiteness in his book, thus creating an odd yet characteristically maskilic blend of innovation and conservativism. I would suggest that these two conflicting trends represent Lindau's two primary motivations for straying from Raff's source: on the one hand, the desire to present a complete and up-to-date scientific lexicon, and on the other, the desire to produce a text that would comply with the political, moral, and religious requirements of the Jewish Haskalah. While the choice to include a taxonomy in the discussion stems from the former desire for innovation, Lindau's choice to employ archaic notions of color within this same innovative taxonomy is politically motivated and stems directly from the author's Jewish background. For Lindau and other maskilic authors, the question of difference and its meanings simply hit too close to home.

RENOUNCING THE JUNGLE IN
THE JEWISH ENLIGHTENMENT

Frantz Fanon once claimed that "every colonized people—in other words, every people in whose soul an inferiority complex has been created by the death and burial of its local cultural originality—finds itself face to face with the language of the civilizing nation. . . . The colonized is elevated above his jungle status in proportion to his adoption of the mother country's cultural standards. He becomes whiter as he renounces his blackness, his jungle."[125] Fanon was, of course, referring not to late eighteenth-century Jews but rather to twentieth-century Blacks in this discussion, but perhaps a lesson is to be learned here on the Haskalah. Throughout the eighteenth and early nineteenth centuries, maskilic authors did their utmost to present Jews as radically acculturable creatures who could, with the aid of science, education, and legislation, become Europeanized. The environmental discourse of the eighteenth century was a particularly useful tool in this maskilic endeavour. As we have seen, most maskilic writers on issues such as natural history, geography, and anthropology tended to associate the physical and "mental" characteristics of different ethnic groups with their various cultural and nutritional practices, as well as with the different climates in which they lived. Not surprisingly, similar environmental explanations of human difference also played a role in the writings of both Jewish and Christian apologists for Jews. Writing in 1789, the Polish French intellectual Zalkind Hourwitz stressed that "it is well known to all physicians that the physical constitution of the Jews is absolutely the same as all other nations that inhabit the same climate."[126] A second Jewish apologist, the Portuguese Dutch Isaac De Pinto, also harnessed the eighteenth century's fluid notions of difference to account for the physical and mental "traits" of the Jews. In a letter written to the French philosopher Charles Marie de La Condamine sometime around 1746, De Pinto stated that "transplanted nations gradually assume the colours that characterize the countries in which they settle. . . . They assume not only the habits of their new compatriots, but also the exterior composition of their bodies, as well as the interior disposition of their spirit. This is quite evident today in Holland, where the descendants of the Spanish, the Portuguese, and the French have become 'Holland-ized,' so to speak, in their colour, temperament, and moods."[127] As noted, De Pinto returned to these statements in a later, better known correspondence with Voltaire, this time claiming that "the Jew is a chameleon who everywhere takes on the colours of the various climates in which he lives, of the various people with whom he associates, and of the various forms of government under which he lives."[128] Jewish "faults" were thus explained by such authors by turning not to anatomical difference, but to such contingencies as the effects of religious institutions, poor nutrition, lack of education, and, most importantly, their subaltern social and political status. However, as the century progressed, discourse surrounding the Jews began to change. In an essay on craniology from 1790, for instance, Blumenbach explained that the Jewish skull is quite clearly distinct and differs visibly from that of a European.[129] Other writers stressed the singularity of the Jewish facial angle and especially of the Jewish nose.[130] The bourgeoning debate on the biological uniqueness of the Jews served the agendas of anti-Jewish thinkers. The latter used the new deterministic discourse surrounding Jewishness as scientific corroboration of their pessimism in respect to the possibility of the integration of the Jews in Europe.

When viewed against the context of late eighteenth-century discourse surrounding the Jews, Lindau's rejection of the chromatism and physical anthropology of his time assumes the form of a political agenda, which is primarily preoccupied with the question of *Jewish* Whiteness. Indeed, even though Lindau does not account for the place of Jews in his taxonomy, his widening of the borders of Whiteness *ad absurdum* leaves little room for doubt as to his views on the racial classification of the Jews. In the political language of the late eighteenth century, to be White was to be worthy. For proponents of emancipation, this simply meant that Jewish darkness was to be whitewashed.

Evidence of a maskilic awareness of the political dimensions of the anthropological debates of the late eighteenth century is found in a wide range of Hebrew texts from the period. Most maskilim demonstrated a reluctance to abandon the environmentalist paradigm, and climatic and cultural explanations for physical variety continued to dominate Jewish texts on natural history well after such explanations had been rendered obsolete by non-Jewish authors. In Joseph Schönhak's 1841 geography, for instance, we read that "even though the appearance of Man, his size and complexion will change according to his place of residence, still his potential and other traits testify that we are all creatures born of the same womb, and there is one father to us all."[131] Indeed, even after scientific racism was introduced to Jewish and, as we shall presently see, Hebrew literature, in the second half of the nineteenth century many Jewish authors still continued to promote an environmentalist approach. Adolph Neubauer, for instance, claimed in 1885 that Jewish physiology was determined primarily by climate and intermarriage, indicating that the Jews are not a distinct race. Similar sentiments are found in an 1890 Jewish geography of Russia in which we are informed that "the animals too will change their natural form in the different countries, and in the torrid countries we find the largest and most beautiful animals in the world."[132] These and other examples point to the exceptional popularity of radical environmentalism in nineteenth-century Jewish literature.[133]

Of course, there were also some exceptions to the rule. As early as Spinoza we find doubts amongst a minority of Jewish authors concerning the effects of climate or environment on the constitution of Man.[134] Such doubts seem to have infiltrated even the maskilic camp, affecting such authors as Lindau and Shenfeld, both of whom appear to have had some reservations concerning the effects of climate. However, even the most skeptical maskilim preferred not to offer their readers alternative explanations to natural variety, or to resort to such radical cultural options as biological determinism, let alone polygenism. An intriguing example is found in Mordecai Aharon Günzberg's 1823 *Massa Columbus o galut ha-arez ha-hadasha*. As is well known, Günzberg's book is a Hebrew translation of Joachim Campe's late eighteenth-century description of the discovery of America. However, toward the end of the translation Günzberg added an appendix that does not appear in Campe's original, and in which he discussed American politics, the issue of slavery, and even the possibility of a Jewish settlement in the "new" continent. This appendix is based on William Robertson's 1777 *The History of the Discovery and Settlement of America*. Günzberg's use of German words throughout the text points to his use of a German mediating text, most probably the anonymously published *Historisch-geographische Beschreibung von Amerika für Jünglinge*.[135] In a characteristic maskilic maneuver, Günzberg peppered Robertson's discussion with observations of his own. Amongst these original additions there is one of particular interest to our discussion. Toward the end of his appendix, Günzberg writes: "The question of the origin of the Americans is a great and profound enigma which is difficult to solve. . . . But what use is there for idle speculation where nature herself holds her tongue? Nature shows us different kinds of inanimate objects, plants and animals, and the men of science toil in vain to understand its limits and causes. [Even] the [biblical] story begins in a real and known age, and does not attempt to penetrate the realms of illusion and fantasy. And as regarding whatever happened before this time, each and every scholar may conduct his own investigations and find ancient chronicles as pleases his wisdom, but he should not confuse such fabrications with the true story."[136]

It was only toward the end of the nineteenth century that biological determinism made a dominant appearance in Jewish, and later even in Hebrew, literature. One of the earliest expressions of the racial turn in Jewish thought is found in Moses Hess's 1862 *Rom und Jerusalem*, in which the author expressed polygenistic views and even harnessed these views to promote his proto-Zionist agenda.[137] Another early author to reject the climatic and circumstantial approach was German Jewish naturalist Aaron Bernstein, who claimed that racial and national traits are innate and are not subject to the whims of weather or the effects of customs. Bernstein, whose work was translated into Hebrew in 1880 by David Frischmann, was one of the earliest Jewish authors to make use of the tools and methodology of the comparative anthropologist. He claimed that the shape of the skull, which differs from one race to the other, indicates the different intellectual capacities of the various peoples. He made particular note of the "negro forehead," which, he explained, portrays the "diminished intelligence" of the "negro race," and is a testimony of Africans' distance from Europeans on the one hand and their close proximity to apes on the other.[138] Other early examples of Jewish authors who embraced modern racism are found in the works of the Italian criminologist Cesare Lambroso and the Russian maskil Kalman Schulmann, who in 1871 explained that the Australians are endowed with inferior intelligence, the outcome of a relatively small and narrow brain.[139]

A particularly instructive discussion is found in Joseph Klausner's 1900 anthropological treatise, *Ha-adam ha-kadmon*. Throughout the book, Klausner makes a great deal of use of physical and comparative anthropology and chastises previous Jewish authors who, he explains, "wish to show that we [the Jews] are not inferior to the nations amongst which we live, and there is therefore no basis for racial anti-Semitism." However, he maintained, difference does not necessarily imply inferiority: "Humanity needs difference and separation, a multitude of colours and characteristics, they and only they . . . are the basis on which lies eternal and supreme harmony."[140]

It appears, then, that toward the end of the nineteenth century, environmentalism, as a viable anthropological explanation, became obsolete, and Jewish naturalists were no longer able to ignore the discourse of scientific racism. John Efron explains that Jewish disillusionment with emancipation and acculturation, combined with the growing antisemitism of 1870s and 1880s led, toward the end of the century, to an increase in Jewish interest in the sciences of race and in physical anthropology. However, he notes that their adoption of the new racial discourse notwithstanding, Jewish thinkers continued to stress the power of environment and the basic equality of men. "It is a crucial feature of the Jewish scientists . . . that despite using the contemporary language, and sometimes the methodology of race science, they all thoroughly rejected its use for chauvinistic purposes," he adds.[141] Similar to most other studies on Jewish attitudes on race, Efron's discussion centers exclusively on Jewish anthropologists' attitudes toward the Jews themselves and toward other Europeans. It is hardly surprising that Jewish scientists rejected the chauvinistic uses of racial discourse in discussing Jews or Christians. However, Efron does not take into account Jewish discussions of non-European peoples in which, as we have seen, there is no small degree of chauvinism to be found. Indeed, during the last decades of the nineteenth century, Jewish thinkers had no reservations regarding what they often understood to be the innate inferiority of Africans, Native Americans, Australians, or other colonial peoples.

I would suggest that Jewish acceptance of modern racial discourse was made possible, at least in part, by the rise of nationalism and the articulation of a Zionist ideology, which allowed Jews to give new meaning to the essentialist discourse on race. Indeed, as has previously been demonstrated by Efron, Mitchell Hart, Amos Morris-Reich, and others, early Zionists such as Moses Hess, Arthur Ruppin, and Elias Auerbach harnessed the repertoire of racism to the Zionist cause. In the writings of these authors, those same skull shapes and facial angles, which had been dreaded and uncomfortably ignored by earlier Jewish writers, were now put to use to prove the Jews' innate connection to the Orient. The Jews were now presented as part of a Semitic race, a race physically designed and destined for the Eastern climate and landscape; a race whose revival may be achieved not through emancipation, acculturation, or assimilation, but rather by a return to its native home, and a realization of its natural and historical purpose.[142] Previous studies have treated the rise of race in late nineteenth-century Jewish discourse in the context of Jewish-Christian or Jewish-Arab relations; however, turn-of-the-century Jewish thinkers' treatment of colonial peoples reinforces the notion that toward the end of the nineteenth century something changed in the ways Jews understood the meaning and implications of race.

Needless to say, the possibility of "disciplining" race by harnessing it to a Zionist agenda was not available for the maskilim. For these Jews, race, as it emerged in the last decades of the eighteenth century, was a wild and untameable concept, which threatened to deliver a crucial blow to the maskilic project of acculturation and emancipation. These Jews often held a dismal view of the present state of their Jewish contemporaries, a view that could very well compete with the most anti-Jewish treatises of their time. However, the environmental paradigm permitted an exceeding degree of "optimism" as to the prospect of Jewish "regeneration." For many authors during the period, abandoning this paradigm was tantamount to giving up one of the most fundamental tools in the struggle for the emancipation of the Jews.

ABRAHAM BEN ELIJAH: A CASE STUDY IN TRADITIONALIST REACTIONS TO RACE

Our examination of Baruch Lindau's taxonomy has led us to an overview of maskilic attitudes toward race and Whiteness. As we have seen, maskilic authors were weary of the racial turn, and attempted to uphold an environmentalist approach, which would permit them to renounce their own cultural and physical "darkness." But beyond the pale of the Haskalah, Whiteness bore different meanings. In 1800 there appeared in Berlin the first Hebrew translation of several parts of Buffon's magnum opus, the *Histoire Naturelle*. The translation was produced by Abraham ben Elijah of Vilna, a writer who differs in his background, education, and lifestyle from the maskilic authors discussed thus far. Ben Elijah was the son of the famous Vilna Gaon and a renowned talmudist in his own right. Not surprisingly, his text is not an emblematic maskilic translation. Rather, it is a rare and somewhat odd encounter between a devout rabbinical scholar and a controversial French deist. Accordingly, while he embraced some maskilic writing conventions, including the choice to translate the French source through a mediating German text or to conceal the identity of the original author, he rejected some of the most basic tropes of maskilic prose.[143] Most conspicuously, contrary to the vast majority of maskilic translations of its period, Ben Elijah's translation does not take part in Jewish apologetics; it does not begin with the standard maskilic lament of the present state of the Jews, or with bitter musings on the absence of Jewish scientific education. Rather, he presents science as merely a new and somewhat amusing way to enjoy the work of God and to sing his praise. Thus, in this text, Ben Elijah offers a glimpse into a unique kind of Jewish translation, which does not necessarily view itself as inferior to its Christian source.

Ben Elijah's unique position vis-à-vis his source text receives its expression in the translator's own take on the question of skin color. He seems to have been far less concerned with the question of Jewish integration in Europe than were his maskilic contemporaries. In contrast to Lindau and other maskilim, or to such Jewish apologists as De Pinto or Zalkind Hourwitz, who, as noted, rejected the notion of innate Jewish physical or mental attributes and portrayed the differences between Jews and Christians as resulting from differences in mode of living, Ben Elijah embraced the idea of Jewish physical uniqueness and even attempted to uphold it against his source text. In a short chapter discussing the Jews, Buffon writes: "It has been pretended, that the Jews, who came originally from Syria and Palestine, still have the same brown complection [sic] they had formerly. But . . . the Jews of Portugal alone are tawny. As they always marry with their own tribe, the complection of the parents is transmitted to the child, and thus with little diminution preserved, even in the northern countries. The German Jews of Germany, those of Prague, for example, are not more swarthy than the other Germans."[144] In his translation, Ben Elijah chose to deviate from his source text to deliver a message that was in direct opposition to Buffon. Whereas Buffon utilized the Jews to further his circumstantial notions of human difference, Ben Elijah explained that the Jews in general (not only the Portuguese Jews) do not intermarry with other nations and are thus always of a darker complexion than their European compatriots. To reinforce his message, Ben Elijah added a footnote in which he emphasized (following Isaiah 61:9) that "all that see them shall acknowledge them, that they are the seed which the Lord hath blessed, and say: who is like your people, one nation in the world and one language."[145] In Ben Elijah's account, then, Jewish darkness is viewed as an indication of the genealogical "purity" of the Jewish people, and as something in which a Jew is to take pride, not attempt to conceal. In contrast to the Jewish apologists of his time who attempted to explain away Jewish uniqueness, Ben Elijah chose to celebrate it.

The turn of the eighteenth century has been defined as the advent of modern notions of identity. Signifiers of difference such as race, religion, and culture underwent some dramatic transformations, and began acquiring new meanings. Well versed in the intellectual trends of their time, Jewish writers confronted these changes by turning their gaze to the New Worlds of the eighteenth century. Sometimes, this was a subversive gaze, which aimed to challenge European notions of identity and alterity. Other gazes were inspired by these same notions, and utilized the Others out there as a means to establish Jews as part of the White European world. However, whether longing or loathing, subversive or conservative, the European Jewish gaze Eastward and Westward was almost always also a gaze inward. In their scrutinizing of the non-European Other, Jewish thinkers attempted to delineate the borders of their own "racial," cultural, or political identity, in many different and often conflicting ways. In what follows, we continue our discussion of the introspective uses of colonial discourse by looking at what was undoubtedly one of the most popular genres of maskilic prose in the first decades of the nineteenth century, the genre of travel books for children.

Fantasies of Acculturation

Campe's Savages in the Service of the Haskalah

But whence should this savior come to the Hebrews? Hardly from among the Egyptians themselves, for how should one of them intercede on behalf of a nation foreign to him, whose language was incomprehensible to him, which he would certainly take no trouble to learn, a nation which must seem to him as unworthy as incapable of a better fate? Even less from their own midst, for what had the inhumanity of the Egyptian in the course of some centuries finally made of the Hebrew people? The coarsest, the most malicious, the most despised people of the Earth, turned savage by three hundred years of neglect. . . . How, out of such a depraved race of people, should a free man rise forth, an enlightened mind, a hero, or a statesman? . . . Thus, what solution did fortune elect? It took a Hebrew, but prematurely tore him forth from his own coarse people, and let him partake of the enjoyment of Egyptian wisdom; and thus did a Hebrew, Egyptian-educated, become the instrument through which this nation escaped from slavery.
—FRIEDRICH SCHILLER, 1790

It is normally supposed that something always gets lost in translation: I cling, obstinately, to the notion that something can also be gained.
—SALMAN RUSHDIE, 1991

In his definitive discussion of the Enlightenment, Peter Gay characterizes the shift of consciousness that took place during the eighteenth century in the following terms: "Whatever the Christians thought of man . . . the point of Christian anthropology was that man is a son, dependent on God. Whatever the *philosophes* thought of man . . . the point of the Enlightenment's anthropology was that man is an adult, dependent on himself."[1] But not all men were considered adults in eighteenth-century eyes. In fact, it was precisely during this period that a new kind of thinking about children and childhood emerged. New notions of childhood, as a unique time of life, resulted in the formation of a library of books specifically tailored for children. Hebrew writers joined this intellectual trend somewhat late in the game, toward the end of the century, and began creating a new genre of Hebrew children's literature almost from scratch. Browsing through these early Hebrew children's books, it is possible to detect an intense preoccupation with a second class of humans who, like children, were not necessarily perceived as adults in Enlightenment eyes. Africans, Americans, Greenlanders, and other "exotic peoples" enticed the imaginations of eighteenth- and nineteenth-century writers for children. These exotic images were perceived by Jewish authors as a kind of literary bait, which would lure the child reader into the pages of the book. Exotic images were thus invoked in a wide range of turn-of-the-century science books, geographies, and anthologies for children written in Hebrew and Yiddish. But their most pervasive use is to be found in what was perhaps the most popular genre of early Jewish children's literature, the genre of travel.

From its earliest beginnings in the second half of the eighteenth century, children's literature has been home to a plethora of travelers. Some travelers, like Robinson Crusoe, Gulliver, or the Baron Münchhausen began their journeys in more "prestigious" literary seas, but like so many other discoverers, navigators, and adventurers of their time, they too were swept by the tide of late eighteenth-century writing for children, and have since found themselves safely anchored to the shelves of the nursery cupboard. Indeed, during the eighteenth century travel was such a popular form of writing for children that even authors who dedicated their books to domestic themes, such as Thomas Day, Maria Edgeworth, and Stephanie Genlis, made a point of peppering them with tales of travel or anecdotes of savage nations.[2] To this day, it seems, children's authors still cling to the notion, expressed already in 1798 by Maria Edgeworth, according to which "voyages and travels . . . interest young people universally."[3] But the ubiquity of travel in children's books does not stem merely from the desire to satisfy the young readers' appetite for adventure. In fact, the inscription of travel into children's literature began in an age that valued instruction over entertainment, or, to paraphrase Mary Thwaite's famous formulation, primers over pleasure.[4] This holds particularly true for early Hebrew children's literature. Indeed, the maskilim seem not to have been deeply preoccupied with the question of enticing the young reader; they tended to employ much duller storytelling techniques than their non-Jewish peers and addressed their readers in a language and style which, for the most part, they simply could not understand. Accordingly, most maskilic travel books for children were rarely read by anyone save proponents of the Haskalah. Thus, as Zohar Shavit has convincingly argued, it was ideology and not demand that dictated the selection of themes in early Jewish children's literature.[5]

Travel, then, was deemed appropriate for young readers not merely because of its purported appeal for children, but, more importantly, because of what late eighteenth-century authors took to be its deeply didactic value. In Diderot and D'Alembert's famous *Encyclopédie*, for instance, it is explained that travel is "the most essential ingredient of the education of the young. [Travels] develop and raise the level of the mind, enrich it through knowledge, and cure it of national prejudices."[6] Similar ideas were expressed by Jewish authors, such as Naphtali Herz Wessely, who wrote that it is imperative that children be exposed to the reading of travel literature on a daily basis. The stories of travelers, he stressed, are beneficial both to the cultivation of the mind and to the reinforcement of religious faith.[7] The first Jewish writers for children shared these sentiments, and thus, throughout the first three decades of the nineteenth century, there emerged a modest library of Hebrew and Yiddish books, vaguely addressed to children, and dominated to a great degree by travel. The vast majority of these texts were thoroughly "Judaized" adaptations of German children's books, with an emphasis on tales of conquest and colonization. Between the pages of these books, travel intertwined with translation to promote and to represent the motivations, ideals, and self-perception of the Jewish Enlightenment.

For the maskilim, travel was not only a beneficial educational tool. It was also a powerful metaphor to discuss the very foundations of the Haskalah project itself. The hazards and travails of travel by sea, and the wonders viewed by those few who dared to set sail to new lands, provided maskilic authors with a compelling platform for discussing the goals and limitations of their movement, which also embarked on a new and hazardous voyage in Jewish tradition and culture. In addition, the stories of the acculturation and cultural assimilation of savage peoples throughout the world served as a platform to discuss and promote the maskilim's more subtle form of colonial aspirations, the desire for the acculturation and cultural integration of the Jews. Read thus as an allegory for the maskilic project, Jewish travel writing for children emerges as a raw manifestation of the fantasies and fears, the hopes and anxieties of the first generation of modern Jewish men. The maskilic "masa" is a melting pot of motifs of colonialism and acculturation, reaction and reform, mimicry and monstrosity, education and Enlightenment. It is to a review of these motifs that the present chapter is dedicated.

JOACHIM HEINRICH CAMPE AND THE FORMATION OF A JEWISH CHILDREN'S LIBRARY

In the world of late eighteenth-century German pedagogy, Campe was a genuine superstar, second perhaps only to Rousseau. His influence extended well beyond German-speaking lands, and his works were translated into French, English, Dutch, Russian, Latin, and, of course, Jewish languages.[8] In a pioneering study on Campe's influence on the Hebrew literary system, Shavit counts nine separate Hebrew translations of Campe's work, published during the first three decades of the nineteenth century. In the following decades Campe's popularity dwindled somewhat, but his works continued to be translated and mimicked by Jewish authors well into the twentieth century.[9] To the Hebrew translations mentioned by Shavit, we must add two editions of Campe's work in German written in Hebrew characters that appeared in 1784 and 1813, as well as at least three more Yiddish translations that appeared during the early decades of the nineteenth century.[10] The most popular of Campe's works were his travel stories for children, particularly his 1779 adaptation of Defoe's *Robinson Crusoe*, entitled *Robinson der Jüngere*; and his account of the first European voyages to America, published in 1781–82 and titled *Die Entdeckung von Amerika*. Both these works were translated into Jewish languages several times during the eighteenth and nineteenth centuries. Three stories were also translated into Hebrew and Yiddish from Campe's 1785–93 collection of travel stories entitled *Sammlung interessanter und zweckmäßig abgefasster Reisebeschreibungen für die Jugend*. Two of these translations were produced by the Polish maskil Menachem Mendel Lefin, and the third is also often attributed to this maskil.[11] Another of Campe's works that seems to have been popular with the maskilim was the children's guidebook *Sittenbüchlein für Kinder*, which was translated into Hebrew first in 1811 by Baruch Shenfeld and then again in 1819 by David Zamość. Unlike other Jewish adaptations of Campe's works produced during the first three decades of the nineteenth century, *Sittenbüchlein für Kinder* is not a travel adventure; however, as we have seen in Chapter 1, it does contain a travel story, perhaps the most famous one of its time, the tale of Inkle and Yarico. It seems that, as a rule, the maskilim favored Campe's tales of exotica and exploration over his other works. His 1783 popular children's guidebook, *Theophron*, which did not contain any such tales, was translated into Hebrew only in 1863. Similarly, other works by Campe that did not feature exotic tales of travel, such as his *Letters from Paris*, his thoughts on the French revolution, his German dictionary, or his European travel tales, were, to the best of my knowledge, entirely overlooked by Jewish translators.[12]

The inclination amongst Campe's Jewish translators to favor tales of travel and exotica is compatible with the tendency prevalent amongst early Jewish authors and translators for children to favor texts in which distant peoples and lands were discussed. This tendency is evident in a plethora of turn-of-the-century maskilic texts in natural history and geography such as Lindau's *Reshit limudim* and the anonymous 1802 *Kleyne yeografie*, both of which discuss a litany of exotic peoples, animals, and lands. Early nineteenth-century anthologies for children, such as those by David Zamość and Leib Stark, also included stories and poems on feral children, savage peoples, and various geographic discoveries. A wide range of anthropological exotica was also invoked by the earliest Hebrew and German Jewish readers for children, compiled by such maskilim as Joseph Perl, Moshe Bock, Shlomo Keysir, Hyman Shvebacher, and Israel ben Chaim.[13] Thus, it seems safe to say that early Jewish authors for children were enticed by the image of the exotic and used it excessively in their various works.

As a rule, the Jewish translations of Campe's works adhere to the norms of maskilic translations discussed in Chapter 3, such as the tendency to domesticate the source text and render it suitable for Hebrew or Jewish readership. Most translators were exceedingly liberal in their attitude to Campe's source texts and added and omitted details, sentences, and whole chapters as they saw fit. These additions and omissions have been the focus of several studies, as scholars have become increasingly aware of the pivotal role played by Jewish translations of Campe's works in the formation of a modern Jewish library for children. And yet even though scholarly attention has begun to focus on maskilic translations, very little attention has been given to the colonial aspects of these translations or to their treatment of such issues as race, anthropological description, and difference.[14] Indeed, most studies have focused on the pedagogical or literary aspects of the translations and have tended to overlook their colonial dimensions. And yet I would suggest that the Jewish translations of Campe's works must be read against the context of the increasing interest amongst late eighteenth-century children's writers in colonial fantasies, travel stories, or stories of the colonization and "acculturation" of savage peoples and lands.

EXOTICISM IN EARLY CHILDREN'S LITERATURE

In order to adequately understand early children's authors' preoccupation with travel and exoticism, we must take into account the functionalist views that dominated children's literature from roughly the second half of the eighteenth century into the mid-nineteenth century. The primary purpose of most children's books produced during this era was to educate and acculturate the young readers, to mold them into "appropriate adults." The enjoyment afforded by the act of reading was a secondary consideration and was only deemed desirable insofar as it promoted the didactic aspects of the book.[15] A gradual change in views would be felt during the second half of the nineteenth century with the publication of such books as *Alice's Adventures in Wonderland* (1865) or Charles Kingsley's *The Water Babies* (1863), whose primary or perhaps sole purpose was to amuse and entertain the young reader.[16] However, it would be wrong to claim that early children's authors overlooked entirely the importance of entertainment. Authors as early as John Locke had noted the importance of enjoyment for the process of education and recommended that children be given pleasant and easy reading material, which would interest as well as educate them. In the absence of books deliberately designed for the consumption of children, Locke himself recommended the fables of Aesop.[17] In the second half of the eighteenth century, however, travel began taking the place of fables as an excellent means for pleasurable instruction.[18] The travel narrative fit in perfectly with the didactic intentions of early writers for children: journeys to foreign lands were an attractive means to promote knowledge of the world and its peoples, and to relate information on natural history or what would later become zoology, botany, biology, and other branches of knowledge deemed especially appealing in eighteenth-century eyes. In addition,

Enlightenment authors were able to utilize the travails of travel, such as the perils of the sea, encounters with foreign peoples and religions, and the difficulties of leading a life outside of civilization (meaning, of course, Europe), in order to deliver various messages on such values as the importance of education, industriousness, resourcefulness, and physical or mental fortitude.

But tales of travel and exoticism were deemed appropriate for children not only because of their instructional value. Public demands for such tales, and particularly children's own demand for them, may also have played a role in their popularity amongst eighteenth-century authors. Let us not forget that travel was an immensely popular genre of writing during the eighteenth century, and that even before the emergence of children's literature as a separate genre of writing, children had long been consumers of travel stories in the form of chapter books and folk tales.

In addition, there seems to have been something almost natural in late eighteenth-century authors' choice to designate colonial writing to children, due to the discursive proximity between the image of the child as it emerged in the second half of the eighteenth century and the contemporaneous image of the savage. Like savages, children were perceived as representing a kind of natural, primeval humanity, at once ideal and flawed, a source for imitation on the one hand and correction on the other. Like savages, they too were thought of as unable to represent, govern, or acculturate themselves, and were thus understood to be in need of constant supervision.[19] The discursive proximity between childhood and savagery is evident in a wide range of late eighteenth-century texts and practices. Thus, for instance, in the last quarter of the century anthropological observations on children became quite popular amongst scientists. In 1803 French physician Alphonse Leroy justified these observations: "We strive to know the morals of savage man, and we find them in children. In them alone we must investigate the anatomy of our faculties."[20] And yet, it is important to bear in mind that children's literature began at that same historical moment in which philosophical interest in savages declined. Philosopher George Boas claims that it is precisely this process of the decline of the noble savage that should serve as a context for the rise of the image of the natural child: "One might think that when it was proved that the only remaining examples of primitive man did not meet the requirements of the cultural primitivist, that the idea would have disappeared.

Quite the contrary. A search was then made for a new exemplar that would be, if not the chronological *Urmensch*, at least the cultural."[21] And indeed, the conflation of children with savages dovetails with the increasing racialization of late eighteenth-century discourse, and it was not long before non-European peoples began to be depicted as eternal children, desperately in need of adult, i.e., European, guidance and supervision. The paternalism of late eighteenth-century colonial discourse is evident, for instance, in Schiller's discussion of Europe's relationship with its colonies: "The discoveries, which our European sea-travellers have made in distant seas and remote coasts, provide us with an instructive and entertaining spectacle. They show us people who have remained in various degrees of education all around us, like children surrounding an adult and through their own example remind him of what he once was, and from whence he came."[22] Schiller's formulation gives tantalizing expression to the colonial uses of the child analogy. By conflating the colonies with children and Europe with adults, European writers were able to present colonial hegemony as serving the better interests of the colonized, who are incapable of governing themselves.[23] However, the child analogy served not only to promote the actual colonization of the non-European world, but also more domestic purposes. By utilizing the image of the savage, with which children were thought to naturally identify, children's authors attempted to acculturate and, in a sense, colonize the European child.[24]

The discursive proximity between children and savages is especially evident in Campe's works, in which, as Zantop explains, "education is metaphorically equated with colonization and colonization with education, the domestication of little savages."[25] Through the story of the conquest of distant lands, Campe conquers his child-readers, and in relating to them tales of the acculturation of savage peoples he in turn promotes their own acculturation and integration into bourgeois European society, the only version of civilization known to eighteenth-century writers. As Richard Apgar explains, for Campe, the defining feature of civilization is education. Anyone without education is, in effect, a savage.[26] This emphasis on the importance of education and its effects on man and society is one of the most pervasive themes of Campe's works.[27] It is this radical belief in reform through education that was, I would suggest, one of the primary reasons for the maskilim's extreme devotion to this particular author.[28]

As we have seen in the previous chapter, in its very essence, the Haskalah was a pedagogic project, aimed at the education and acculturation of the Jews. It was a project that sprung from feelings of intellectual inferiority, which tied to a zealous belief in the all-encompassing power of education. Indeed, it was something of a maskilic consensus that education can create an actual revolution within Judaism and raise Jews from the depths of illiteracy and ignorance to the forefront of scientific and intellectual development. As famed Jewish physician Markus Herz stated: "The ḥokhmot [חכמות, meaning secular studies] satisfy the hungry soul . . . and alleviate it from the level of animals and beasts."[29] Mendelssohn-Frankfurt agreed, claiming that "without the ḥokhmot man has no advantage over beasts, indeed, he is worse than a beast."[30] The significance of these statements is not to be underestimated; during the eighteenth century secular studies were often viewed by the Jewish religious elite as redundant and even hazardous for Jews. The maskilim's identification of the ḥokhmot, as opposed to revelation, as the essential signifier of civilization, is perhaps the most subversive element of the early conservative Haskalah. It was to this struggle for the legitimization of secular studies that the maskilim harnessed Campe's savages.

CAMPE IN MASKILIC GARB

That Campe's work had its unique maskilic uses has long been recognized by scholars. Nancy Sinkoff and Leah Garrett have demonstrated how maskilim such as Mendel Lefin and Joseph Vitlin utilized Campe's travel narratives as a means to challenge Jewish separatism, and to call for the integration of Jews into European political and communal life.[31] Elsewhere, I have argued that Jewish translations of the works of Campe served the maskilim as a means to argue for the radical changebility or acculturability of the Jews. By designating children's literature to adult Jews, maskilic translators equated Jews with children, thus introducing the element of change into the age-old image of the obstinate Jew.[32] And as Sinkoff and Ken Frieden have demonstrated, another important maskilic use of Campe was to deliver anti-hasidic messages and promote an ideology of self-reliance and industriousness, which stood in stark contrast to the contemporaneous hasidic discourse of miracles and divine intervention.[33]

The most pervasive maskilic use of Campe's work to promote the reform of Jewish curriculum, however, has been largely overlooked by scholars. And yet examples are ubiquitous. Take, for instance, the various Jewish translations of Campe's *Robinson der Jüngere*. Campe's adaptation of Defoe's novel was inspired by Rousseau's endorsement of the novel in his *Émile*. In order to better adapt Defoe's exceedingly religious novel to the ideas of Rousseau, Campe did away with Defoe's excessive religious musings, at best turning them into marginal anecdotes. In their stead, he inserted into the book didactic allegories and morals, informative discussions on science and geography and vehement objections to the transatlantic slave trade.[34] But perhaps the most important difference between Defoe's and Campe's renderings of the tale was that in stark contrast to Defoe's Crusoe, who had been cast away on the island with a plethora of Western artifacts that played a paramount role in his (both mental and physical) survival, and over which Crusoe often obsessed, Campe's Krusoe was stranded on the island with nothing save his own industriousness. Thus, while the original Crusoe's survival was a celebration of divine providence, the German Krusoe's survival was a tribute to individual industry and learning. This difference is vital and a function of the different morals inlaid in the two texts. Indeed, while Defoe's novel bears a distinct theological moral, corresponding with the author's Dissentist sympathies, Campe's version of the book is purely pedagogical: its morals have little to do with religion and everything to do with education. Thus, whereas Crusoe often laments his former religious negligence, Campe's Krusoe regrets not his neglect of religion, but his neglect of studies: "Oh, he often sighed, how little did I understand my own advantage in the years of my childhood, in not watching my own interest better and taking notice of everything that I saw or heard! Oh! If I could grow young again, how attentive would I be to everything that is executed by the hands or industry of men! There is not a trade nor an art of which I would not endeavour to learn some part."[35] Similarly, while in Defoe's novel the difference between civilized Europe and the savage America lies in the importance of religion, for Campe, the difference between civilized men and savages lies, as we have now come to expect, in education. Thus, for instance, whereas Defoe attributes Caribbean cannibalism to the absence of divine revelation, Campe views it as a testimony to the depths of degeneracy "to which men may fall when they are left to fend for themselves, without education and instruction!"[36]

Such passages, which conflate lack of learning with savagery, would clearly take on special meaning when translated into Hebrew or Yiddish and addressed to a Jewish audience.[37] Jewish readers lived in a world in which secular studies, even where accepted, were always thought of as marginal to religious learning. And yet here was a man whose entire existence was dependent not on his religious education, his knowledge of the Talmud, or his proficiency in the works of the sages, but rather on his secular education, on his industriousness and skill. Robinson on his island has no use for rabbinical knowledge, but rather for geography, agronomy, biology, medicine, carpentry, and so on. It is plain to see why such a message would have appealed greatly to the maskilim. Indeed, Krusoe's island is a tantalizing literary demonstration of Wessely's outrageous (yet often reiterated) assertion that "a Talmudic scholar . . . who has no education . . .— a carcass is better than he."[38]

In the works of some translators, Campe's quest for education and Enlightenment took on the form of a militant maskilic manifesto. One such text is Mendelssohn-Frankurt's 1807 Hebrew translation of the first part of Campe's *Discovery of America*. Similarly to other Hebrew translators of his time, Mendelssohn-Frankfurt treated Campe's text with great liberty, omitting the dialogic form of the source text as well as a great deal of moral, didactic, and scientific detail. And yet, in stark contrast to his tendency to abbreviate in most parts of the book, the translator did not spare his readers Campe's tedious descriptions of Kolumbus's travails before or during his journey to the new continent. Moreover, not only did Mendelssohn-Frankfurt deliver these descriptions in full, he even added some more descriptions and details of his own.

Kolumbus's troubles begin already in Europe while seeking support for his expedition. A patriot who wishes to devote the fruits of his future discoveries to his native country, he begins by presenting his plan before the senate in Genoa, but his offer is declined in humiliating fashion. Rather than becoming discouraged, writes Campe, the bold discoverer, "having satisfied the duty he owed to his country, . . . turned his thoughts towards Lisbon."[39] As Apgar convincingly argues, Campe uses the image of Kolumbus to signify the author himself and his fellow Enlighteners, who strove for the acculturation, education, and advantage of their respective countries and Europe in general.[40] But what happens to this emblem of Aufklärung, when he becomes a symbol of the Haskalah? Mendelssohn-Frankfurt's treatment of the episode is telling. Let us read his version of the Kolumbus's Genoan escapades:

And [Kolumbus] went on his journey and he came to the heads of state who sit in the city of Genoa in the land of Italy, and he spoke with his countrymen and said: thus and thus did I council, and now, therefore, rise and assist me. But he seemed as one who mocked unto them, for they could not understand his words, and they mocked him and sent him empty-handed. And Kolumbus was greatly saddened upon seeing that none of his own people would hear him. . . . For this is the way of all who are wise in their own eyes, they will not forgive the man who awakens to discover novelties, which they could not. For it is better for them to sit alone idly, than to awake from their slumber and investigate houses filled with everything the world has to offer.[41]

In contrast to Campe's Kolumbus, who "was not discouraged" by the refusal of the Genoan senate, Mendelssohn-Frankfurt's description takes on a somewhat melodramatic form. The "Jewish Kolumbus" is so shaken by the senate's refusal that he continues to dwell on the episode later in the book, bitterly remarking that "I set out to benefit my people but they would not hear me."[42] Similarly to Campe, Mendelssohn-Frankfurt uses the image of Kolumbus as an emblem for the author himself and his fellow maskilim, and yet, in the move from the German literary system to the Hebrew one, the image of the Genoan discoverer receives added value. Indeed, it is hard to imagine that a contemporaneous reader of the translation could have read these passages, as well as many other such utterances in the book, and not understand the reference to the Haskalah. For Mendelssohn-Frankfurt and his fellow maskilim, the image of Kolumbus could serve as a paradigm for the Jewish maskil, an ambitious reformer who wishes to better the situation of his people, but in return encounters ridicule, antagonism, and, in the case of some maskilim, even persecution. Interestingly, in his conflation of the two images of the European colonizer and the Jewish maskil, Mendelssohn-Frankfurt touches upon one of the most complex and volatile aspects of the Jewish translations of Campe's works. Indeed, whereas Campe utilized colonial discourse to promote education, in what may be viewed as a kind of pedagogical colonialism—still a far cry from the actual colonial subjection of subaltern peoples—his Jewish translators were promoting not merely the education of children in their works but also the actual cultural colonization of an underprivileged minority group within Europe, the Jews. In fact, as Shavit has argued, maskilic translations of children's books were often ambiguous in defining their target audience and appear to have been designated for, and read by, both adolescents and adults.[43] Of course, this ambiguity corresponds with the maskilim's feelings of inferiority vis-à-vis their source texts, and the sense amongst Jewish translators that cultural revival may be achieved only by subjugating Jewish culture to Christian culture. The translation of Christian children's literature, to be consumed by all members of Jewish society, adults and children, was a means of doing just that. Thus, in the works of Campe's Jewish translators, education and colonization informed and reinforced one another in complex and often revelatory ways.

CAMPE AND THE COLONIZATION OF EUROPEAN JEWRY

I have mentioned above that the colonial dimension of the Jewish translations of Campe's works has been largely overlooked by scholars. In fact, Garrett argues that it is precisely *the complete absence* of colonial aspirations that differentiates the Jewish versions of the island adventure from the non-Jewish versions of authors such as Campe and Defoe. "Tropes such as 'island,' 'home,' 'colony,' and 'adventure,'" she writes, "speak differently to a Jewish East European readership than to German or English readers."[44] The latter point is undoubtedly true, and in discussing Campe's Jewish translations one must consider their unique context. Moreover, as we have seen in the first chapter, early Ashkenazi texts tended to exhibit a kind of colonial indifference, which negated the political, cultural, and social expansion of the Jews, preferring instead exclusion, separatism, and the preservation of difference between Jews and Others. Clearly, however, this is not the approach adopted by turn-of-the-century maskilim. In contrast to Glikl or Ber and Bella Perlhefter, who adapted the ubiquitous tale of erotic intercultural encounter into a uniquely non-colonialist version, later Jewish tales describing colonial encounters are deeply entrenched in colonialist discourse. In all these texts, the intercultural encounter is articulated by use of colonialist symbols and tropes, such as the native-child analogy discussed above, the deification of the European colonizer, the feminization of the native, or the discourse of acculturation, conversion, enslavement, and conquest.[45] Some Jewish texts even include outright justifications for European overseas expansion. We have witnessed an early expression of this tendency already in Horowitz's *Amudey beyt Yehudah*, discussed in Chapter 2 above, and later examples abound. Thus, in Zamość's translation of *Robinson der Jüngere* we are told (following Campe) that it is common sense that justifies the subjugation of indigenous peoples to foreign European rule: "For if there is found a country which has no government, the discoverer has the right to government. Thus Robinson on his island is the rightful governor."[46] As we have seen in the second chapter, Campe's Jewish translators also exhibited an acute awareness of European colonial needs in their discussion of the issue of slavery, and offered their readers various "Enlightened justifications" for the continuation of the practice. Indeed, much like his German predecessor, the Jewish Robinson is modeled after the paradigmatic late eighteenth-century image of the reluctant slave owner, whose only interest in perpetuating the institution of slavery is his justified fear of the enslaved. This may be a far cry from the blunt and unapologetic colonialism of Defoe's Crusoe, but in his assumption that enslavement may be tolerated, both by Europeans as well as by the enslaved themselves, the German and Jewish Robinson is a prototypical product of the late eighteenth-century colonialist mindset.[47]

The investment of turn-of-the-century maskilim in colonialism is not to be underestimated. These authors were fascinated by colonial encounters and conquests and viewed them as a powerful metaphor to discuss their own movement. They employed colonial discourse to discuss external and internal European matters, thus harnessing the conquest, enslavement, and disenfranchisement of non-European peoples in order to promote their own interests. They did not, at any point, contest direct, overseas colonialism, but rather viewed it as financially, politically, morally, and pedagogically instrumental. They employed colonialist tropes, myths, and stereotypes in their discussion of non-European peoples. But most importantly, they assumed the cultural superiority of Europe over all other peoples, and supported, and in practice promoted, the imposition of this culture on politically inferior groups, particularly the Jews.

This last point bears no small significance for our present discussion, for, in essence, maskilic translations of Campe's works are not only sympathetic to European colonial aspirations, they also actively participated in bringing them about. In fact, any reading of these texts as non-colonialist entails a problematic understanding of colonialism as a simple, one-dimensional phenomenon, which pertains only to European interests overseas. And yet, as we have seen numerous times throughout this study, colonialist discourse often bears purely domestic implications, and is often directed to non-hegemonic groups within the domestic-European sphere, such as women, children, ethnic minorities, or underprivileged classes.[48] This close connection between external and internal colonialism crystallizes in maskilic literature. The maskilim used the stories of the colonization and acculturation of non-European peoples and lands as a model for Jewish acculturation and integration within Europe. In the writings of these Jewish authors, savages were conflated with Jews, and the Jewish encounter with modernity was viewed through the colonialist lens. The widespread Jewish interest in the exotic was, therefore, closely linked to an interest in acculturation and the means to achieve it.

The conflation of Jews with savages is achieved through a variety of literary tools and tactics, the most important of which is, I would suggest, intertextuality. By carefully selecting various phrases and passages, most often from the Bible, but also from other Jewish sources, Hebrew translators and authors were able to establish an identification between the subjects of the text and its objects. An interesting example is offered by Shenfeld's 1825 description of the races of Man, discussed in the previous chapter. Taken at face value, Shenfeld's piece is merely a Hebrew adaptation of Blumenbach's famous human taxonomy. However, a closer reading reveals that even though the author makes no explicit mention of Jews throughout the text, he still aims to deliver a powerful message concerning the state of the Jews in Europe. Here is what Shenfeld has to say on savage nations: "This is the fate of the nation on which the light of morals and reason does not shine, and [which] without eyes stumbles as a blind man in darkness. And to this day there are many more nations in the distant islands [who are] ignorant, shameless and immodest, until they receive help from afar, and educated men [maskilim] rise to open their eyes so that they may see that they are naked in body and soul, and be ashamed. It is then that they will cease their wild ways and begin treading in the path of civilized man . . . and they will have the Torah of man [torat adam, תורת אדם], and live a righteous life in the realms of knowledge and Torah."[49] Upon a first reading, Shenfeld appears to be offering a somewhat detached discussion of savage nations. By using such terms as "distant islands" and "help from afar," he creates an impression of foreignness and exoticism. And yet, like so many Hebrew texts of its time, Shenfeld's piece is written in a kind of maskilic code, which would have been easily decipherable for a turn-of-the-century reader. I am referring particularly to the author's use of the term torat ha-adam toward the end of his discussion. The term originates in the writings of the fourteenth-century sage

Nachmanides, where it denotes halakhot or ritual laws pertaining to matters of illness, death, and mourning. However, in his sensational 1782 *Divrey shalom ve-emet* Naphtali Herz Wessely reappropriated the term to denote secular studies and the teachings of civilization. In subsequent years, the term became popular amongst maskilim and was regularly invoked in the debates surrounding the revision of Jewish curriculum. In fact, it became so identified with this debate and with the maskilim in general, and Wessely in particularly, that it is hard to imagine that a contemporaneous Hebrew reader would have read it in Shenfeld's piece without being inevitably reminded of Wessely's book. Indeed, the application of the term *torat ha-adam* to "distant islanders" is sure to have struck a chord with maskilic readers. By conjuring Wessely's maskilic arch-text, Shenfeld frames his discussion of savagery and civilization within the context of the maskilic agenda and the Jewish curriculum debates. It is, indeed, not savages that are being discussed here at all, but rather Jews. As Wessely himself explained: "There is only one nation on earth, that has not paid adequate attention to the Torah of man, and in their youth and the homes of their rabbis ceased the study of civility, nature and science: we, the Children of Israel in Europe, . . . and more so the inhabitants of Ashkenaz and Poland."[50]

The conflation of Jews and savages is perfected in the Campe translations.[51] A remarkable use of the analogy is found in Lefin's 1815 translation of one of Campe's travel tales, which describes the English "discovery" of the Pacific island of Palau. During their tour of the island, the English sailors befriend a Palauan native. The latter is described as a reckless, hedonistic youth who is enchanted by the sophisticated Christian visitors and who "clings to the ways of the British with all his might, and does his utmost to resemble them."[52] When the English sailors resolve to leave the island, the young man expresses his wish to join them, but the leaders of the tribe object to the journey and accuse him of turning his back on his people and family and preferring an alien culture over his own native one. The tribe leader then suggests that a second native, the Palauan prince Libou, accompany the British in order to acquire from them "those things required for the advancement of his people."[53] The allegory here is almost blunt; the first native, the Palauan youth, represents the assimilationist, the mimic man, whose travels outside the borders of Palau/Judaism, Lefin suggests, serve only his own libertine or hedonistic desires. This is the image of the radical Jewish intellectual, dreaded by traditionalists and conservative maskilim alike.

Conversely, Libou, the noble savage, is tailored after the image of the moderate maskil, whose sole purpose in his journeys outside Jewish tradition is to acquire knowledge and tools with which to strengthen Jewish tradition and society. Like Mendelssohn-Frankfurt's Kolumbus, this traveler serves as an emblem of the Haskalah. Indeed, the reader immediately recognizes in the image of Libou the literary corollary of the translator himself, Lefin, and of his fellow maskilim. As Sinkoff explains, these maskilim also made the conceptual or physical journey Westward, to "civilized Europe" where, like Libou, they hoped to be able to acquire the tools necessary to "regenerate" their "backward" people.[54] And yet the similarity between Mendelssohn-Frankfurt's Kolumbus and Lefin's Libou is not complete, for unlike Kolumbus, Libou is not a European colonist, but rather a savage in his own right. In this sense, the Lefin-Libou analogy sheds light on the problematic self-perception of the maskilic translator. In choosing this self-colonizing native as an allegory for the Jewish maskil, Lefin betrays perhaps an awareness to the ambivalent position of the maskilic translator, who is at once an agent of acculturation and its subject.

This ambivalent position of the Jewish translator, as both acculturator and acculturated, is expressed in other parts of the translation as well. Indeed, throughout the text, Lefin's choice of language reflects the translator's identification not only with the savage Palauans, but also with the British colonizers. Thus, for instance, in an allusion to the biblical story of the spies in Numbers 13, Lefin explains that the British "decided to send spies [מרגלים] that they may search the land [לתור את הארץ]."[55] The biblical allusion at once renders Palau as the biblical Canaan, and the English as the biblical colonizers of the land, the Children of Israel. In a separate translation also attributed to Lefin and entitled *Oniyah soarah,* the story of the Exodus is once again invoked to describe colonial exploration. The author describes how the Dutch explorer William Bontekoe and his crew encounter a storm on their quest to the East Indies. The sailors express their anxieties thus: "Behold, we die, we perish, we all perish."[56] The sailors' cries are an allusion to Numbers 17:27: "And the Children of Israel spake unto Moses, saying, Behold, we die, we perish, we all perish." The Dutch sailors' choice to articulate their anxieties in the language of the Children of Israel not only transforms them from modern European sailors to biblical Jews, but also converts their leader, Bontekoe, from a seventeenth-century explorer to the biblical Moses. This last analogy is particularly instructive and appears not only in *Oniyah soarah*, but also in other maskilic translations, most conspicuously in Mendelssohn-Frankfurt's *Meziat ha-arez*.

In the case of Mendelssohn-Frankfurt, the choice of biblical verse seems to play a crucial part in the construction of meaning within the text. In his description of Kolumbus's adventures, the author invokes numerous biblical allusions to the story of the Exodus, at once conflating the Children of Israel with European colonizers as well as with non-European victims of colonization. A fascinating example is found in Mendelssohn-Frankfurt's description of the horrors of colonization: "Heaven help us when we consider all the cruelties which the Europeans pursued in the New World! With evil designs in heart they came to a foreign country to worsen the situation of its inhabitants. . . . And the cries of the Indians came up unto God, and God heard their groaning and said: I shall avenge the blood of the innocents! . . . And God spilled his cup of wrath upon those nations, who came to unjustly inherit foreign lands, and He inflicted upon them a famine and a plague; and every man's sword shall be set against his brother, and His hand is stretched out still to punish the nations for their evil."[57] This description is ripe with biblical allusions that echo the story of the Children of Israel's enslavement in Egypt (e.g., Exodus 2:13–14). The same rhetoric is repeated elsewhere in the book, for instance when Mendelssohn-Frankfurt writes that "the children of India sighed by reason of the bondage,"[58] once again invoking Exodus 2:24. Such allusions would not have been lost on the contemporaneous Hebrew reader, who would have identified the implicit analogy drawn here between the Children of Israel's travails in Egypt and the Native American's plight. Further allusions to the plight of the Israelites in the context of the colonized appear throughout the text and are used not only to describe the woes of the Native Americans but also those of African slaves.[59]

The resource to the biblical story of the enslavement of the Israelites in order to describe the conquest and enslavement of colonial peoples is a recurring theme in this maskilic text. Taken at face value, it seems to imply a Jewish identification with the woes of other minority groups, a sympathy between subalterns, as it were. However, reading through Mendelssohn-Frankfurt's book, it is not long before the reader realizes that allusions to the Exodus serve the translator not only to discuss the colonized, but also to describe their colonizers. Indeed, in Mendelssohn-Frankfurt's text, Kolumbus is consistently likened not to the Egyptian Pharaoh, but rather to the biblical image of Moses, leading the Children of Israel through the desert. In a classic maskilic maneuver of domestication of the non-Jewish narrative, the exotic becomes the exodic, and the modern colonial journey is phrased through the language of the biblical journey of the Israelites from Egypt into the Promised Land. Thus, Mendelssohn-Frankfurt describes how during the long journey to the "New World," Kolumbus is forced to handle the skepticism, suspicion, and despair of his ship's crew: "As they went on their way the wind was against them. And the bread which had sustained them for the past eight months had all but gone, and they had but a few crumbs of bread which were dry and mouldy, and [which had] bred worms from the heat of the day. . . . And the soul of the people was much discouraged and loatheth the light bread and they spake against Kolumbus. . . . And they gathered themselves together against Kolumbus and said unto him is it a small thing that thou hast brought us up out of our land to kill us in a foreign place?"[60] These passages include unmistakable allusions to the story of the Israelites, as described in Exodus 16:20: "Notwithstanding they hearkened not unto Moses; but some of them left of it until the morning, *and it bred worms*, and stank: and Moses was wroth with them." Similarly, in Numbers 21:4–5: "And they journeyed from Mount Hor by the way of the Red Sea, to compass the land of Edom: and the soul of the people was much discouraged because of the way. And the people spake against God, and against Moses, Wherefore have ye brought us up out of Egypt to die in the wilderness? For [there is] no bread, neither [is there any] water; and our soul loatheth this light bread." Or Numbers 16:3: "And they gathered themselves together against Moses and against Aaron," and 16:13: "Is it a small thing that thou hast brought us up out of a land that floweth with milk and honey, to kill us in the wilderness[?]" Elsewhere in the book, Mendelssohn-Frankfurt uses the same biblical passages quoted some two dozen pages earlier to describe the plight of the natives, this time to describe Kolumbus's travails: "And Kolumbus cried and sighed by reason of the bondage."[61]

Mendelssohn-Frankfurt's extensive usage of intertextuality and maskilic code creates, then, a tangled web of analogies, in which the Children of Israel are at once identified with the colonizer and with the colonized, thus complicating the translator's identification with the one or the other group. A closer look at this complex analogical matrix reveals yet another analogy that runs through the text. As we have seen, in Mendelssohn-Frankfurt's book Kolumbus is likened not only to the biblical Moses, but also to the Jewish Haskalah. Similarly to Lefin's Palauan Libou, Mendelssohn-Frankfurt's Kolumbus is portrayed as a bold modernizer, struggling to pave his way Westward, to great treasures and discoveries, through the thicket of ignorance, superstition, and obstinance. Under Mendelssohn-Frankfurt's treatment, then, Kolumbus at once becomes a prototypical maskil and a modern-day Moses. In this manner, the translator draws an indirect analogy between the biblical image of Moses and the Jewish maskilim. A similar analogy is found, it will be recalled, in Lefin's *Oniyah soarah*, where the Dutch navigator Willem Ysbradsz Bontekoe is likened at once to the narrating maskil and to the biblical Moses. And indeed, much like the great biblical liberator, the maskilim viewed their project as an attempt to break the social, cultural, and political bonds that restrained the Jews of their time. In addition, similar to Moses, who, as the epigraph to this chapter suggests, was a hybrid being, trapped between the world of the hegemonic Egyptians and the subaltern Israelites, so too the maskilim were trapped between the new science, philosophy, and norms of the Enlightenment on the one hand and Jewish faith and traditions on the other, making it difficult to find the golden mean between the two worlds.[62] Finally, the implicit analogy drawn between Moses and the maskilim reveals an interesting aspect in the pedagogical program of the Haskalah. Indeed, similar to Moses, who withheld the Holy Land from the Exodus generation, so too the maskilim assigned the new world of knowledge, acculturation, and emancipation not to their own generation of Jews, but rather to a new generation of Jewish children, who would be brought up on the values of the European Enlightenment and the Jewish Haskalah.

THE RACIALIZATION OF *ROBINSON CRUSOE* FROM DEFOE TO THE JEWISH CAMPE

The various translations and adaptations of *Robinson Crusoe* afford a bird's-eye view of the changes that occurred in notions of ethnic difference, from the days of Defoe to the early nineteenth century. In this context, it is particularly instructive to see how the image of Friday, or Freitag in Campe's version, was constructed by different authors throughout the period. Defoe, it will be recalled, molded the image of his noble savage in compliance with the literary norms of his time, contrasting him with other savages on the one hand, and likening him to Europeans on the other. Let us recall the description as it appears in the original 1719 text:

> He [Friday] was a comely handsome Fellow, perfectly well made; with straight strong Limbs, not too large; tall and well shap'd, and as I reckon, about twenty six Years of Age. He had a very good Countenance, not a fierce and surly Aspect, but seem'd to have something very manly in his Face, and yet he had all the Sweetness and Softness of an European in his Countenance too, especially when he smil'd. His Hair was long and black, not curl'd like Wool; his Forehead very high, and large, and a great Vivacity and sparkling Sharpness in his Eyes. The Colour of his Skin was not quite black, but very tawny, and yet not of an ugly yellow nauseous tawny, as the Brazilians, and Virginians and other Natives of America are; but of a bright kind of a dun olive Colour, that had in it something very agreeable; tho' not very easy to describe. His Face was round, and plump; his Nose small, not flat like the Negroes, a very good Mouth, thin Lips, and his fine Teeth well set, and white as Ivory.[63]

Friday, then, is depicted as a young man of a masculine yet not savage appearance. The color of his skin is contrasted with that of other Native Americans, whereas his other physiognomic traits are contrasted, either explicitly or implicitly, with those of Africans. Similar descriptions of Europeanized noble savages are ubiquitous in early eighteenth-century literature. Thus, for instance, Behn's West African noble savage, Oroonoko, is described as "pretty tall, but of a shape the most exact that can be fancied; . . . . His face was not of that brown, rusty black which most of that nation are, but a perfect ebony, or polished jet. . . . His nose was rising and Roman, instead of African and flat. His mouth, the finest shaped that could be seen; far from those great turned lips, which are so natural to the rest of the Negroes."[64] We find here once again the same technique used by Defoe: the savage is rendered noble by being contrasted to his fellow savages, on the one hand, and being likened to a European, on the other. This technique betrays a latent assumption that to be noble is emphatically to be European; there is no other form of aristocracy. And yet, as the eighteenth century progressed, the tendency to focus on the similarities between Europeans and non-Europeans gave way to an increasing interest in difference, particularly anatomical difference. As we have seen, one of the most significant foci of late eighteenth-century anthropology was the question of skin color. The last quarter of the century saw a rise in the importance of complexion, for all its complexities. This preoccupation with pigmentation left its mark on Campe's works. Consider Campe's description of Freitag, as it appears in the early editions of *Robinson der Jüngere*: "He was a well-made young man, about twenty years old. His skin was blackish-brown and brilliant [*schwarzbraun und glänzend*]; his hair black, but not woolly [*nicht wollicht*], like the hair of the Moors [*Mohren*], but long, his nose was short, but not flat [*kurz, aber nicht flach*]; his lips were small [*klein*] and his teeth white, like ivory. In his ears he wore various feathers and shells, ornaments on which he seemed to lay no small value. Otherwise he was entirely naked from head to toe."[65] Not surprisingly, the description is much shorter than Defoe's, and differs considerably from it. As we have seen, in *Robinson Crusoe*, Defoe was deeply preoccupied with the mutability, indeed, impossibility, of identity. Throughout his novel he toyed with such notions as European cannibalism, savagery, and slavery, and contested the boundaries between Europe and its Others only to rebuild them with the tools of revelation. For Defoe, the physical description of Friday served as a means to further test the elasticity of identity. Friday's description collapses rigid categories of difference; he (indeed, like Crusoe himself) is depicted as being at once savage and civilized, same and Other, European and Caribbean. But all this was of little interest to Campe, who had an altogether different project and target audience in mind. Accordingly, Campe's description of Freitag's physique is an extremely simplified version of the original, which lacks the complexities and uncertainties that characterize Defoe's treatment of the Caribbean body. Campe retains the contrast between Freitag's nose and hair to that of Africans, but, contrary to Defoe, he makes no attempt to Europeanize the savage. Indeed, difference for Campe is a much simpler phenomenon than it is for Defoe, and its seat is the surface of the skin.

Before reviewing Campe's treatment of skin color, let us briefly review its place in Defoe's earlier text. Similarly to other authors of his time, Defoe treats skin color as an extremely marginal characteristic. Crusoe notes the savage's skin color only after discussing a litany of other physical traits, including height, physical build, age, expressions, hair, forehead, and eyes. In addition, in discussing the savage's skin, he seems to be devoting a great deal more attention to what it is not ("not quite black;" "not of that ugly yellow") than to which color it actually is. Through Defoe's somewhat confusing discussion, the color of Friday's skin emerges as a kind of anti-color that is, to quote the author, "not very easy to describe." In Campe's description of Freitag, on the other hand, color takes on an entirely different meaning. Indeed, not only does Campe change the (anti-)color of the savage's skin to a succinct "blackish brown," but he also promotes the discussion of color to very beginning of the description. In fact, color is one of the first two things the late eighteenth-century Krusoe notices about his savage, the first (not surprisingly, considering the genre of the text) being the savage's age. Hair, physiognomy, and even nudity are demoted to marginal positions in Campe's text, while skin color (at this point, presumably, merely in the sense of formal color) takes center stage. It is difficult to ascertain whether Campe's reorganization of the mise-en-scène of Friday's anatomical components is a deliberate literary maneuver. It is clearly, however, not incidental. The same kind of emphasis on skin color appears in other works by Campe, such as in his *Entdeckung von Amerika*, or his description of Bontekoe's "discovery" of Palau. Once again, in these descriptions, Campe places much more emphasis on skin color than the original authors, who marginalize color, in some cases, to the point of ignoring it completely.[66]

It is a well-known fact that when one gazes at savages, savages often gaze back. And indeed, not surprisingly, skin color plays a central role not only in the German Krusoe's assessment of Freitag, but also in the savage's perception of him. In this corresponding description, color once again plays a central role, so much so that it takes the form of a pervasive colonialist tool. In a demonstration of characteristic savage naïveté, Freitag takes Krusoe to be a kind of deity, a superhuman being. As Gananath Obeyesekere and others have argued, the apotheosis of the European traveler is a recurring motif in early modern discourse of discovery and serves a clear colonial purpose. However, whereas earlier descriptions tied the savage tendency to deify Europeans with their technological backwardness or with their effeminacy, in Campe's description it is Whiteness to which European divinity is attributed. Campe explains: "He [Freitag] was encouraged in this belief by the European whiteness of [Krusoe's] skin, and his long beard, which made him appear completely different from Friday and his blackish-brown and beardless countrymen."[67]

That the differences between Defoe and Campe's treatment of skin color are indicative of a larger cultural trend is evident from some of the later editions, adaptations, and translations of *Robinson der Jüngere*. In an 1827 German adaptation, for instance, the contrast of

Friday/Freitag's physical characteristics (and especially his nose and hair) with those of other savages, and particularly Africans, is abandoned completely. Instead we find the following succinct account: "This [Freitag] was a young and well-built man; his skin was brown [*bräunlich*], his hair black and straight, his teeth as white as ivory."[68] A similar phenomenon is found in Franz Geiger's 1794 adaptation of the book in which Campe's description of the savage appears almost in full, and only the passages contrasting the savage's hair and nose with those of "Moors" have been omitted.[69] The description is complimented by an illustration (fig. 12) in which Freitag appears as black-skinned and curly haired, his visage betraying a flat nose and protruding lips, traits that in contemporaneous discourse were traditionally affiliated with Africans.

The emerging picture of a "Negroization" of the Caribbean savage is reinforced by a reading of some of the Jewish translations of Campe's *Robinson der Jüngere*. In the 1813 German-in-Hebrew-characters edition, we find the following description: "[Freitag] was well built, about twenty, his skin was brown [ברוין], his hair coarse and black [טטארר אונד שווארץ], his nose short [קורצי נאזי], his lips small, his teeth white."[70] In this translation, not only are the passages contrasting the savage with Africans omitted, but Friday/Freitag's once fine hair now becomes coarse. An 1820 Yiddish translation of Campe's book perfects the trend of Negroization by describing Freitag's skin as "black-brown [שְׁוַוארְץ בְּרוֹין] and brilliant like velvet [וויא אַסאַמעט], the hair long and black, the nose short and wide [קוּרְץ אוּנ בְּרֵייט], the lips small but crimson red, the teeth white as snow, healthy and bright as alabaster."[71] In this description, skin color becomes the first (and presumably foremost) marker of the savage's identity. Indeed, the entire description is dominated by a contrasting of colors; the crimson red of the lips compliments the blackness of the skin, which is contrasted with the snowy whiteness of the alabaster teeth. Like many of his predecessors, the author omits Campe's contrasting of the savage's hair with that of "the Moors," as well as his mention of the thinness of his lips, which is another means of distinguishing him from Africans. Instead, he adds to the Caribbean savage a short and wide nose, which stands in direct contrast to Campe's description of Freitag's nose as being "short but not flat."

In the 1849 Hebrew translation of Campe's text, the Negroization of the savage is made explicit, and Freitag is referred to as "a descendant of the Kushites" [מבני כושים הוא]. Similarly, in Zamość's 1824

Figure 12. Robinson and Freitag, from Franz Xavier Geiger, *Der neue Robinson oder Seefahrten und Schicksale eines Deutschen*. 1794; repr. Reutlingen, 1837. Courtesy of the University of Michigan Library.

translation he and his tribesmen are referred to simply as "Blacks" [שחורים].[72] This process is subsequently perfected in the twentieth century, when in both popular and academic imagination Friday assumes the image of a Black African man. Thus, for instance, in 1979 Yiddish scholar David Roskies referred to Freitag as a "Black man," whereas in 1981 a study by Israeli children's literature scholar Uriel Ofek referred to Friday as a "Kushite" [כושי].[73]

This misrepresentation of Friday is not exclusive to scholars of Jewish studies. Roxann Wheeler points to the tendency amongst contemporary English scholars to portray Friday not as an Amerindian but as a Black African. Wheeler ties this misnomer to scholarly anachronism, claiming that the current preoccupation with chromatism amongst American scholars dyes the past in black and white.[74] However, as Wheeler herself notes in a later study, the confusion of Friday with Africans is not a purely contemporary phenomenon, nor is it exclusively characteristic of American scholars. Indeed, the roots of the misnomer may be found already in the frontispiece to the 1720 edition of Defoe's work, in which the Caribbean Islanders appear as Black. Wheeler attributes discrepancy between the text and its illustration particularly to the realities of eighteenth-century colonial slavery and demography. And indeed, whereas in Defoe's novel slavery is at once attributed to Europeans, Muslims, Caribbean Islanders, and Africans, in the years following the publication of the work, because of the massive importation of Black Africans into the Americas, as well as their assimilation with native population, it became more and more associated with Blacks. Thus, the image of the slave was subsequently blackened, and Friday's ambivalent status as a kind of servant-slave rendered him Black in popular as well as scholarly imagination.[75] A similar phenomenon of Negroization is found in the late eighteenth-century treatment of other famous literary slaves, such as Steele's Yarico, who, in several adaptations of the tale, becomes a Black African and Defoe's Xury.[76]

The 1720 frontispiece of *Robinson Crusoe* notwithstanding, however, it appears that the Negroization trend was intensified in the last quarter of the eighteenth century. This process becomes clear from the above comparison of editions of *Robinson der Jüngere* that demonstrates the consistent blackening of Freitag and his countrymen. Viewed thus, in the context of a dynamic historical process, the confusion surrounding Friday's ethnicity becomes part of a larger historical phenomenon. As Pierre Boulle explains: "The confused identification of the Caribs and Blacks, by lumping together two colonial peoples into one inferior non-white group, was a significant step in the emerging racist, Manichaean, vision of the world."[77] And indeed, the emergence of modern notions of race during the late eighteenth century was marked by a growing tendency to describe difference between various groups through the binary terms of "Black" and "White." In the wake of this dichotomizing discourse, ambiguous beings, such as "White Negros," "wild men," or "monsters," which had fascinated early modern thinkers, began to fall out of favor. These creatures were now thought of as tasteless anomalies, from which nothing may be gleaned on the nature of Man. As we have seen, this process bore unique significance for the Jews, whose place in this new regime of identities was shrouded with doubt.

HYBRID HEBREWS: MASKILIC TRANSLATIONS AND THE SELF-COLONIZING JEW

Maskilic translations form a fascinating meeting point between the Jewish and "general" Enlightenments. The relatively lenient norms of maskilic translation allowed the translators to divert freely from their source texts, thus offering an instructive view into the ways in which new notions of identity and difference, which began to dominate late eighteenth-century discourse, were adapted and domesticated as they reached a Jewish reading public. In addition, maskilic translations reveal an intriguing dilemma, one that was integral to the Jewish Haskalah. On the one hand, they demonstrate the desire of maskilic Jews to acculturate themselves by conforming to the standards of a hegemonic culture that they perceived as higher. And indeed, in a great deal of maskilic translations, stories of the colonization and acculturation of savage peoples and lands are harnessed to promote the internal colonization of European Jews. On the other hand, however, the translators often did their utmost to limit the effects of non-Jewish ideas within the translated text. They did so by omitting words, paragraphs, and whole chapters, inserting their own thoughts and ideas, and often radically changing their source texts to comply with the unique limitations and requirements of the Hebrew literary system of their time. In addition, the translators domesticated their source texts by dressing them in Jewish garments and phrasing them in biblical Hebrew. The latter translational norm may be viewed as an attempt to construct a kind of "Jewish authenticity" by assuming the language of the "pre-diasporic Jew." It is worth noting that in shifting the focus from rabbinical to biblical Judaism, the maskilim were conforming with the widespread belief amongst Enlightenment scholars, according to which there was nothing innately wrong with the Jewish bible, but the rabbis, with their scholasticism, their Mishnah, and their Talmud, had corrupted the faith.[78] It should be stressed, however, that even though they accepted Christian standards, ideals, and even assessments of Judaism, and even though they viewed the "improvement" of Jewish culture as achievable only through the importation of non-Jewish influences, still most maskilic authors had no intention of giving up the cultural or religious uniqueness of the Jews. They viewed themselves as a kind of latter-day Moses, who, by combining non-Jewish education with a profound sense of loyalty to Jewish faith, society, and culture, would finally liberate the Jews and lead them to their glorious destiny. What they yearned for was the creation of a kind of hybrid Jew, at once Jewish and European; a Jewish citizen of the state who would conveniently blend into his non-Jewish surroundings without surrendering his Jewish self. Translation was perceived as the ideal means of achieving this goal, allowing for the careful importation of European elements into Jewish culture in domesticated form.

Translation, it is often said, is a negotiation of meanings, the outcome of which is hybridity and newness.[79] Maskilic translations are a prime example. In his attitude toward the hegemonic, non-Jewish (as well as the subaltern Jewish) culture, the maskilic translator is deeply ambivalent; he is simultaneously submissive and subversive; he accepts, yet he adapts; he at once embraces and rejects his source. It is here, in the utterly impassable divide that separates source text from target text, self from other, colonizer from colonized, that the deepest fantasies and anxieties of both the hegemonic and the subaltern cultures are most vividly revealed.

Epilogue. A Terrible Tale

Some Final Thoughts on Jews and Race

The Jew is a chameleon who everywhere assumes the colors of the different climates he inhabits, of the different peoples he frequents, and of the different governments under which he lives.
—ISAAC DE PINTO, 1762

Chameleons are curious creatures. Their ability for camouflage allows them to blend in with their environment, thus both protecting them from predators and allowing them to ambush their own prey undetected. Camouflage is at once a protective and an offensive strategy. It is not a means of waiving difference, but rather of concealing it. The chameleon may resemble its habitat, but it will never become identical with it. It is doubtful that De Pinto would have conceded to such a subversive reading of his famous analogy. His primary interest was merely to suggest the inherent and radical reformability of the Jews, a quality he justifiably took to be most attractive to an Enlightenment thinker like Voltaire, to whom the analogy was addressed. And yet the analogy seems to invite further scrutiny, for the chameleon is not merely known for its ability to camouflage itself. Its other distinctive feature is its eyes, which can rotate and focus independently from one another. These eyes rotate 360 degrees, thus allowing the chameleon to look at two different objects at one and the same time.

Jewish discourse on race was characterized by an even more complex vision. In discussing difference, Jewish authors focused their observations on both the Other without, the savage, as well as the Other within, the Christian, and, finally, upon their own selves. They were at once outsiders looking in, insiders looking out, and Jews looking at themselves. Forever aware of their unique position within European identity discourse, they harnessed this discourse, and the transformations it underwent throughout the century, to promote their own unique agendas. Indeed, in their unique usage of racial discourse, eighteenth-century Jews reveal quite vividly that the appropriation of colonial symbols by subaltern groups is not always as naïve as it may appear at face value. Let us review one final example.

In the course of the previous chapters, we have had several encounters with the Polish maskil David Zamość. A devout follower and Hebrew translator of Campe, and the author of numerous stories, plays, and poems of his own, Zamość was the most prolific children's writer of his time. Amongst his plethora of works, there is one story that deserves particular attention. The story appeared in 1827 under the title "A Terrible Tale" [מעשה נורא], and it affords an invaluable opportunity to discuss the changes that occurred in Jewish uses and representations of race, from Glikl's time to the early nineteenth century.

Zamość tells of two children, Yoḥanan and Miriam, who are stranded alone on an East Indian island. The children spend over a decade alone on the island, until one day they are discovered by a band of "black savages," who take them back with them to their home island. Within a short while, the savage king falls deeply in love with Miriam and offers to marry her. The girl declines and explains her reluctance to marry the king given his cannibalism and polytheism. In response, Yoḥanan decides to redeem the king of his uncouth ways by poisoning the local monkey god. According to his plan, once the savages witness the death of their god, they will realize that he is a simple monkey and not an actual deity. The plan, of course, goes miserably wrong—the savages resent the murder of their god and sentence the children to death. Eventually, the children are saved by the neighboring Spanish colonists, and the story ends happily with Miriam's marriage to the colony's Christian king.[1]

Zamość presents his tale as a translation from the French, but there is reason to suspect that the story is in fact a fictitious translation. As Toury explains, subversive or radically new ideas, when presented in the form of translation, are often more tolerated than the same ideas when they appear in the context of an original work. It is thus tempting for authors working within a system undergoing cultural change "to try and put the cultural gatekeepers to sleep by presenting a text as if it were translated, thus lowering the threshold of resistance to the novelties it may hold in store."[2] The suspicion that "A Terrible Tale" is in fact Zamość's original creation arises from his omission of the name of the original author of the tale, which stands in stark contrast to his custom in both this anthology and other works. It could be that

Zamość chose to omit the name of the original writer simply because the tale had been written by an author of little literary prestige. As we have seen, this was not without precedent in the maskilic literary world. However, the supposition that the story is Zamość's own is further supported by some of its narrative components, most important of which is the protagonists' young age of marriage (Yoḥanan marries at the age of fifteen, whereas Miriam is wed at the tender age of thirteen). Even though French law permitted the marriage of thirteen-year-old girls, the average age of betrothal for eighteenth-century French women was much higher (around twenty-four or twenty-five).[3] Consequently, it may be imagined that had the story originated in France, the young age of the children's marriage would have raised some eyebrows. For eighteenth- and early nineteenth-century East European Jews, on the other hand, early marriage was not uncommon. Indeed, according to Katz, within the Jewish community of the time "sixteen was considered the proper age for a girl, and eighteen at the latest for a boy. Parents were never censured, indeed, they were praised, for arranging a match for daughters of thirteen or fourteen and sons of fifteen or sixteen, and even for marrying off their children at such young ages."[4] Younger brides and grooms were not a rare sight in eighteenth-century Poland; Dov of Bolechow, for instance, was wed at the age of twelve, whereas Salomon Maimon was famously betrothed when he was no older than eleven years old.[5]

Whether or not Zamość's story is an original creation, it is clear that the story has been specially tailored to meet the needs of early nineteenth-century Jewish readership. Like other maskilic translators of his time, Zamość domesticated his tale by lacing the story with biblical verses and Judaizing the narrative setting, to the extent of choosing Jewish names for the protagonists, though with a certain, perhaps sly, allusion to Christianity. The choice of Jewish names permits a reading of the tale as a story depicting an intercultural encounter between Jews, savages, and, toward the end of the story, Christians. Viewed thus, as a Jewish colonial fantasy, we are immediately confronted by the story's startling similarity to Glikl's tale of the savage woman, discussed in Chapter 1. Written over a century apart, both stories deliver the fates of Jews who are stranded in the East Indies, confronted by savages, and saved by Christians. Moreover, in both stories the Jew is depicted as the object of a (literally noble) savage lust, and, in both, the savages' advances are emphatically declined. Also present in both tales is the Christian corollary to the tale of savage pursuit; both stories depict not only savage leaders lusting after Jews, but also Christians suitors. Finally, both tales use the image of the savage to point to certain similarities between Jews and Christians. As we have seen, this last motif is ubiquitous in eighteenth- and early nineteenth-century Jewish literature, appearing also in a third Jewish encounter story, Horowitz's *Amudey beyt Yehudah.*

But there are also some important differences between these three encounter stories, some of which offer a tantalizing example of the changes that occurred in notions of identity and alterity throughout the long eighteenth century. One such difference has to do with the three authors' understanding of the meanings of intercultural encounter and the possibilities that are contained therein. As will be recalled, Glikl's treatment of the colonial encounter offers an unconventional expression of a kind of colonial indifference. The protagonist of Glikl's tale rejects the possibility of a union with the savage woman and, in contrast to other, primarily non-Jewish travelers of his time, he makes no attempt to domesticate, enslave, or conquer her, whether romantically or politically. In Horowitz's tale, on the other hand, the intercultural encounter is framed within a colonialist worldview. Horowitz reads the encounter as an invitation to acculturation both of the savage without (Ira) as well as of the savage within (the Jews). Through the interaction with the Jewish travelers, the savage is rendered civilized and in turn becomes an emblem for the maskilic acculturation project itself.

Like Horowitz before him but to a much greater degree, Zamość too constructs his narrative with the tools of colonialist discourse. Miriam and Yoḥanan's immediate impulse upon encountering the savages is to acculturate them. Indeed, such acculturation is named by Miriam as a precondition for her marriage to the savage king. As we have seen, marital fantasies were ubiquitous in eighteenth-century colonial writing and were a means of imagining a legitimate and "natural" form of European expansionism. And yet in Zamość's version the colonial aspirations of acculturation and betrothal are frustrated by the savages' inability to "evolve" to the level of Europeans. In this sense, Zamość demonstrates a deterministic understanding of savagery, quite different from his predecessors' mutable notions of difference. For Zamość, it appears, savagery cannot be remedied by education; it is not the outcome of climate or customs (in fact, both the Jewish children and the savages are raised in more or less similar circumstances) but rather the product of some innate quality, some essential difference, something, perhaps, like skin color. Indeed, in stark contrast to Glikl and Horowitz, who make no note of skin color or racial traits at all in their tales, in Zamość's story skin color takes the form of a primary marker of difference between savages and Jews. The significance of skin color for Zamość is nowhere more evident than in the author's choice of language to describe his main protagonists, Yoḥanan and Miriam. Prior to their encounter with the savages, the two are consistently referred to as "children," whereas immediately following the encounter with the savages' dark skin, and consistently throughout the remainder of the tale, they are no longer referred to as "children" but rather as "Whites."[6] Whiteness thus supersedes all other signifiers of identity, including geography, religion, and even age. That Zamość is referring to a special kind of Whiteness in his story, not the formal shade of skin that played so central a role in Lindau's taxonomy, may be gleaned from the story's ending, in which we discover that the circumstances of their life, combined with the East Indian climate, has rendered the children so dark that to the eyes of the Spanish colonists they appear black.[7]

The black Whiteness of Yoḥanan and Miriam corresponds with another important point of difference between Zamość's tale and Glikl and Horowitz's earlier accounts. In all three stories the image of the savage serves as a means to establish a close proximity between Christians and Jews. In Glikl and Horowitz's narratives, this proximity is based on religion and culture, whereas for Zamość it is achieved by turning to notions of skin color and race. However, it is not only the ways in which proximity is achieved that is different in the three tales, but also its outcome. In Zamość's tale, the early modern fantasy of the colonial wedding reappears in the story of the wedding between the Jewish girl and the Spanish colonial governor. "And the governor," we are told, "heard the story of Miriam, and thought: this maiden is poor and black [שׁחורה] as the sun hath looked upon her. I would be wise to take her for a wife, instead of a handsome rich man's daughter."[8] In Zamość's tale, then, the colonial fantasy receives an interesting twist, in which the role of the exotic woman, who is subjugated to a hegemonic colonist, is played not by an East Indian native but rather by a Jewish girl who is deemed appealing to a Christian man in her feral wretchedness. This meager child, a victim of her circumstances, serves Zamość as an allegory for the Jewish community. Through the image of Miriam, the author presents the Jews as inferior to Christians as a result of their historical circumstances and (contrary to the savages) not of their nature. This depiction of the Jew as a poor, neglected orphan girl redeemed by a Christian prince stands in direct contrast to Glikl's depiction of the Jewish woman as proud and self-assured. Indeed, let us recall that in Glikl's version of the erotic encounter between the Christian man and the Jewish woman, the woman charms her suitor with her beauty, gentleness, and wit, only to vehemently decline his advances. Zamość's colonial fantasy thus emerges as a kind of inversion of Glikl's tale. Indeed, in contrast to Glikl's protagonist who, at the end of the tale, becomes a ruler over the Judaized Christian sailors, Zamość's Miriam becomes queen by marrying a hegemonic Christian man. This colonial fantasy is, of course, a far cry from Glikl's Judeocentric thought or even from Horowitz's fantasy of a union of equals. For Zamość, a devout maskil and prolific Hebrew translator of German and French texts, the salvation of the Jew can be achieved only by subjugating Jewish culture to Christian culture, thus achieving an unequal union between Christians and Jews.

Glikl, Horowitz, and Zamość offer their readers three stories of stranded Jews ranging from both ends of the long eighteenth century. These three stories demonstrate the changes that occurred in the uses and understandings of race in Jewish thought, from Glikl's time through the early Jewish Enlightenment and into the nineteenth-century Haskalah. These changes correspond with cultural transformations that occurred inside the Jewish community, but they are also inspired by changing notions of identity within Christian Europe, which manifested themselves in Europeans' attitudes toward both the Other without—the savage—as well as toward the Other within—the Jew. Throughout this period, the shifts of meaning in discourse surrounding race played an essential role in Jewish authors' perceptions of both Christians and non-Europeans, as well as in the construction of their own identity. From Glikl's sense of superiority through Horowitz's quest for equality to Zamość's feelings of inferiority, Jewish thinkers utilized the image of the savage as a means to redraw the lines that separated Europe from its Others, and to construct an ideal of fraternity between Jews and Christians to be based on religion and culture, or, conversely, on skin color and race.

NOTES

INTRODUCTION

1. V. S. Naipaul, *The Mimic Men* (1967; repr. Middlesex, 1969), 5.

2. For a discussion of this paradigm and its drawbacks, see Benjamin Isaac, Joseph Ziegler, and Miriam Eliav-Feldon, Introduction to *Origins of Racism in the West*, ed. Isaac, Ziegler, and Eliav-Feldon (Cambridge, 2009), 2.

3. For some of the most important contributions to this field, see Dror Wahrman, *The Making of the Modern Self: Identity and Culture in Eighteenth-Century England* (New Haven, 2004); Roxann Wheeler, *The Complexion of Race: Categories of Difference in Eighteenth-Century British Culture* (Philadelphia, 2000); Felicity Nussbaum, *Torrid Zones: Maternity, Sexuality, and Empire in Eighteenth-Century English Narratives* (Baltimore, 1995).

4. Some notable examples are John H. Zammito, "Policing Polygeneticism in Germany, 1775 (Kames,) Kant, and Blumenbach," in *The German Invention of Race*, ed. Sara Eigen and Mark Larrimore (Albany, 2006); Susanne Zantop, *Colonial Fantasies: Conquest, Family and Nation in Precolonial Germany, 1770–1870* (Durham, NC, 1997).

5. See, e.g., Felicity Nussbaum, "Women and Race: A Difference of Complexion," in *Women and Literature in Britain, 1700–1800*, ed. Vivien Jones (Cambridge, 2000); Julia V. Douthwaite, *Exotic Women: Literary Heroines and Cultural Strategies in Ancien Régime France* (Philadelphia, 1992); Billie Melman, *Women's Orients: English Women and the Middle East: 1718–1918* (London, 1992).

6. Isaac de Pinto, "Réflexions critiques sur le premier chapitre de VIIe. tome des Œuvres de M. de Voltaire, &c." in *Lettres de quelques Juifs Portugais, Allemands et Polonois, à M. de Voltaire*, Vol. 1 (1762; repr., Paris, 1781), 12–13.

7. See, e.g., Eli Faber, *Jews, Slaves, and the Slave Trade: Setting the Record Straight* (New York, 1998); Saul S. Friedman, *Jews and the American Slave Trade* (London, 1998); Harold D. Brackman, *Ministry of Lies: The Truth Behind the Nation of Islam's 'The Secret Relationship Between Blacks and Jews'* (New York, 1994); Joshua Rothenberg, "Black-Jewish

Relations in Eighteenth-Century Newport," *Rhode Island Jewish Historical Notes* 2 (1992): 117–71; Paul H.D. Kaplan, "Jewish Artists and Images of Black Africans in Renaissance Venice," in *Multicultural Europe and Cultural Exchange in the Middle Ages and Renaissance*, ed. James P. Helfers (Turnhout, 2005), 81–90, esp. 89–90. On the polemical nature of this corpus of studies, and its discernible drawbacks, see Jonathan Schorsch, "American Jewish Historians, Colonial Jews and Blacks, and the Limits of 'Wissenschaft': A Critical Review," *Jewish Social Studies* 6, no. 2 (2000): 102–32. A similar focus on Jews and Blacks is also prevalent in scholarship surrounding Jews in the Muslim world. For a recent example, see David M. Goldenberg, "It Is Permitted to Marry a Kushite," *AJS Review* 37, no. 1 (2013): 29–49.

8. Jonathan Schorsch, *Jews and Blacks in the Early Modern World* (Cambridge, 2004), 292. A similar approach is found in Abraham Melamed, *The Image of the Black in Jewish Culture: A History of the Other* (London, 2003).

9. Schorsch, *Jews and Blacks*, 12 and throughout.

10. Two recent exceptions are Martin Jacobs's discussion of Medieval Jewish travel literature to the Orient and Limor Mintz-Manor's dissertation on images of Native Americans in Jewish thought from the sixteenth to the mid-seventeenth century. These studies offer important contributions to the study of Jews and race, and may point to a change in the historiographical approach. See Martin Jacobs, "From Lofty Caliphs to Uncivilized Orientals—Images of the Muslim in Medieval Jewish Travel Literature," *Jewish Studies Quarterly* 18 (2011): 64–90; Limor Mintz-Manor, "Ha-siah al ha-olam ha-hadash ba-tarbut ha-yehudit ba-et ha-hadashah ha-mukdemet" (Ph.D. diss., Hebrew University of Jerusalem, 2011).

11. Roxann Wheeler, "The Complexion of Desire: Racial Ideology and Mid-Eighteenth-Century British Novels," *Eighteenth-Century Studies* 32, no. 3 (1999): 309.

12. For a further discussion of the historiographical discourse surrounding Jews and Blacks, and its shortcomings, see Iris Idelson-Shein, "'Barukh meshaneh ha-briot': Dmuto ve-shimushav shel ha-ekzoty ba-neorut ha-yehudit" (Ph.D. diss., Tel Aviv University, 2010); Mintz-Manor, "Ha-siah," 25–28.

13. Robert Liberles, "'She Sees That Her Merchandise Is Good, and Her Lamp Is Not Extinguished at Nighttime': Glikl's Memoir as Historical Source," *Nashim: A Journal of Jewish Women's Studies & Gender Issues* 7 (2004): 11–27.

14. On the importance of a contextualization of the eighteenth-century Haskalah, see David Sorkin, "Ha-haskalah be-Berlin: Perspektivah hashvaatit," in *Ha-haskalah ligvaneyha: Iyunim hadashim be-toldot ha-haskalah u-sifrutah*, ed. Shmuel Feiner and Israel Bartal (Jerusalem, 2005), 8.

CHAPTER 1

1. For some examples, see Zantop, *Colonial Fantasies*; Louis Montrose, "The Work of Gender in the Discourse of Discovery," *Representations* 33

(1991): 1–41; Margarita Zamora, "Abreast of Columbus: Gender and Discovery," *Cultural Critique* 17 (1990–1991): 127–49.

2. On the problems inherent in the scholarly tendency to focus exclusively on the colonial uses of European discourse on non-Europeans, see Judith Butler, *Bodies That Matter: On the Discursive Limits of "Sex"* (New York, 1993), 18–19. See also Jonathan M. Hess, *Germans, Jews and the Claims of Modernity* (New Haven, 2002), 15; Johann J.K. Reusch, "Germans as Noble Savages and Castaways: Alter Egos and Alterity in German Collective Consciousness During the Long Eighteenth Century," *Eighteenth-Century Studies* 42, no. 1 (2008): 91–129; Traci S. O'Brien, "A 'Daughter of the Occident' Travels to the 'Orient': Ida von Hahn-Hahn's 'The Countess Faustina' and 'Letters from the Orient," *Women in German Yearbook* 24 (2008): 26–27.

3. For a publication history of the memoirs, and a discussion of their reception within Jewish studies circles, see Turniansky, introduction to *Zikhronot Glikl, 1691–1719*, trans. Chava Turniansky (Jerusalem, 2006), 44–60; Dorothy Bilik, "The Memoirs of Glikl of Hameln: The Archeology of the Text," *Yiddish* 8, no. 2 (1992): 5–22.

4. See Turniansky, introduction, 9–44; Davis, *Women on the Margins: Three Seventeenth-Century Lives* (London, 1995), 8–62.

5. On the difference between the economical status of Christian and Jewish women during the period, see Debra Kaplan, "Women and Worth: Female Access to Property in Early Modern Urban Jewish Communities," *Leo Baeck Institute Year Book* 55 (2010): 3, 11, 13–21. On Christian women and work: Heide Wunder, *He Is the Sun, She Is the Moon: Women in Early Modern Germany*, trans. Thomas Dunlap (Cambridge, 1998), 81–83; Martha Howell, "The Gender of Europe's Commercial Economy, 1200–1700," *Gender and History* 20, no. 3 (2008): 519–38; Claudia Ulbrich, *Shulamit und Margarete: Macht, Geschlecht und Religion in einer ländlichen Gesellschaft des 18. Jahrhunderts* (Wien, 1999), 109–15; Merry E. Wiesner, "Having Her Own Smoke: Employment and Independence for Single Women in Germany, 1400–1750," in *Single Women in the European Past, 1250–1800*, ed. Judith M. Bennett and Amy M. Froide (Philadelphia, 1999), 192–213. On Jewish women and work: Yemima Ḥovav, *Alamot ahevukha: Ḥayey hadat ve-ha-ruaḥ shel nashim yehudiyot be-Ashkenaz ba-et ha-ḥadashah ha-mukdemet* (Jerusalem, 2009), 225–56; Frauke von Rohden, introduction to Rivkah bat Meir, *Meneket Rivkah—A Manual of Wisdom and Piety for Jewish Women* (c. 1609, repr. Philadelphia, 2009), trans. Samuel Spinner, ed. Frauke von Rohden, 1–2; Robert Liberles, "On the Threshold of Modernity," in *Jewish Daily Life in Germany 1618–1945*, ed. Marion A. Kaplan (Oxford, 2005), 59–61.

6. I have chosen to utilize Chava Turniansky's excellent critical edition of Glikl's memoirs, which includes the entire memoirs in their original Yiddish version as well as a Hebrew translation. In my English citations of Glikl, I have consulted Beth-Zion Abrahams's 1962 English translation, which I have checked against Glikl's original Yiddish. References to both sources appear parenthetically in the text, where G. Tur. refers to the Yiddish text and G. Abr. to the English translation. I have often chosen to modify the Abrahams

translation according to the Yiddish text. For the above quotation, see G. Tur., 501; G. Abr., 500.

7. On the literary nature of the memoirs, see Turniansky, "Dmut ha-ishah be-zikhronoteyah shel Glikl Hamel," in *Eros, erusin ve-isurin: Mini-yut u-mishpaḥah ba-historiah*, ed. Israel Bartal and Isaiah Gafni (Jerusalem, 1998), 179–80. Early modern memoirists often tended to open their texts with stories of the family's past. See, e.g., Pinchas Katzenelbogen, *Yesh manḥilin* (eighteenth century; repr. Jerusalem, 1986), especially pp. 81, 156–57; Yehudah Arieh Leon Modena, *Ḥayey Yehudah* (1648; repr. Jerusalem, 1968), 17–20; Anon./Alexander Marx, "A Seventeenth-Century Autobiography" [English and Hebrew], *Jewish Quarterly Review* 8, no. 3 (1918): 276–78; Salomon Maimon, *Geschichte des eigenen Lebens* (1792; repr. Berlin, 1935), 4–13.

8. Maimon, *Geschichte*, esp. 26–125; Henriette Herz, "Jugenderinnerungen von Henriette Herz," in *Henriette Herz: Ihr Leben und ihre Zeit*, ed. H. Landsberg (c. 1823/1850; repr. Weimar, 1913), 101–54; Mordecai Aharon Günzberg, *Aviezer* (Vilnius, 1863).

9. See Turniansky's brief discussion in "Dmut ha-ishah," 182; Turniansky and Chana Amit, Interview, *Davka: Eretz Yiddish u-tarbutah* 2 (2007): 4.

10. Chaim's death is described in details in G. Tur., 360–69. For the descriptions of the deaths of her children, see G. Tur, 232–35, 350–51, 414–15, 552–55.

11. Asher Ha-levi, *Sefer zikhronot* (1598–1635; repr. Berlin, 1913), 8–10, 18, 35; Jacob Emden, *Megilat sefer* (c. 1776, repr. Warsaw, 1896), 62, 64–65, 84, 114, 151, 160–61. Following J. J. Schacter's justified critique of the more recent edition of *Megilat sefer*, ed. Bick, I have chosen to utilize the older edition of the memoirs. See Jacob J. Schacter, "History and Memory of Self: The Autobiography of Rabbi Jacob Emden," in *Jewish History and Jewish Memory: Essays in Honor of Yosef Hayim Yerushalmi*, ed. Elisheva Carlebach, John Efron, David M. Myers (Hanover, NH, 1998), 446n13.

12. Marcus Moseley, *Being for Myself Alone: Origins of Jewish Autobiography* (Stanford, 2006), 164–65.

13. On laundresses in early modern Germany, see Wiesner, "Her Own Smoke," 204.

14. See Davis, *Women on the Margins*, 245n138–39; "Glikl bas Judah Leib—ein jüdisches, ein europäisches Leben," in *Die Hamburger Kauffrau Glikl: Jüdische Existenz in der frühen Neuzeit*, ed. Monika Richarz (Hamburg, 2001), 43–44; Turniansky, "Ha-sipurim be zikhronot Glikl me-Hameln u-mekorteyhem," *Meḥkarey Yerushalayim be-folklor Yehudy* 16 (1983): 56–63.

15. Riemer, "Some Parallels of Stories in Glikl of Hameln Zikhroynes," *Pardes: Zeitschrift der Vereinigung für Jüdische Studien* 14 (2008): 125–48. Riemer offers a comparison only of the other two stories, and mentions in passing the occurrence of this tale in both texts. Cf., however, G. Tur., 80; Beila and Baer Perlhefter, *Beer sheva*, Paris edition, 9a (Paris Alliance Israelite Universelle, Ms. no. 295, photocopy at National Library Israel [NLI], reel no. F3301); Frankfurt edition, 18b: Frankfurt am Mein Stadt- und

Universitaets bibliothek, photocopy at NLI, reel no. F22030. On the Perl-hefters, see Riemer, *Zwischen Tradition und Häresie: ,Beer sheva'—eine Enzyklopädie des jüdischen Wissens der frühen Neuzeit* (Wiesbaden, 2010), 24–66. Glikl mentions that she found the story in a book written by a man named Präger (G. Tur., 106). She may be referring to the Perlhefters, who were natives of Prague, or to some other presently unknown writer.

16. Turniansky, "Introduction," 17–19. See also Moseley, *Myself Alone*, 164–65, 170.

17. For a comparison between the two versions of the story, see Riemer, "Parallels," 132–42.

18. Robert Liberles, "'She Sees That Her Merchandise Is Good, and Her Lamp Is Not Extinguished at Nighttime': Glikl's Memoir as Historical Source," *Nashim: A Journal of Jewish Women's Studies & Gender Issues* 7 (2004): 19. See also Noa Sophie Kohler, "Schutzjuden and Opportunistic Criminality in the Early Modern Period," *Leo Baeck Institute Yearbook* 55, no. 1 (2010): 144.

19. G. Abr. 4; *Zikhronot Glikl*, trans. A. Z. Rabinovich (Tel Aviv, 1929), 147.

20. For doubts concerning Glikl's image as the prototypical Yiddishe Mame and devout Jewish woman, see Turniansky, Introduction, 30–31; "Dmut ha-ishah," 186; Davis, *Women on the Margins*, 50–60; Moseley, *Being for Myself*, 166–67.

21. Richard Steele, *The Spectator*, no. 11, Tuesday, 13 March 1711, repr. in *English Trader, Indian Maid: Representing Race, Gender and Slavery in the New World*, ed. Frank Felsenstein (Baltimore, 1999), 84–85; for a discussion of the story and its sources, see 1–14.

22. For a more nuanced discussion of Steele's version of the "Inkle and Yarico" tale, see Nicole Horejsi, "'A Counterpart to the Ephesian Matron': Steel's 'Inkle and Yarico' and a Feminist Critique of the Classics," *Eighteenth-Century Studies* 39 (2006): 201–26; Peter Hulme, *Colonial Encounters: Europe and the Native Caribbean 1492–1797* (London, 1992), 239. For a selection of popular versions of the story, see Felsenstein, *English Trader*; Lawrence M. Price, *Inkle and Yarico Album* (Berkeley, 1937).

23. English translation according to Amerigo Vespucci, "Letter to Pier Soderini," 1504; repr. in *The English Literatures of America, 1500–1800*, ed. M. Jehlin and M. Warner (New York, 1997), 20, 22. For other early accounts of similar nature, see Zamora, "Abreast of Columbus," 127–49; Montrose, "Gender in the Discourse of Discovery," 2–42.

24. For some examples, see William Dampier, "A New Voyage Round the World," 1691, repr. in *The World Displayed; Or, A Curious Collection of Voyages and Travels, Selected from the Writers of All Nations* (London, 1761), 6:85; Nicholas Creswell, *The Journal of Nicholas Cresswell, 1774–1777* (New York, 1924), 108; Mauritius A. Benyowsky, *Memoirs and Travels of Mauritius Augustus Count de Benyowsky*, 2 vols. (London, 1790), 2:11–14; William Clark and Meriwether Lewis, *The Journals of Lewis and Clark* (1804–1806; repr. New York, 2003), 243. On the uses of colonial

erotica in early modern visual art, see Sergio Perosa, *From Islands to Portraits: Four Literary Variations* (Amsterdam, 2000), 35–40.

25. Walter Raleigh, "The Discovery of the Large, Rich, and Beautiful Empire of Guiana," 1595, repr. in *The Works of Sir Walter Raleigh, Kt.* (Oxford, 1829), 8:464. For an interesting discussion of the image of land as woman and woman as land see Pamela Cheek, *Sexual Antipodes: Enlightenment, Globalization, and the Placing of Sex* (Stanford, 2003), 85–123.

26. Thomas Morton, *New English Canaan* (1637; repr. Scituate, 1999), 7; Roger Wolcott, "A Brief Account," 1725, repr. in *Specimens of American Poetry*, ed. Samuel Kettel (Boston, 1829), 24.

27. For a discussion of the colonial uses of the erotic encounter, see Wheeler, *Complexion of Race*, 137–75; Zantop, "Domesticating the Other: European Colonial Fantasies 1770–1830," in *Encountering the Other(s): Studies in Literature, History, and Culture*, ed. G. Brinker-Gabler (Albany, 1995), 269–83; Ashish Nandi, *The Intimate Enemy: Loss and Recovery of Self under Colonialism* (New York, 1983) 4–11; Elliott Horowitz, "The New World and the Changing Face of Europe," *Sixteenth Century Journal* 28, no. 4 (1997): 120; Hulme, *Colonial Encounters*, 140–41; Idelson-Shein, *Haekzoty*, 40–49.

28. Zantop, "Domesticating the Other," 271.

29. See ibid., 269–83; Zantop, *Colonial Fantasies*, 121–40; Wheeler, "Complexion of Desire," 316–17, 328; Hulme, *Colonial Encounters*, 140–41; Mary L. Pratt, *Imperial Eyes: Travel Writing and Transculturation* (London, 1992), 96–100.

30. Colman, "Inkle and Yarico: An Opera," 1787, repr. in Felsenstein, *English Trader*, 172–233.

31. Ligon, "History of the Island of Barbadoes," 1673, repr. in Felsenstein, *English Trader*, 74.

32. Salomon Gessner, "Inkel und Yariko," 1756, repr. in *Schriften*, 3 vols. (Zürich, 1795), 3:268.

33. Jean Mocquet, *Voyages en Afrique, Asie, Indes Orientales, & Occidentales faits par Jean Mocquet* (1616; repr. Rouen, 1665), 150. For a comparison between Mocquet's tale and later versions of "Inkle and Yarico," see Hulme, *Colonial Encounters*, 257–58.

34. Joachim Heinrich Campe, *Sittenbüchlein für Kinder aus gesitteten Ständen* (1777; repr. Frankfurt, 1785), 102; David Zamość, *Tokhaḥot musar* (Breslau, 1819), 176–77; Baruch Shenfeld, *Musar haskel* (1811; repr. Berlin, 1859), 53–54.

35. Davis, *Women on the Margins*, 40. In light of the narrative similarities between Glikl and the Perlhefter's tales, the analysis below applies also to the tale appearing in *Beer sheva*.

36. Mintz-Manor, "Ha-siaḥ," 107–9. For a discussion of the much more colonialist Sepharadi-Jewish view, see 252–61, 281–84.

37. Jacobs, "Images of the Muslim," 64–90. For similar observations on a later period of Jewish writing, see Kathrin Wittler, "Good to Think: (Re)Conceptualizing German-Jewish Orientalism," in *Orientalism, Gender, and the Jews: Literary and Artistic Transformations of European National*

Discourses, ed. Ulrike Brunotte, Anna-Dorothea Ludewig, and Axel Stähler (Berlin, forthcoming).

38. There were, of course, some exceptions to this rule, in the form of Ashkenazi women in the colonies. An interesting example of such a woman is the English American Abigaill Levi Franks, whose letters to her son in London constitute a further rare example of early modern Jewish feminine writing. See *The Letters of Abigaill Levy Franks 1733–1748*, ed. Edith B. Gelles (New Haven, 2004). On the marginal role played by Ashkenazi Jews in the colonial project, see Schorsch, *Jew and Blacks*, 5–6. On Jewish involvement in colonialism in general, see Bernardini and Fiering, *The Jews and the Expansion of Europe to the West* (New York, 2001).

39. I utilize the term "rape" here in its present-day meaning, based on Glikl's description: "And the pious Jew must lie with her at night" (G. Tur., 88). See, however, the discussion of the problematic definition of rape in the eighteenth century in Sharon Block, *Rape and Sexual Power in Early America* (Chapel Hill, 2006), 16–28. Interestingly, the Babylonian Talmud specifically discusses the possibility of a Jewish man being coerced by idolaters into sexual relations with a woman, but does not recognize this as rape, as it takes erection as a token of willingness. See BT Yebamoth 53b. A similar approach is expressed in Joseph Karo's authoritative halakhic manual, *Shulḥan aruḥ*, *Even ha-ezer*, 166:7.

40. A further difference is that in both Glikl and the Perlhefters' texts, the story is located in the East Indies rather than in the West Indies, as in all other version. This difference could be a result of the fact that the East Indies were much more familiar to seventeenth-century Jews, who often traded in goods imported from the East. For a short discussion of this difference, see Idelson-Shein, *Ha-ekzoty*, 36–37.

41. Stories of the rape of European women by native men, though less rare, are also surprisingly few. The relative scarcity of such rape accounts could be connected to the colonial image of the Native American men as frigid. Some changes in this image occurred toward the end of the eighteenth century. See Block, *Rape and Sexual Power*, 222–23; June Namias, *White Captives: Gender and Ethnicity on the American Frontier* (Chapel Hill, 1993), 36–48, 99–100.

42. John Thelwall, *Incle and Yarico* (1792; repr. Madison, 2006), 52.

43. Denis Diderot, "Supplément au Voyage de Bougainville," 1772, repr. In *Œuvres Completes* (Paris, 1989), 602. For another example, see Pratt, *Imperial Eyes*, 82.

44. On this practice of adopting Europeans in place of deceased tribesmen, see Namias, *White Captives*, 3–4. Interesting examples are found in James Smith, "An Account of the Captivity of Col. James Smith," in *A Selection of Some of the Most Interesting Narratives, Or the Outrages Committed by the Indians in Their Wars with the White People*, 2 vols., ed. Archibald Loudon (1808–1811; repr. Carlisle, 1888), 1:128–31; Eastburn, "A Faithful Narrative," in Loudoun, *Selection*, 2:28–33.

45. Tobias Smollett, *The Expedition of Humphry Clinker* (1771; repr. New York, 1836), 233–34.

46. Ibid., 234.

47. Ibid., 197.

48. Jonathan Swift, *Gulliver's Travels* (1726/1735; repr. New York, 1970), 95–96, 232–33.

49. Henry Fielding, *The Adventures of Joseph Andrews and His Friend Mr. Abraham Adams* (1742; repr. London, 1749), 14–17, 19–22, 28–33, 91–92.

50. John Cleland, *Fanny Hill, or, Memoirs of a Woman of Pleasure* (1748; repr. London, 2001), 197–202.

51. Maimon, *Lebensgeschichte*, 514–15. English translation according to Maimon, *Autobiography*, trans. J. Clark Murray (1888; repr. Champaign, 2001), 250.

52. Patricia Spacks, *Desire and Truth: Functions of Plot in Eighteenth-Century English Novels* (Chicago, 1994), 61. An interesting exception to this point is offered by Sade, whose literary heroines occasionally partake in the raping of both other women and, less frequently, men. These heroines' sexual aggression and acts of rape are no laughing matter. See, e.g., Donatien Alphonse François Sade, *Juliette*, 1797, repr. and trans. Austryn Wainhouse (New York, 1968), 90–91, 138, 289, 300, 326–33, 360.

53. In a previous discussion of the male-rape theme, I referred to another Jewish story of female sexual aggression that appears in the 1979 edition of Jacob Emden's *Megilat sefer*, edited by Avraham Bick. I have since found, however, that the scene does not appear in the original manuscript of Emden's memoirs, on which Bick based his edition. Compare Jacob Emden, "Megilat sefer," 155, Oxford Bodleian Library, MS Mich. 587, available in microfilm at NLI, reel no. F17754; *Megilat sefer*, ed. Avraham Bick (Jerusalem, 1979), 107.

54. Davis, *Women on the Margins*, 40, 246n. A version of the story appears in Sarah Zfatman, *Nisuey adam ve-shedah* (Jerusalem, 1987), 34–35. For a discussion of the folkloristic trope of a marriage between a man and a she-demon, see Tamar Alexander, "Ha-iẓuv ha-z'aneri shel sipurey shedim: Nisuyim beyn gever le-shedah," in *Ashnav le-ḥayeyhen shel nashim ba-ḥevrah ha-yehudit*, ed. Yael Aẓmon (Jerusalem, 1995), 291–307. Also relevant are the folktales which center on the image of Lilith. See Howard Schwartz, *Tree of Souls: The Mythology of Judaism* (Oxford, 2004), 215.

55. For these stories, see Zfatman, *Adam ve-shedah*, 25–27, 32–34, 71–72, 109–10, 119–41.

56. The tale survived in a Polish translation only. For a contemporary retranslation into Yiddish, see Zfatman, *Adam ve-shedah*, 140. A Hebrew translation is given on page 110.

57. See Nicholas Hudson, "'Why God No Kill the Devil?': The Diabolical Disruption of Order in 'Robinson Crusoe,'" *Review of English Studies*, n.s., 39, no. 156 (1988): 494–501; Hayden White, "The Forms of Wildness: Archeology of an Idea," in *The Wild Man Within: An Image in Western Thought from the Renaissance to Romanticism*, ed. Edward Dudley and Maximillian E. Novak (London, 1972), 22; Mintz-Manor, "Ha-siaḥ," 138.

See also Jeremy Dauber, *In the Demon's Bedroom: Yiddish Literature and the Early Modern* (New Haven, 2010), 144.

58. For some examples, see Eli Yassif, *Sipurey Ben Sira bi-yemey ha-beynayim* (Jerusalem, 1985), 50–59; Raphael Patai, *The Hebrew Goddess* (New York, 1967), 238.

59. On shame as a designator of the human, see Brian Cummings, "Animal Passions and Human Sciences: Shame, Blushing and Nakedness in Early Modern Europe and the New World," in *At the Borders of the Human: Beasts, Bodies and Natural Philosophy in the Early Modern Period*, ed. Erica Fudge, Ruth Gilbert, and Susan Wiseman (New York, 2002), 26–50.

60. David E. Stannard, *American Holocaust: The Conquest of the New World* (Oxford, 1992), 169.

61. On the doubts concerning the hairiness of savages, and the rise of the "hairless savage," see Gordon M. Sayre, *Les Sauvages Américains Representations of Native Americans in French and English Colonial Literature* (Chapel Hill, 1997), 154–56; Olive Patricia Dickason, *The Myth of the Savage, and the Beginnings of French Colonialism in the Americas* (Edmonton, 1984), 77–80.

62. Carl Linnaeus, *Systema Naturae per Regna Tria Naturae* (Holmiae [Stockholm], 1766), 28. For a later use of the hairy feral child motif, see Georg Christian Raff, *Naturgeschichte für Kinder* (1778; repr. Göttingen, 1781), 625. All references to Raff's *Naturgeschichte* are to this edition unless otherwise stated. For a different view, see Susi Colin, "The Wild Man and the Indian in Early 16th Century Book Illustration," in *Indians and Europe: An Interdisciplinary Collection of Essays*, ed. Christian F. Feest (Aachen, 1989), 22, 29.

63. Memmie Leblanc's appetite for frogs was infamous during the eighteenth century. See, e.g., in Baruch Lindau's discussion of Leblanc: Baruch Lindau, *Reshit limudim* (Berlin, 1788), 100b; Raff, *Naturgeschichte*, 627–31. All references to Lindau's book are to this edition unless otherwise stated. The source for the rumor was probably the famous description of the girl attributed to Condamine: [Charles Marie Condamine?]/Mme Hecquet, *Histoire d'une Jeune Fille Sauvage, Trouvée dans les Bois à l'âge de dix ans* (Paris, 1755), 21–22.

64. Anon., "Bito shel Tarzan be-harey midbar Yehudah," *Iton meyuḥad* (Adar, 1937), 6. I am grateful to Ofri Ilani for bringing the article to my attention.

65. See Ingrid Maisch, *Mary Magdalene: The Image of a Woman Through the Centuries* (Collegeville, MN, 1998), 48; Charles A. Williams, *The German Legends of the Hairy Anchorite* (Urbana, 1935); Colin, "Wild Man," 8.

66. See reproduction in Mary E. Fissel, "Hairy Women and Naked Truths: Gender and the Politics of Knowledge in Aristotle's Masterpiece," *William and Mary Quarterly* 60, no. 1 (2003): 68. Hairy women featured prominently in early modern "monster" literature as well. See Fissel, "Hairy Women," 43–73; Idelson-Shein, *Ha-ekzoty*, 74–80.

67. On these manuscripts, known in Hebrew as "sifrey evronot," and their illustrations, see Elisheva Carlebach, *Palaces of Time: Jewish Calendar*

and Culture in Early Modern Europe (Cambridge, MA, 2011), 79–114. Interestingly, a Yemenite folktale draws another parallel between Eve and Glikl's savage woman by depicting Eve as paedophagic. According to the tale, Eve was seduced by Samael and bore him a son. When Adam discovered the child, he killed it and boiled its remains. The remains were then eaten by Adam and Eve, and thus evil entered the heart of man. See Schwartz, *Tree of Souls*, 454.

68. Angela Rosenthal, "Raising Hair," *Eighteenth-Century Studies* 38, no. 1 (2004): 1–2. See also Julia Kristeva, *Powers of Horror: An Essay on Abjection*, trans. Leon. S. Roudiez (1980; repr. New York, 1982), 1–4.

69. Diane Wolfthal, *Images of Rape: The "Heroic" Tradition and Its Alternatives* (Cambridge, 1999), 162.

70. Genesis 12, 20, 34; Esther 2:5–17. For a discussion of the coerced nature of Esther's relationship with Ahasuerus, see Merav Schnitzer-Maimon, "Ha-yaḥas le-ones ba-parshanut ha-yehudit bi-yemey ha-bey-nayim" (master's thesis, Tel Aviv University, 2005), 14; Gershon Malbar, "Ones ve-aveyrot inus nosafot ba-ḥok ha-yehudy ve-ha-angly" (Ph.D. diss., Hebrew University of Jerusalem, 1960), 70–72. The motif of rape by a non-Jew also appears in early modern Jewish folktales. See, e.g., Juspa of Worms, "Sefer maaseh minhagim," c. 1678, repr. in *R' Juspa shamash d'kehilat Worms*, ed. and trans. Shlomo Eidelberg (Jerusalem, 1991), 62–63, 86–87.

71. BT Kiddushin, 39b–40a.

72. Deuteronomy 7:3.

73. Moseley, *Being for Myself Alone*, 163–64. Davis also speculates that perhaps Glikl showed some sympathy for the savage woman's travails. See Davis, "Glikl," 44.

74. On the appreciation of the "effeminate male" in premodern Jewish culture, and in Glikl's memoirs in particular, see Daniel Boyarin, *Unheroic Conduct: The Rise of Heterosexuality and the Invention of the Jewish Man* (Berkeley, 1997), 54–55.

75. See further examples in Wetenhall Wilkes, "A Letter of Genteel and Moral Advice to a Young Lady," 1740/1766, repr. in *Women in the Eighteenth-Century: Constructions of Femininity*, ed. Vivien Jones (Routledge, 1990), 29–30; Richard Steele and Joseph Addison, *The Spectator*, no. 99, 23 June 1711, repr. in *The Spectator: A New Edition* (London, 1852), 116. On similar notions within the early modern Jewish community, see Ḥovav, *Alamot ahevukha*, 61–63.

76. Elsewhere, I have suggested that given the close connection between hairiness and monstrous births, as well as her own belief in the power of the maternal imagination, Glikl may have associated the "savage child" in the story with a monstrous birth. See Idelson-Shein, *Ha-ekzoty*, 60–79.

77. Davis, *Women on the Margins*, 41.

78. See Deuteronomy 28:53; 2 Kings 6:24–29; Lamentations 4:10; Josephus, "The Jewish War," in *The New and Complete Works of Josephus*, trans. William Whiston (Grand Rapids, 1999), 893; Yehudah Ha-hasid, *Sefer Hasidim* (n.d.; repr. Sudylkiv, 1826), 73a. For some further examples,

see Merrall L. Price, *Consuming Passions: The Uses of Cannibalism in Late Medieval and Early Modern Europe* (New York, 2003), 65–82.

79. See Gustav Jahoda, *Images of Savages: Ancient Roots of Modern Prejudice in Western Culture* (London, 1999), 105.

80. See discussions in Ronald C. Finucane, *The Rescue of Innocents: Endangered Children in Medieval Miracles* (New York, 1997), 33; John Boswell, *The Kindness of Strangers* (1988; repr. Chicago, 1998), 60, 89, 106, 291–93; Ottavia Niccoli, *Prophecy and People in Renaissance Italy* (Princeton, 1990), 32–33. For a discussion of Jewish attitudes, see Elisheva Baumgarten, *Mothers and Children: Jewish Life in Medieval Europe* (Princeton, 2004), 174; Ephraim Shoham-Steiner, *Harigim beal korham: Meshugayim u-mezuraim ba-hevrah ha-yehudit bi-yemey ha-beynayim* (Jerusalem, 2008), 246–49.

81. For a discussion of the case, see Carlebach, *The Death of Simon Abeles: Jewish-Christian Tension in Seventeenth-Century Prague* (New York, 2001). On the accusation in general, see Frank Felsenstein, *Anti-Semitic Stereotypes: A Paradigm of Otherness in English Popular Literature 1660–1839* (Baltimore, 1995), 109–10. Also relevant are the reports of filicidal martyrdom, which is said to have taken place during the 1096 Crusades. For a discussion of these, see Israel Yuval, "Ha-nakam ve-ha-kelalah, ha-dam ve-ha-alilah: Me-alilot kedoshim le-alilit dam," *Zion* 58 (1993): 66–73.

82. Anon., *Maaseh Book*, 1602, repr. and trans. by Moses Gaster, 2 vols. (Philadelphia, 1934), 2:443–45.

83. For an enlightening discussion of the infanticidal motif in Hogarth's painting and in other eighteenth-century sources, see Toni Bowers, *The Politics of Motherhood: British Writing and Culture, 1680–1760* (Cambridge, 1996), 1–3, 91–150.

84. See Josephine McDonagh, "Infanticide and the Boundaries of Culture from Hume to Arnold," in *Inventing Maternity: Politics, Science and Literature 1650–1865*, ed. Susan C. Greenfield and Carol Barash (Lexington, KY, 1999), 217; *Child Murder and British Culture, 1720–1900* (New York, 2003), 3–4; Kerstin Michalik, "The Development of the Discourse on Infanticide in the Late Eighteenth-Century and the New Legal Standardization of the Offense in the Nineteenth Century," in *Gender in Transition: Discourse and Practice in German-Speaking Europe 1750–1830*, ed. Ulrike Gleixner and Marion W. Gray (Ann Arbor, 2006), 53–54; Peter C. Hoffer and N.E.H. Hull, *Murdering Mothers: Infanticide in England and New England, 1558–1803* (New York, 1981), 17–31; Bowers, *The Politics of Motherhood*, 93–96.

85. On this halakhic prohibition, see Baumgarten, *Mothers and Children*, 123–24, 170; Israel Ta-Shma, "Children in Medieval Germanic Jewry: A Perspective on Ariés from Jewish Sources," *Studies in Medieval and Renaissance History* 12 (1991): 268–69. For a different view, see Simcha Goldin, "Pen yavou ha-arelim halalu ve-yitfesum hayim ve-yihiyu mekuyamin be-taatuyim: Yeladim yehudim ve-misionerizaziya nozrit," in *Eros, erusin ve-isurim: Miniyut u-mishpahah ba-historiah*, ed. Israel Bartal and Isaiah Gafni (Jerusalem, 1998), 102–3. Goldin suggests that the prohibition of remarriage does not reflect anxieties about the stability of maternal love,

but rather about the quality of breast milk produced by a remarried woman. However, several of the sources brought forth by Baumgarten and Ta-Shma are explicit in their skepticism regarding the remarried mother's concern for the well-being of her child from an earlier marriage.

86. Bernard Mandeville, *The Fable of the Bees*, 1732, repr. in 2 vols. (Indianapolis, 1988), 1:71.

87. See note 10 above.

88. Zvi Hirsch Kaidanover, *Sefer kav ha-yashar* (Frankfurt, 1705), 13a–b.

89. Daniel Defoe, *The Fortunes and Misfortunes of the Famous Moll Flanders* (1722; repr. London, 1993), 134–35.

90. See Alysa Levene, "The Estimation of Mortality at the Lindon Foundling Hospital, 1741–99," *Population Studies* 59 (2005): 87–97.

91. Defoe, *Moll Flanders*, 46.

92. On Glikl's negligence toward her grandchildren, see Turniansky, "Introduction," 30–31.

93. Dov mi-Bolichov, *Zikhronot* (c. 1723–1805; repr. Krakow, 2006), 123.

94. Maimon, *Geschichte*, 6–7.

95. The story of the "Negro Woman" originally appeared in the memoirs of John Stuart of Augusta, Virginia, probably written during the 1760s. The earliest version of the story I have found appears in *Collections of the Virginia Historical and Philosophical Society* (Richmond, 1833), 39–40.

96. Samuel Gardner Drake, *Tragedies of the Wilderness* (c. 1839; repr. Boston, 1844), 286. For a discussion of the development of the ideal of maternal sacrifice in the late eighteenth century, see Elisabeth Badinter, *L'amour en plus: Histoire de l'amour maternal, XVIIe-Xxe siècle* (Paris, 1980), 264–70. Some examples of (mostly) late eighteenth-century stories of maternal sacrifice appear in Carolyn D. Williams, "Women Behaving Well: Early Modern Images of Female Courage," in *Presenting Gender: Changing Sex in Early-Modern Culture*, ed. Chris Mounsey (Lewisburg, PA, 2001), 70.

97. Wahrman, *Modern Self*, 12.

98. For the Yiddish song, see Carlebach, "Death of Abeles." For some late eighteenth- and nineteenth-century rationalizations of infanticidal behavior in biological mothers, see, e.g., William *Robertson, The History of the Discovery and Settlement of America* (1777; repr. New York, 1856), *154;* August von Kotzebue, *Die Negersklaven, ein historisch-dramatiches Gemälde in drey Akten* (1796; repr. Leipzig, 1821), 191; Harriet Beecher Stowe, *Uncle Tom's Cabin or Life Among the Lowly*, 2 vols. (Boston, 1852), 2:204–10, 315.

99. On these changes, see McDonagh, "Infanticide," 216–21, 228–31; Hoffer and Hull, *Murdering Mothers*, 66–91; Nussbaum, "'Savage' Mothers: Narratives of Maternity in the Mid Eighteenth-Century," *Eighteenth-Century Life* 16, no. 1 (1992): 163–84; Mark Jackson, *Newborn Child Murder: Women, Illegitimacy and the Courts in Eighteenth-Century England* (Manchester, 1996), 110–28. On the larger context of the changes, see Lawrence Stone, *The Family, Sex and Marriage in England, 1500–1800* (New

York, 1977), 405–78; Mary Poovey, *The Ideological Work of Gender in Mid-Victorian England* (London, 1989), 6–15.

100. Maria Tatar, *The Hard Facts of the Grimm's Fairy Stories* (1987; repr. Princeton, 2003) 36–37, 49–50; Kay Stone, "Three Transformations of Snow White," in *The Brothers Grimm and Folktale*, ed. James M. McGlathery (Urbana, 1988), 57–58.

101. Baruch Shenfeld, "Yelalat em al mot ben-riḥmah," *Bikurey ha-itim* (1827): 141; Yossef Perl, *Ẓir neeman li-shnat 5576* (Ternopol, 1815), 17a. For a more detailed discussion, see Idelson-Shein, *Ha-ekzoty*, 106–16.

102. Quoted in Anon., "Review: The Physiognomical System of Drs. Gall and Spurtzheim," *Medical and Physical Journal* 33, no. 191 (1815): 498–99.

103. To be sure, the infanticidal woman was often labeled "unnatural mother" in seventeenth- and eighteenth-century English literature and law, and the act of infanticide was termed an "unnatural crime"; still, the term appears to have been primarily meant to stress the horrendous and immoral nature of the crime rather than to suggest an actual deviation from nature. See Idelson-Shein, *Ha-ekzoty*, 96n. For a different view of pre-modern Jewish formulations of maternal love, see Baumgarten, *Mothers and Children*, 162–71; Avraham Grossman, *Ḥasidot u-mordot: Nashim Yehudiyot be-Eropah bi-yemey ha-beynayim* (Jerusalem, 2001), 225–27.

104. See excerpt in Zamora, *Reading Columbus* (Berkeley, 1993), 167. Earlier reports of parenting practices amongst wild men were just as dismal. See White, "Wild Man," 20.

105. Quoted in Mintz-Manor, "Ha-siaḥ," 77.

106. John Locke, "An Essay Concerning Human Understanding," in *The Works of John Locke, Esq.* (1690; repr. London, 1714), I:15; Adam Smith, *The Theory of Moral Sentiments* (1759; repr. London, 1761), 322–23.

107. See Roy Porter, "The Exotic as Erotic: Captain Cook in Tahiti," in *Exoticism in the Enlightenment*, ed. Roy Porter and G. S. Rousseau (Manchester, 1990), 128–29.

108. Voltaire, *Quéstions sur l'Encyclopédie* (London, 1771), 7:270. Voltaire was inconsistent in his attitude toward parental devotion. He claimed, for instance, vis-à-vis Rousseau, that all parents love their child, even when he is still in the womb. See Voltaire, *Quéstions sur l'Encyclopédie*, 7:102.

109. Jean-François Marmontel, *Les Incas, ou la destruction de l'empire du Pérou*, 2 vols. (Paris, 1777), 1:16.

110. Georges-Louis Leclerc de Buffon, "Animaux communs aux deux continents," in *Œuvres complètes de Buffon*, vol. 21, part 6 (1761; repr. Paris, 1825), 53. Several other discussions on the effects of climate on familial relations appear in Julie Kipp, "Naturally Bad or Dangerously Good: Romantic-Era Narratives of Murderous Motherhood," in *Writing British Infanticide: Child-Murder, Gender and Print, 1722–1859*, ed. Jennifer Thorn (Cranbury, NJ, 2003), 241–42.

111. Buffon, "Variétés dans l'espèce humaine," 1748–1778, repr. in *De l'homme* (Paris, 1971), 278.

112. James Boswell, *The Life of Samuel Johnson*, 2 vols. (London, 1791), 2:449. For a discussion of Johnson's attitudes toward maternity see

Nussbaum, *Torrid Zones*, 63. For further examples of doubts concerning the maternal instincts in savage mothers, see Bridget Orr, "Stifling Pity in a Parent's Breast: Infanticide and Savagery in Late Eighteenth-Century Travel Writing," in *Travel Writing and Empire: Postcolonial Theory in Transit*, ed. Steve Clark (London, 1999), 131–46.

113. Schorsch, *Jews and Blacks*, esp. 292; Melamed, *Image of the Black*, esp. 32–33.

114. Aphra Behn, "Oroonoko," 1688, repr. in *Oroonoko, The Rover and Other Works* (London, 1992), 121.

115. See Chapter 2, "Confronting the Savage Body," below.

116. Wheeler, *Complexion of Race*, esp. 3–9, 21–28, 30–33; Wahrman, *Making of the Modern Self*, esp. 83–126. See also Mark Harrison, *Climates and Constitutions: Health, Race, Environment and British Imperialism in India: 1600–1850* (New York, 1999).

117. Buffon, "Variétés," esp. 23; *Histoire Naturelle, Générale et Particulière* (Paris, 1753), 4:317. See also Henri Grégoire, *De la littérature des nègres* (Paris, 1808), 18–19.

118. See, e.g., John Adams, *A View of Universal History, from the Creation to the Present Time*, 3 vols. (London, 1795), 3:52–55; Louis B. Wright, "Introduction" to *The History and Present State of Virginia*, by Robert Beverley (Chapel Hill, 1947), xvii. I thank Denis Todd for this reference.

119. Isaac De Pinto, Letter to Charles Marie La Condamine [1745–46], British Library London, Eggerton Collection, Bentinck Papers, manuscript no. EG. 1745, ff.184a–185a. For other examples, see Harrison, *Climates and Constitutions*, esp. 10–11, 16–17.

120. See e.g., Campe, *Die Entdekkung* [sic] *von Amerika, einangenehmes und nützliches Lesebuch für Kinder und junge Leute*, part 1 (Hamburg, 1781), 95–96; Moshe Mendelssohn-Frankfurt, *Meziat ha-arez ha-hadashah kolel kol ha-gevurot ve-ha-maasim asher naasu le-et mezo ha-arez ha-zot* (Altona, 1807), 36; Günzberg, *Masa Kolombus o galut ha-arez ha-hadashah al yedey Kristof Kolombus* (Vilnius, 1823), 16. All references to Campe's *Entdekkung* and Günzberg's *Kolombus* are to these editions unless otherwise stated.

121. See Mintz-Manor, "Ha-siah," 74, 149n, 216, 283. See also Schorsch, *Jews and Blacks*, 22–38, 144–45. For some exceptions, see Mintz-Manor, "Ha-siah," 148–49.

122. Elyakim ben Avraham (Hart), *Milhamot ha-shem* (London, 1794), 23b. On Hart, see David Ruderman, *Jewish Enlightenment in an English Key* (Princeton, 2000), 188–200.

123. Mordecai Gumpel Schnaber Levison, *Maamar ha-torah ve-ha-hohmah* (London, 1771), part 1, 24. On Levison, see Heinz Moshe Graupe, "Mordechai Schnaber-Levison: The Life, Works and Thought of a Haskalah Outsider," *Leo Baeck Institute Yearbook* 41, no. 1 (1996): 3–20; Ruderman, *Jewish Thought and Scientific Discovery in Early Modern Europe* (New Haven, 1995), 332–68.

124. This seems to be a mistranslation of Campe's original, in which it is claimed that the sailors' bodies were distorted by the hunger and travails of

the journey. Compare Anon. [Menachem Mendel Lefin?], *Oniyah soarah* (c. 1815; repr. Warsaw, 1854), 57; Campe, "Wilhelm Isbrand Bonteku's merkwürdige Abentheuer auf einer Reise aus Holland nach Ostindien," in *Sammlung interessanter und durchgängig zwekmäßif abgefaßter Reisebeschreibung für die Jugend* (Reutlingen, 1794), 5:56–57. The attribution of dark color to the Dutch is also missing in the other German editions of the book I have consulted; see, e.g., Campe, *Interessanter und durchgängig zwekmäßg abgefaßter Resebeschreibungen für die Jugend* (Reutlingen, 1801), 5:56; *Sammlung merkwürdiger Reisebeschreiben für die Jugend* (Stuttgart, 1823), 4:30. On the identity of the translator, see Sinkoff, *Out of the Shtetl: Making Jews Modern in the Polish Borderlands* (Providence, 2004), 195–96n.

125. Zalkind Hourwitz, *Apologie des Juifs* (Paris, 1789; facs. repr. Paris, 1968), 67. See also De Pinto, *Letter to Condamine*, 184b.

126. Shimshon Bloch, *Sefer sheviley olam*, 2 parts (1822–1828; repr. Warsaw, 1894), 1:4a.

127. Tuviah Ha-cohen, *Maaseh Tuviah* (1707; repr. Krakow, 1908), 67b; see also 61a–62b.

128. Shlomo ben Yossef Keysir, "Kohelet Shlomo" (1818), 4a, Levy Collection, Hamburg Staats- und Universitätsbibliothek, Hamburg, Germany, ms. 172, available in microfilm at the NLI, reel no. F1600. An almost identical description appears in Joseph Perl's "Teḥunat anshey Greenland" (1813–17), draft version for Ẓir Neeman, 11a–b, ARC 4° 1153/96, Josef Perl Archive, NLI, 11a–b. For a comparison between the three texts, see Idelson-Shein, *Ha-ekzoty*, appendix a, 403–5.

129. [Abraham ben Elijah of Vilna], *Gevulot arez* (Berlin, 1801), 9b. For a discussion of this text and its source, see Idelson-Shein, "Abraham Ben Elijah of Vilna Encounters the Spirit of Mr. Buffon," *AJS Review* 36, no. 2 (2012): 295–322. The above paragraph is in all probability the translator's original addition. For a discussion of the Hebrew translational norms of the period, see Chapter 3 below.

130. Diderot, "Supplément," 579–644; Françoise de Graffigny, *Lettres d'une Péruvienne* (1747; repr. Paris, 1983).

131. Yehudah Horowitz, *Amudey beyt Yehudah* (Amsterdam, 1766). Hereafter AMBY.

132. See, e.g., G. Tur., 116, 146, 194. For a discussion of Glikl's ambivalent portrayal of Christians see Robert Liberles, "Die Juden und die anderen—Das Bild des Nichtjuden in Glikls Memoiren," in *Die Hamburger Kauffrau Glikl: Jüdische Existenz in der frühen Neuzeit*, ed. Monika Richarz (Hamburg, 2001), 135–46; Davis, *Women on the Margins*, 36–38. For an opposing view, see Turniansky, "Introduction," 44; she contends that Glikl's representation of non-Jews is usually either neutral or positive.

133. Nussbaum, *Torrid Zones*, 53; see also Bowers, *Politics of Motherhood*, 94–96, 122.

134. See G. Tur., 80 and 86. On other aspects of the reversal of traditional gender roles in the story, see Moseley, *Being for Myself Alone*, 162.

135. See G. Tur., 500–504.

136. On the feminine ideal in Christian conduct literature, see Bowers, *Politics of Motherhood*, 156–67; and Martha Howell, "The Gender of Europe's Commercial Economy, 1200–1700," *Gender and History* 20, no. 3 (2008): 526–27. Ḥovav shows that these ideals were also shared by early modern Jews. However, another competing ideal of the virtuous woman as an industrious woman may also be gleaned from the sources. See Ḥovav, *Alamot ahevukha*, 225–56. See also Moshe Rosman, "Lihiyot ishah Yehudiyah be-Polin-Lita be-reshit ha-et ha-ḥadashah," in *Kiyum va-shever: Yehudey Polin le-doroteyhem*, ed. Israel Bartal and Israel Guttman (Jerusalem, 2001), 415–16.

137. Sylvia Hahn, "Women in Older Ages—'Old' Women?," *History of the Family* 7, no. 1 (2002): 45–52; Wiesner, "Having Her Own Smoke," 198–99, 209; Rosman, "Ishah Yehudiyah," 430–33; Ḥovav, *Alamot ahevukha*, 211–12; Ulbrich, *Shulamit und Margarete*, 109–15.

138. Bowers, *Politics of Motherhood*, 125–35.

139. *Maaseh Book*, 1:341–43.

140. Marx, "Autobiography," 276; English translation according to Marx, 278, modified to better reflect original. See also Emden, *Megilat sefer*, 64; G. Tur., 70–79. For a discussion of Glikl's attitude toward her grandmother, see Turniansky, "Dmut ha-ishah," 182–84. See also further examples below.

141. Tiktiner, *Meneket Rivkah*, 240–44. For a discussion of the sources of the story and its other appearances during the early modern period, see von Rohden, "Introduction" to *Meneket Rivkah*, 138n.

142. For some further examples see G. Tur., 262–63, 494–97, 552.

143. Turniansky, "Dmut ha-ishah," 185.

144. Marx, "Autobiography," 277; English translation, 288.

145. Yeḥezkel Landau, *Responsa noda be-Yehudah*, Mahadurah kamma (1776), Even ha-ezer, 9.

146. Emden, *Megilat sefer*, 148, 151, 157.

147. On this understanding of women's work as a means to their husband's piety, see Ḥovav, *Alamot ahevukha*, 41–44.

148. Rosman, "Lihiyot ishah Yehudiyah," 426; see also 426–34. In addition, see Ḥovav, *Alamot ahevukha*, 56–247, 307–14; Liberles, "Threshold of Modernity," 38–39, 57–61; Ulbrich, *Shulamit und Margarete*, 211–15. On the similar reality in non-Jewish homes, see Ulbrich, *Shulamit und Margarete*, 108–15; Wunder, *He Is the Sun*, 63–112; and Olwen H. Hufton, "Women and the Family Economy in Eighteenth-Century France," *French Historical Studies* 9, no. 1 (1975): 1–22.

149. Yet Glikl's story does not comply with the trend found in the literature of such other women writers on the exotic as Françoise de Graffigny or Marie-Josephine de Monbart, as explained by Julia Douthwaite: "The exotic heroines of women's novels exemplify loyalty, intelligence and moral decency." Douthwaite, *Exotic Women*, 18.

CHAPTER 2

1. See, e.g., Antonio Pigafetta, *First Voyage Around the World, 1519–1522: An Account of Magellan's Expedition* (1525; repr. Toronto, 2007), 78;

Henry Schooten, *The Hairy Giants: or a Description of Two Islands in the South Sea Called by the Name of Bengaga and Coma* (London, 1671); Matithiahu Delakrut, *Zel ha-olam* (16th cent.; repr. Munkács, 1897), 8a; Yossef Ha-cohen, *Sefer ha-Indeah ha-ḥadashah* (1557; repr. Lancaster, 2002), 27.

2. Anthony Ashley-Cooper (Third Earl of Shaftesbury), *Characteristics of Men, Manners, Opinions, Times* (1711; repr. Cambridge, 1999), 153–57. Ironically, Shaftesbury himself was also wont to make philosophical use of non-European peoples. See, e.g., 156–57.

3. In my translations of Horowitz, I have attempted to keep some of the spirit of the original, which was written in biblical Hebrew and rhymed prose in the style of the medieval maqama. I have often preferred adequacy over a literal translation, and I have attempted to keep the verses in rhyme and the biblical allusions intact.

4. See 2 Samuel 20:26, as well as 21:18–19 for an integration of all three names.

5. Horowitz was not alone in viewing these two groups as the main threat to Jewish tradition. See Shmuel Feiner, *The Origins of Jewish Secularization in Eighteenth-Century Europe*, trans. Chaya Naor (2010; repr. Philadelphia, 2011), 36; and on the increasing secularizing trends in the Jewish community of the 1760s and the early maskilic reaction to these, see 103–18.

6. Feiner, "Beyn ananey ha-siḥlut le-or ha-muskalot: Yehudah Horowitz, maskil mukdam ba-meah ha-18," in *Be-maagaley ḥasidim: Koveẓ meḥkarim le-zikhro shel profesor Mordecai Vilensky*, ed. Israel Bartal and Elchanan Reiner (Jerusalem, 1999); Shmuel Werses, "Hatafah maskilit be-maḥleẓot shel prozah meḥurezet," *Meḥkary yerushalaim be-sifrut ivrit* 10–11 (1988). In earlier studies by Klausner, Dinur, Mahler, and others Horowitz is mentioned only in passing.

7. For a characterization of the early Haskalah, see Feiner's definitive work *The Jewish Enlightenment*, trans. Chaya Naor (2002; repr. Philadelphia, 2004).

8. Jonathan Israel, *Radical Enlightenment: Philosophy and the Making of Modernity 1650–1750* (New York, 2001), 11, and see also 12–13; Jonathan Israel, *Enlightenment Contested* (Oxford, 2006), 3–15; John G.A. Pocock, "Conservative Enlightenment and Democratic Revolutions: The American and French Cases in British Perspective," *Government and Opposition* 24, no. 1 (1989): 82–105; John G.A. Pocock, *Barbarism and Religion*, vol. 1, *The Enlightenments of Edward Gibbon* (Cambridge, 1999), 6–9. Israel uses the terms "conservative Enlightenment" and "moderate Enlightenment" interchangeably. However, it seems to me that the latter term inadvertently assumes only one "true" Enlightenment, against which all other "pseudo-Enlightenments" are to be measured. I would suggest, conversely, that conservativism is an essential part of the kind of Enlightenment purported by such thinkers as Mendelssohn or Horowitz, and not a caveat that moderates their investment in the Enlightenment project. For a major discussion of the religious Enlightenment, see David Sorkin, *The Religious Enlightenment: Protestants, Jews, and Catholics from London to Vienna* (Princeton, 2008).

9. AMBY, 8a. On the ideology of moderation in the early Haskalah and in other religious Enlightenments, see Sorkin, *Religious Enlightenment*, esp. 11–14, 30–31; Nancy Sinkoff, "Tradition and Transition: Mendel Lefin of Satanow and the Beginnings of the Jewish Enlightenment in Eastern Europe, 1749–1826" (Ph.D. diss., Columbia University, 1996), 137–38.

10. Horowitz's date of birth is revealed in his book *Kerem Ein Gedy* (Königsburg, 1764), 2a. See Feiner, "Yehudah Horowitz," 117n19. Regarding his place of birth, though modern studies identify Horowitz as a native of Vilnius, nineteenth-century sources tend to present him as Paduan by origin. See Shmuel Yossef Fün, *Knesset Israel* (Warsaw, 1886), 394; *Kiryah neemanah* (Vilnius, 1860), 171–73; Reuven J. Wunderbar, *Geschichte der Juden in den Provinzen Liv- und Kurland* (Mitau, 1853), 71 (art. XIX); Johann F. Von Recke and Karl E. Napiersky, *Algemeinem Schrifsteller und Gelehrten Lexicon der Provinzen Livland, Esthland und Korland* (Mitau, 1831), 3:53.

11. On the enigma of Horowitz's academic education, see Feiner, "Yehudah Horowitz," 118–19. On Jewish physicians during the early modern period, see John M. Efron, "Interminably Maligned: The Conventional Lies about Jewish Doctors," in *Jewish History and Jewish Memory: Essays in Honor of Yosef Hayim Yerushalmi*, ed. Elisheva Carlebach, John Efron, and David Myers (Hanover, NH, 1998), 298. That Horowitz served as a physican may be gleaned from his books, where he is presented as such both by himself as well as by others who supplied haskamot and recommendations. See, e.g., title page to Horowitz, *Hayey ha-nefesh u-nizhiyutah* (Poritzk, 1786), as well as AMBY, [3].

12. Horowitz, *Megilat sdarim* (1793; repr. Prague, 1884). For a discussion of the book, see Werses, "Hatafah," 253–70.

13. Horowitz, *Megilat sdarim*, 6–47.

14. See Feiner, "Yehudah Horowitz," 120–21, 151. Other early maskilim, such as Israel of Zamość or Naphtali Herz Wessely, shared similar fates. See Feiner, *Jewish Enlightenment*, 87–104; Edward Breuer, "Naphtali Herz Wessely and the Cultural Dislocation of an 18th Century Maskil," in *New Perspectives on the Haskalah*, ed. Shmuel Feiner and David Sorkin (London, 2001), 27–47; Mordecai Eliav, *Ha-hinuh ha-Yehudy be-Germaniyah bi-yemey ha-haskalah ve-ha-emanzipaziyah* (Jerusalem, 1960), 33–36.

15. Horowitz, "Musar haskel," in *Koz Yehudah*, 1790–1791, MS no. B 574, St. Petersburg Inst. of Oriental Studies of the Russian Academy, microfilm at NLI, reel no. F69310.

16. On the genre of the maskilic maqama, see Nurit Govrin, "Signon ha-maqama ba-sifrut ha-Ivrit ba-dorot ha-aharonim," *Measef* 8–9 (1968): 394–417.

17. Some scholars find in Linnaeus and Hume exceptions to this rule. To be sure, Linnaeus tended to view nature in a more synchronous manner than many of his contemporaries and generally refrained from discussing the origins of human variety; still, he too divided human beings into separate varieties based on geography, thus implying, I think, a kind of subtle environmentalism, not entirely different from the kind of environmentalism

endorsed by such thinkers as Buffon or Blumenbach. On Hume, see Wahrman, *Modern Self*, 91.

18. David Hume, *Dialogues Concerning Natural Religion* (1777; repr. London, 1779), 8–9.

19. Moshe Mendelssohn, *Sefer netivot ha-shalom ve-hu hibur kolel hameshet humshey torah im tirgum Ashkenazy u-biyur* (1783; repr. Vienna, 1795), vol. 2: Exodus, 96b.

20. David Frisenhausen, *Mosdot tevel* (Vienna, 1820), 86a. See also Wessely, "Magid hadashot," *Ha-measef* (1798): 155; Isaac Satanov, *Mishley Assaf*, part 2 (Berlin 1792), 47a.

21. See, e.g., Joachim Heinrich Campe, "Kapitän Wilson's Schiffbruch bei den Pelju-Inseln," in *Sämmtliche Kinder- und Jugendschriften von Joachim Heinrich Campe* (1791; repr. Braunschweig, 1830), part 9, vol. 25, p. 177; Mary Wortley Monatgu, "Letters: Volume II," *Monthly Review: or Literary Journal: by Several Hands* 28 (1763): 461.

22. Abraham ben Naphtali Tang, "Behinat adam" (1772), 70a–71b, MS no. EVR II A22, St. Petersburg National Library, microfilm at NLI, reel no. F63945. On this debate, its sources of inspiration and its place in Tang's thought, see Ruderman, *Jewish Enlightenment*, 113.

23. Mendelssohn, *Jerusalem oder über religiöse Macht und Judentum* (Berlin, 1783), part 2, 84–85.

24. Ibid.; Biyur: Deuteronomy, 73a–b. For a discussion of these views, see Hess, *Claims of Modernity*, 127–28; Jan Assman, "Pictures Versus Letters: William Warburton's Theory of Grammatological Iconoclasm," in *Representation in Religion: Studies in Honor of Moshe Barasch*, ed. Assman and A. I. Baumgarten (Leiden, 2001), 297–311.

25. On Heinicke, see Shulamit Volkov, "Ha-hershim ke-kvuzat miyut: Reshit ha-maavak al sefat ha-simanim," *Historiah* 1 (1998): 86–87. For Ben Avraham's views, see Ben Avraham, *Milhamot*, 2a–5a.

26. Mendelssohn, *Jerusalem*, 2, 95; English translation, *Jerusalem or on Religious Power and Judaism*, trans. Allan Arkush (Hanover, NH, 1983), 118.

27. Satanov, Commentary to *Sefer ha-kuzary* (Berlin, 1795), 32a; Levison, *Maamar ha-torah*, 80–91.

28. Campe, *Wilson's Schiffbruch*, 177.

29. Menachem Mendel Lefin, *Masaot ha-yam* (1818; repr. Lemberg, 1859), 69. The only extant copy of the original edition is incomplete. I have therefore chosen to utilize the later edition, which is almost identical.

30. Feiner, *Secularization*, 1–2, 127–28.

31. See Ruderman, *Jewish Enlightenment*, 102; Feiner, *Secularization*, 137.

32. [Euchel], "Igrot Meshulam ben Uriah ha-Ashtemoy," letter 2, *Ha-measef* (1789): 44.

33. Euchel's attitude toward religion has been a point of contention amongst scholars. See, e.g., Moshe Pelli, *The Age of Haskalah: Studies in Hebrew Literature of the Enlightenment in Germany* (Leiden, 1979),

193–97, 201–11, 221–26; Yehuda Friedlander, *Prakim ba-satirah ha-Ivrit*, part 1 (Tel Aviv, 1979), 29.

34. Feiner, *Jewish Enlightenment*, 52–53. For a comparison between the two books see Idelson-Shein, "Gilguley pere: Hashvaah beyn 'Robinson Crusoe' le-Daniel Defoe le-Amudey beyt Yehudah le-Yehudah Horowitz," *Historiah* 21 (2008): 31–83. It is quite probable that Horowitz was familiar with Defoe's book, as the book's popularity did not pass over the early maskilim. It was translated into Yiddish as early as 1764, and would continue to appear in Jewish languages throughout the eighteenth century (see Chapter 4 below). These various translations all point to the novel's positive reception amongst the maskilim. Additionally, it stands to reason that Horowitz, who was, as will be demonstrated, an avid reader of Rousseau, would have made a point of reading a book that came so highly recommended by the Swiss philosopher. For Rousseau's recommendation of *Robinson Crusoe*, see Jean Jacques Rousseau, *Émile ou de l'éducation* (1762; repr. Paris, 1961), 210–11. On the early Yiddish translation, see Moritz Steinschneider, "Hebräische Drucke in Deutschland," *Zeitschrift für die Geschichte der Juden in Deutschland* 2 (1892): 156.

35. Defoe, *Robinson Crusoe* (1719; repr. New York, 1975), 169.

36. Ibid., 171. For some discussions of the Devil debate, see Nicholas Hudson, ",Why God No Kill the Devil?': The Diabolical Disruption of Order in 'Robinson Crusoe,'" *Review of English Studies*, n.s., 39, no. 156 (1988): 494–504; Timothy C. Blackburn, "Friday's Religion: Its Nature and Importance in Robinson Crusoe," *Eighteenth-Century Studies* 18, no. 3 (1985): 372–74; J. P. Hunter, "Friday as a Convert: Defoe and the Accounts of Indian Missionaries," *Review of English Studies*, n.s., 14, no. 55 (1963): 243–48. See also Israel, *Radical Enlightenment*, 375–405, for a discussion of Enlightenment attitudes toward the concept of the Devil. Also instructive are Defoe's musings on the importance of revelation in his other writings, e.g., Defoe, *The Family Instructor* (1726; repr. Bungay, 1826), 15–17, and *An Essay on the Original of Literature* (1726; repr. New York, 1999), 3–4, 16–17, 21, 62.

37. Idelson-Shein, "Gilguley pere," 59–62.

38. Quoted in Feiner, "Y. L. Margaliyot ve-paradoks ha-haskalah ha-mukdemet," *Zion* 63 (1998): 62, and see also 66–74; Ruderman, *Scientific Discovery*, 356, 368; Pelli, *Age of Haskalah*, 37–43.

39. Satanov, *Mishley Assaf*, part 2, 18b, and see also 4a–b, 12b, 37a–38; Euchel, "Igrot Meshulam," letter 2, 46–47.

40. See also AMBY, 3a, 26b–27a, 81b–82a. And see discussion in Feiner, "Yehudah Horowitz," 144–45; Israel Zinberg, *Toldot sifrut Israel*, 7 vols. (Tel Aviv, 1971), 3:311–12.

41. Horowitz is referring specifically to Maimonides. On the importance of Maimonides and his *Guide to the Perplexed* in the Haskalah, see Ismar Schorsch's seminal "The Myth of Sepharadic Supremacy," *Leo Baeck Institute Yearbook* 34 (1989): 47–66.

42. There are some exceptions in which Hushai also contributes rabbinical knowledge to the discussion. See, e.g., AMBY, 17a–b. However, even in these cases, Ittai still has the last word.

43. For some other examples, see AMBY, 5b, 12a. On the desirability yet insufficiency of reason for religion in the works of thinkers of the religious Enlightenment, see Sorkin, *Religious Enlightenment*, 13–14, 81–82.

44. See, e.g., AMBY, 29b–30a. And see discussion in Feiner, "Yehudah Horowitz," 145–50.

45. For a similar attempt to present Judaism as a natural religion, based on rational consent, see Satanov, *Mishley Assaf*, part 2, 18b n. 14.

46. Horowitz, *Hayey ha-nefesh*, [41].

47. Rousseau, *Émile*, 192; in English as *Emile or on Education*, trans. Christopher Kelly and Allan Bloom (Lebanon, NH, 2010), 317.

48. On Rousseau's influence in the early Haskalah, see Eliav, *Ha-hinukh*, 53, 59, 70; Sinkoff, *Tradition and Transition*, 116–19. A German translation of the book was available as early as 1762. See Kurt Christ, *F. H. Jacobi: Rousseaus deutscher Adept: Rousseauismus in Leben und Frühwerk* (Würzburg, 1998), 161–62.

49. Anon. [Schnaber Levison?], "Sefer Gidul Bonim," 1771, trans. Siegfried Stein, in *Remember the Days: Essays on Anglo-Jewish History presented to Cecil Roth*, ed. John M. Shaftesley (London, 1966), 149–50.

50. Maimon, *Geschichte*, 43–49. For some further examples, see [David Friedländer], *Sendschreiben an Seine Hochwürden, Herrn ... Teller ... von einigen Hausvätern jüdischer Religion* (Berlin, 1799; facsimile repr. Jerusalem, 1975), 6; Emden, *Megilat sefer*, 56. See also Eliav, *Ha-hinukh*, 143–48; Avner Holtzman, "Ben hokaah le-hitrapkut: Ha-heder be-sifrut ha-zikhronot u-ba-sifrut ha-ivrit," in *Ha-heder: Mehkarim, pirkey sifrut u-zikhronot*, ed. Immanuel Etkes and David Assaf (Tel Aviv, 2010), 77–80.

51. On Jewish pedagogical discourse before the Haskalah, see Azriel Shohat, *Im hilufey ha-tekufot: Reshit ha-haskalah be-yahadut Germaniyah* (Jerusalem, 1960), 123–38; Morris M. Faierstein, Introduction to Isaac Wetzlar, *The Libes Briv of Isaac Wetzlar* (1749; repr. Atlanta, 1996), 19, 40–41.

52. Lazarus Bendavid, *Etwas zur Characteristik der Juden* (Leipzig, 1793; facsimile repr. Jerusalem, 1994), 25–27.

53. Franks, *Letters*, 68. For further examples of the negative attitude toward the Talmud, see Feiner, *Jewish Enlightenment*, 139, 294, 333, and elsewhere.

54. See Ronald Schechter, *Obstinate Hebrews: Representations of Jews in France, 1715–1815* (Berkeley, 2003), 44–46, 64, 88–89, 127–28. For some examples, see Grégoire, *Essai sur la Régénération physique, morale et politique des Juifs* (1789; repr. Paris, 1988), 103–5; Christian W. Dohm, "Concerning the Amelioration of the Civil Status of the Jews," in *The Jew in the Modern World*, 27–29.

55. Naphtali Herz Wessely, *Divrey shalom ve-emet* (Berlin, 1782), [2].

56. The ideological affinity between Wessely and Horowitz is also attested to by the inclusion of a "friendship song" by Wessely in the preface to AMBY, [19].

57. See Feiner, "Laakor et ha-hohmah mi-ha-olam: Oyvey ha-neorut u-shorshey ha-emdah ha-haredit," *Alpayim* 26 (2004): 166–75.

58. See Immanuel Etkes, *Rabbi Israel Salanter and the Mussar Movement: Seeking the Torah of Truth* (Philadelphia, 1993), 133–34; David Assaf, *Neeḥaz ba-svakh: Pirkey mashber u-mevukhah be-toldot ha-Ḥasidut* (Jerusalem, 2006), 42–48; Yehoshua Mondshein, "Haskamot shtukot mi-Valozhyn u-Vilnah: Kabel et ha-emet mi-my she-amarah?," *Or Israel* 4, no. 16 (1999): 151–59; Israel Nathan Heshel, "Daatam shel gedoley ha-dor be-milḥamtam neged ha-maskil Naphtali Herẓ Wessely," *Koveẓ beyt Aharon ve-Israel* 5, no. 47 (1993): 146n26; Yoel Katan, "Kabel et ha-emet mi-mi she-amarah," *Ha-maayan* 32, no. 3 (1992): 54–55; Noah Rosenblum, "Ha-Malbim ve-filosofiyah modernit," *Proceedings of the American Society for Jewish Research* 52 (1985): 1–41; Shohat, *Ḥilufey ha-tekufot*, 198–241.

59. Jossef Klausner, "Ha-Haskalah ha-clalit ve-ha-Ivrit be-Lita," in *Yahadut Lita*, vol. 1 (Tel Aviv, 1984), 405; Werses, "Hatafah maskilit," 268.

60. Mendelssohn, "Sendschreiben an den Herrn Magister Lessing in Leipzig," 1756, repr. in *Gesammelte Schriften*, vol. 2: Schriften zur Philosophie und Ästhetik, ed. Fritz Bamberger and Leo Strauss (Berlin, 1931), 83–96. And see discussion in Matt Erlin, "Reluctant Modernism: Moses Mendelssohn's Philosophy of History," *Journal of the History of Ideas* 63, no. 1 (2002): 88–90; Avi Lifschitz, *Language and Enlightenment: The Berlin Debates of the Eighteenth Century* (Oxford, 2012), 82–87.

61. Satanov, *Igeret Adar ha-yakar* (Berlin, 1772), 2a. See also *Mishley Assaf*, part 2, 4b, 25a; *Ḥelek rishon min sefer ha-midot le-Aristotalis*, Hebrew trans. and commentary by Satanov (1784; repr. Lemberg, 1867), 6a. For some famous non-Jewish objections, see Voltaire, *Quéstions*, part 7, 100–105; Joseph de Maistre, *Against Rousseau: 'On the State of Nature' and 'On the Sovereignty of the People'*, 1796, trans. Richard A. Lebrun (Montreal, 1996), 3–33.

62. On free will as the defining feature of the human, see AMBY, 2b, 57a. Horowitz is, however, somewhat inconsistent in his treatment of the issue, and in other places in the book he repeats the more conventional approach, according to which man differs from the animals in reason and speech. See AMBY, 58a.

63. Alexander Pope, "The Dunciad," 1743, repr. in *Alexander Pope: Selected Poetry and Prose* (New York, 1963), 431. For some further examples, see Buffon, "Nomenclature des Singes," 1766, repr. in *Oeuvres philosophiques de Buffon* (Paris, 1954), 389. The use of language as an exclusively human trait is also characteristic of Jewish medieval philosophy and reappears in Jewish eighteenth-century literature. See, e.g., Wetzlar, *Libes Briv*, 5a, 8a, 10b–11a; David Levy, *Lingua Sacra* (London, 1786), part 2, [39]; Israel Ha-levi mi-Zamość, Commentary to *Ruaḥ ḥen*, by Yehudah Ibn Tibbon (1744; repr. Yosifov, 1889), 34.

64. Rousseau, *Discours sur l'origine et les fondements de l'inégalité parmi les hommes* (1754; repr. Paris, 1965), 56–58, 170.

65. Another maskil who rejected language as an essential characteristic of man was Isaac Satanov, who claimed that deaf persons and feral children, though they do not possess language, are still human. See Satanov, *Sefer*

ha-gderim oder leksikon fon visenshaften (Berlin, 1798), 4a; Kuzary commentary, 8a.

66. Lazarus Bendavid, "Über den Menschen als Kunstwerk," *Neue Berlinische Monatsschrift* 18 (1807): 270.

67. Rousseau, *de l'inégalité*, 55. Translation according to Rousseau, *Discourse on the Origins of Inequality (Second Discourse)*, trans. Judith R. Bush, Roger D. Masters, Christopher Kelly, and Terence Marshall (Hanover, NH, 1992), 25.

68. Rousseau himself recommended a more "natural" diet, and in *Émile* expressed his support for vegetarianism. See *Émile*, 165, 168–69.

69. Rousseau, *de l'inégalité*, 54

70. See Wahrman, *Modern Self*, 177–79; Linda Colley, "Going Native, Telling Tales: Captivity, Collaborations and Empire," *Past and Present* 168 (2000): 178–79.

71. Shmuel Romanelli, *Masa ba-Arav* (Berlin, 1792), 26–27, 34.

72. Euchel, "Igrot Meshulam," letter 1, 40, 43; Mordecai M. Noah, "She Would Be a Soldier," 1819, repr. in Noah, *Selected Writings* (Westport, CT, 1999), 39–62; Lefin, *Masaot ha-yam*, 10, 12.

73. Buffon, "Variétés," 319–20.

74. Abraham ben Elijah, Gevulot arez, 14b–15a. Though, as I have shown elsewhere, the majority of the text is a translation of Buffon's *Histoire Naturelle*, the story of the feral children does not originate in Buffon. It may be Ben Elijah's own edition, or a translation of a different, yet unknown text.

75. Lindau, *Reshit limudim* (Berlin, 1788), 74b. References to *Reshit limudim* appear hereafter as RL, parenthetically. Keysir, "Kohelet Shlomo," 4b. There was also a gender dimension to diet. See Douthwaite, *Dangerous Experiments*, 39–40.

76. Defoe, *Robinson Crusoe*, 17–19.

77. Ibid., 146. On the Enlightenment's preoccupation with European and non-European cannibalism, see Gananath Obeyesekere, *Cannibal Talk: The Man-Eating Myth and Human Sacrifice in the South Seas* (Berkeley, 2005), 16–20.

78. Wheeler, "'My Savage,' 'My Man': Racial Multiplicity in Robinson Crusoe," *English Literary History* 62, no. 4 (1995): 842.

79. Swift, *Gulliver's Travels*, 199, and see also 204–6, 209, 227–28, 243.

80. AMBY, 2b. On undressing in eighteenth-century travel narratives see Wheeler, *Complexion of Race*, 19–21; Melman, *Women's Orients*, 89–91; Mary L. Pratt, "Scratches on the Face of the Country; or, What Mr. Burrows Saw in the Land of the Bushmen," in *"Race," Writing and Difference*, ed. Henry Louis Gates Jr. (Chicago, 1986), 150–51.

81. See, e.g., Schorsch, *Jews and Blacks*, 254–61, 267–93.

82. Klausner, *Historiah shel ha-sifrut ha-Ivrit ha-ḥadashah* (1936; repr. Jerusalem, 1952), 2: 360.

83. See, e.g., Friedman, *Jews and the Slave Trade*, 203; Garrett, "Jewish Robinson," 226. For a more subtle yet not entirely different approach, see Hess, *Claims of Modernity*, 91–135.

84. Wylie Sypher, *Guinea's Captive Kings: British Anti-Slavery Literature of the XVIIIth Century* (1942; repr. New York, 1969), 259.

85. See discussion in Idelson-Shein, "Gilguley pere," 59–62.

86. Campe, *Robinson der Jüngere* (Strasbourg, 1784), 46–47.

87. Richard B. Apgar, "Taming Travel and Disciplining Reason: Enlightenment and Pedagogy in the Work of Joachim Heinrich Campe" (Ph.D. diss., University of North Carolina, Chapel Hill, 2008), 39.

88. Leah Garrett, "The Jewish Robinson Crusoe," *Comparative Literature* 54, no. 3 (2002): 226.

89. See, e.g., David Zamość, *Robinzohn der eingere: Ein lezebuch fir kinder* (Breslau, 1824), 95–96; Anon. *Historiye odr zeltzame und vunderbahre bgebenheyten eynes yungen zee fahrers* (Prague, 1784), 23b; Anon., *Historiye fon den zeefahrer Robinzohn* (Frankfurt am Oder, 1813), [6]; Anon. [Yossef Vitlin], *Robinzohn: Di geshichte fun Alter Leb, eyne vahre und vunderbare geshichte tzum lezen* (1820, repr. Vilnius, 1894), part 2, 26a. For a discussion of these and other Jewish translations of Campe's works, see Chapter 4 below.

90. Kotzebue, *Die Negersklaven*, 89.

91. Maria Edgeworth, *Tales and Novels by Maria Edgeworth* (London, 1870), 2:399–419.

92. George Boulukos, *The Grateful Slave: The Emergence of Race in Eighteenth-Century British and American Culture* (Cambridge, 2008), 4–13.

93. Thomas Jefferson, "Notes on the State of Virginia," 1781, repr. in *Race and the Enlightenment: A Reader*, ed. Emmanuel C. Eze (Cambridge, 1997), 97. See further examples in Henri Grégoire, *An Inquiry Concerning the Intellectual and Moral Faculties of Negroes* (New York, 1997), 144; Adams, *Universal History*, 3:19.

94. Boulukos, *Grateful Slave*, 10. See also Boulukos's discussion of the English Amelioration act of 1798, and the ameliorationist discourse surrounding other legislative acts during the period, as well as David Brion Davis, *The Problem of Slavery in the Age of Revolution, 1770–1823* (Oxford, 1999), 412–20.

95. Bendavid, *Characteristik der Juden*, 15.

96. Quoted in Peter Gay, *The Enlightenment: An Interpretation, vol. 2: The Science of Freedom* (1969; repr. New York, 1977), 4, and see also 29–45; Moira Ferguson, *Subject to Others: British Women Writers and Colonial Slavery, 1670–1834* (New York, 1992), 91–94, 101.

97. Schorsch, *Jews and Blacks*, 292.

98. Romanelli, *Masa ba-Arav*, 35. English translation according to *Travail in an Arab Land*, trans. Yedida K. Stillman and Norman A. Stillman (Tuscaloosa, 1989), 70.

99. The question of the origin of the myth of Ham's Blackness is complex and has been the focus of somewhat heated scholarly debate. However, it is widely accepted amongst scholars that whereas Ham possessed variable identities during the ancient and medieval periods, by the seventeenth century he became predominantly regarded as the forefather of Black

Africans. For a discussion of the myth and its evolution, see Goldenberg, *The Curse of Ham: Race and Slavery in Early Judaism, Christianity and Islam* (Princeton, 2003), esp. pp. 1–6, 99–101, 141–44; Schorsch, *Jews and Blacks*, 19–39, 135–41, 274–76, 292; Benjamin Braude, "The Sons of Noah and the Construction of Ethnic and Geographical Identities in the Medieval and Early Modern Periods," *William and Mary Quarterly*, 3rd ser., 54, no. 1 (1997): 103–42. The earliest known Jewish illustration that depicts Ham as Black, in direct connection with the Curse, appeared in a mid-sixteenth-century illuminated Pentateuch by the Venetian painter Moisè dal Castellazzo. The illustration is reprinted in Kaplan, "Jewish Artists," 82, fig. 7. See also Kaplan's discussion on pp. 83–84.

100. Satanov, *Kuzary*, 2b. English translation according to Schorsch, *Jews and Blacks*, 280.

101. Schorsch, *Jews and Blacks*, 280.

102. Joseph Baran, "Divrey ha-yamim le-mamleḥot ha-araẓot," *Hameasef* 4 (1788): 371; Maimon, "Givat ha-moreh," in *Sefer moreh nevoḥim la-rav ha-gadol . . . Moshe ben Maimon* (1791; repr. Solzbach, 1800), 51b. For Mendelssohn's thoughts on the issue, see Hess, *Claims of Modernity*, 91–93, 96.

103. Ben Elijah, *Gevulot areẓ*, 7a; Khaykl Hurwitz, *Tsofnas paneyakh* (Bardichev, 1817), part 1, 50a–52a; Mendelssohn-Frankfurt, *Meẓiyat ha-areẓ*, 155–65; Günzberg, *Masa Kolombus*, part 2, 51.

104. See Isaac Weld, "Isaac Weld's des Jüngern Reisen durch die Staaten von Nordamerika und die Provinzen Ober- und Nieder-Canada während den Jahren 1795, 1796 und 1797," trans. Henriette Herz, in *Magazin von merkwürdigen neuen Reisebeschreibungen aus fremden Sprachen übersetzt*, vol. 20 (Berlin, 1800); Grégoire, *Die Neger. Ein Beitrag zur Staats- und Menschenkunde von H. Gregoire*, trans. Saul Asher (Berlin, 1809).

105. Bloch, *Sheviley olam*, part 1, 7a. On sentimentalism in abolitionist discourse, see Srividhya Swaminathan, *Debating the Slave Trade: Rhetoric of British National Identity, 1759–1815* (Surrey, 2009), esp. 100–110; Brycchan Carey, *British Abolitionism and the Rhetoric of Sensibility: Writing, Sentiment, and Slavery, 1760–1807* (New York, 2005). Another Jewish writer to employ sentimental abolitionism was Mordecai Noah, in his 1820 "Of Slavery": Noah, *Selected Writings* (Westport, CT, 1999), 103.

106. A rare exception may be found in Bendavid, *Characteristick der Juden*, 14–15.

107. Norbert Elias, *The Civilizing Process*, 1939, trans. Edmund Jephcott (Malden, MA, 2000), 34–35.

108. On cultural codes, see Shulamit Volkov, "Antisemitism as a Cultural Code: Reflections on the History and Historiography of Antisemitism in Imperial Germany," *Leo Baeck Institute Yearbook* 33 (1978): 25–46.

109. Rousseau, *de l'inégalité*, 160. English translation according to Rousseau, "Second Discourse," 76.

110. James Burnett, Lord Monboddo, *Of the Origin and Progress of Language* (Edinburgh, 1774), 1:226. See also Diderot, "Supplément," 579–644; Michel Adanson, *Histoire naturelle du Sénégal* (Paris, 1757), 31; John

Hawkesworth, *An Account of the Voyages undertaken by the order of his present Majesty for making Discoveries in the Southern Hemisphere* (Dublin, 1775), 2:36–40, 188, 250–51, 262–63.

111. Shalom Ha-cohen, *Amal ve-Tirẓah: Shirat dodim bi-shloshah ḥalakim* (Rödelheim, 1812), 29, 41–42; Aaron Wolfssohn-Halle, *Avtalyon, ve-hu mavo ha-limud le-naarey bney Yisrael u-le-khol ha-ḥafeẓim bi-lshon avar* (Berlin, 1790), 52; Zamość, *Toar ha-zman* (Dyhernfurth, 1821), 2.

112. For Elijah's story, see 1 Kings 19:1–16; for Rashby's tale: BT Shabbat 33b. See also Jeremiah 9:1–5.

113. See Percy Adams, *Travelers and Travel Liars* (London, 1962), 8–9, 11, 80–131, 183–91.

114. Quoted in Carla Gardina Pestana, *The English Atlantic in an Age of Revolution, 1640–1661* (Cambridge, 2004), 206.

115. The same dualistic significance of the cave is also found in the Arabian Nights, well known in the period and translated into English, French, and even Yiddish. Consider, e.g., Ali Baba's cave, which offers both treasures and death.

116. See, e.g., Outram's reading of the novel as an exemplary primitivistic text: Dorinda Outram, *The Enlightenment* (Cambridge, 1995), 64.

117. See, e.g., Crusoe's father's depiction of the "middle state" in Defoe, *Robinson Crusoe*, 5–6.

118. Ibid., 87; see also 32–33, 53, 77, 108, 179.

119. Ibid., 133.

120. Quoted in Richard Nash, *Wild Enlightenment: The Borders of Human Identity in the Eighteenth Century* (Charlottesville, 2003), 84.

121. Interestingly, the relationship between nature and culture is expressed in the geography of the island itself. The island's western, acculturated shore—inhabited by Crusoe—is a safe haven, while the eastern, wild shore is the location of cannibalistic feasts. Defoe, *Robinson Crusoe*, 129–30.

122. Buffon, "Animaux communes," 52.

123. I. Bernard Cohen, "Anquetil-Duperron, Benjamin Franklin, and Ezra Stiles," *Isis* 33, no. 1 (1941): 17.

124. Shenfeld, "Ha-adam," *Bikurey ha-itim* (1825): 86.

125. White, "Forms of Wildness," 28.

126. Similar rhetoric is found in Yossef Ha-cohen's *Sefer ha-Indeah*, 29. Another "natural man" said to have mated with animals is the biblical Adam. According to the great medieval sage Rashi, before the creation of Eve, Adam mated with every beast and animal. For a discussion of this theory and its reception, see Eric Lawee, "The Reception of Rashi's Commentary on the Torah in Spain: The Case of Adam's Mating with the Animals," *Jewish Quarterly Review* 97, no. 1 (2007): 33–66.

127. See Ofri Ilany, "From Divine Commandment to Political Act: The Eighteenth-Century Polemic on the Extermination of the Canaanites," *Journal of the History of Ideas* 73, no. 3 (2012): 437–61. Evidence of the Jewish reception of the negative attitude toward the story of the seven nations is found in Pinchas Horowitz's *Sefer ha-brit*. The author, a staunch though somewhat unconventional defender of the faith, vehemently objects to the

new approach to the story. See Pinchas Horowitz, *Sefer ha-brit ha-shalem* (1797; repr. Jerusalem, 1990), 531.

128. Thomas Hobbes, *Leviathan or the Matter, Forme and Power of a Common Wealth Ecclesiasticall and Civil* (1651; repr. Cambridge, 1991), 88–89.

129. Ibid., 89.

130. Feiner, "Yehudah Horowitz," 141–42.

131. See Jacob Katz, *Exclusiveness and Tolerance: Studies in Jewish-Gentile Relations in Medieval and Modern Times* (New York, 1961), 174–75.

132. Mendelssohn's letter to Yaacov Emden, 26 October 1773, and Emden's response dated November 1773, in Mendelssohn, *Gesammelte Schriften*, vol. 16: *Hebräische Schriften 3: Briefwechsel* (transcript and facsimile of ms., Berlin, 1929), 178–83.

133. The image of the hirsute Eve, discussed above, offers perhaps another example. As noted, early modern imagination tended to attribute hairiness to wild men, the counter image of the noble Savage. The Edenic couple, on the other hand, served as a paragon of natural nobility. By depicting Eve as hairy, therefore, early modern illustrators tied together the images of the wild man and the noble savage, to form a "noble wild woman," as it were.

134. Defoe, *Robinson Crusoe*, 132.

135. Rousseau, *de l'inégalité*, 95. English translation: *Second Discourse*, 48–49.

136. Boulukos, *Grateful Slave*, 10. See also Davis, *Age of Revolution*, 412–20.

137. Kant, *Was ist Aufklärung: Ausgewählte kleine Schriften* (1784; repr. Hamburg, 1999), 21. English translation: "An Answer to the Question: What is Enlightenment?," trans. Lara Denis, in *Groundwork for the Metaphysics of Morals* (Toronto, 2005), 120.

138. Voltaire, *Dictionnaire Philosophique* (London, 1767), 1:208. Translated according to Voltaire, *Philosophical Dictionary*, trans. Theodore Besterman (London, 2004), 183–84.

139. Grégoire, *des Juifs*, 63, 140.

140. Mendelssohn, *Jerusalem*, 2:45. English version according to Arkush translation, 96.

141. Horowitz, *Ḥayey ha-nefesh*, [41]. An almost identical discussion appears in Satanov, *Mishley Assaf*, part 2, 43b.

142. Horowitz, *Ḥayey ha-nefesh*, [39].

143. See John G.A. Pocock, *Virtue, Commerce and History: Essays on Political Thought and History, Chiefly in the Eighteenth-Century* (Cambridge, 1985), 196; "Conservative Enlightenment," 82–105. See also Israel, *Enlightenment Contested*, 6–15; Sorkin, *Religious Enlightenment*, 5–6.

144. See also Horowitz, *Ḥayey ha-nefesh*, [41].

145. Romanelli, *Masa ba-Arav*, 57; see also pp. 3–4, 6. For a different view, see Andrea Schatz, "Detours in a 'Hidden Land': Shmuel Romanelli's *Masa' ba'rav*," in *Jewish Studies at the Crossroads of Anthropology and History: Authority, Diaspora, Tradition*, ed. Ra'anan S. Boustan, Oren Kosansky, and Marina Rustow (Philadelphia, 2011), 164–84.

146. Hobbes, *Leviathan*, 244.

147. Locke, *Two Treatises of Government* (1690; repr. Cambridge, 1988), 276.

148. See, e.g., Henry Redhead Yorke, *Letters from France, in 1802* (London, 1804), 56–57, 117, 331. For a discussion of this imagery in the German-speaking world, see Andreas Mielke, "Hottentots in the Aesthetic Discussion of Eighteenth-Century Germany," *Monatshefte* 80, no. 2 (1988):144 ; and in England: Alan Bewell, *Romanticism and Colonial Disease* (Baltimore, 1999), 141–47; Obeyesekere, *Cannibal Talk*, 28–29. I thank Amnon Yuval for referring me to the works of Yorke and Gillray.

149. Rousseau, *Émile*, 211. Translation according to Rousseau, *Emile or on Education*, 332.

150. Anon. [attr. to Yonatan Eybeschütz], "Divrey yonat elem," 1824, Ms. Heb. 8° 2497, NLI. microfilm available at NLI, reel no. F 10505; Jacob Harif, *Amudey Yaavez* (Manchester, 1897). On the latter, see Leybovich, "Sefer amudey Yaavez," *Ha-zofeh le-hohmat Israel* 9, no. 1 (1925): 121–23.

CHAPTER 3

1. For a discussion of the stadial theory in the Scottish Enlightenment, see Karen O'Brien, *Women and Enlightenment in Eighteenth-Century Britain* (Cambridge, 2009), 69–109.

2. Pinto, "Réflexions," 1:13. English translation according to Paul Mendes-Flohr and Jehuda Reinharz, *The Jew in the Modern World: A Documentary History* (New York, 1980), 254.

3. For a discussion of these changes in various national contexts, see, e.g., Wheeler, *Complexion of Race*, 3–9, 21–28, 30–33; Wahrman, *Modern Self*, 104–26; Zantop, *Colonial Fantasies*, 66–80; Harrison, *Climates and Constitutions*, 92–110. For a different view, see Miriam Eliav-Feldon, "Vagrants or Vermin? Attitudes Towards Gypsies in Early Modern Europe," in *Origins of Racism*, 276–91.

4. For a bird's-eye view of this cultural shift, see Wahrman, *Modern Self*, esp. 127–66.

5. Quoted in Sander Gilman, "The Jewish Nose: Are Jews White? Or, the History of the Nose Job," in *The Other in Jewish Thought and History: Constructions of Jewish Culture and Identity*, ed. Laurence J. Silberstein and Robert L. Cohn (New York, 1994), 371. The passage is often mistakenly dated to the 1792 German translation; however, the original Dutch version appeared in 1786.

6. For White's quotation, see Wahrman, *Modern Self*, 108–9.

7. See my discussion in "Renouncing the Jungle" below.

8. My use of the term "translation" to describe these texts is inspired by Gideon Toury's discussion of the problems inherent in any essentialistic definition of "translation." Toury suggests that translation, by its very nature, eludes rigid, ahistorical definitions, and must be defined contextually, according to the manner in which it is perceived in the target culture. See Gideon Toury, "The Notion of 'Assumed Translation'—An Invitation

to a New Discussion," in *Letterlijkheid, Woordelijheid*, ed. H. Bloemen, E. Hertog, and W. Segers (Antwerpen/Harmelen, 1995), 141–47. For a further discussion of the problems inherent in differentiating between translations and adaptations, see Georges L. Bastin, "Adaptation," in *Routledge Encyclopedia of Translation Studies*, ed. Mona Baker (New York, 1998), 3–6.

9. For centuries, the Gaon's attitude toward secular studies has been the focus of heated controversy. For some recent discussions, see Eliyahu Stern, *The Genius: Elijah of Vilna and the Making of Modern Judaism* (New Haven, 2013), esp. 26, 37–38; Immanuel Etkes, *The Gaon of Vilna: The Man and His Image*, trans. Jeffrey M. Green (Berkeley, 2002), 46–56. For a discussion and references to further studies, see Idelson-Shein, "Strange Things," 318–22.

10. Idelson-Shein, "Strange Things," 295–322.

11. On the book's target audience and its popularity, see Tal Kogman, "Yezirat dimuyey ha-yeda ba-arazot dovrot ha-germanit bi-tkufat ha-haskalah" (Ph.D. diss., Tel Aviv University, 2000), 47–49, 85–89; Moshe Pelli, *Haskalah and Beyond: The Reception of the Hebrew Enlightenment and the Emergence of Haskalah Judaism* (Lanham, MD, 2010), 59–60.

12. Ḥanokh Zundel, *Sefer knaf renanim: Biyur neḥmad al midrash perek shirah* (Krotoszyn, 1842), 205; Euchel, *Sefer Mishley im tirgum Ashkenazy u-biyur me-et ha-ḥaham ha-torany Izḥak Euchel z"l* (1790; repr. 1834), 27; Joel Brill, "Mavo ha-sefer," in *Sifrey kodesh im tirgumim u-biyurim mi-meḥabrim shonim*, ed. Moshe ha-levi Landau (1788; repr. Prague, 1834), 51a. For some other examples, see Bloch, *Sheviley olam*, 2: 6a, 8a, 40a–41a; Shmuel Ashkenazy (Deutschlander), *Sefer mareh ha-Levanon ve-hu ḥibur kolel megilat shir ha-shirim im biyur al-pi ḥakirah amitit ve-gam tirgum Ashkenazy u-perush ha-milot* (Pressburg, 1847), 45a. On Horowitz's use of Lindau, see Rosenblum, *Iyuney sifrut ve-hagut mi-shilhey ha-meah ha-shmoneh-esreh ad yameynu* (Jerusalem, 1989), 5–7, 36; Kogman, "Dimuyey ha-yeda," 85–86.

13. Feiner, *Jewish Enlightenment*, 210.

14. Lindau, "Besorat sfarim ḥadashim," *Ha-measef* (1787): 15.

15. There were, of course, important exceptions such as Lefin or Satanov, who incorporated rabbinical Hebrew in their works, or Khaykl Hurwitz and Joseph Vitlin, who wrote in Yiddish. However, the use of biblical Hebrew was so widespread amongst the maskilim that it subsequently came to be identified with maskilic affiliations. For an amusing example, see Perl, *Megaleh temirin* (Vienna, 1819), 2a–b. Some maskilim even apologized for occasionally resorting to rabbinical Hebrew. See, e.g., Leib Stark, *Agudat shoshanim* (Prague, 1817), 88; Mendelssohn-Frankfurt, *Meziat ha-arez*, [9]; Günzberg, *Masa Kolombus o galut ha-arez ha-ḥadashah al yedey Kristof Kolombus* (1823; repr. Warsaw, 1883), 4. The introduction is missing in the earlier edition. On maskilic language as encompassing a wide array of styles, see Jeremy Dauber, *Antonio's Devils: Writers of the Jewish Enlightenment and the Birth of Modern Hebrew and Yiddish Literature* (Stanford, 2004), 32–34.

16. My translation. See Friedlander and Shoham, "Introduction," 28.

17. Zamość, *Tokhaḥot*, 172–76. On Zamość's treatment of Campe's book, see Idelson-Shein, *Ha-ekzoty*, 38.

18. Horowitz, *Sefer ha-brit*, 4–6, 9. For a discussion see Rosenblum, *Iyuney sifrut*, 20–22.

19. Anon., "Bikoret Sefer ha-brit," parts 1 and 2, *Ha-measef* (1808): 130–37, 140–41. For some other contemporaneous criticisms of this literary norm, see Bloch, *Sheviley olam*, 1:2; Mendelssohn-Frankfurt, *Meziat ha-arez*, [7]. Interestingly, Mendelssohn-Frankfurt's critique notwithstanding, he too was unable to refrain from stressing the theological value of secular studies. See Mendelssohn-Frankfurt, *Meziat ha-arez*, [3]–[4].

20. Mendelssohn, *Jerusalem*, 39–40. English version according to Arkush translation, 93. For other examples see Levison, *Shlosh esreh yessodey ha-torah* (Altona, 1791), 17a–21a; Lefin, Moda le-vinah (Berlin, 1788), 2b, 7b–8a, 10a–b; Euchel, "Igeret le-Michael Friedländer," *Ha-measef* (1785): part 1, 116–17, part 2, 137–42. For a discussion of this view in the Jewish Enlightenment, see Feiner, *Jewish Enlightenment*, 267–68; Sinkoff, *Tradition and Transition*, 171–83. On similar trends in the non-Jewish Enlightenment, see Israel, *Radical Enlightenment*, 456–62.

21. See discussion in Kogman, "Dimuyey ha-yeda," 82–84.

22. Horowitz, *Sefer ha-brit*, 199. See also Rosenblum, *Iyuney Sifrut*, 6. On Horowitz's use of Lindau, see Kogman, "Dimuyey ha-yeda." Horowitz also took whole chapters out of Baruch Schick's *Sefer tiferet ha-adam* and incorporated them into his own book. Cf. Schick, "Sefer tiferet ha-adam," in *Sefer amudey ha-shamayim* (Berlin, 1776), 4b, 21b–22a, 27a; Horowitz, *Sefer ha-brit*, 244–45.

23. Kogman, "Dimuyey ha-yeda," 54–62. Kogman shows that other maskilim also made some use of Raff's book; see "Dimuyey ha-yeda," 57, 100–105, and her "Magayim beyn-tarbutiyim be-tekstim shel ha-haskalah al madaey ha-teva," in Feiner and Bartal, *Ha-haskalah li-gvaneyhah*, 35–36.

24. Adams, *Travel Liars*, 11, 17.

25. For a discussion of these new translational norms see Fania Oz-Salzberger, *Translating the Enlightenment: Scottish Civic Discourse in Eighteenth-Century Germany* (Oxford, 1995), 77–85; Louis Kelly, "The Eighteenth Century to Tytler," in *The Oxford History of Literary Translation in English: 1660–1790*, ed. Stuart Gillespie and David Hopkins (Oxford, 2005), 3:67–77; Miriam Salama-Carr, "French Tradition," in Baker, *Translation*, 407–9.

26. For some other examples, see [Herz], *Weld's Reisen*; Asher, *Die Neger*. For a discussion of these translations, see Idelson-Shein, *Ha-ekzoty*, 222–24.

27. For a discussion of Mendelssohn's two translations, see Idelson-Shein, "Strange Things," 305–6, and *Ha-ekzoty*, 224–25. On Mendelssohn's treatment of Rousseau's *Discours* see Lifschitz, *Language and Enlightenment*, 81–83.

28. On acceptability as one of the main characteristics of early maskilic translations, see Toury, *Descriptive Translation Studies and Beyond* (Amsterdam, 1995), 131–32, and "Reshit ha-tirgum ha-moderny le-Ivrit: Od manbat eḥad," *Dapim le-meḥkar be-sifrut* 11 (1997): 110–11. For a discussion of the

differences between the translational norms prevalent amongst the maskilim and those adhered to by members of other Enlightenments, and some further examples, see Idelson-Shein, *Ha-ekzoty*, 220–25; "Strange Things," 304–8.

29. See Zohar Shavit, "Literary Interference between German and Jewish-Hebrew Children's Literature During the Enlightenment: The Case of Campe," *Poetics Today* (Children's Literature) 13, no. 1 (1992): 52–53; "From Friedländer's Lesebuch to the Jewish Campe: The Beginning of Hebrew Children's Literature in Germany," *Leo Baeck Institute Yearbook* 33 (1988): 402, 407, 410; Toury, "Hebrew [Translation] Tradition," in Baker's *Encyclopedia of Translation Studies*, 443; *Descriptive Translation*, 132–3; Yehudah Friedlander and Chaim Shoham, Introduction to *Mot Adam*, by Friedrich Klopstock, trans. Zvi Ben-David (Prague, 1817), 7–8.

30. Kogman, "Magayim," 32–35.

31. For a discussion of this practice, see Kogman, "Haskalah Scientific Knowledge in Hebrew Garment: A General Statement and Two Examples," *Target* 19, no. 1 (2007): 72–80; Rebecca Wolpe, "Judaizing Robinson Crusoe: Maskilic Translations of Robinson Crusoe," *Jewish Culture and History* 13, no. 1 (2012): 42–67; Garrett, "Jewish Robinson Crusoe," 215–27; Idelson-Shein, *Ha-ekzoty*, 225–28.

32. For a discussion of these different motivations, and some examples, see Idelson-Shein, "Strange Things," 309–18.

33. See Toury, "Reshit ha-tirgum," 114–19; Shavit, "Friedländer's Lesebuch," 404.

34. [Ferri, Giovanni di San Constante,] *Génie de M. de Buffon* (Paris, 1778). On Ferry, see Anon., *Biographie des Hommes Vivants* (Paris, 1817), 3:79. For a comparison between the two texts, see Idelson-Shein, "Strange Things," 295–322. For another example of mediated translation through children's books, see Kogman's discussion of Isaac Satanov in "Magayim," 32–40.

35. Ferri, *Büffons Geist, oder Kern seiner Naturgeschichte*, trans. Anon. (St. Petersburg, 1783). On Ben Elijah's knowledge of French, see Etkes, *The Gaon*, 45.

36. Kogman, "Dimuyey ha-yeda," 56.

37. I discuss this issue in some detail in a forthcoming essay on the uses of travel in early maskilic children's literature.

38. For a discussion of these Jewish translations see Shavit, "Literary Interference," 41–61; Garrett, "Jewish Robinson Crusoe," 215–28; Ken Frieden, "Neglected Origins of Modern Hebrew Prose: Hasidic and Maskilic Travel Narratives," *AJS Review* 33 (2009): 3–43; Kogman, "A Case Study," 277–304; Idelson-Shein, *Ha-ekzoty*, 214–33, 324–32. This may also explain the maskilim's tendency to omit distinctly childish features from their translations. On this tendency, see Kogman, "Dimuyey ha-yeda," 58–61, 74–84; Shavit, "Ha-rihut shel hadar ha-Haskalah be-Berlin," in *Ke-minhag Ashkenaz u-Polin: Sefer yovel le-Hone Shmeruk*, ed. Israel Bartal, Ezra Mendelsohn, and Chava Turniansky (Jerusalem, 1993), 194–207; "Literary Interference," 51–57.

39. Linnaeus, *Systema Naturae*, 33.

40. Schnaber-Levison, *Yesodey ha-torah*, 96a.

41. Sholem Avramovich, *Sefer toldot ha-tevah* (Leipzig, 1862), xxi.

42. Buffon, "Variétés," 224–25; English translation, *Natural History*, trans. James Smith Barr (London, 1792), 191–96.

43. On the Borandians, see, e.g., Voltaire's sarcastic reference to Buffon: "Histoire de l'Empire de Russie sous Pierre le Grand," 1759, repr. in *Collection complète des œuvres de M. de Voltaire* (Genève, 1768), 2:334.

44. Ferry's adaptation of Buffon, which was used by Ben Elijah, makes no mention of the Ostyaks, and could not serve as Lindau's source. Another German source in which Buffon's description of the northerners appears almost in its entirety is Campe's account of the voyage of Heemskerk and Barenz. This account was translated into Hebrew by Lefin in 1818. However, Campe's account does not include the other peoples described by Buffon, and which similarly appear in RL. Compare Buffon, "Variétés," 224; Ferri, *Génie de Buffon*, 307; Campe, "Jakob Heemkerks und Wilhelm Barenz nördliche Entdeckungsreise," 1786, repr. in *Sammlung interessanter und durchgängig zwekmäßig abgefaßter Reisebeschreibung für die Jugend* (Reutlingen, 1796), 1:76–81. On the problems inherent in identifying the use of mediating texts in maskilic translations, see Toury, *Descriptive Translation*, 134.

45. Cf. RL, 75a; Buffon, "Variétés," 229–34.

46. Compare Perl, Draft for Zir Neeman, 11a; Keyser, *Kohelet Shlomo*, 4a. For Hurwitz's reference to Büsching, see Hurwitz, *Tsofnas paneyakh*, part 3, 180b. Though the book is a Yiddish translation of Campe's *Entdeckung von Amerika*, the reference to Büsching is Hurwitz's own addition.

47. On Büsching and his geography, see Wilhelm Michel, "Anton Friedrich Büsching," *Allgemeine deutsch Biographie und neue deutsche Biographie* (Berlin, 1957), 3:3–4.

48. See Theodor Brüggermann and Hans-Heino Ewers, *Handbuch zur Kinder- und Jugendliteratur* (Stuttgart, 1982), 1014.

49. Compare Anton Friedrich Büsching, *Neue Erdbeschreibung* (1754; repr. Hamburg, 1770), 1:386–98; Lindau, RL, 105a–b; Raff, *Geographie für Kinder* (Göttingen, 1776), 287–96; *Geographie für Kinder zum Gebrauch auf Schulen* (Tübingen, 1786), 381. Unfortunately, I have been unable to locate the first edition of Raff's book; however, I have checked both extant editions—the second and the fourth.

50. Compare Büsching, *Erdbeschreibung*, 1:67–68; Raff, *Naturgeschichte*, 624.

51. Büsching, *Erdbeschreibung*, 1:69.

52. RL, 75a, 81a.

53. On Raff's primary sources, see Idelson-Shein, *Ha-ekzoty*, 253–55. On the other sources used by Raff, see Klaus-Ulrich Pech, "Raff, Georg Christian," in *Lexikon der Kinder und Jugendliteratur*, ed. Klaus Doderer (Weinheim, 1979), 3:120; Brüggermann and Ewers, *Handbuch*, 3:1023, 1026.

54. Büsching, *Erdbeschreibung*, 393.

55. Perl, "Greenland," 11a; Keysir, "Kohelet Shlomo," 4a.

56. See, e.g., Buffon, "Variétés," 319; Kant, "Physische Erdbeschreibung: Zweiter Theil," 1802, repr. in *Kants Werke: Akademie Textausgabe*, vol. 9:

Logik, Physische Geographie, Pädagogik (Berlin, 1968), 311; Johann Friedrich Blumenbach, "Of the Anthropological Variety of Mankind, Ed. 1795,"
in *The Anthropological Treatises of Johann Friedrich Blumenbach*, trans.
Thomas Bendyshe (London, 1865), 265; Georges Léopold Cuvier, "Animal
Kingdom (Excerpt)," 1797, repr. in Eze, *Race and the Enlightenment*, 104.

57. Defoe, *Robinson Crusoe*, 160.

58. Sander L. Gilman, "The Figure of the Black in German Aesthetic Theory," *Eighteenth-Century Studies* 8, no. 4 (1975): 373–91; Mielke, "Hottentots," 135–41, 144. Oddly, we find the theory of universal fear of Blackness
reiterated in some contemporary works. A striking example is found in Abraham Melamed's *Image of the Black*, esp. 15–25. Schorsch criticizes Melamed
for his resource to the theory of universal negrophobia, justifiably claiming
that "there is nothing inevitable about the way various 'Others' are characterized." See Schorsch, "Review: Abraham Melamed, the Image of the Black
in Jewish Culture: A History of the Other," *Jewish History* 21 (2007): 212.

59. For a discussion of the purported swarthiness of the Jews in eighteenth-century thought, see Felsenstein, *Antisemitic Stereotypes*, 55–56, 80.

60. Mendelssohn-Frankfurt, *Meziat ha-arez*, [7].

61. Shenfeld, "Ha-adam," 86.

62. See Zamość, *Agudat shoshanim* (Breslau, 1827), 24; Abraham ben
Elijah, *Gevulot*, 8a.

63. Johann Gottfried Herder, "Letters for the Advancement of Human-
ity—Tenth Collection," 1793–97, repr. in *Philosophical Writings*, trans.
Michael N. Forster (Cambridge, 2002), 383; Johann Georg Zimmermann,
An Essay on National Pride (1758; repr. London, 1805), 20; Grégoire,
Nègres, 28; Bloch, *Sheviley olam*, 7a; Mendelssohn-Frankfurt, *Meziat
ha-arez*, 31, 34. Compare Campe, *Die Entdeckung* (1781), 90–91; *Die Ent-
deckung* (1784), 55; *Die Entdeckung* (1830), 57. On Brown, see Gilman,
"Figure of the Black," 382.

64. See Mielke, "Hottentots," 135–37, 143; Gilman, "Figure of the
Black," 380–87. For some examples, see Buffon, "Variétés," 238, 278–79,
287; Campe, "Wilson's Schiffbruch," 175; Robertson, *Settlement of America*, 176; Lefin, *Masaot ha-yam*, 69; Abraham ben Elijah, *Gevulot*, 6b.

65. Romanelli, *Masa ba-Arav*, 5. English translation according to *Travail*,
23. I have slightly modified the translation to make it more compatible with
Romanelli's original Hebrew.

66. Stanley Diamond, *In Search of the Primitive* (New Brunswick, NJ,
1974), 109–10.

67. Kogman, "Dimuyey ha-yeda," 66–70. There is, it must be admitted,
a certain degree of anachronism in using the term "polygenism" in the context of late eighteenth-century thought. In fact, the term was introduced only
during the second half of the nineteenth century. However, since the term has
become commonplace in eighteenth-century studies, it is used here without
quotation marks.

68. Ben Elijah, *Gevulot arez*, 1a.

69. Buffon, "Variétés," 223, and see also 320–21; Ferry, *Génie de Buffon*,
107; *Büffon's Geist*, 74.

70. Aharon Gumpertz, *Megaleh sod* (Hamburg, 1765), [4].

71. Buffon, *Histoire naturelle*, 4:385–86. English translation according to Buffon, *Natural History*, 5:189. For a discussion of Buffon's "reproduction criterion," see Robert Bernasconi, "Who Invented the Concept of Race? Kant's Role in the Enlightenment Construction of Race," in *Race*, ed. Robert Bernasconi (Oxford, 2001), 16.

72. See, e.g., Rousseau, *L'inégalité*, 171; Kant, "Von den verschiendenen Racen der Menschen," 1775, repr. in *Kants gesammelte Schriften*, vol. 2 (Berlin, 1912), 435. See also Darwin's own discussion of Buffon's influence on the meaning of "species": Charles Darwin, *The Origin of Species by Means of Natural Selection* (1859; repr. New York, 1979), 53–63. See also Bernasconi, "Concept of Race," 16–17; Richards, "Species," 174–77. Some initial doubts concerning Buffon's criterion were expressed by Linnaeus, Blumenbach, and even, at one point, Buffon himself. See, e.g., Blumenbach, "Anthropological Variety, 1775," 73–81; "Anthropological Variety, 1795," 188. And see discussion in Peter J. Bowler, *Evolution: The History of an Idea* (1983; repr. Berkeley, 2003), 70; Jacques Roger, *Buffon*, trans. Sarah L. Bonnefoi (Ithaca, 1997), 326–27; Lord Henry Home Kames, *Sketches of the History of Man* (Edinburgh, 1774), 6–7.

73. Kant, "Verschiedenen Rassen," 435.

74. For one polygenist's attempt to tackle this problem, see Virey, *Histoire des mœurs et de l'instinct des animaux* (Paris, 1822), 1:251, and *De la puissance vitale considérée dans ses fonctions physiologiques chez l'homme* (Paris, 1823), 373.

75. Zammito, "Policing Polygeneticism," 35–54. On Spinoza's preadamism, see Asa Kasher and Shlomo Biderman, "Why Was Baruch de Spinoza Excommunicated?," in *Sceptics, Millenarians, and Jews*, ed. David S. Katz and Jonathan I. Israel (Leiden, 1990), 138–41.

76. Kames, *Sketches*, 1:39–40. For some earlier anthropological uses of the story of the tower of Babel see Goldenberg, *Curse of Ham*, 98–99.

77. Grégoire, *Nègres*, 30–31. Translation according to Grégoire, *Cultural Achievements of Negroes*, 17.

78. Satanov, *Mishley Assaf*, 2:4a–4b.

79. Ben Avraham, *Milḥamot*, 8a.

80. Gumpertz, *Megaleh sod*, [4].

81. Ben Elijah, *Gevulot areẓ*, 8a. Compare *Büffon's Geist*, 114. See also, e.g., *Gevulot*, 10a. For a more detailed discussion of Ben Elijah's monogenism, see Idelson-Shein, "Strange Things," 310–15.

82. For some examples of the maskilic usage of the term in its medieval sense, see, e.g., Satanov, *Sefer ha-gderim*, 66a; "Sefer holeḥ tamim," in *Beyur milot ha-higayon* (Berlin, 1795), 1a–2a; *Mishley Assaf*, 2:21a(n); Mendelssohn, *Milot ha-higayon*, 15a, 17b, 28b, 31a–33a; Israel mi-Zamość, *Ruaḥ hen*, 29, 34–35; Horowitz, *Sefer ha-brit*, 24–29. For some medieval examples, see Baḥya Ibn Paquda, *Ḥovot ha-levavot* (1080; repr. Jerusalem, 1973), 59; *Ḥovot ha-levavot*, trans. Yehudah Ibn Tibbon (1161; repr. Jerusalem, 1973), 18b; Iẓḥak Abravanel, *Perush ha-torah* (15th cent.; repr. Warsaw, 1862), Exodus 20: 37a.

83. See, e.g., Ben Elijah, *Gevulot*, 6a (compare *Büffon's Geist*, 103; *Génie de Buffon*, 148); Moshe ben Zvi Bock, *Moda le-yaldey bney Israel* (Berlin, 1812), 118; Levi, *Lingua Sacra*, 3: Letter S., Sug; Ben-Zeev, *Ozar ha-shorashim*, 70b–71a; Horowitz, *Sefer ha-brit*, 211; Wetzlar, *Libes briv*, 4b–5a, 9a–b.

84. See, e.g., Horowitz, *Sefer ha-brit*, 208–10 and throughout.

85. See, e.g., Emden, *Megilat sefer*, 10; Shalom Ha-cohen, *Kore ha-dorot* (Warsaw, 1838), 224. For a discussion of the ambiguity of the term in English and French, see Joanna Lipkin, "'Others', Slaves and Colonists in 'Oroonoko,'" in *The Cambridge Companion to Aphra Behn*, ed. Dereck Hughes and Janet Todd (Cambridge, 2004), 167–70; Pierre H. Boulle, "In Defense of Slavery: Eighteenth-Century Opposition to Abolition and the Origins of a Racist Ideology in France," in *History from Below*, ed. Fredrick Kranz (Oxford, 1988), 221. For some of the earliest modern uses of the term in Hebrew, see Kalman Shulman, *Mosdey arez* (Vilnius, 1871), 11; Julius Lippert, *Toldot hashlamat ha-adam*, trans. David Frischmann (Warsaw, 1894), 1:216.

86. See, e.g., Buffon, "Variétés," 224, 290. For some further examples, see Kames, *Sketches*, 1:1, 6, 7, 10, 12, 26, and throughout. For a discussion of the taxonomic ambiguities prevalent in non-Jewish literature during the eighteenth century, see Bernasconi, "Concept of Race," 17–18; Nicholas Hudson, "From 'Nation' to 'Race': The Origin of Racial Classification in Eighteenth-Century Thought," *Eighteenth-Century Studies* 29, no. 3 (1996): 247–64; Frank Spencer, *History of Physical Anthropology* (New York, 1997), 170.

87. See, e.g., Blumenbach, *Handbuch der Naturgeschichte* (1779; repr. Göttingen, 1825), 55; Greogoire/[Asher], *Die Neger*, 1, 5, 34; Kant, "Verschiedenen Rassen," 435.

88. Joseph Klausner, *Ha-adam ha-kadmon: Yesodot ha-antropologiyah* (Warsaw, 1900), v, and see also vii; Avramovich, *Toldot ha-teva*, 2.

89. For a discussion of this process, see Kogman, "Dimuyey ha-yeda," 68.

90. Shenfeld, "Ha-adam," 86. Compare Blumenbach, "The Anthropological Variety, 1795," 265–66; *Handbuch*, 55–57; in an earlier edition of *De generis humani varierate nativa*, Blumenbach identified only four varieties of man; however, the 1795 edition spoke of five races.

91. Shenfeld, "Ha-adam," 86. For Blumenbach's views on climate see Blumenbach, "Anthropological Variety, 1775," 71–73, 101–29. The Hebrew term "nof"—usually meaning "scenery"—is used here in its more archaic sense as "climate." On such usage in early modern Hebrew, see Mintz-Manor, "Ha-siah," 209(n).

92. Shenfeld, "Ha-adam," 86.

93. Harrison, *Climates and Constitutions*, 106, and see also 15–16, 103–6; Wahrman, *Modern Self*, 111–12; Hess, *Claims of Modernity*, 52–54, 84–87.

94. RL, 34b, 35a, 40a–b. On Lindau's discussion of the zebra, see Kogman, "A Case Study," 295.

95. Ruderman, *Jewish Thought*, 260–67.

96. Ibid., 265; Bowler, *Evolution*, 45.

97. On the radical potential of spontaneous generation, see Bowler, *Evolution*, 45–83; Israel, *Radical Enlightenment*, 456–57; Gordon Wattles, "Buffon, d'Alembert and Materialist Atheism," *Studies on Voltaire and the Eighteenth Century* 266 (1989): 289–92.

98. See Ruderman, *Jewish Thought*, 260–61.

99. Israel mi-Zamość, "Oẓar neḥmad," 1771, repr. in *Sefer ha-kuzary*, by Yehudah Ha-levi (Tel Aviv, 1959), 66.

100. Satanov, *Kuzary*, 47b. On other early modern Jewish responses to spontaneous generation, see Ruderman, *Jewish Thought*, 260–67, 342–43, 366–67.

101. Levison, *Yesodey ha-Torah*, 30a. See also Levison's reference to Dutch naturalist Antony van Leeuwenhoek, one of the great opponents of spontaneous generation: Levison, *Yesodey ha-Torah*, 31–32. Levison demonstrates here an awareness of another relatively recent scientific discovery, that of plant sexuality. This discovery is often attributed to Linnaues, but the notion that plants reproduce sexually originates already in the late seventeenth century. Linnaeus, however, was one of the great popularizers of this discovery, and it stands to reason that Levison first encountered the notion through his work.

102. Gershon ben Shlomo, *Shaarey ha-shamayim* (13th cent.; repr. Warsaw, 1876), 13. For other early examples, see Richard H. Popkin, *Isaac La Peyrère (1596–1676)* (Leiden, 1987), 39–40, 134; Anthony Pagden, "The Peopling of the New World: Ethnos, Race and Empire in the Early-Modern World," in *Origins of Racism*, 307–8.

103. Paul Erickson, "The Anthropology of Charles Caldwell, M.D.," *Isis* 72, no. 2 (1981): 255.

104. Johann Wolfgang Goethe/Johann Peter Eckermann, *Gespräche mit Goethe in den Letzten Jahren seines Lebens*, 1823–1832 (Leipzig, 1836), 2:22. And see also Popkin, "La Peyrére," 134.

105. Raff, *Naturgeschichte*, 125.

106. RL, 59b. The addition is also absent in other editions of Raff's book I have checked. See Raff, *Naturgeschichte* (1780), 126; *Naturgeschichte* (1788), 126; *Naturgeschichte* (1793), 119. See also Pinchas Horowitz's outraged reaction to Lindau's rejection of spontaneous generation, which is reminiscent of Briel's position earlier in the century: Horowitz, *Sefer ha-brit*, 222.

107. See discussion in Winthrop D. Jordan, *White over Black: American Attitudes Toward the Negro, 1550–1812* (Kingsport, NC, 1968), 518–21.

108. BT Sanhedrin 108b. On the anthropological uses of the curse, see Schorsch, *Jews and Blacks*, 19–39, 135–41; Braude, "Cham et Noé," 93–125; Goldenberg, *Curse of Ham*, 1–6, 99–101, 141–44.

109. This understanding of the phenomenon of albinism is discernible, e.g., in the talmudic requirement that upon encountering an albino one should say the blessing "Blessed is the changer of beings" [ברוך משנה הבריות]. See BT Berachot 58b.

110. Voltaire, "Homme," 301–2.

111. Buffon, "Variétés," 303–4. On Rush's views, see Martin, *The White African Body: A Cultural and Literary Exploration* (New York, 2002), 41–43.

112. [Anon.], "Negres blancs," 1765, in *Encyclopédie, ou dictionnaire raisonné des sciences, des arts et des métiers*, ed. Denis Diderot and Jean le Rond D'Alembert (repr. Chicago: University of Chicago ARTFL Encyclopédie Projet, Winter 2008), 11:79. The author cites also other widespread explanations for the phenomenon, such as the effects of maternal imagination, or the possibility that the albinos are the product of an unnatural union between African women and apes. For a discussion of these and similar theories, see Julia V. Douthwaite, *The Wild Girl, Natural Man and the Monster: Dangerous Experiments in the Age of Enlightenment* (Chicago, 2002), 207.

113. William Nicholson, ed., *The British Encyclopedia or Dictionary of Arts and Sciences* (London, 1809), 4:[238].

114. See, e.g., Friedrich Anton Brockhaus, *Konversation-Lexikon* (1796–1808; repr. Leipzig, 1827), 6:5; Joseph Uihlein, *Unterricht in der Geographie* (1806; repr. Frankfurt, 1820), 12; Pierre-Louis Moreau Maupertuis, "Vénus Physique," 1745, repr. in *Oeuvres* (Lyon, 1768; repr. Hildesheim, 1965), 115–16; Blumenbach, "Natural Variety, 1775," 130.

115. Hawkesworth, *Voyages*, 3:23. For a preliminary discussion of these changes, see Wahrman, *Modern Self*, 112–13.

116. Virey, "Nègre," in *Nouveau Dictionnaire d'Histoire Naturelle* (Paris, 1818), 22:459.

117. Samuel Thomas von Sömmering, *Ueber die körperliche Verschiedenheit des Negers vom Europäer* (Frankfurt, 1785), table of contents article 2. See also pp. 1–2ff. See also a discussion of the importance of other anatomical traits besides skin color in turn-of-the-century scientific discourse in Wheeler, *Complexion of Race*, 295.

118. On Behn, see discussion in Chapter 1 above. On Stibbs see Wheeler, *Complexion of Race*, 4.

119. šćAgudat shoshanim120. Virey, *Histoire Naturelle du Genre Humain* (1801; repr. Paris, 1824), 1:170.

121. Schorsch, *Jews and Blacks*, 116.

122. Ben Elijah, *Gevulot arez*, 4b.

123. On the differences between the two terms in eighteenth-century German, see May Opitz, "Racism, Sexism, and Precolonial Images of Africa in Germany," in *Showing Our Colors: Afro-German Women Speak Out*, ed. May Opitz, Katharina Oguntoye, and Dagmar Schultz (Amherst, 1986), 4–9.

124. See, e.g., RL, 79b, 81a. Compare Raff, *Naturgeschichte*, 635–36. *Reshit limudim* appears, in fact, to have been the first Hebrew text to mention the existence of a fifth part of the world. The next Hebrew author to convey a familiarity with the discoveries made in the South Pacific was Wessely, who in 1789 mentioned the travels of James Cook to the South Seas. See Wessely, *Shirey tiferet*, part 1 (1789; repr. Warsaw 1883), IV. Other contemporaneous Hebrew or Yiddish mentions of the "new world" of the late eighteenth century are rare. For some exceptional discussions,

see Anon., *Kleyne yeografye oder erd beshreybung* (Frankfurt, 1802), 16; Keysir, "Kohelet Shlomo," 3a; Bock, *Moda*, 93; Lefin, *Masaot ha-yam*, part 1. To the best of my knowledge, the earliest reference made by a Jewish author to the South Sea voyages is found in Mendelssohn's *Jerusalem*, 2:84–85. As for the physical presence of Jews in Oceania, there are reports of a few Jewish convict laborers in Australia already in 1788. A small Jewish community was established on the continent, but only in the late 1820s. An amusing mention of Jews in South Seas travel literature is found in Ebenezer Townsend's late eighteenth-century travel diary, in which the author claims that upon arriving in Hawaii in 1798 he was greeted by the king, Kamehameha I, and his Jewish cook. See Ebenezer Townsend, "Diary," repr. in *Papers of the New Haven Colony Historical Society* 4 (1888): 74. I thank James W. Campbell of the Whitney Library in New Haven for his help in obtaining this source.

125. Frantz Fanon, *Black Skin, White Masks* (1952; repr. London, 1986), 18.

126. Hourwitz, *Apologie*, 67.

127. Pinto, Letter to Condamine, f. 184b.

128. Pinto, "Réflexions," 1:13.

129. See Léon Poliakov, *The History of Anti-Semitism*, vol. 3: *From Voltaire to Wagner* (1968; repr. London, 1975), 138–39.

130. See Gilman, "Jewish Nose," 371; Wahrman, *Modern Self*, 108–10; Efron, *Defenders of the Race: Jewish Doctors and Race Science in Fin-de-Siècle Europe* (New Haven, 1994); Michael Ragusis, *Theatrical Nation: Jews and Other Outlandish Englishmen in Georgian Britain* (Philadelphia, 2010), 36–38.

131. Schönhak, *Toldot ha-arez* (Warsaw, 1841), 1:2

132. Shoa Ish Bialistok, *Sheviley erez Russiah* (Warsaw, 1893), 18. For Neubauer's view, see Efron, "Scientific Racism," 83–84.

133. Volkov, "Talking of Jews, Thinking of Germans—The Ethnic Discourse in 19th Century Germany," *Tel Aviver Jahrbuch für deutsche Geschichte* 30 (2002): 47–49; Mitchell B. Hart, *Social Science and the Politics of Modern Jewish Identity* (Stanford, 2000), 178–81; Efron, *Defenders of the Race*, 58–90, 100–122.

134. One Jewish thinker who rejected climatic theory was Isaac Disraeli, who deemed the theory one of the "follies of the wise." However, Disraeli was not opposed to environmentalism in general, and he explained that differences between nations are purely the outcome of education, liberty, and customs. See Isaac Disraeli, *Miscellanies; or Literary Recreations* (London, 1796), 288–309; Wahrman, *Modern Self*, 111.

135. Compare Günzberg, *Galut ha-arez*, 49–51; Anon., *Historisch-geographische Beschreibung von Amerika für Jünglinge* (Nürnberg, 1784), 26–27; Robertson, *Settlement of America*, 356–58. On the German adaptation of Robertson's book, see *Allgemeine deutsche Bibliothek* 66, no. 2 (Berlin, 1786), 525–27.

136. Günzberg, *Galut ha-arez*, 50–51.

137. See Ken Koltun-Fromm, *Moses Hess and Modern Jewish Identity* (Bloomington, 2001), 76–77. For another example, see Jacob Shavit and

Jehudah Reinharz, *Darwin u-khama mi-bney mino* (Jerusalem, 2009), 240, and see also therein the discussion of Hess's ambivalence toward race, 256–57.

138. See Aaron Bernstein, *Yediyot ha-teva*, trans. David Frischmann (1880; repr. 1884), 11:14–15, 33.

139. Schulmann, *Mosdey arez*, 11. On Lambroso, see Mary Gibson and Nicole Hahn Rafter, introduction to *Criminal Man*, by Cesare Lombroso, trans. Gibson and Rafter (Durham, NC, 2006), 17–19.

140. Klausner, *Ha-adam*, 137–38.

141. Efron, *Defenders of the Race*, 9. See also Shavit and Reinharz, *Darwin*, 241–43.

142. See Hart, *Social Science*, 181–93; Efron, *Defenders of the Race*, 123–74; "Scientific Racism," 89–96; Amos Morris-Reich, "Arthur Ruppin's Concept of Race," *Israel Studies* 11, no. 3 (2006): 1–30. See also Volkov, "Talking of Jews," 47–49; Shavit, "Thunat ha-arez," 400–403, 410–12; Shavit and Reinharz, *Darwin*, 241; Hanan Harif, "Asiatic Brothers, European Strangers: Eugen Hoeflich and Pan-Asian Zionism in Vienna," in *Against the Grain: German-Jewish Intellectuals in Hard Times*, ed. Ezra Mendelsohn, Stefani Hoffman, and Richard I. Cohen (New York, 2013), 171–185.

143. On Ben Elijah's translation, and its style, content, and source, see Idelson-Shein, "Strange Things," 295–322.

144. Buffon, *Variétés*, 266, translation according to Buffon, *Natural History*, 4:262.

145. *Gevulot arez*, 4b. See 1 Chronicles 17:21. For a more detailed discussion of this and other deviations, see Idelson-Shein, "Strange Things," 308–18.

CHAPTER 4

1. Gay, *The Enlightenment: Science of Freedom*, 174.

2. See, e.g., Edgeworth, *Tales and Novels*, 1:3, 147–51; 2: 399–412; Stephanie F. Genlis, "Les esclaves, Ou le pouvoir de la bienfaisance," 1784, repr. in *Les veillées du château* (Paris, 1851), 345–61; Thomas Day, *The History of Sandford and Merton* (1783; repr. New York, 1856), 49–52, 83, 101, 115–18, 225–29, 273–78, 279–92, 299, 328.

3. Quoted in Geoffrey Summerfield, *Fantasy and Reason: Children's Literature in the Eighteenth Century* (London, 1984), 135–36.

4. Mary F. Thwaite, *From Primer to Pleasure in Reading* (Boston, 1963).

5. Shavit, "Jewish Campe," 389. An exception to this rule is the 1820 Yiddish translation of Campe's *Robinson*, which attracted some readership and was printed in no fewer than five editions, most recently in 1907.

6. Louis de Jaucourt, "Travel," 1765, repr. in *The Encyclopedia of Diderot & d'Alembert Collaborative Translation Project*, trans. Nelly S. Hoyt and Thomas Cassirer, University of Michigan Library, 2003, http://hdl.handle.net/2027/spo.did2222.0000.169 (accessed 18 July 2012).

7. Wessely, *Divrey shalom*, part 2, [34].

8. On Campe's status amongst non-Jewish educators in Germany and Europe in general, see Zantop, *Colonial Fantasies*, 103; Apgar, *Taming Travel*, 11–13, 29, 86.

9. Shavit, "Literary Interference," 56–58. In a later study, Shavit cites a tenth translation, Leib Stark's *Agudat shoshanim*. See Shavit and Ewers, *Deutsch-judische Kinder- und Jugendliteratur* (Stuttgart, 1996), 1:233. However, Stark's book is not a translation of Campe, but rather an anthology of the poems of such writers as Christian Felix Weise and William Lisle Bowles, as well as Hebrew writers such as Judah Jeiteles. See Stark, *Agudat shoshanim*, 2, 78–80, and compare 17–18, 76–77; Christian Felix Weise, "Der Fleiß," in *Kleine lyrische Gedichte* (Leipzig, 1772), 3:55–57; William Lisle Bowles, "The Butterfly and the Bee," in *The Little Villager's Verse Book* (n.d., repr. London, 1826), 23. There is also some uncertainty as to the existence of an 1810 translation of Campe's *Die Entdeckung,* which Shavit attributes to Hirsch Ber Hurwitz. See Frieden, "Neglected Origins," 7n; Rebecca Wolpe, "The Sea Voyage Narrative as an Educational Tool in the Early Haskalah" (master's thesis, Hebrew University of Jerusalem, 2006), 83.

10. On these Yiddish translations, see Shavit, "Literary Interference," 50; Frieden, "Neglected Origins," 3–35; Garett, "Jewish Robinson," 215–29; Wolpe, "Sea Voyage," 81–105; "Judaizing Robinson," 53–54; Z. Reyzn, "Campes 'Entdekung fon Amerike' in Yiddish," *Yivo bleter* 5 (1933): 29–40; Ber Shlosberg, "Hurwitz's Tsofnas paneyakh," *Yivo bleter* 7 (1937): 546–58; Meir Wiener, *Tsu der geshikhte fun der Yidisher literature in 19th yorhundert* (New York, 1945), 255–64.

11. See Sinkoff, *Out of the Shtetl*, 195–96n.

12. On the popularity of *Theophron* outside the Hebrew system, see John Gorton, *A General Biographical Dictionary*, 3 vols. (London, 1847), 3: appendix, s.v. Campe.

13. RL, 74a–75b and throughout; Zamość, *Resisey ha-meliẓah* (Dyhernfurth, 1822), 2:8, 27, 30; *Agudat shoshanim*, 20–24, 36–37 (based on a talmudic tale); Stark, *Agudat shoshanim*, 22–43, 47–54, 81–82; Bock, *Moda*, 93, 103–29; Hyman Shvebacher, *Hadrakhat ha-yeled oder erster unterrikht fir kinder fon dreye bis finf yahren* (1812, repr. Fürth, 1824), 16, 28; Israel ben Chaim mi-Belgrad, *Limudey ha-kriah oder unterrikht im lezen fir di israelitishen yugend fon 3 biz 5 yahren* (before 1807; repr. Vienna, 1823), 22–36.

14. For some exceptions see Sinkoff, *Tradition and Transition*, 162; Sinkoff, "Strategy and Ruse," 93; Garrett, "Jewish Robinson," 223. However, these studies tend to mention the colonial aspect merely in passing, or, in Garrett's case, to stress that the translations are emphatically not colonialist texts.

15. There were, of course, exceptions to this rule; however, it is widely agreed that most eighteenth- and early nineteenth-century children's authors viewed entertainment as secondary to instruction. For a more nuanced discussion of the development of children's literature "from instruction to delight," see, e.g., Jan Susina, *The Place of Lewis Carroll in Children's Literature* (New York, 2010), esp. 3–4, 108–11.

16. See Dennis Butts, "The Birth of the Boy's Story and the Transition from the 'Robinsonnades' to the Adventure Story," *Revue de literature compare* 304, no. 4 (2002): 445–54.

17. Locke, *Some Thoughts Concerning Education* (1693; repr. London, 1779), 226.

18. See Charles L. Batten Jr., *Pleasurable Instruction* (Berkeley, 1978).

19. See Adriana S. Benzaquén, "Childhood, Identity and Human Science in the Enlightenment," *History Workshop Journal* 57 (2004): 50–51; Perry Nodelman, "The Other: Orientalism, Colonialism and Children's Literature," *Children's Literature Association Quarterly* 17 (1992): 29–35.

20. Quoted in Benzaquén, "Childhood," 35, and see also 44–53.

21. George Boas, *The Cult of Childhood* (1966; repr. London, 1996), 8.

22. Johann Christoph Friedrich Schiller, "Was heißt und zu welchem Ende studiert man Universalgeschichte," 1789, repr. in *Schillers sämtliche Werke* (Stüttgart, 1838), 10:369. For a contemporaneous "Jewish" use of the child analogy see, e.g., Mendelssohn-Frankfurt, *Meẓiyat ha-areẓ*, 49. The relevant passage appears to be Mendelssohn-Frankfurt's original addition. Compare Campe, *Die Entdeckung* (1781), 116–17; (1784), 70–71; (1830), 71–72. For a later example, see Schulmann, *Mosdey areẓ*, 12.

23. See Alan C. Cairns, *The Clash of Cultures: Early Race Relations in Central Africa* (New York, 1965), 85–96.

24. On children's literature as inherently colonialist, see Jacqueline Rose's controversial *The Case of Peter Pan or the Impossibility of Children's Literature* (1982; repr. Philadelphia, 1992).

25. Zantop, *Colonial Fantasies*, 105. See also Apgar, *Taming Travel*, 41, 78, 124–40. Apgar's discussion of the domestic uses of the colonial in Campe's works is convincing; however, it appears that in his zeal to contest Zantop's earlier reading of Campe as a purely colonialist writer, he overemphasizes the non-colonial aspects of his work. In so doing, he oversimplifies the relationship between external and internal colonialism. For more on this issue, see my discussion of the colonial aspect of the Jewish translations of Campe's works below.

26. Apgar, *Taming Travel*, 132–33.

27. See ibid., esp. 26–29, 71–72, 90–91, 104, 108, 116, 120–22, 132–33.

28. For other explanations, focusing on Campe's philosemitism, his friendship with Mendelssohn, or his prestige in the European literary world, see Israel Bartal, "Mordecai Aaron Günzburg: A Lithuanian Maskil Faces Modernity," in *From East and West: Jews in a Changing Europe, 1750–1870*, ed. Frances Malino and David Sorkin (Oxford, 1991), 142–43; Shavit, "Literary Interference," 48–52; "Friedländer's Lesebuch," 405; Frieden, "Neglected Origins," 26.

29. Herz, "Letter to Lindau," in RL [7].

30. Mendelssohn-Frankfurt, *Meẓiyat ha-areẓ*, [1]. For some other examples, see Lefin, *Ḥeshbon ha-nefesh* (1808; repr. Vilnius, 1844), 8–9; Shenfeld, "Ha-adam," 86. For some more radical formulations of this idea, see, e.g., Bendavid, *Characteristick der Juden*, 25–28; Naphtali Herz Homberg, "Igeret el roey she pzurah Israel," *Ha-measef* (1788): 228.

31. Sinkoff, "Strategy and Ruse," 93–94; Garrett, "Jewish Robinson," 224–25.

32. I discuss this in detail in a forthcoming essay on early maskilic travel literature.

33. Sinkoff, *Tradition and Transition*, 163–68; Frieden, "Neglected Origins," 17–24.

34. For an instructive comparison between Defoe's *Robinson Crusoe* and Campe's adaptation of the book, see Zantop, *Colonial Fantasies*, 102–20.

35. Campe, *Robinson* (1807), 166–67. English translation according to Campe, *Robinson the Younger*, trans. John Timaeus (Brunswick, 1816), 121.

36. Campe, *Robinson* (1807), 270–71.

37. See, e.g., Zamość, *Robinson*, 55, 87.

38. Wessely, *Divrey shalom*, part 1, [4].

39. Campe, *Die Entdeckung* (1781), 23.

40. Apgar, *Taming Travel*, 90–91.

41. Mendelssohn-Frankfurt, *Meẓiat ha-areẓ*, 10–11. The additions do not appear in other editions of Campe's *Entdeckung*, or in the other Hebrew translation of the book by Günsberg. See, e.g., Campe, *Die Entdeckung* (1781), 23; (1784), 14–15; (1830), 16; Günsberg, *Galut ha- areẓ*, 4.

42. Mendelssohn-Frankfurt, *Meẓiat ha-areẓ*, 12. Compare Campe, *Die Entdeckung* (1781), 33; (1784), 20; (1830), 22; Günsberg, *Galut ha- areẓ*, 11.

43. Shavit, "Literary Interference," 53.

44. Garrett, "Jewish Robinson," 219, and see also 220, 223–24, 226.

45. See, e.g., Mendelssohn-Frankfurt, *Meẓiyat ha-areẓ*, 31–33, 52, 80–81; Günsberg, *Galut ha-areẓ*, 15, 18, 20–21; Lefin, *Masaot ha-yam*, 7–8.

46. Zamość, *Robinson*, 124. Compare Campe, *Robinson* (1784), 2:116. For other direct justifications, see, e.g., Shenfeld, "Ha-adam," 87.

47. Zamość, *Robinson*, 95–96. Compare Campe, *Robinson* (1784), 2:46–47.

48. For a critical discussion of this problematic one-dimensional view, see Hess, *Claims of Modernity*, 15.

49. Shenfeld, "Ha-adam," 87.

50. Wessely, *Divrey shalon*, [7–8].

51. For some further examples, see Idelson-Shein, *Ha-ekzoty*, 253–62.

52. Lefin, *Masaot ha-yam*, 47.

53. Lefin, *Masaot ha-yam* (1818, repr. Lemberg, 1859), 50.

54. Sinkoff, "Strategy and Ruse," 93–94. Sinkoff mistakenly attributes the anthropological description of the Palauans in *Masaot ha-yam* to Lefin himself, claiming that it is the translator's original addition. In reality the description appears already in Campe's source. Lefin simply reorganized the narrative, placing the description, which appears in the middle of Campe's book, at the end of his translation. See Sinkoff, *Tradition and Transition*, 162; Sinkoff, "Strategy and Ruse," 93n3. And cf. Lefin, *Masaot ha-yam*, 64–71; Campe, *Pelju Inseln*, 163–85.

55. Lefin, *Masaot ha-yam*, 4.

56. [Lefin?], *Oniyah soarah* (1854), [1]. The earlier edition is missing the first page.

57. Mendelssohn-Frankfurt, *Meẓiyat ha-areẓ*, 85–86. Compare Campe, *Die Entdeckung* (1781), 190–91.

58. Mendelssohn-Frankfurt, *Meẓiyat ha-areẓ*, 89.

59. See, e.g., ibid., 89, 163. Compare Campe, *Die Entdeckung* (1781), 374; Exodus 1:13.

60. Mendelssohn-Frankfurt, *Meẓiyat ha-areẓ*, 137, 146.

61. Ibid., 114.

62. On hybridity in the image of Moses, see Jan Assman, *Moses the Egyptian: The Memory of Egypt in Western Monotheism* (London, 1997); F. V. Greifenhagen, *Egypt on the Pentateuch's Ideological Map: Constructing Biblical Israel's Identity* (London, 2002), 156. Some radical authors tended to present Moses as a mere translator of Egyptian lore. It would perhaps be tempting to think of the relationship between this view of Moses as translator and the rhetorical use of the image of Moses in the translational project of the Haskalah, but we must bear in mind that the kind of Jewish authors involved in this translational project were far removed from the more radical thought of their time.

63. Defoe, *Robinson Crusoe*, 160.

64. Behn, *Oroonoko*, 80–81.

65. Campe, *Robinson* (1781), 2, 58; (1784), 2, 45–46; (1807), 298.

66. Compare Campe, *Die Entdeckung* (1781), 1:92; "Bonteku's Abentheuer" (1794), 5:22; Willem Ysbrandsz Bontekoe, *Journael ofte Gedenckwaerdige beschrijvinghe van de Oost-Indische Reyse* (1646; repr. Amsterdam, 1648), 7. For a discussion of Columbus's descriptions of the Native Americans and some further examples, see Tzveten Todorov, *The Conquest of America: The Question of the Other*, 1982, trans. Richard Howard (New York, 1984), 34–50.

67. Campe, *Robinson* (1781), 2, 73; (1784), 2, 58–59; (1807), 315–16. See also Zamość, *Robinson*, 100. On apotheosis and its uses, see Gananath Obeyesekere, *The Apotheosis of Captain Cook: European Mythmaking in the Pacific* (Princeton, NJ, 1992). The tales of native deification of Europeans in South America and the Pacific are familiar. Less familiar is the story of the deification of Hans Egede, the Norwegian missionary who arrived in Greenland in 1721. The myth appears also in Raff's *Geographie* [1786], 382.

68. Luise Hölder, *Rückreise Robinsons der Jüngern nach seinem Eilande in Begleitung seiner Kinder* (Nürnberg, 1827), 24.

69. Franz Xavier Geiger, *Der neue Robinson oder Seefahrten und Schicksale eines Deutschen* (1794; repr. Reutlingen, 1837), 42.

70. Anon., *Robinson* (1813), [6]. I am grateful to Chaim Levy for his help in translating the word "טטארר."

71. Anon., [Vitlin?], *Alter Leb* (1851), [86]–[87]. The original edition, presumably published around 1820, has been lost. For the purpose of the above translation I have utilized the earliest extant edition from 1851. The description, however, appears in slight variations also in other extant editions. See *Alter Leb* (1894), 2, 13; (1907), 2, 13. The only remaining copy of the 1898 edition is missing the relevant pages; however, it is identical to the 1907 edition.

72. Eliezer ben Shimon ha-Cohen Bloch, *Maaseh Robinzohn* (Warsaw, 1849), 31; Zamość, *Robinson*, 100. Compare Campe, *Robinson* (1781), 2, 73; (1784), 2, 58–59; (1807), 315–16. For an example from the English-speaking world, see, e.g., F. Fortescue, *Robinson Crusoe or, the Island of Juan Fernandez, An Operatic Drama in Three Acts* (Boston, 1822), 11.

73. David Roskies, "The Medium and Message of the Maskilic Chapbook," *Jewish Social Studies* 41, no. 3 (1979): 283; Uriel Ofek, "Al Robinson ve-Robinsonim: Bi-mlot 250 shanah le-mot Daniel Defoe," *Sifrut yeladim va-noar* (1981): 32.

74. Wheeler, "Racial Multiplicity," esp. 824–25.

75. Wheeler, *Complexion of Race*, 81–84.

76. Ibid., 61–62; Felsenstein, *English Trader*, 18–19, 32–33.

77. Boulle, "Defense of Slavery," 232.

78. See Schechter, *Obstinate Hebrews*, 45–46, 89.

79. Homi K. Bhabha, *The Location of Culture* (London, 1994), 223–29.

EPILOGUE

1. Zamość, *Agudat shoshanim*, 22–23.

2. Toury, "Enhancing Change," 4.

3. Stéphane Minvielle, "Le mariage précoce des femmes à Bordeaux au XVIIIe siècle," *Annales de démographie Historique* 1 (2006): 159–76; David B. Grigg, *Population Growth and Agrarian Change: An Historical Perspective* (Cambridge, 1980), 113; George F.E. Rudé, *Europe in the Eighteenth Century: Aristocracy and the Bourgeois Challenge* (Cambridge, 1972), 18.

4. Katz, *Tradition and Crisis*, 116.

5. Jacob Goldenberg, "Jewish Marriage in Eighteenth-Century Poland," *Polin* 10 (1997): 14.

6. Zamość, *Agudat shoshanim*, 20–24.

7. Ibid., 24.

8. Ibid.

Abraham ben Elijah of Vilna. *Gevulot areẓ.* Berlin, 1801.

Abravanel, Iẓhak. *Perush ha-torah.* 15th century. Repr. Warsaw, 1862.

Adams, John. *A View of Universal History, from the Creation to the Present Time.* 3 vols. London, 1795.

Adams, Percy. *Travelers and Travel Liars.* London, 1962.

Adanson, Michel. *Histoire naturelle du Sénégal.* Paris, 1757.

Aikin, Lucy. *Epistles on Women, exemplifying their character and condition in various ages and nations. With Miscellaneous Poems.* London, 1810.

Alexander, Tamar. "Ha-iẓuv ha-z'anery shel sipurey shedim: Nisuyim beyn gever le-shedah." In *Ashnav le-ḥayeyhen shel nashim ba-ḥevrah ha-yehudit,* ed. Yael Aẓmon. Jerusalem, 1995.

Allgemeine deutsche Bibliothek 66, no. 2. Berlin, 1786.

Anon. "Bikoret sefer ha-brit." Parts 1 and 2. *Ha-measef* (1808).

Anon. *Biographie des hommes vivants, ou histoire par ordre alphabétique de la vie publique de tous les hommes qui se sont fait remarquer par leurs actions ou leurs écrits.* Vol. 3. Paris, 1817.

Anon. "Bito shel Tarzan be-harey midbar Yehudah." *Iton meyuḥad.* Adar, 1937.

Anon. [attributed to Yonatan Eybeschütz]. "Divrey Yonat Elem." 1824. Ms. Heb.8° 2497. National and University Library, Jerusalem. Microfilm available at National Library Israel, reel no. F10505.

Anon. *Historisch-geographische Beschreibung von Amerika für Jünglinge.* Nürnberg, 1784.

Anon. *Historiye odr zeltzame und vunderbahre bgebenheyten eynes yun-gen zee fahrers.* Prague, 1784.

Anon. *Historiye fon den zeefahrer Robinzohn.* Frankfurt am Oder, 1813.

Anon. *Kleyne yeografye oder erd bshreybung.* Frankfurt, 1802.

Anon. *Maaseh Book.* 1602. Repr. and trans. Moses Gaster. 2 vols. Philadelphia, 1934.

Anon. "Negres Blancs." 1765. In *Encyclopédie, ou dictionnaire raisonné des sciences, des arts et des métiers.* Vol. 11. Ed. Denis Diderot and Jean le Rond D'Alembert. Repr. Chicago: University of Chicago ARTFL Encyclopédie Projet (Winter 2008), ed. Robert Morrissey. http://artflx. uchicago.edu/cgi-bin/philologic/getobject.pl?p.80:80.encyclopedie0110.

Anon. "Review: The Physiognomical System of Drs. Gall and Spurtzheim." *Medical and Physical Journal* 33, no. 191 (1815).

Anon. [Joseph Vitlin?]. *Robinzohn: Di geshichte fun Alter Leb, eyne vahre und vunderbare geshichte tzum lezen.* 1820. Repr. Lvov, 1851.

———. *Robinzohn: Di geshichte fun Alter Leb.* Repr. Vilnius, 1894.

———. *Robinzohn: Di geshichte fun Alter Leb.* Repr. Krakow, 1907.

Anon. [Schnaber Levison?]. "Sefer gidul bonim." 1771. Trans. Siegfried Stein. In *Remember the Days: Essays on Anglo-Jewish History Presented to Cecil Roth,* ed. John M. Shaftesley. London, 1966.

Anon. Memoir. Repr. in English and Hebrew in "A Seventeenth-Century Autobiography." By Alexander Marx. *Jewish Quarterly Review* 8, no. 3 (1918).

Apgar, Richard B. "Taming Travel and Disciplining Reason: Enlightenment and Pedagogy in the Work of Joachim Heinrich Campe." Ph.D. diss., University of North Carolina, Chapel Hill, 2008.

Ashkenazy, Shmuel (Deutschlander). *Sefer mareh ha-Levanon ve-hu ḥibur kolel megilat shir ha-shirim im biyur al-pi ḥakirah amitit ve-gam tirgum Ashkenazy u-perush ha-milot.* Pressburg, 1847.

Ashley-Cooper, Anthony (Third Earl of Shaftesbury). *Characteristics of Men, Manners, Opinions, Times.* 1711. Repr. Cambridge, 1999.

Assaf, David. *Neeḥaz ba-svakh: Pirkey mashber u-mevuḥah be-toldot ha-Ḥasidut.* Jerusalem, 2006.

Assman, Jan. *Moses the Egyptian: The Memory of Egypt in Western Monotheism.* London, 1997.

———. "Pictures Versus Letters: William Warburton's Theory of Grammatological Iconoclasm." In *Representation in Religion: Studies in Honor of Moshe Barasch,* ed. Assman and A. I. Baumgarten. Leiden, 2001.

Avramovich, Sholem. *Sefer toldot ha-teva.* Leipzig, 1862.

Badinter, Elisabeth. *L'amour en plus: Histoire de l'amour maternal, XVIIe–XXe siècle*. Paris, 1980.

Baran, Joseph. "Divrey ha-yamim le-mamlehot ha-arazot." *Ha-measef* (1788).

Bartal, Israel. "Mordecai Aaron Günzburg: A Lithuanian Maskil Faces Modernity." In *From East and West: Jews in a Changing Europe, 1750–1870*, ed. Frances Malino and David Sorkin. Oxford, 1991.

Bastin, Georges L. "Adaptation." In *Routledge Encyclopedia of Translation Studies*, ed. Mona Baker. New York, 1998.

Batten, Charles L. Jr. *Pleasurable Instruction*. Berkeley, 1978.

Baumgarten, Elisheva. *Mothers and Children: Jewish Life in Medieval Europe*. Princeton, 2004.

Behn, Aphra. "Oroonoko." 1688. Repr. in *Oroonoko, The Rover and Other Works*. London, 1992.

Ben Abraham (Hart), Elyakim. *Milhamot ha-shem*. London, 1794.

Ben Chaim, Israel mi-Belgrad. *Limudey ha-kriah oder unterrikht im lezen fir di israelitishen yugend fon 3 biz 5 yahren*. Before 1807. Repr. Vienna, 1823.

Bendavid, Lazarus. *Etwas zur Characteristik der Juden*. Leipzig, 1793. Facsimile repr. Jerusalem, 1994.

———. "Über den Menschen als Kunstwerk." *Neue Berlinische Monatsschrift* 18 (1807).

Benyowsky, Mauritius A. *Memoirs and Travels of Mauritius Augustus Count de Benyowsky*. 2 vols. London, 1790.

Benzaquén, Adriana S. "Childhood, Identity and Human Science in the Enlightenment." *History Workshop Journal* 57 (2004).

Bernardini, Paolo, and Norman Fiering, eds. *The Jews and the Expansion of Europe to the West, 1450–1800*. New York, 2001.

Bernasconi, Robert. "Who Invented the Concept of Race? Kant's Role in the Enlightenment Construction of Race." In *Race*, ed. Robert Bernasconi. Oxford: Blackwell, 2001.

Bernstein, Aaron. *Yediyot ha-teva*. Trans. David Frischmann. 1880. Repr. 1884.

Bewell, Alan. *Romanticism and Colonial Disease*. Baltimore, 1999.

Bhabha, Homi K. *The Location of Culture*. London: Routledge, 1994.

Bilik, Dorothy. "The Memoirs of Glikl of Hameln: The Archeology of the Text." *Yiddish* 8, no. 2 (1992).

Blackburn, Timothy C. "Friday's Religion: Its Nature and Importance in Robinson Crusoe." *Eighteenth-Century Studies* 18, no. 3 (1985).

Bloch, Eliezer ben Shimon ha-Cohen. *Maaseh Robinzohn*. Warsaw, 1849.

Bloch, Shimshon. *Sefer sheviley olam.* 2 parts. 1822–1828. Repr. Warsaw, 1894.

Block, Sharon. *Rape and Sexual Power in Early America.* Chapel Hill, 2006.

Blumenbach, Johann Friedrich. *The Anthropological Treatises of Johann Friedrich Blumenbach.* Trans. Thomas Bendyshe. London, 1865.

———. *Handbuch der Naturgeschichte.* 1779. Repr. Göttingen, 1825.

Boas, George. *The Cult of Childhood.* 1966. Repr. London, 1996.

Bock, Moshe ben Ẓvi. *Moda le-yaldey bnei Israel.* Berlin, 1812.

Bontekoe, Willem Ysbrandsz. *Journael ofte Gedenckwaerdige beschrijvinghe van de Oost-Indische Reyse.* 1646. Repr. Amsterdam, 1648.

Boswell, James. *The Life of Samuel Johnson.* 2 vols. London, 1791.

Boswell, John. *The Kindness of Strangers.* 1988. Repr. Chicago, 1998.

Boulle, Pierre H. "In Defense of Slavery: Eighteenth-Century Opposition to Abolition and the Origins of a Racist Ideology in France." In *History from Below,* ed. Fredrick Kranz. Oxford, 1988.

Boulukos, George. *The Grateful Slave: The Emergence of Race in Eighteenth-Century British and American Culture.* Cambridge, 2008.

Bowers, Toni. *The Politics of Motherhood: British Writing and Culture, 1680–1760.* Cambridge, 1996.

Bowler, Peter J. *Evolution: The History of an Idea.* 1983. Repr. Berkeley, 2003.

Boyarin, Daniel. *Unheroic Conduct: The Rise of Heterosexuality and the Invention of the Jewish Man.* Berkeley, 1997.

Brackman, Harold D. *Ministry of Lies: The Truth Behind the Nation of Islam's "The Secret Relationship Between Blacks and Jews."* New York, 1994.

Braude, Benjamin. "The Sons of Noah and the Construction of Ethnic and Geographical Identities in the Medieval and Early Modern Periods." *William and Mary Quarterly.* 3rd ser. 54, no. 1 (1997).

Breuer, Edward. "Naphtali Herz Wessely and the Cultural Dislocation of an 18th Century Maskil." In *New Perspectives on the Haskalah,* ed. Shmuel Feiner and David Sorkin. London, 2001.

Brill, Joel. "Mavo ha-sefer." In *Sifrey kodesh im tirgumim u-biyurim mi-meḥabrim shonim,* ed. Moshe ha-levi Landau. 1788. Repr. Prague, 1834.

Brockhaus, Friedrich Anton. *Conversations-Lexikon.* 1796–1808. Repr. Leipzig, 1827.

Brüggermann, Theodor, and Hans-Heino Ewers. *Handbuch zur Kinder- und Jugendliteratur.* Stuttgart, 1982.

Buffon, Georges-Louis Leclerc de. "Animaux communs aux deux continents." In Œuvres complètes de Buffon. 1761. Repr. Paris, 1825.

———. Histoire naturelle, générale et particulière. Vol. 4. Paris, 1753.

———. Natural History. Trans. James Smith Barr. London, 1792. Vols. 4
and 5.

———. "Nomenclature des singes." 1766. Repr. in Oeuvres philosophiques
de Buffon. Paris, 1954.

———. "Variétés dans l'espèce humaine." 1748–1778. Repr. in De
l'homme. Paris, 1971.

Büsching, Anton Friedrich. Neue Erdbeschreibung. 1754. Repr. Hamburg,
1770.

Butler, Judith. Bodies That Matter: On the Discursive Limits of "Sex."
New York, 1993.

Butts, Dennis. "The Birth of the Boy's Story and the Transition from the
'Robinsonnades' to the Adventure Story." Revue de literature compare
304, no. 4 (2002).

Cairns, H. Alan C. The Clash of Cultures: Early Race Relations in Central
Africa. New York, 1965.

Campe, Joachim Heinrich. Columbus, oder die Entdekkung von Westin-
dien. Strasbourg, 1784.

———. "Die Entdeckung von Amerika." In Sämmtliche Kinder- und
Jugendschriften von Joachim Heinrich Campe. Vol. 9. Braunschweig,
1830.

———. Die Entdeckung von Amerika, ein Unterhaltungsbuch für Kinder
und junge Leute. Part 3. Braunschweig, 1817.

———. Die Entdekkung von Amerika, ein angenehmes und nützliches
Lesebuch für Kinder und junge Leute. Part 1. Hamburg, 1781.

———. "Jakob Heemkerks und Wilhelm Barenz nördliche Entdeckungsreise." 1786. Repr. in Sammlung interessanter und durchgängig zweckmäßig abgefaßter Reisebeschreibung für die Jugend. Vol. 1. Reutlingen,
1796.

———. "Kapitän Wilson's Schiffbruch bei den Pelju-Inseln." 1791. In
Sämmtliche Kinder- und Jugendschriften von Joachim Heinrich Campe.
Repr. Braunschweig, 1830. Part 9, Vol. 25.

———. Robinson der jüngere. 1779. Repr. Frankfurt and Leipzig, 1781.

———. Robinson der jüngere. Repr. Strasbourg, 1784.

———. Robinson der jüngere. Repr. Braunschweig, 1807.

———. Sittenbüchlein für Kinder aus gesitteten Ständen. 1777. Repr.
Frankfurt, 1785.

———. "Wilhelm Isbrand Bonteku's merkwürdige Abentheuer auf einer

Reise aus Holland nach Ostindien." In *Sammlung interessanter und durchgängig zweckmäßig abgefaßter Reisebeschreibung für die Jugend.* Vol. 5. Reutlingen, 1794.

Carey, Brycchan. *British Abolitionism and the Rhetoric of Sensibility: Writing, Sentiment, and Slavery, 1760–1807.* New York, 2005.

Carlebach, Elisheva. *The Death of Simon Abeles: Jewish-Christian Tension in Seventeenth-Century Prague.* New York, 2001.

———. *Palaces of Time: Jewish Calendar and Culture in Early Modern Europe.* Cambridge, MA, 2011.

Cheek, Pamela. *Sexual Antipodes: Enlightenment, Globalization, and the Placing of Sex.* Stanford, 2003.

Christ, Kurt. *F. H. Jacobi: Rousseaus deutscher Adept: Rousseauismus in Leben und Frühwerk.* Würzburg, 1998.

Clark, William, and Meriwether Lewis. *The Journals of Lewis and Clark.* 1803–1806. Repr. New York, 2003.

Cleland, John. *Fanny Hill, or, Memoirs of a Woman of Pleasure.* 1748. Repr. London, 2001.

Cohen, Bernard I. "Anquetil-Duperron, Benjamin Franklin, and Ezra Stiles." *Isis* 33, no. 1 (1941).

Colin, Susi. "The Wild Man and the Indian in Early 16th Century Book Illustration." In *Indians and Europe: An Interdisciplinary Collection of Essays,* ed. Christian F. Feest. Aachen, 1989.

Collections of the Virginia Historical and Philosophical Society. Vol. 1. Richmond, 1833.

Colley, Linda. "Going Native, Telling Tales: Captivity, Collaborations and Empire." *Past and Present* 168 (2000).

Colman, George the Younger. "Inkle and Yarico: An Opera, in Three Acts." 1787. Repr. in *English Trader, Indian Maid: Representing Race, Gender and Slavery in the New World,* ed. Frank Felsenstein. Baltimore, 1999.

[Condamine, Charles Marie ?]/Mme Hecquet. *Histoire d'une jeune fille sauvage, trouvée dans les bois à l'âge de dix ans.* Paris, 1755.

Creswell, Nicholas. *The Journal of Nicholas Cresswell, 1774–1777.* New York, 1924.

Cummings, Brian. "Animal Passions and Human Sciences: Shame, Blushing and Nakedness in Early Modern Europe and the New World." In *At the Borders of the Human: Beasts, Bodies and Natural Philosophy in the Early Modern Period,* ed. Erica Fudge, Ruth Gilbert, and Susan Wiseman. New York, 2002.

Cuvier, Georges Léopold. "Animal Kingdom (Excerpt)." 1797. Repr. in *Race and the Enlightenment—A Reader,* ed. Emmanuel C. Eze. Cambridge, 1997.

Dampier, William. "A New Voyage Round the World." 1691. Repr. in *The World Displayed; Or, A Curious Collection of Voyages and Travels, Selected from the Writers of All Nations*. London, 1761.

Darwin, Charles. *The Origin of Species by Means of Natural Selection*. 1859. Repr. New York, 1979.

Dauber, Jeremy. *Antonio's Devils: Writers of the Jewish Enlightenment and the Birth of Modern Hebrew and Yiddish Literature*. Stanford, 2004.

———. *In the Demon's Bedroom: Yiddish Literature and the Early Modern*. New Haven, 2010.

Davis, David Brion. *The Problem of Slavery in the Age of Revolution, 1770–1823*. Oxford, 1999.

Davis, Natalie Zemon. "Glikl bas Judah Leib—ein jüdisches, ein europäisches Leben." In *Die Hamburger Kauffrau Glikl: Jüdische Existenz in der frühen Neuzeit*, ed. Monika Richarz. Hamburg, 2001.

———. *Women on the Margins: Three Seventeenth-Century Lives*. London, 1995.

Day, Thomas. *The History of Sandford and Merton*. 1783. Repr. New York, 1856.

Delakrut, Matithiahu. *Ẓel ha-olam*. 16th century. Repr. Munkács, 1897.

Defoe, Daniel. *An Essay on the Original of Literature*. 1726. Repr. New York, 1999.

———. *The Family Instructor*. 1726. Repr. Bungay, 1826.

———. *The Fortunes and Misfortunes of the Famous Moll Flanders*. 1722. Repr. London, 1993.

———. *Robinson Crusoe*. 1719. Repr. New York, 1975.

Diamond, Stanley. *In Search of the Primitive*. New Brunswick, NJ, 1974.

Dickason, Olive Patricia. *The Myth of the Savage, and the Beginnings of French Colonialism in the Americas*. Edmonton, 1984.

Diderot, Denis. "Supplément au voyage de Bougainville." 1772. Repr. in *Œuvres completes*. 25 volumes. Paris, 1989.

Disraeli, Isaac. *Miscellanies; or Literary Recreations*. London, 1796.

Douthwaite, Julia V. *Exotic Women: Literary Heroines and Cultural Strategies in Ancien Régime France*. Philadelphia, 1992.

———. *The Wild Girl, Natural Man and the Monster: Dangerous Experiments in the Age of Enlightenment*. Chicago, 2002.

Dov mi-Bolichov. *Zikhronot*. C. 1723–1805. Repr. Krakow, 2006.

Drake, Samuel Gardner. *Tragedies of the Wilderness*. C. 1839. Repr. Boston, 1844.

Eastburn, Robert. "A Faithful Narrative." In *A Selection of Some of the Most Interesting Narratives, Or the Outrages Committed by the*

Indians in Their Wars with the White People, ed. Archibald Loudon. 1808–1811. Repr. Carlisle, 1888.

Edgeworth, Maria. *Tales and Novels by Maria Edgeworth.* London, 1870.

Efron, John M. *Defenders of the Race: Jewish Doctors and Race Science in Fin-de-Siècle Europe.* New Haven, 1994.

———. "Interminably Maligned: The Conventional Lies about Jewish Doctors." In *Jewish History and Jewish Memory: Essays in Honor of Yosef Hayim Yerushalmi*, ed. Elisheva Carlebach, John M. Efron, and David N. Myers. Hanover, NH, 1998.

Elias, Norbert. *The Civilizing Process.* 1939. Trans. Edmund Jephcott. Malden, 2000.

Eliav, Mordecai. *Ha-ḥinukh ha-Yehudy be-Germaniyah bi-yemey ha-haskalah ve-ha-emanzipaziyah.* Jerusalem, 1960.

Eliav-Feldon, Miriam. "Vagrants or Vermin? Attitudes Toward Gypsies in Early Modern Europe." In *Origins of Racism in the West*, ed. Miriam Eliav-Feldon, Benjamin Isaac, and Joseph Ziegler. Cambridge, 2009.

Emden, Jacob. *Megilat sefer.* C. 1776. Oxford, Bodleian Library. MS Mich. 587. Microfilm available at the National Library Israel, reel no. F17754.

———. *Megilat sefer*, ed. David Kahana. Warsaw, 1896.

———. *Megilat sefer*, ed. Abraham Bick. Jerusalem, 1979.

Erickson, Paul. "The Anthropology of Charles Caldwell, M.D." *Isis* 72, no. 2 (1981).

Erlin, Matt. "Reluctant Modernism: Moses Mendelssohn's Philosophy of History." *Journal of the History of Ideas* 63, no. 1 (2002).

Etkes, Immanuel. *The Ga'on of Vilna: The Man and His Image.* Trans. Jeffrey M. Green. Berkeley, 2002.

———. *Rabbi Israel Salanter and the Mussar Movement: Seeking the Torah of Truth.* Philadelphia, 1993.

Euchel, Isaac. "Igeret le-Michael Friedländer." *Ha-measef* (1785).

———. "Igrot Meshulam ben Uriah ha-Ashtemoy." *Ha-measef* (1789).

———. *Sefer Mishley im tirgum Ashkenazy u-biyur me-et ha-ḥakham ha-torany Izḥak Euchel z"l.* 1790. Repr. 1834.

Faber, Eli. *Jews, Slaves, and the Slave Trade: Setting the Record Straight.* New York, 1998.

Fanon, Frantz. *Black Skin, White Masks.* 1952. Repr. London, 1986.

Feiner, Shmuel. "Beyn ananey ha-siḥlut le-or ha-muskalot: Yehudah Horowitz, maskil mukdam ba-meah ha-18." In *Be-maagaley ḥasidim: Kovez meḥkarim le-ziḥro shel profesor Mordecai Vilensky*, ed. Israel Bartal and Elchanan Reiner. Jerusalem, 1999.

———. *The Jewish Enlightenment*. 2002. Trans. Chaya Naor. Philadelphia, 2004.

———. "Laakor et ha-ḥokhmah mi-ha-olam—Oyvey ha-neorut u-shorshey ha-emdah ha-ḥaredit." *Alpayim* 26 (2004).

———. *The Origins of Jewish Secularization in Eighteenth-Century Europe*. 2010. Trans. Chaya Naor. Philadelphia, 2011.

———. "Y. L. Margaliyot ve-paradoks ha-Haskalah ha-mukdemet." *Zion* 63 (1998).

Felsenstein, Frank. *Anti-Semitic Stereotypes: A Paradigm of Otherness in English Popular Literature 1660–1839*. Baltimore, 1995.

Ferguson, Moira. *Subject to Others: British Women Writers and Colonial Slavery, 1670–1834*. New York, 1992.

[Ferri, Giovanni di San Constante.] *Génie de M. de Buffon*. Paris, 1778.

[———.] *Büffons Geist, oder Kern seiner Naturgeschichte*. Trans. Anon. St. Petersburg, 1783.

Fielding, Henry. *The Adventures of Joseph Andrews and His Friend Mr. Abraham Adams*. 1742. Repr. London, 1749.

Finucane, Ronald C. *The Rescue of Innocents: Endangered Children in Medieval Miracles*. New York, 1997.

Fissel, Mary E. "Hairy Women and Naked Truths: Gender and the Politics of Knowledge in Aristotle's Masterpiece." *William and Mary Quarterly* 60, no. 1 (2003).

Fortescue, F. *Robinson Crusoe or, the Island of Juan Fernandez, An Operatic Drama in Three Acts*. Boston, 1822.

Franks, Abigaill Levy. *The Letters of Abigaill Levy Franks 1733–1748*, ed. with an introduction by Edith B. Gelles. New Haven, 2004.

Frieden, Ken. "Neglected Origins of Modern Hebrew Prose: Hasidic and Maskilic Travel Narratives." *AJS Review* 33 (2009).

[Friedländer, David]. *Sendschreiben an seine Hochwürden, Herrn . . . Teller . . . von einigen Hausvätern jüdischer Religion*. Berlin, 1799. Facsimile repr. Jerusalem, 1975.

Friedlander, Yehuda. *Prakim ba-satirah ha-Ivrit*. Vol. 1. Tel Aviv, 1979.

Friedlander, Yehuda, and Chaim Shoham. Introduction to *Mot Adam* by Friedrich Klopstock. Trans. Ẓvi Ben-David. Prague, 1817.

Friedman, Saul S. *Jews and the American Slave Trade*. London, 1998.

Frisenhausen, David. *Mosdot tevel*. Vienna, 1820.

Fün, Shmuel Joseph. *Kiryah neemanah*. Vilnius, 1860.

———. *Knesset Israel*. Warsaw, 1886.

Garrett, Leah. "The Jewish Robinson Crusoe." *Comparative Literature* 54, no. 3 (2002).

Gay, Peter. *The Enlightenment: An Interpretation*. Vol. 2: *The Science of Freedom*. 1969. Repr. New York, 1977.

Geiger, Franz Xavier. *Der neue Robinson oder Seefahrten und Schicksale eines Deutschen*. 1794. Repr. Reutlingen, 1837.

Genlis, Stéphanie F. "Les esclaves, ou le pouvoir de la bienfaisance." 1784. Repr. in *Les veillées du château*. Paris, 1851.

Gershon ben Solomon. *Shaarey ha-shamayim*. 13th century. Repr. Warsaw, 1876.

Gessner, Salomon. "Inkel und Yariko." 1756. Repr. in *Schriften*. 3 vols. Zürich, 1795.

Gibson, Mary, and Nicole Hahn Rafter. Introduction to *Criminal Man*, by Cesare Lombroso. Trans. Gibson and Hahn Rafter. Durham, NC, 2006.

Gilman, Sander L. "The Figure of the Black in German Aesthetic Theory." *Eighteenth-Century Studies* 8, no. 4 (1975).

———. "The Jewish Nose: Are Jews White? Or, the History of the Nose Job." In *The Other in Jewish Thought and History: Constructions of Jewish Culture and Identity,* ed. Laurence J. Silberstein and Robert L. Cohn. New York, 1994.

Glikl. *The Life of Glückel of Hameln, 1624–1724: Written by Herself.* Trans. Beth Zion Abrahams. London, 1962.

———. *Zikhronot Glikl, 1691–1719*. Trans. Chava Turniansky. Jerusalem, 2006.

Goethe, Johann Wolfgang/Johann Peter Eckermann. *Gespräche mit Goethe in den Letzten Jahren seines Lebens*, 1823–1832. Vol. 2. Leipzig, 1836.

Goldenberg, David M. *The Curse of Ham: Race and Slavery in Early Judaism, Christianity and Islam*. Princeton, 2003.

———. "It Is Permitted to Marry a Kushite." *AJS Review* 37, no. 1 (2013).

Goldenberg, Jacob. "Jewish Marriage in Eighteenth-Century Poland." *Polin* 10 (1997).

Goldin, Simḥa. "Pen yavou ha-arelim halalu ve-yitfesum ḥayim ve-yihiyu mekuyamin be-taatuyim—yeladim yehudim ve-misionerizaẓiya noẓrit." In *Eros, erusin ve-isurim: Mimiyut u-mishpaḥah ba-historiah*, ed. Israel Bartal and Isaiah Gafni. Jerusalem, 1998.

Gorton, John. *A General Biographical Dictionary*. 3 vols. London, 1847.

Govrin, Nurit. "Signon ha-maqama ba-sifrut ha-Ivrit ba-dorot ha-aḥaronim." *Measef* 8–9 (1968).

Graffigny, Françoise de. *Lettres d'une Péruvienne*. 1747. Repr. Paris, 1983.

Graupe, Heinz Moshe. "Mordechai Shnaber-Levison: The Life, Works and Thought of a Haskalah Outsider." *Leo Baeck Institute Yearbook* 41, no. 1 (1996).

Grégoire, Henri. *De la littérature des nègres*. Paris, 1808.

———. *Die Neger. Ein Beitrag zur Staats- und Menschenkunde von H. Gregoire*. [Trans. Saul Asher]. Berlin, 1809.

———. *Essai sur la régénération physique, morale et politique des Juifs*. 1789. Repr. Paris, 1988.

———. *An Inquiry Concerning the Intellectual and Moral Faculties of Negroes*. New York, 1997.

———. *On the Cultural Achievements of Negroes*. Trans. Thomas Cassirer and Jean-François Brier. Boston, 1996.

Greifenhagen, F. V. *Egypt on the Pentateuch's Ideological Map: Constructing Biblical Israel's Identity*. London, 2002.

Grigg, David B. *Population Growth and Agrarian Change: An Historical Perspective*. Cambridge, 1980.

Grossman, Abraham. *Ḥasidot u-mordot: Nashim Yehudiyot be-Eropah bi-yemey ha-beynayim*. Jerusalem, 2001.

Gumpertz, Aharon. *Megaleh sod*. Hamburg, 1765.

Günzberg, Mordecai Aharon. *Aviezer*. Vilnius, 1863.

———. *Masa Kolombus o galut ha-areẓ ha-ḥadashah al yedey Kristof Kolombus*. Vilnius, 1823.

———. *Masa Kolombus o galut ha-areẓ ha-ḥadashah al yedey Kristof Kolombus*. Warsaw, 1883.

Ha-cohen, Joseph. *Sefer ha-Indeah ha-ḥadashah*. 1557. Repr. Lancaster, 2002.

Ha-cohen, Shalom. *Amal ve-Tirẓah: Shirat dodim bi-shloshah ḥalakim*. Rödelheim, 1812.

———. *Kore ha-dorot: Divrey ha-yamim le-ameynu zera Yaakov . . . mi-yemey malkhut beyur ha-Ḥeshmonayim ad ha-yom hazeh*. Warsaw, 1838.

Ha-cohen, Tuviah. *Maaseh Tuviah*. 1707. Repr. Krakow, 1908.

Hahn, Sylvia. "Women in Older Ages—'Old' Women?" *History of the Family* 7, no. 1 (2002).

Hall, Joseph. *The Works of the Right Reverend Joseph Hall*. 1598. Repr. Oxford, 1863.

Harif, Hanan. "Asiatic Brothers, European Strangers: Eugen Hoeflich and Pan-Asian Zionism in Vienna." In *Against the Grain: German-Jewish Intellectuals in Hard Times*, ed. Ezra Mendelsohn, Stefani Hoffman, and Richard I. Cohen. New York, 2013.

Harif, Jacob. *Amudey Yaaveẓ*. Manchester, 1897.

Harrison, Mark. *Climates and Constitutions: Health, Race, Environment and British Imperialism in India: 1600–1850*. New York, 1999.

Hart, Mitchell B. *Social Science and the Politics of Modern Jewish Identity*. Stanford, 2000.

Ha-hasid, Yehudah. *Sefer ha-ḥasidim*. N.d. Repr. Sudylkiv, 1826.

Ha-levi, Israel mi-Zamość. Commentary to *Ruaḥ ḥen*, by Yehudah Ibn Tibbon. 1744. Repr. Yosifov, 1889.

———. "Oẓar neḥmad." 1771. Repr. In Yehudah Ha-levi, *Sefer ha-kuzary*. Tel Aviv, 1959.

Hawkesworth, John. *An Account of the Voyages undertaken by the order of his present Majesty for making Discoveries in the Southern Hemisphere*. Dublin, 1775.

Herder, Johann Gottfried. "Letters for the Advancement of Humanity—tenth collection." 1793–97. Repr. in *Philosophical Writings*. Trans. Michael N. Forster. Cambridge, 2002.

Herz, Henriette. "Jugenderinnerungen von Henriette Herz." In *Henriette Herz: Ihr Leben und ihre Zeit*, ed. H. Landsberg. C. 1823/1850. Repr. Weimar, 1913.

Heshel, Israel Nathan. "Daatam shel gedoley ha-dor be-milḥamtam neged ha-maskil Naphtali Herẓ Wessely." *Koveẓ beyt Aharon ve-Israel* 5, no. 47 (1993).

Hess, Jonathan M. *Germans, Jews and the Claims of Modernity*. New Haven, 2002.

Hobbes, Thomas. *Leviathan or the Matter, Forme and Power of a Common Wealth Ecclesiasticall and Civil*. 1651. Repr. Cambridge, 1991.

Hoffer, Peter C., and N. E. H. Hull. *Murdering Mothers: Infanticide in England and New England, 1558–1803*. New York, 1981.

Hölder, Luise. *Rückreise Robinsons der Jüngern nach seinem Eilande in Begleitung seiner Kinder*. Nürnberg, 1827.

Holtzman, Avner. "Ben hokaah le-hitrapkut: Ha-ḥeder be-sifrut ha-zikhronot u-ba-sifrut ha-ivrit." In *Ha-ḥeder: Meḥkarim, pirkey sifrut u- zikhronot*, ed. Immanuel Etkes and David Assaf. Tel Aviv, 2010.

Homberg, Naphtali Herz. "Igeret el roey seh pzurah Israel." *Ha-measef* (1788).

Horejsi, Nicole. "'A Counterpart to the Ephesian Matron': Steel's 'Inkle and Yarico' and a Feminist Critique of the Classics." *Eighteenth-Century Studies* 39 (2006).

Horowitz, Elliott. "The New World and the Changing Face of Europe." *Sixteenth Century Journal* 28, no. 4 (1997).

Horowitz, Pinchas. *Sefer ha-brit ha-shalem*. 1797. Repr. Jerusalem, 1990.

Horowitz, Yehudah. *Amudey beyt Yehudah*. Amsterdam, 1766.

———. *Ḥayey ha-nefesh u-nitzḥiyutah*. Poritzk, 1786.

———. *Megilat sdarim.* 1793. Repr. Prague, 1884.

———. "Musar haskel." In *Koz Yehudah.* 1790–1791. MS# B 574, St. Petersburg Inst. of Oriental Studies of the Russian Academy. Microfilm available at the National Library Israel, reel no. F69310.

———. *Sefer kerem Eiyn Gedy.* Königsburg, 1764.

Hourwitz, Zalkind. *Apologie des Juifs.* Paris, 1789. Facsimile reproduction. Paris, 1968.

Hovav, Yemima. *Alamot ahevukha: Hayey ha-dat ve-ha-ruah shel nashim yehudiyot be-Ashkenaz ba-et ha-hadashah ha-mukdemet.* Jerusalem, 2009.

Howell, Martha. "The Gender of Europe's Commercial Economy, 1200–1700." *Gender and History* 20, no. 3 (2008).

Hudson, Nicholas. "From 'Nation' to 'Race': The Origin of Racial Classification in Eighteenth-Century Thought." *Eighteenth-Century Studies* 29, no. 3 (1996).

———. "'Why God No Kill the Devil?': The Diabolical Disruption of Order in 'Robinson Crusoe.'" *Review of English Studies*, new ser., 39, no. 156 (1988).

Hufton, Olwen H. "Women and the Family Economy in Eighteenth-Century France." *French Historical Studies* 9, no. 1 (1975).

Hulme, Peter. *Colonial Encounters: Europe and the Native Caribbean, 1492–1797.* London, 1992.

Hume, David. *Dialogues Concerning Natural Religion.* 1777. Repr. London, 1779.

Hunter, J. P. "Friday as a Convert: Defoe and the Accounts of Indian Missionaries." *Review of English Studies.* new ser., 14, no. 55 (1963).

Hurvitz, Khaykl. *Tsofnas paneyakh.* Bardichev, 1817.

Ibn Paquda, Bahya. *Hovot ha-levavot* [Arabic]. 1080. Repr. Jerusalem, 1973.

———. *Hovot ha-levavot* [Hebrew]. Trans. Yehudah Ibn Tibbon. 1161. Repr. Jerusalem, 1990.

Idelson-Shein, Iris. "'Barukh meshaneh ha-briot': Dmuto ve-shimushav shel ha-ekzoti ba-neorut ha-yehudit." Ph.D. diss., Tel Aviv University, 2010.

———. "Gilguley pere: Hashvaah ben 'Robinson Crusoe' le-Daniel Defoe le-Amudey beyt Yehudah le-Yehudah Horowitz." *Historiah* 21 (2008).

———. "'Their Eyes Shall Behold Strange Things': Abraham Ben Elijah of Vilna Encounters the Spirit of Mr. Buffon." *AJS Review* 36, no. 2 (2012).

Ilany, Ofri. "From Divine Commandment to Political Act: The Eighteenth-

Century Polemic on the Extermination of the Canaanites." *Journal of the History of Ideas* 73, no. 3 (2012).

Isaac, Benjamin, Joseph Ziegler, and Miriam Eliav-Feldon. Introduction to *Origins of Racism in the West*, ed. Isaac, Ziegler, and Eliav-Feldon. Cambridge, 2009.

Israel, Jonathan. *Enlightenment Contested*. Oxford, 2006.

———. *Radical Enlightenment: Philosophy and the Making of Modernity 1650–1750*. New York, 2001.

Jackson, Mark. *Newborn Child Murder: Women, Illegitimacy and the Courts in Eighteenth-Century England*. Manchester, 1996.

Jacobs, Martin. "From Lofty Caliphs to Uncivilized Orientals—Images of the Muslim in Medieval Jewish Travel Literature." *Jewish Studies Quarterly* 18 (2011).

Jahoda, Gustav. *Images of Savages: Ancient Roots of Modern Prejudice in Western Culture*. London, 1999.

Jaucourt, Louis, Chevalier de. "Travel." *The Encyclopedia of Diderot & d'Alembert Collaborative Translation Project*. Trans. Nelly S. Hoyt and Thomas Cassirer. Ann Arbor: University of Michigan Library, 2003. http://hdl.handle.net/2027/spo.did2222.0000.169, accessed 18 July 2012. Originally published as «Voyage." *Encyclopédie ou Dictionnaire raisonné des sciences, des arts et des métiers*, 17:476–477. Paris, 1765.

Jefferson, Thomas. "Notes on the State of Virginia." 1781. Repr. in *Race and the Enlightenment: A Reader*, ed. Emmanuel C. Eze. Cambridge, 1997.

Jordan, Winthrop D. *White over Black: American Attitudes Toward the Negro, 1550–1812*. Kingsport, 1968.

Josephus. "The Jewish War." In *The New and Complete Works of Josephus*. Trans. William Whiston. Grand Rapids, 1999.

Juspa of Worms. "Sefer maase nissim." C. 1678. Repr. in *R' Juspa shamash d'kehilat Worms*, ed. and trans. Shlomo Eidelberg. Jerusalem, 1991.

Kaidanover, Zvi Hirsch. *Sefer kav ha-yashar*. Frankfurt, 1705.

Kames, Lord Henry Home. *Sketches of the History of Man*. Edinburgh, 1774.

Kant, Immanuel. "An Answer to the Question: What Is Enlightenment?" Trans. Lara Denis. In *Groundwork for the Metaphysics of Morals*. Toronto, 2005.

———. "Physische Erdbeschreibung: Zweiter Theil." 1802. Repr. in *Kants Werke: Akademie Textausgabe*. Vol. 9, *Logik, Physische Geographie, Pädagogik*. Berlin, 1968.

———. "Von den verschiendenen Racen der Menschen." 1775. Repr. in *Kant's gesammelte Schriften*. Berlin, 1912.

———. *Was ist Aufklärung: Ausgewählte kleine Schriften.* 1784. Repr. Hamburg, 1999.

Kaplan, Debra. "Women and Worth: Female Access to Property in Early Modern Urban Jewish Communities." *Leo Baeck Institute Year Book* 55 (2010).

Kaplan, Paul H.D. "Jewish Artists and Images of Black Africans in Renaissance Venice." In *Multicultural Europe and Cultural Exchange in the Middle Ages and Renaissance,* ed. James P. Helfers. Turnhout, 2005.

Kasher, Asa, and Shlomo Biderman. "Why Was Baruch de Spinoza Excommunicated?" In *Sceptics, Millenarians, and Jews,* ed. David S. Katz and Jonathan I. Israel. Leiden, 1990.

Katan, Yoel. "Kabel et ha-'emet mi-mi she'amrah." *Ha-maayan* 32, no. 3 (1992).

Katz, Jacob. *Exclusiveness and Tolerance: Studies in Jewish-Gentile Relations in Medieval and Modern Times.* New York, 1961.

———. *Tradition and Crisis: Jewish Society and the End of the Middle Ages.* 1958. Repr. Trans. Bernard Dov Cooperman. New York, 2000.

Katzenelbogen, Pinchas. *Yesh manḥilin.* Eighteenth-Century. Repr. Jerusalem, 1986.

Kelly, Louis. "The Eighteenth-Century to Tytler." In *The Oxford History of Literary Translation in English: 1660–1790.* Vol. 3. Ed. Stuart Gillespie and David Hopkins. Oxford, 2005.

Keysir, Shlomo ben Yosef. "Kohelet Shlomo." 1818. Levy Collection, Hamburg Staats- und Universitätsbibliothek, Hamburg, Germany, ms. 172. Microfilm available at the National Library Israel, reel no. F1600.

Kipp, Julie. "Naturally Bad or Dangerously Good: Romantic-Era Narratives of Murderous Motherhood." In *Writing British Infanticide: Child-Murder, Gender and Print, 1722–1859,* ed. Jennifer Thorn. Cranbury, NJ, 2003.

Klausner, Joseph. *Ha-adam ha-kadmon: Yesodot ha-antropologiyah.* Warsaw, 1900.

———. "Ha-haskalah ha-clalit ve-ha-Ivrit be-Lita." In *Yahadut Lita.* Vol. 1. Tel Aviv, 1984.

———. *Historiah shel ha-sifrut ha-Ivrit ha-ḥadashah.* 1936. Repr. Jerusalem, 1952.

Kogman, Tal. "Haskalah Scientific Knowledge in Hebrew Garment: A General Statement and Two Examples." *Target* 19, no. 1 (2007).

———. "Magaim beyn-tarbutiyim be-tekstim shel ha-haskalah al madaey ha-teva." In *Ha-haskalah li-gvaneyhah: Iyunim ḥadashim be-toldot ha-haskalah u-sifrutah,* ed. Shmuel Feiner and Israel Bartal. Jerusalem, 2005.

———. "Yeẓirat dimuyey ha-yeda ba-araẓot dovrot ha-germanit bi-tkufat ha-haskalah." Ph.D. diss., Tel Aviv University, 2000.

Koltun-Fromm, Ken. *Moses Hess and Modern Jewish Identity*. Bloomington, 2001.

Kotzebue, August von. *Die Negersklaven, ein historisch-dramatisches Gemälde in drey Akten*. 1796. Repr. Leipzig, 1821.

Kristeva, Julia. *Powers of Horror: An Essay on Abjection*. 1980. Trans. Leon. S. Roudiez. New York, 1982.

Landau, Yeḥezkel. *Responsa noda be-Yehudah*. Mahadurah kamma. 1776.

Lawee, Eric. "The Reception of Rashi's *Commentary on the Torah* in Spain: The Case of Adam's Mating with the Animals." *Jewish Quarterly Review* 97, no. 1 (2007).

Lefin, Menachem Mendel. *Ḥeshbon ha-nefesh*. 1808. Repr. Vilnius, 1844.

———. *Masaot ha-yam*. 1818. Repr. Lemberg, 1859.

———. *Moda le-vinah*. Berlin, 1788.

[Lefin?]. *Oniyah soarah*. 1815. Repr. Warsaw, 1854.

Levene, Alysa. "The Estimation of Mortality at the Lindon Foundling Hospital, 1741–99." *Population Studies* 59 (2005).

Levison, Mordecai Gumpel Schnaber (George). *Maamar ha-torah ve-ha-ḥokhma*. Part 1. London, 1771.

———. *Shlosh esreh yesodey ha-torah*. Altona, 1791.

Levy, David. *Lingua Sacra*. 3 vols. London, 1786.

Leybovich, N. S. "Sefer amudey Yaaveẓ." *Ha-ẓofeh le-ḥokhmat Israel* 9, no. 1 (1925).

Liberles, Robert. "Die Juden und die anderen—Das Bild des Nichtjuden in Glikls Memoiren." In *Die Hamburger Kauffrau Glikl: Jüdische Existenz in der Frühen Neuzeit*, ed. Monika Richarz. Hamburg, 2001.

———. "On the Threshold of Modernity." *Jewish Daily Life in Germany 1618–1945*, ed. Marion A. Kaplan. Oxford, 2005.

———. "'She Sees That Her Merchandise Is Good, and Her Lamp is Not Extinguished at Nighttime': Glikl's Memoir as Historical Source." *Nashim: A Journal of Jewish Women's Studies & Gender Issues* 7 (2004).

Lifschitz, Avi. *Language and Enlightenment: The Berlin Debates of the Eighteenth Century*. Oxford, 2012.

Ligon, Richard. "Histoy of the Island of Barbadoes." 1673. Repr. in *English Trader, Indian Maid: Representing Race, Gender and Slavery in the New World*, ed. Frank Felsenstein. Baltimore, 1999.

Lindau, Baruch. "Besorat sfarim ḥadashim." *Ha-measef* (1787).

———. *Reshit limudim*. Berlin, 1788.

Linne, Caroli (Linnaeus). *Systema Naturae per Regna Tria Naturae*. Holmiae [Stockholm], 1766.

Lipkin, Joanna. "'Others', Slaves and Colonists in 'Oroonoko.'" In *The Cambridge Companion to Aphra Behn*, ed. Dereck Hughes and Janet Todd. Cambridge, 2004.

Lippert, Julius. *Toldot hashlamat ha-adam*. Trans. David Frischmann. Warsaw, 1894.

Locke, John. "An Essay Concerning Human Understanding." In *The Works of John Locke, Esq.* 1690. Repr. London, 1714.

———. *Some Thoughts Concerning Education*. 1693. Repr. London, 1779.

———. *Two Treatises of Government*. 1690. Repr. Cambridge, 1988.

Maimon, Salomon. *Autobiography*. Trans. J. Clark Murray. 1888. Repr. Champaign, 2001.

———. *Geschichte des eigenen Lebens*. 1792. Repr. Berlin, 1935.

———. "Givat ha-moreh." In *Sefer moreh nevohim la-rav ha-gadol . . . Moshe ben Maimon*. 1791. Repr. Solzbach, 1800.

Maisch, Ingrid. *Mary Magdalene: The Image of a Woman Through the Centuries*. Collegeville, MN, 1998.

Maistre, Joseph Marie Comte de. *Against Rousseau: "On the State of Nature' and 'On the Sovereignty of the People."* 1796. Trans. Richard A. Lebrun. Montreal, 1996.

Malbar, Gershon. "Ones ve-aveyrot inus nosafot ba-hok ha-yehudy ve-ha-angly." Ph.D diss., Hebrew University of Jerusalem, 1960.

Mandeville, Bernard. *The Fable of the Bees*. 1732. Repr. in 2 vols. Indianapolis, 1988.

Marmontel, Jean-François. *Les Incas, ou la destruction de l'empire du Pérou*. 2 vols. Paris, 1777.

Martin, Charles D. *The White African Body: A Cultural and Literary Exploration*. New York, 2002.

Maupertuis, Pierre-Louis Moreau. "Vénus Physique." 1745. Repr. in *Oeuvres*, 2 vols. Hildesheim, 1965.

McDonagh, Josephine. *Child Murder and British Culture, 1720–1900*. New York, 2003.

———. "Infanticide and the Boundaries of Culture from Hume to Arnold." In *Inventing Maternity: Politics, Science and Literature, 1650–1865*, ed. Susan C. Greenfield and Carol Barash. Lexington, KY, 1999.

Melamed, Abraham. *The Image of the Black in Jewish Culture: A History of the Other*. 2002. Trans. Betty Sigler Rozen. London, 2003.

Melman, Billie. *Women's Orients: English Women and the Middle East: 1718–1918*. London, 1992.

Mendelssohn, Moses. *Gesammelte Schriften*. Vol. 16: Hebräische Schriften III: Briefwechsel. Berlin, 1929.

―――. *Jerusalem oder über religiöse Macht und Judentum*. Berlin, 1783.

―――. *Jerusalem, or on Religious Power and Judaism*. Trans. Allan Arkush. Hanover, NH, 1983.

―――. *Sefer netivot ha-shalom ve-hu ḥibur kolel ḥameshet ḥumshey torah im tirgum Ashkenazy u-biyur*. 1783. Repr. Vienna, 1795.

―――. "Sendschreiben an den Herrn Magister Lessing in Leipzig." 1756. Repr. in *Gesammelte Schriften*. Vol. 2: Schriften zur Philosophie und Ästhetik, ed. Fritz Bamberger and Leo Strauss. Berlin, 1931.

Mendelssohn-Frankfurt, Moshe. *Meẓiat ha-areẓ ha-ḥadashah kolel kol ha-gevurot ve-ha-maasim asher naasu le-et meẓo ha-areẓ ha-zot*. Altona, 1807.

Mendes-Flohr, Paul R., and Jehuda Reinharz, ed. *The Jew in the Modern World: A Documentary History*. New York, 1980.

Michalik, Kerstin. "The Development of the Discourse on Infanticide in the Late Eighteenth-Century and the New Legal Standardization of the Offense in the Nineteenth Century." In *Gender in Transition: Discourse and Practice in German-Speaking Europe, 1750–1830*, ed. Ulrike Gleixner and Marion W. Gray. Ann Arbor, 2006.

Michel, Wilhelm. "Anton Friedrich Büsching." *Allgemeine deutsch Biographie und neue deutsche Biographie*. Vol. 3. Berlin, 1957.

Mielke, Andreas. "Hottentots in the Aesthetic Discussion of Eighteenth-Century Germany." *Monatshefte* 80, no. 2 (1988).

Mintz-Manor, Limor. "Ha-siaḥ al ha-olam ha-ḥadash ba-tarbut ha-yehudit ba-et ha-ḥadashah ha-mukdemet." Ph.D. diss., Hebrew University of Jerusalem, 2011.

Minvielle, Stéphane. «Le mariage précoce des femmes à Bordeaux au XVIIIe siècle.» *Annales de démographie historique* 1 (2006).

Mocquet, Jean. *Voyages en Afrique, Asie, Indes Orientales, & Occidentales faits par Jean Mocquet*. 1616. Repr. Rouen, 1665.

Modena, Yehudah Arieh Leon. *Ḥayey Yehudah*. 1648. Repr. Jerusalem, 1968.

Monboddo, Lord James Burnett. *Of the Origin and Progress of Language*. Edinburgh, 1774.

Mondshein, Yehoshua. "Haskamot shtukot mi-Valozhyn u-Vilna: Kabel et ha-emet mi-my she-amarah?" *Or Israel* 4, no. 16 (1999).

Montagu, Mary Wortley. "Letters: Volume II." *Monthly Review: or Literary Journal: by Several Hands*, 28 (1763).

Montrose, Louis. "The Work of Gender in the Discourse of Discovery." *Representations* 33 (1991).

Morris-Reich, Amos. "Arthur Ruppin's Concept of Race." *Israel Studies* 11, no. 3 (2006).

Morton, Thomas. *New English Canaan*. 1637. Repr. Scituate, 1999.

Moseley, Marcus. *Being for Myself Alone: Origins of Jewish Autobiography*. Stanford, 2006.

Nadler, Allan. *The Faith of the Mithnagdim: Rabbinic Responses to Hasidic Rapture*. Baltimore, 1999.

Naipaul, V. S. *The Mimic Men*. 1967. Repr. Harmondsworth, Middlesex, 1969.

Namias, June. *White Captives: Gender and Ethnicity on the American Frontier*. Chapel Hill, 1993.

Nandi, Ashish. *The Intimate Enemy: Loss and Recovery of Self under Colonialism*. New York, 1983.

Nash, Richard. *Wild Enlightenment: The Broders of Human Identity in the Eighteenth Century*. Charlottesville, 2003.

Niccoli, Ottavia. *Prophecy and People in Renaissance Italy*. Princeton, 1990.

Nicholson, William, ed. *The British Encyclopedia or Dictionary of Arts and Sciences*. London, 1809.

Noah, Mordecai Manuel. *Selected Writings*. Westport, 1999.

Nodelman, Perry. "The Other: Orientalism, Colonialism and Children's Literature." *Children's Literature Association Quarterly* 17 (1992).

Nussbaum. "'Savage' Mothers: Narratives of Maternity in the Mid-Eighteenth-Century." *Eighteenth-Century Life* 16, no. 1 (1992).

———. *Torrid Zones: Maternity, Sexuality, and Empire in Eighteenth-Century English Narratives*. Baltimore, 1995.

———. "Women and Race: A Difference of Complexion." In *Women and Literature in Britain, 1700–1800*, ed. Vivien Jones. Cambridge, 2000.

Obeyesekere, Gananath. *The Apotheosis of Captain Cook: European Mythmaking in the Pacific*. Princeton, NJ, 1992.

———. *Cannibal Talk: The Man-Eating Myth and Human Sacrifice in the South Seas*. Berkeley, 2005.

O'Brien, Karen. *Women and Enlightenment in Eighteenth-Century Britain*. Cambridge, 2009.

O'Brien, Traci S. "A 'Daughter of the Occident' Travels to the 'Orient': Ida von Hahn's 'The Countess Faustina' and 'Letters from the Orient.'" *Women in German Yearbook* 24 (2008).

Ofek, Uriel. "Al Robinson ve-Robinsonim: Bi-mlot 250 shanah le-mot Daniel Defoe." *Sifrut yeladim va-noar,* 1981.

Opitz, May. "Racism, Sexism, and Precolonial Images of Africa in Germany." In *Showing Our Colors: Afro-German Women Speak Out,* ed. May Opitz, Katharina Oguntoye, and Dagmar Schultz. Amherst, 1986.

Orr, Bridget. "Stifling Pity in a Parent's Breast: Infanticide and Savagery in Late Eighteenth-Century Travel Writing." In *Travel Writing and Empire: Postcolonial Theory in Transit,* ed. Steve Clark. London, 1999.

Outram, Dorinda. *The Enlightenment.* Cambridge, 1995.

Oz-Salzberger, Fania. *Translating the Enlightenment: Scottish Civic Discourse in Eighteenth-Century Germany.* Oxford, 1995.

Pagden, Anthony. "The Peopling of the New World: Ethnos, Race and Empire in the Early-Modern World." In *Origins of Racism in the West,* ed. Miriam Eliav-Feldon, Benjamin Isaac, and Joseph Ziegler. Cambridge, 2009.

Patai, Raphael. *The Hebrew Goddess.* New York, 1967.

Pech, Klaus-Ulrich. "Raff, Georg Christian." In *Lexikon der Kinder und Jugendliteratur,* ed. Klaus Doderer. Weinheim, 1979.

Pelli, Moshe. *The Age of Haskalah: Studies in Hebrew Literature of the Enlightenment in Germany.* Leiden, 1979.

Perl, Joseph. *Megaleh temirin.* Vienna, 1819.

———. "Teḥunat anshey Greenland" (1813–17). Draft version for Ẓir Neeman, ARC 4° 1153/96, Josef Perl Archive, National Library Israel.

———. *Ẓir neeman li-shnat 5576.* Ternopol, 1815.

Perlhefter, Beila, and Baer Perlhefter. *Beer sheva.* Frankfurt edition: Frankfurt am Mein Stadt- und Universitaetsbibliothek, Microfilm available at National Library Israel, reel no. F22030.

———. *Beer sheva.* Paris edition: Paris Alliance Israelite Universelle, Ms. no. 295. Microfilm available at National Library Israel, reel no. F3301.

Perosa, Sergio. *From Islands to Portraits: Four Literary Variations.* Amsterdam, 2000.

Pestana, Carla Gardina. *The English Atlantic in an Age of Revolution, 1640–1661.* Cambridge, 2004.

Pigafetta, Antonio. *First Voyage Around the world, 1519–1522: An Account of Magellan's Expedition.* 1525. Repr. Toronto, 2007.

Pinto, Isaac De. Letter to Charles Marie La Condamine [1745–6], Eggerton Collection, Bentinck Papers, manuscript no. EG. 1745, ff. 181–199. British Library London.

———. "Réflexions critiques sur le premier chapitre du VIIe. tome des

Œuvres de M. de Voltaire, &c." In *Lettres de quelques Juifs Portugais, Allemands et Polonois, à M. de Voltaire*. 1762. Repr. Paris, 1781.

Pocock, John G.A. *Barbarism and Religion*, vol. 1: *The Enlightenments of Edward Gibbon*. Cambridge, 1999.

———. "Conservative Enlightenment and Democratic Revolutions: The American and French Cases in British Perspective." *Government and Opposition* 24, no. 1 (1989).

———. *Virtue, Commerce and History: Essays on Political Thought and History, Chiefly in the Eighteenth Century*. Cambridge, 1985.

Poovey, Mary. *Uneven Developments: The Ideological Work of Gender in Mid-Victorian England*. London, 1989.

Pope, Alexander. "The Dunciad." 1743. Repr. in *Alexander Pope: Selected Poetry and Prose*. New York, 1963.

Popkin, Richard H. *Isaac La Peyrère (1596–1676)*. Leiden, 1987.

Porter, Roy. "The Exotic as Erotic: Captain Cook in Tahiti." In *Exoticism in the Enlightenment*, ed. Roy Porter and G. S. Rousseau. Manchester, 1990.

Pratt, Mary L. *Imperial Eyes: Travel Writing and Transculturation*. London, 1992.

———. "Scratches on the Face of the Country; or, What Mr. Burrows Saw in the Land of the Bushmen." In *"Race," Writing and Difference*, ed. Henry Louis Gates Jr. Chicago, 1986.

Price, Lawrence M. *Inkle and Yarico Album*. Berkeley, 1937.

Price, Merrall L. *Consuming Passions: The Uses of Cannibalism in Late Medieval and Early Modern Europe*. New York, 2003.

Raff, Georg Christian. *Geographie für Kinder*. Göttingen, 1776.

———. *Geographie für Kinder zum Gebrauch auf Schulen*. Tübingen, 1786.

———. *Naturgeschichte für Kinder*. 1778. Repr. Frankfurt and Leipzig, 1780.

———. *Naturgeschichte für Kinder*. Göttingen, 1781.

———. *Naturgeschichte für Kinder*. Tübingen, 1788.

———. *Naturgeschichte für Kinder*. Göttingen, 1793.

Raleigh, Walter. "The Discovery of the Large, Rich, and Beautiful Empire of Guiana." 1595. Repr. in *The Works of Sir Walter Raleigh, Kt*. Vol. 8. Oxford, 1829.

Recke, Johann F., and Karl E. Napiersky. *Algemeines Schrifsteller und Gelehrten Lexicon der Provinzen Livland, Esthland und Korland*. Vol. 3 (L-R). Mitau, 1831.

Reusch, Johann J.K. "Germans as Noble Savages and Castaways: Alter

Egos and Alterity in German Collective Consciousness during the Long Eighteenth-Century." *Eighteenth-Century Studies* 42, no. 1 (2008).

Reyzen, Z. "Campes 'Entdekung fon Amerike' in Yiddish." *Yivo bleter* 5 (1933).

Riemer, Nathanael. "Some Parallels of Stories in Glikl of Hameln Zikhroynes." *Pardes: Zeitschrift der Vereinigung für Jüdische Studien* 14 (2008).

———. *Zwischen Tradition und Häresie: ‚Beer sheva'—eine Enzyklopädie des jüdischen Wissens der Frühen Neuzeit.* Wiesbaden, 2010.

Rivkah (Tiktiner) bat Meir. *Meneket Rivkah—A Manual of Wisdom and Piety for Jewish Women.* C. 1609. Repr. and trans. Samuel Spinner. Ed. Frauke von Rohden. Philadelphia, 2009.

Robertson, William. *The History of the Discovery and Settlement of America.* 1777. Repr. New York, 1856.

Roger, Jacques. *Buffon.* Trans. Sarah L. Bonnefoi. Ithaca, 1997.

Romanelli, Shmuel. *Masa ba-Arav.* Berlin, 1792.

———. *Travail in an Arab Land.* Trans. Yedida K. Stillman and Norman A. Stillman. Tuscaloosa, 1989.

Rose, Jacquelin. *The Case of Peter Pan or the Impossibility of Children's Literature.* 1982. Repr. Philadelphia, 1992.

Rosenblum, Noah. "Ha-Malbim ve-filosofiyah modernit." *Proceedings of the American Society for Jewish Research* 52 (1985).

———. *Iyuney sifrut ve-hagut mi-shilhey ha-meah ha-shmoneh-esreh ad yameynu.* Jerusalem, 1989.

Rosenthal, Angela. "Raising Hair." *Eighteenth-Century Studies* 38, no. 1 (2004).

Roskies, David. "The Medium and Message of the Maskilic Chapbook." *Jewish Social Studies* 41, no. 3 (1979).

Rosman, Moshe (Murray). "Lihiyot ishah Yehudiah be-Polin-Lita be-reshit ha-et ha-hadashah." In *Kiyum va-shever: Yehudey Polin le-doroteyhem,* ed. Israel Bartal and Israel Guttman. Jerusalem, 2001.

Rothenberg, Joshua. "Black-Jewish Relations in Eighteenth-Century Newport." *Rhode Island Jewish Historical Notes* 2 (1992).

Rousseau, Jean Jacques. *Discours sur l'origine et les fondements de l'inégalité parmi les hommes.* 1754. Repr. Paris, 1965.

———. *Discourse on the Origins of Inequality (Second Discourse).* Trans. Judith R. Bush, Roger D. Masters, Christopher Kelly, and Terence Marshall. Hanover, NH, 1992.

———. *Emile or On Education.* Trans. Christopher Kelly and Allan Bloom. Lebanon, NH, 2010.

———. *Émile ou de l'éducation*. 1762. Repr. Paris, 1961.

Rudé, George F.E. *Europe in the Eighteenth-Century: Aristocracy and the Bourgeois Challenge*. Cambridge, 1972.

Ruderman, David B. *Jewish Enlightenment in an English Key*. Princeton, 2000.

———. *Jewish Thought and Scientific Discovery in Early Modern Europe*. New Haven, 1995.

Sade, Donatien Alphonse François. *Juliette*. 1797. Trans. Austryn Wainhouse. New York, 1968.

Salama-Carr, Myriam. "The French [Translation] Tradition." In *Routledge Encyclopedia of Translation Studies*, ed. Mona Baker. New York, 1998.

Satanov, Isaac. Commentary to *Sefer ha-kuzary*. Berlin, 1795.

———. *Ḥelek rishon min sefer ha-midot le-Aristotalis*. 1784. Repr. Lemberg, 1867.

———. *Igeret Adar ha-yakar*. Berlin, 1772.

———. *Mishley Assaf*. Part 2. Berlin, 1792.

———. *Sefer ha-gderim oder leksikon fon vissenshaften*. Berlin, 1798.

———. "Sefer holekh tamim." In *Beyur milot ha-higayon la-Rambam z"l*, with commentaries by Mendelssohn and Satanov. Berlin, 1795.

Sayre, Gordon M. *Les Sauvages Américains: Representations of Native Americans in French and English Colonial Literature*. Chapel Hill, 1997.

Schacter, Jacob J. "History and Memory of Self: The Autobiography of Rabbi Jacob Emden." In *Jewish History and Jewish Memory: Essays in Honor of Yosef Hayim Yerushalmi*, ed. Elisheva Carlebach, John Efron, and David M. Myers. Hanover, NH, 1998.

Schatz, Andrea. "Detours in a 'Hidden Land': Shmuel Romanelli's *Masa' ba'rav*." In *Jewish Studies at the Crossroads of Anthropology and History: Authority, Diaspora, Tradition*, ed. Ra'anan S. Boustan, Oren Kosansky, and Marina Rustow. Philadelphia, 2011.

Schechter, Ronald. *Obstinate Hebrews: Representations of Jews in France, 1715–1815*. Berkeley, 2003.

Schick, Baruch of Shklov. "Sefer tiferet ha-adam." In *Sefer amudey ha-shamayim*. Berlin, 1776.

Schiller, Johann Christoph Friedrich. "Was heißt und zu welchem Ende studiert man Universalgeschichte." 1789. Repr. in *Schillers sämmtliche Werke*. Vol. 10. Stüttgart, 1838.

Schnitzer-Maimon, Merav. "Ha-yaḥas le-ones ba-parshanut ha-yehudit bi-yemey ha-beynayim." Master's thesis, Tel Aviv University, 2005.

Schönhak, Joseph ben Binyamin Dov. *Toldot ha-areẓ*. Warsaw, 1841.

Schooten, Henry. *The Hairy Giants: or a Description of Two Islands in the South Sea Called by the Name of Bengaga and Coma*. London, 1671.

Schorsch, Ismar. "The Myth of Sepharadic Supremacy." *Leo Baeck Institute Yearbook* 34 (1989).

Schorsch, Jonathan. "American Jewish Historians, Colonial Jews and Blacks, and the Limits of 'Wissenschaft': A Critical Review." *Jewish Social Studies* 6, no. 2 (2000).

———. *Jews and Blacks in the Early Modern World*. New York, 2004.

———. "Review: Abraham Melamed, the Image of the Black in Jewish Culture: A History of the Other." *Jewish History* 21 (2007).

Schwartz, Howard. *Tree of Souls: The Mythology of Judaism*. Oxford, 2004.

Shavit, Jacob, and Judah Reinharz. *Darwin u-khama mi-bney mino: Evoluẓiya, geza, svivah ve-tarbut—Yehudim korim et Darwin, Spencer, Buckle ve-Renan*. Jerusalem, 2009.

Shavit, Zohar. "From Friedländer's Lesebuch to the Jewish Campe: The Beginning of Hebrew Children's Literature in Germany." *Leo Baeck Institute Yearbook* 33 (1988).

———. "Ha-rihut shel ḥadar ha-haskalah be-Berlin." In *Ke-minhag Ashkenaz u-Polin: Sefer yovel le-Ḥone Shmeruk*, ed. Israel Bartal, Ezra Mendelsohn, and Chava Turniansky. Jerusalem, 1993.

———. "Literary Interference between German and Jewish-Hebrew Children's Literature During the Enlightenment: The Case of Campe." *Poetics Today* (Children's Literature) 13, no. 1 (1992).

Shavit, Zohar, and Hans H. Ewers. *Deutsch-judische Kinder- und Jugendliteratur. Von der Haskalah bis 1945. Die deutsch- und hebräischsprachigen Schriften des deutschsprachigen Raums. Ein bibliographisches Handbuch*. Stuttgart, 1996.

Shenfeld, Baruch. "Ha-adam." *Bikurey ha-itim* (1825).

———. "Yelalat em al mot ben-riḥmah." *Bikurey ha-itim* (1827).

Shlosberg, Ber. "Khaykl Hurvitz's Tsofnas paneyakh." *Yivo bleter* 7 (1937).

Shoa Ish Bialistok. *Sheviley ereẓ Russiah*. Warsaw, 1893.

Shoham-Steiner, Ephraim. *Ḥarigim beal korḥam: Meshugayim u-meẓuraim ba-ḥevrah ha-yehudit bi-yemey ha-beynayim*. Jerusalem, 2008.

Shoḥat, Azriel. *Im ḥilufey ha-tekufot: Reshit ha-haskalah be-yahadut Germaniyah*. Jerusalem, 1960.

Shulman, Kalman. *Mosdey areẓ*. Vilnius, 1871.

Shvebacher, Hyman. *Hadrakhat ha-yeled oder erster unterrikht fir kinder fon dreye bis finf yahren*. 1812. Repr. Fürth, 1824.

Sinkoff, Nancy. *Out of the Shtetl: Making Jews Modern in the Polish Borderlands*. Providence, 2004.

——. "Strategy and Ruse in the Haskalah of Mendel Lefin of Satanov." In *New Perspectives on the Haskalah*, ed. Shmuel Feiner and David Sorkin. London, 2001.

——. "Tradition and Transition: Mendel Lefin of Satanow and the Beginnings of the Jewish Enlightenment in Eastern Europe, 1749–1826." Ph.D. diss., Columbia University, 1996.

Smith, Adam. *The Theory of Moral Sentiments*. 1759. Repr. London, 1761.

Smith, James. "An Account of the Captivity of Col. James Smith." In *A Selection of Some of the Most Interesting Narratives, Or the Outrages Committed by the Indians in Their Wars with the White People*. 2 vols. Ed. Archibald Loudon. 1808–1811. Repr. Carlisle, 1888.

Smollet, Tobias. *The Expedition of Humphry Clinker*. 1771. Repr. New York, 1836.

Sömmering, Samuel Thomas. *Ueber die körperliche Verschiedenheit des Negers vom Europäer*. Frankfurt, 1785.

Sorkin, David. "Ha-haskalah be-Berlin: Perspektivah hashvaatit." In *Ha-haskalah ligvaneyhah: Iyunim hadashim be-toldot ha-haskalah u-sifrutah*, ed. Shmuel Feiner and Israel Bartal. Jerusalem, 2005.

——. *The Religious Enlightenment: Protestants, Jews, and Catholics from London to Vienna*. Princeton, 2008.

Spacks, Patricia A.M. *Desire and Truth: Functions of Plot in Eighteenth-Century English Novels*. Chicago, 1994.

Spencer, Frank. *History of Physical Anthropology*. New York, 1997.

Stannard, David E. *American Holocaust: The Conquest of the New World*. Oxford, 1992.

Stark, Leib. *Agudat shoshanim*. Prague, 1817.

Steele, Richard. *The Spectator*, no. 11. Tuesday, 13 March 1711. Repr. in *English Trader, Indian Maid: Representing Race, Gender and Slavery in the New World*, ed. Frank Felsenstein. Baltimore, 1999.

Steele, Richard, and Joseph Addison. *The Spectator*, no. 99. 23 June 1711. Repr. in *The Spectator: A New Edition*. London, 1852.

Steinschneider, Moritz. "Hebräische Drucke in Deutschland." *Zeitschrift für die Geschihcte der Juden in Deutschland* 2 (1892).

Stern, Eliyahu. *The Genius: Elijah of Vilna and the Making of Modern Judaism*. New Haven, 2013.

Stone, Kay. "Three Transformations of Snow White." In *The Brothers Grimm and Folktale*, ed. James M. McGlathery. Urbana, 1988.

Stone, Lawrence. *The Family, Sex and Marriage in England, 1500–1800.* New York, 1977.

Stowe, Harriet Beecher. *Uncle Tom's Cabin or Life Among the Lowly.* 2 vols. Boston, 1852.

Summerfield, Geoffrey. *Fantasy and Reason: Children's Literature in the Eighteenth Century.* London, 1984.

Susina, Jan. *The Place of Lewis Carroll in Children's Literature.* New York, 2010.

Swaminathan, Srividhya. *Debating the Slave Trade: Rhetoric of British National Identity, 1759–1815.* Surrey, 2009.

Swift, Jonathan. *Gulliver's Travels.* 1726/1735. Repr. New York, 1970.

Sypher, Wylie. *Guinea's Captive Kings: British Anti-Slavery Literature of the XVIIIth Century.* 1942. Repr. New York, 1969.

Ta-Shma, Israel. "Children in Medieval Germanic Jewry: A Perspective on Ariés from Jewish Sources." *Studies in Medieval and Renaissance History* 12 (1991).

Tang, Abraham ben Naphtali. "Beḥinat adam." 1772. MS no. EVR II A22, St. Petersburg National Library. Microfilm available at National Library Israel. Reel no. F63945.

Tatar, Maria. *The Hard Facts of the Grimms' Fairy Tales.* 1987. Repr. Princeton, 2003.

Thelwall, John. *Incle and Yarico.* 1792. Repr. Madison, 2006.

Todorov, Tzveten. *The Conquest of America: The Question of the Other.* 1982. Trans. Richard Howard. New York, 1984.

Toury, Gideon. *Descriptive Translation Studies and Beyond.* Amsterdam, 1995.

———. "Hebrew [Translation] Tradition." In *Routledge Encyclopedia of Translation Studies*, ed. Mona Baker. New York, 1998.

———. "The Notion of 'Assumed Translation'—An Invitation to a New Discussion." In *Letterlijkheid, Woordelijheid*, ed. H. Bloemen, E. Hertog, and W. Segers. Antwerpen/Harmelen, 1995.

———. "Reshit ha-tirgum ha-moderny le-Ivrit: Od mabat eḥad." *Dapim le-meḥkar be-sifrut* 11 (1997).

Townsend, Ebenezer. "Diary." Repr. in *Papers of the New Haven Colony Historical Society* 4 (1888).

Turniansky, Chava. "Dmut ha-ishah be-zikhronoteyhah shel Glikl Hamel." In *Eros, erusin ve-isurim: Miniyut u-mishpaḥah ba-historiyah*, ed. Israel Bartal and Isaiah Gafni. Jerusalem, 1998.

———. "Ha-sipurim be zikhronot Glikl me-Hameln u-mekorteyhem." *Meḥkarey Yerushalayim be-folklor Yehudy* 16 (1983).

Turniansky, Chava, and Chana Amit. "Interview." *Davkah: Erez Yiddish ve-tarbutah* 2 (2007).

Uihlein, Joseph. *Unterricht in der Geographie.* 1806. Repr. Frankfurt, 1820.

Ulbrich, Claudia. *Shulamit und Margarete: Macht, Geschlecht und Religion in einer ländlichen Gesellschaft des 18. Jahrhunderts.* Vienna, 1999.

Vespucci, Amerigo. "Letter to Pier Soderini." 1504. Repr. in *The English Literatures of America, 1500–1800*, ed. M. Jehlin and M. Warner. New York, 1997.

Virey, Julien-Joseph. *De la puissance vitale considérée dans ses fonctions physiologiques chez l'homme.* Paris, 1823.

———. *Histoire des moeurs et de l'instinct des animaux.* Vol. 1. Paris, 1822.

———. *Histoire naturelle du genre humain.* 1801. Repr. Paris, 1824.

———. *Nouveau dictionnaire d'histoire naturelle.* Vol. 22. Paris, 1818.

Volkov, Shulamit. "Antisemitism as a Cultural Code: Reflections on the History and Historiography of Antisemitism in Imperial Germany." *Leo Baeck Institute Yearbook* 33 (1978).

———. "Ha-ḥershim ke-kvuẓat miyut: Reshit ha-maavak al sefat ha-simanim." *Historiah* 1 (1998).

———. "Talking of Jews, Thinking of Germans—The Ethnic Discourse in 19th Century Germany." *Tel Aviver Jahrbuch für deutsche Geschichte* 30 (2002).

Voltaire. *Dictionnaire philosophique.* Tome 1. London, 1767.

———. "Histoire de l'empire de Russie sous Pierre le Grand." 1759. Repr. in *Collection complète des oeuvres de M. de Voltaire.* Vol. 2. Geneva, 1768.

———. *Philosophical Dictionary.* Trans. Theodore Besterman. London, 2004.

———. *Quéstions sur l'Encyclopédie.* London, 1771.

Wahrman, Dror. *The Making of the Modern Self: Identity and Culture in Eighteenth-Century England.* New Haven, 2004.

Wattles, Gordon. "Buffon, d'Alembert and Materialist Atheism." *Studies on Voltaire and the Eighteenth Century* 266 (1989).

Weise, Christian Felix. "Der Fleiß." In *Kleine lyrische Gedichte.* Vol. 3. Leipzig, 1772.

Weld, Isaac. "Isaac Weld's des Jüngern Reisen durch die Staaten von Nordamerika und die Provinzen Ober- und Nieder-Canada während den Jahren 1795, 1796 und 1797." Trans. Herz Henriette. In *Magazin von merkwürdigen neuen Reisebeschreibungen aus fremden Sprachen übersetzt.* Vol. 20. Berlin, 1800.

Werses, Shmuel. "Hatafah maskilit be-maḥleẓot shel prozah meḥurezet." *Meḥkary Yerushalayim be-sifrut ivrit* 10–11 (1988).

Wessely, Naphtali Herz. *Divrey shalom ve-emet.* Berlin, 1782.

———. "Magid ḥadashot." *Ha-measef* (1789).

———. *Shirey tiferet.* Part 1. 1789. Repr. Warsaw, 1883.

Wetzlar, Isaac. *The Libes Briv of Isaac Wetzlar.* 1749. Repr. Atlanta, 1996.

Wheeler, Roxann. "The Complexion of Desire: Racial Ideology and Mid-Eighteenth-Century British Novels." *Eighteenth-Century Studies* 32, no. 3 (1999).

———. *The Complexion of Race: Categories of Difference in Eighteenth-Century British Culture.* Philadelphia, 2000.

———. "'My Savage,' 'My Man': Racial Multiplicity in Robinson Crusoe." *English Literary History* 62, no. 4 (1995).

White, Hayden. "The Forms of Wildness: Archeology of an Idea." In *The Wild Man Within: An Image in Western Thought from the Renaissance to Romanticism,* ed. Edward Dudley and Maximillian E. Novak. London, 1972.

Wiener, Meir. *Tsu der geshikhte fun der Yidisher literature in 19th yorhundert.* New York, 1945.

Wiesner, Merry E. "Having Her Own Smoke: Employment and Independence for Single Women in Germany, 1400–1750." In *Single Women in the European Past, 1250–1800,* ed. Judith M. Bennett and Amy M. Froide. Philadelphia, 1999.

Wilkes, Wetenhall. "A Letter of Genteel and Moral Advice to a Young Lady." 1740/1766. Repr. in *Women in the Eighteenth Century: Constructions of Femininity,* ed. Vivien Jones. Routledge, 1990.

Williams, Carolyn D. "Women Behaving Well: Early Modern Images of Female Courage." In *Presenting Gender: Changing Sex in Early-Modern Culture,* ed. Chris Mounsey. Lewisburg, PA, 2001.

Williams, Charles A. *The German Legends of the Hairy Anchorite.* Urbana, 1935.

Wittler, Kathrin. "Good to Think: (Re)Conceptualizing German-Jewish Orientalism." In *Orientalism, Gender, and the Jews: Literary and Artistic Transformations of European National Discourses,* ed. Ulrike Brunotte, Anna-Dorothea Ludewig, and Axel Stähler. Berlin, forthcoming.

Wolcott, Roger. "A Brief Account." 1725. Repr. in *Specimens of American Poetry,* ed. Samuel Kettel. Boston, 1829.

Wolfssohn Halle, Aaron. *Avtalyon, ve-hu mavo ha-limud le-naarey bney Israel u-le-khol ha-ḥafeẓim bi-lshon avar.* Berlin, 1790.

Wolfthal, Diane. *Images of Rape: The "Heroic" Tradition and Its Alternatives.* Cambridge, 1999.

Wolpe, Rebecca. "Judaizing Robinson Crusoe: Maskilic Translations of Robinson Crusoe." *Jewish Culture and History* 13, no. 1 (2012).

———. "The Sea Voyage Narrative as an Educational Tool in the Early Haskalah." Master's thesis. Hebrew University of Jerusalem, 2006.

Wright, Louis B. Introduction to Robert Beverly's *The History and Present State of Virginia.* Chapel Hill, 1947.

Wunder, Heide. *He Is the Sun, She Is the Moon: Women in Early Modern Germany.* Trans. Thomas Dunlap. Cambridge, 1998.

Wunderbar, Reuven J. *Geschichte der Juden in den Provinzen Liv- und Kurland.* Mitau, 1853.

Yassif, Eli. *Sipurey Ben Sira bi-yemey ha-beynayim.* Jerusalem, 1985.

Yorke, Henry Redhead. *Letters from France, in 1802.* London, 1804.

Yuval, Israel. "Ha-nakam ve-ha-kelalah, ha-dam ve-ha-alilah: Me-alilot kedoshim le-alilit dam." *Zion* 58 (1993).

Zammito, John H. "Policing Polygeneticism in Germany, 1775 (Kames,) Kant, and Blumenbach." In *The German Invention of Race,* ed. Sara Eigen and Mark Larrimore. Albany, 2006.

Zamora, Margarita. "Abreast of Columbus: Gender and Discovery." *Cultural Critique* 17 (1990–1991).

———. *Reading Columbus.* Berkeley, 1993.

Zamość, David. *Agudat shoshanim.* Breslau, 1827.

———. *Resisey ha-melizah.* Dyhernfurth, 1822.

———. *Robinzohn der eingere: Ein lezebuch fir kinder.* Breslau, 1824.

———. *Toar ha-zman.* Dyhernfurth, 1821.

———. *Tohahot musar.* Breslau, 1819.

Zantop, Susanne. *Colonial Fantasies: Conquest, Family and Nation in Precolonial Germany, 1770–1870.* Durham, NC, 1997.

———. "Domesticating the Other: European Colonial Fantasies 1770–1830." In *Encountering the Other(s): Studies in Literature, History, and Culture,* ed. G. Brinker-Gabler. Albany, 1995.

Zimmermann, Johann Georg. *An Essay on National Pride.* 1758. Repr. London, 1805.

Zinberg, Israel. *Toldot sifrut Israel.* 7 vols. Tel Aviv, 1971.

Zfatman, Sarah. *Nisuey adam ve-shedah.* Jerusalem, 1987.

Zundel, Hanokh. *Sefer knaf renanim: Biyur nehmad al midrash perek shirah.* Krotoszyn, 1842.

INDEX

ACKNOWLEDGMENTS

This project has been a long time in the making, and throughout this time I have incurred numerous debts of gratitude. My greatest debt is to Shulamit Volkov, a model of superb scholarship and an unfailing source of insight and inspiration. Shula's influence is felt on every page of this book. I am deeply grateful to her for her dedicated guidance, invaluable advice, and unwavering support throughout the years. I owe a great intellectual and personal debt to Shmuel Feiner, whose studies on the Jewish Enlightenment paved the way to my own research, and who has supported and encouraged me throughout. I am also deeply grateful to David Ruderman, whose work on early modern Jewish culture and thought continues to be a source of inspiration and insight, and without whose active encouragement and support this book would probably still be a work in progress. It has been an honor and a pleasure to work with such great minds and such generous scholars.

Throughout the writing of this work I have benefited from the help of numerous friends and colleagues. Very heartfelt thanks go to my close friends and brilliant colleagues Amir Engel, Hanan Harif, Roni Ratzkovsky, and Amnon Yuval, who carefully read and reread the different chapters of this study. Their insightful comments, criticism, and advice have improved this work to a great degree. Michèle Bokobza Kahan, Tova Cohen, Aya Elyada, Sharon Gordon, Tal Kogman, Limor Mitz-Manor, and Merav Schnitzer-Maimon provided invaluable support and advice during the various stages of this project, and I am thankful to them all. I am especially grateful to Jonathan M. Hess and Felicity Nussbaum, who reviewed the book for Penn Press. I could not have hoped for more thoughtful, generous, and educative readings of my work.

At Tel Aviv University, I would like to thank my teachers, and especially David Assaf, José Brunner, Snait Gissis, and Igal Halfin, all of whom challenged and fascinated me as a student, and whose influence on my thought is discernible still today. Thanks also to the learned and friendly staff at the Sourasky central library in Tel Aviv, the library at the Katz Center for Advanced Judaic Studies in Philadelphia, and the Israel National Library in Jerusalem. I would also like to thank the wonderful editorial staff at Penn Press and the Modern Language Initiative, and especially Jerome Singerman, senior humanities editor, for what has been an educative and enjoyable process.

During the writing of this work I was fortunate to be a fellow at the Franz Rosenzweig-Minerva Center for German-Jewish Thought, the Leo Baeck Institute for German-Jewish History, and the Herbert D. Katz Center for Advanced Judaic Studies at the University of Pennsylvania. I am grateful to these institutions and centers and to their directors, staff, and donors for the generous support that enabled me to carry out this work. I am particularly thankful to Yfaat Weiss of the Rosenzweig Center and Raphael Gross of the LBI for their kind encouragement and support. My co-fellows at all three centers have been an important source of stimulation and friendship, and I am deeply indebted to them all. Particular thanks are due the exceptional scholars I encountered at the Katz Center for Advanced Judaic Studies, who made my stay there a truly remarkable and joyous experience: Asher Salah, Chaim Noy, Dimitry Shumsky, Eitan Bar Yosef, Elliott Horowitz, Jack Kugelmass, Martin Jacobs, Miriam Frenkel, Oded Irshai, Orit Bashkin, and Vered Madar.

I am thankful to Tel Aviv University, the Goldstein-Goren Institute for the History of Polish Jewry, and the Lessing Memorial Foundation for generous support of this project in its early stages. The final stages of the work were carried out during my stay as a Minerva fellow in the Ludwig Maximilians University in Munich and the Goethe University in Frankfurt. I would like to thank my hosts in Germany, Christian Wiese and Michael Brenner, for making my stay so very pleasant and educational.

Few living people have suffered more from eighteenth-century Ashkenazi racialism than my husband, Mark Shein-Idelson, who endured my love-hate relationship with this project with unending patience. A brilliant scholar and perceptive reader, Mark treated every page of this work with thoroughness, thoughtfulness, and love, and challenged me to reach the clarity, precision, and depth that characterize his own work. He has inspired me more than he knows, and to a great degree shaped this book into what it is. Many thanks also to my wonderful sister, Daphna Idelson, for precious advice, ideas, laughs, and encouragement, and to my incredible son, Adam, who has endured our journeys throughout the globe with patience and grace well beyond his modest years.

I have dedicated almost a decade to studying racism, and I am still confounded by it. I owe my lifelong interest in this subject to my parents, Tmima Idelson and Arie Idelson, who taught me to accept, nay, appreciate difference in both myself and in others. Their inspired education, unending support, and unshakable belief in me (often against all odds) have been the driving force behind this project. It is with great love and the deepest gratitude that I dedicate this book to them.